"THE WOMAN WILL OVERCOME THE WARRIOR"

"THE WOMAN WILL OVERCOME THE WARRIOR"

A Dialogue with the Christian/Feminist Theology of Rosemary Radford Ruether

Nicholas John Ansell

UNIVERSITY
PRESS OF
AMERICA

Lanham • New York • London

Copyright © 1994 by
University Press of America® Inc.
4720 Boston Way
Lanham, Maryland 20706

3 Henrietta Street
London WC2E 8LU England

Copublished by arrangement with the
Institute for Christian Studies

Library of Congress Cataloging-in-Publication Data
Ansell, Nicholas John.
The woman will overcome the warrior : a dialogue with
the Christian/feminist theology of Rosemary Radford Ruether /
Nicholas John Ansell.
p.   cm.
Includes bibliographical references and index.
1. Ruether, Rosemary Radford—Contributions in feminist theology.
2. Feminist theology.   3. Feminism—Religious aspects—
Christianity.   I. Title.
BT83.55.A57   1994   230'.092—dc20   94–17167 CIP

ISBN 0–8191–9545–6 (cloth : alk. paper)
ISBN 0–8191–9546–4 (pbk. : alk. paper)

IN MEMORY

OF MY GRANDMOTHER

MARY ISOBEL STRICKLAND WALLER

Contents

Dedication   v
Contents   vii
Acknowledgments   ix
Introduction   1

PART ONE: WRESTLING WITH THE PAST: THE NEGATION
AND AFFIRMATION OF WOMAN IN THE CHRISTIAN
TRADITION   15

Chapter 1: Ruether's Critique of the Theological Tradition 17
   I. Theological Anthropology   18
   II. Evil   25
   III. Mariology   27
   IV. Ecclesiology   30
   V. Christology   33
   VI. Nature   36
   VII. Eschatology   39
   VIII. God   41
   IX. An Initial Response   45

Chapter 2: The Methodological Foundations of Ruether's Feminist
Theology   51
   I. When a Tradition Faces a Crisis   51
   II. Ruether's Critique of the Bible   53
   III. Usable Tradition   60

Chapter 3: Towards an Evangelical-Reformational Feminism 77
   I. A Place to Stand   78
   II. Experience, Faith, and Revelation   81
   III. Tradition, Story, and the Language of Faith   88
   IV. The Relationship Between Bible, Word, and Spirit   95

V. Towards a Redemptively-Sensitive Hermeneutic   103
VI. Male and Female in the Scriptures   113
VII. Some Concluding Hermeneutical Comments   148

PART TWO: GIVING BIRTH TO THE FUTURE: TOWARDS
A CHRISTIAN FEMINIST THEOLOGY   173

Chapter 4: Ruether's Proposals for a Feminist Theology   173
I. Theological Anthropology   174
II. Evil   188
III. Mariology   193
IV. Ecclesiology   198
V. Christology   206
VI. Nature   212
VII. Eschatology   224
VIII. God   246

Chapter 5: The Sins of the Fathers?   285
I. Patriarchy as a Global Concept   285
II. The Rise and Development of Patriarchy   289
III. The Origin and Nature of Patriarchy   298
IV. Towards a Multi-Faceted Liberation Theology   313

Conclusion   327
I. Anthropology/Cosmology   328
II. The Biblical Drama   338
III. Towards an Integral Christian Feminist Theology   348

Bibliography   363
Index   381

Acknowledgements

This work on Rosemary Ruether's theology began as a thesis for the Master of Philosophical Foundations degree at the Institute for Christian Studies in Toronto, where it was defended in 1990. Since then it has been substantially revised and extended to incorporate comments on Ruether's work up until the end of 1992. During my work on this project, I have received help and support from a number of people, which I am very happy to acknowledge.

Professor Ellen Leonard of St. Michael's College at the University of Toronto, and Professors James Olthuis, Hendrik Hart and Brian Walsh, all Senior Members at the Institute for Christian Studies, each gave me valuable feedback on the thesis version of this study. Brian has also commented on the shape it has taken since then as has Jim, who deserves special thanks not only for serving as supervisor for my initial work on this project, but also for having read almost as many drafts of this manuscript as I have! While I have learned much from all of the Senior Members (and from many fellow Junior Members) at the ICS, the references to Jim and Henk's work in the following pages indicate something of the special debt I owe to them.

I am very grateful for the detailed and thoughtful comments I received from Christiane Carlson-Thies and from an outside reader who I would like to thank by name, but who was sadly anonymous. My thinking on feminist theology and its relation to reformed and reformational scholarship has been helped by the opportunity to hear and respond to a paper given at the ICS by Douglas Schuurman. Similarly, the chance to respond to a paper on Ruether's view of nature by Steve Bouma-Prediger was also timely. My thanks also to Mary Stewart Van Leeuwen and fellow members of her 1987 "Psychology of Women" course. Chapter 3 of this study has benefited from the questions and comments of those who heard some of my ideas on hermeneutics and exegesis in "Biblical Foundations" classes at the Institute for Christian Studies between 1988 and 1990. Special thanks to those who took my "Bible, Sex and Gender" course between 1990 and 1992 for their feedback to an early draft of this chapter.

While the comments of others have greatly enhanced this work, I am solely responsible for any weaknesses that remain, especially as I have stubbornly resisted some suggestions. Some of my own ideas presented in these pages have been worked out more fully in *The Troubled Marriage of Adam and Eve*, which was to be published by Regius Press in Bristol, England, until its sad demise. I hope this will appear elsewhere.

I would like to acknowledge my thanks to Rosemary Ruether for the consistently challenging and stimulating nature of her theology, as it has made this an exciting and rewarding project to work on. While I suspect that she may not entirely agree with my analysis of her work, I nevertheless sincerely hope that she will find this study to be responsive to her concerns and to represent a worthwhile attempt to grapple with issues of gender justice and authentic spirituality that face us all, and that are best faced together.

My thanks to the ICS publications committee and to Henk Hart for originally suggesting that my thesis could become a book. Thanks also to Bob VanderVennen and Willem Hart for preparing the text and diagrams for publication, to Claude Primeau of HarperCollins for getting hold of an early copy of *Gaia and God* for me, to Claude Bilodeau of Compuvisit for extracting chapter 4 from a resistant floppy disk, to David Collins and Bill Rowe for their support at a crucial time, and to Richard and Janice Russell for introducing me to the Reformational tradition of Christian scholarship practised at ICS, and for their hospitality to my family and I while I worked on the final proofreading of this manuscript soon after our return to England.

My studies in Toronto would not have been possible without the support of my parents, David and Molly Ansell, and my late uncle, Tony Ansell. Furthermore, this book simply could not have been finished without the constant encouragement of my wife, Gloria Nelson, and the patience of our son, Daniel. I'm very grateful! One of the themes of this study is that the past is not always something that we need to be emancipated from as it may provide us with a rich legacy of precious memories that can empower us to face the evils of our generation with hope. It is therefore very fitting that I dedicate this book to the memory of my Grandmother, with thanks to God for the wonderful gift of her life.

Nik Ansell
Bath, England
Lent, 1994

Introduction

My intellectual questions have never been purely theoretical. I have in every case dealt with existential questions about how I was to situate my life, my identity, my commitments. I have never taken up an intellectual issue which did not have direct connections with clarifying and resolving questions about my personal existence, about how I should align my existence with others, ideologically and socially. (Rosemary Radford Ruether)[1]

It is ironic that one of the most famous quotations from the history of ideas calls the very nature and legitimacy of that history into question. In his eleventh thesis on Feuerbach, Karl Marx asserts, "The philosophers have only *interpreted* the world, in various ways; the point, however, is to *change* it."[2] Since Marx spent much of his own life interpreting the world, it might seem paradoxical to those who have visited his tomb in London's Highgate cemetery that it is this saying, which clearly relativizes theory in relation to action, that has been chosen to grace the monument erected to his memory.

While Marx's famous dictum is supposed to goad us into action rather than mere speculation, it is, nevertheless, extremely thought-provoking. We might wonder whether Marx's apparent elevation of praxis above theory is falsified by the fact that it has been Marx's *ideas*—including this famous saying—which have proven to be so instrumental in changing the world, or at least those countries with governments that have described themselves with his name. Alternatively, the impact that Marx's thought has had may lead us to interpret this saying not as a call to replace theory with praxis so much as a challenge to engage in the kind of scholarship that has social transformation as its goal. Seen in this light, the eleventh thesis on Feuerbach is a fitting epitaph for Marx's life after all.

In the helpful discussion of the relationship between theory and praxis which he presented during the 1981 Kuyper Lectures at the Free University of Amsterdam, Nicholas Wolterstorff distinguished between two very different ways of engaging in scholarship. First there is the well-known "ivory tower" approach that is taken by those scholars who have no desire to see theoretical work as a means to change the world. "As Rotterdam burns," says Wolterstorff wryly, "they study Sanskrit verb forms." In contrast to those who aspire to "pure theory," however, he also notes with approval that there are scholars who have made structural reform the governing interest of their theorizing. Wolterstorff describes such "scholarship of social commitment" as "praxis-oriented theorizing."[3]

This second approach to the academic enterprise is very clearly exemplified by the American Catholic theologian who had delivered the Kuyper Lectures of the previous year: Rosemary Radford Ruether. One need only look at her careful analysis of the rhetorical technique of Gregory of Nazianzus to see that she could have had a successful career devoted to the kind of detailed and disciplined work exemplified by those of us who choose to concentrate on "Sanskrit verb forms."[4] Yet with the exception of this doctoral dissertation, all of Ruether's published work—whether in systematic theology, church history or contemporary cultural analysis—is clearly animated by her desire to uncover the roots of our present social problems and find solutions. It is no coincidence that the material on Christology and cultural criticism that she delivered at the Kuyper Lectures was later published under the title *To Change the World*.[5]

Her passionate, provocative, and praxis-oriented approach to theology is undoubtedly one of the reasons why William M. Ramsey placed her in the exalted company of Walter Rauschenbusch, Martin Luther King, and Gustavo Gutierrez when he selected her work for special attention in his book *Four Modern Prophets.*[6] The title of this work testifies to Ruether's importance as a contemporary theologian.

Although Ruether is best known as a feminist theologian, she is more accurately described as a liberation theologian for whom women's liberation is one of a large number of concerns. This is not to deny that feminist issues feature very prominently within her corpus. But even in those of her writings that are completely devoted to feminist theology, she frequently connects her feminist concerns with her analysis of anti-Semitism, heterosexism, racism, cosmological dualism, capitalism and the ecology crisis. When Ruether came to the Institute for Christian Studies in Toronto in 1983 to give the Christianity and Learning Lectures, Bernard Zylstra succinctly captured both the nature and scope of her work when he introduced her by saying,

> She is a theologian who, in a sense parallel to Marx, searches for the alienating chasms between God and humanity, humanity and the world, spirit and body, male and female, in the very roots of history and fabric of the world's major civilizations, including our own.[7]

To say that Rosemary Ruether is a prolific writer is something of an understatement. To date, in addition to having written over five hundred articles and essays, she has either authored, co-authored, edited or co-edited twenty-three books![8] These have all been published within a twenty-five year period in which she has also been academically busy as a teacher and public speaker. By the end of Ruether's career, these figures will no doubt be even more impressive.

While the fact that Ruether has been concerned with the oppression and liberation of women since the beginning of her academic career can be seen in some of her earliest essays and articles,[9] the special attention that she has given to issues germane to feminist theology is most evident in her writings that have been published in book form. The future direction of much of her research is clearly anticipated in two studies in her fourth book,

Liberation Theology: Human Hope Confronts Christian History and American Power, published in 1972.[10] "Is Christianity Misogynist? The Failure of Women's Liberation in the Church," focuses on the sexism of the Church Fathers to which Ruether will refer repeatedly in her later works. "Mother Earth and the Megamachine: A Theology of Liberation in a Feminine, Somatic and Ecological Perspective," as its title suggests, correlates sexism, the domination of nature, and dualistic thinking in a way that characterizes her cultural analysis to this day. It also shows an interest in the counter-patriarchal potential of Ancient Near Eastern religion, which Ruether has continued to explore. All of these concerns can be seen in her most recent work, *Gaia and God: An Ecofeminist Theology of Earth Healing*.[11]

1974 saw the publication of the first of five books to date that Ruether has either edited or co-edited which consist of important essays by a number of feminist scholars on the relationship between women and religion in the history of Western culture. *Religion and Sexism: Images of Woman in the Jewish and Christian Traditions*[12] was followed in 1979 by *Women of Spirit: Female Leadership in the Jewish and Christian Traditions*, co-edited with Eleanor McLaughlin.[13] A three volume documentary history entitled *Women and Religion in America* appeared between 1981 and 1986.[14] This was co-edited with Rosemary Skinner Keller, a colleague at Garrett Evangelical Theological Seminary in Evanston, Illinois. These works, including Ruether's own essays in them, have made a very significant contribution to feminist historiography.

With the sole exception of *Faith and Fratricide: The Theological Roots of Anti-Semitism*,[15] which also appeared in 1974, the next fourteen of her books published after *Religion and Sexism* all contain studies that focus on the oppression and liberation of women. Indeed, no fewer than ten of these are exclusively devoted to feminist theology. The works in this latter category which I have not yet mentioned include: *New Woman/New Earth: Sexist Ideologies and Human Liberation* (1975),[16] *From Machismo to Mutuality: Essays on Sexism and Woman-Man Liberation*, co-authored with Eugene C. Bianchi (1976),[17] *Mary—The Feminine Face of the Church* (1977),[18] *Sexism and God-Talk: Towards a Feminist Theology* (1983), *Woman-*

guides: Readings Toward a Feminist Theology (1985),[19] and *Women-Church: Theology and Practice of Feminist Liturgical Communities* (1986).[20] While these works make it easy to understand why Ruether is best known as a feminist theologian, the minimal attention to feminist concerns in her first three books and in two of her three most recent works serve to remind us that she is a thinker who cannot be classified so narrowly.[21]

This study will focus on Ruether's feminist theology, although some attention will be given to the question of how it is interwoven with other aspects of her overall theology of liberation. While the discussion is deliberately wide-ranging in order to reflect something of the breadth of Ruether's theological reflection, there is one fundamental question which I wish to explore in relation to Ruether's thought which provides the unifying thread in the following chapters: How is it possible to develop a theology that is simultaneously feminist and Christian? Or, to put it another way, what does it mean to develop a feminist theology in a distinctively Christian way, and what does it mean to develop a Christian theology in a distinctively feminist way?

There are, of course, many ways of defining both "feminism" and "Christianity." Minimally, however, I suggest that to be a feminist one must be committed to opposing all that oppresses women and robs them of their full humanity. While different worldviews will understand what constitutes the "full humanity" of women in different ways, thus allowing for the possibility of a number of feminist perspectives, any authentically feminist position will take very seriously what women themselves experience as liberating and dehumanizing. In other words, it will honour the authority of women's experience. There is nothing in this definition that rules out the possibility of a feminist also being a Christian or a Humanist or a Hindu. Consistency demands, however, that to the extent that one's own religious tradition is judged to be responsible for oppressing women, it too must be called to change.

To be a *Christian* feminist carries with it the additional minimal requirement that one nurture a positive relationship to at least some aspects of the Christian tradition to the extent that they are allowed to shape one's feminist vision and praxis. While many Christian feminists reject large parts of the Christian tradition, none of them, by definition, reject all of it. It would be hard to imagine a Christian feminist wanting to continue in the Christian faith if she or he concluded, for example, that Jesus is part of the problem and in no way part of the solution. By the same token, no one who has noted the largely negative view of the Christian tradition in Mary Daly's first book *The Church and the Second Sex* can be too surprised by her move to a "postchristian" feminist position in her later works.[22]

A Christian feminist position, therefore, needs to maintain significant continuities with the Christian tradition even when it calls for extensive change. Christian feminists engaged in trying to bring reformation to the church and to theology, have to decide which resources they will draw upon and which norms they will appeal to. If the resources chosen do not include resources from the Christian tradition, and if the norms to which appeal is made are not demonstrably Christian in character, the very possibility of a distinctly Christian feminism is inevitably called into question.

In her book *Feminist Theology/Christian Theology: In Search of Method,* Pamela Dickey Young argues persuasively that the way we view the normative relationship between past Christian tradition and the present experience of women that has been ignored for so long by traditional theology profoundly affects the shape of our theologizing and accounts for many of the differences between contemporary Christian feminists. Some of the pertinent questions that she raises in this context include:

> In what ways should a Christian feminist theology be continuous with past Christian tradition? With which Christian tradition or traditions should it be continuous? In what ways should a Christian feminist theology reformulate, rework, and rethink these traditions in order to deal with the pressing questions of the present? What should be the norm or norms that determine how all these questions are answered?[23]

Whether Ruether's own approach to such foundational and methodological questions allows her to construct an integrally Christian feminist theology is a question which will never be far beneath the surface in the following chapters.

This study is divided into two parts which are respectively entitled *Wrestling With The Past: The Negation and Affirmation of Woman in the Christian Tradition*, and *Giving Birth To The Future: Towards a Christian Feminist Theology*. Taken together, these titles point to the two main foci of the study: How should we evaluate the Christian tradition that we have inherited with respect to its view of woman? and How can we draw on that tradition in order to construct a woman-affirming theology for our times?

Part One directly concerns foundational issues. It looks at Ruether's evaluation of previous Christian thought, with a particular focus on those elements of our heritage that she believes feminist theologians should continue to affirm and those which she believes they (we) must reject. Chapter 1 summarizes her critique of past and current thinking in eight major areas of Christian theology. Chapter 2 explores the options we have when a tradition is in crisis. It also describes Ruether's positive and negative conclusions about the Bible and looks briefly at some areas of "usable tradition" in Christian (and non-Christian) thought which she believes can contribute to the formation of a feminist theology. Chapter 3, which concludes Part One, offers a preliminary assessment of Ruether's basic stance towards tradition and normativity and sets out an alternative hermeneutical and exegetical basis for a Christian feminist theology.

Ruether and I both agree that the way we assess the past inevitably affects the way we will attempt to construct the future. Thus, while these first three chapters all look at material that is foundational to Part Two in which I examine Ruether's constructive proposals, chapter 3 is more specifically intended to give support to the particular way in which I assess and respond to these proposals in later chapters.

While Part One primarily concerns the criticism of tradition, Part Two addresses the task of creative reconstruction. Chapter 4 parallels the beginning of Part One by summarizing and responding to Ruether's constructive proposals for the same eight areas of theological thought selected for examination in chapter 1. Chapter 5 focuses on some aspects of her cultural analysis, paying special attention to the nature of patriarchy. Finally, in the conclusion, I offer some closing comments on what I see as the overall strengths and weaknesses of Ruether's Christian feminist theology.

The title of this book, *The Woman Will Overcome The Warrior*, is taken from Jer. 31:22.[24] Ruether quotes this text at the beginning of her book *New Woman/New Earth*. In its original context, the passage from which it comes describes Israel's future return from exile. Its powerful counter-patriarchal language, however, is suggestive of the prophetic imagination and hope that Christian feminists such as Ruether and I believe the church needs to nurture today as it finds itself in a patriarchal world that is deeply alienated from its true calling.

The wording of the subtitle—*A Dialogue with the Christian/ Feminist Theology of Rosemary Radford Ruether*—is also significant. *Firstly*, it points to the deliberately broad scope of this study. My conviction that so much of what Ruether has to say is important has led me to try to pay attention to her feminist theology as a whole rather than attempt to "master" one particular facet of her thought in great detail. *Secondly*, the fact that I have attempted a *dialogue* with her thought rather than merely an *analysis* of it, reflects my belief that she intends her writings to provoke a discussion not just of her own ideas but of the *issues* with which she grapples. I am convinced that to attempt a "detached" examination of her work that brackets one's own response to these issues is to fail to take the nature of her work seriously. As many of the proposals that I put forward in these pages took shape as a result of wrestling with Ruether's writings, I would feel that the following study was incomplete if I left them out. *Thirdly*, the virgule or slash in the phrase "Christian/Feminist Theology" is important as it hints at my conviction that Ruether's feminist theology, for all its many strengths, is not as integrally Christian as it could be in the final analysis.

This sympathetic critique of Ruether's thought is not aimed at Christians who are fundamentally hostile towards any attempt to construct a Christian feminist theology. If I had written with such an audience in mind, I would have produced a completely different book. My primary concern has been to engage those who are either comfortable with, or open to, Ruether's position. Nevertheless, I am also aware that there are many convinced Christian feminists, whose views I respect, who locate themselves far closer to the "conservative" end of the theological spectrum than Ruether and her followers. For this reason, they may find many of her more "unconventional" or "unorthodox" ideas less appealing or worth wrestling with than I do. I have therefore tried to write in such a way that both my own views and those of Ruether can be heard as easily as possible by fellow Christians who locate themselves (as I do) somewhere within the broad tradition of contemporary evangelicalism.

I also hope to make contact with those who, like myself, are philosophically and theologically indebted to the "reformational" tradition of Christian scholarship associated with Abraham Kuyper, Herman Dooyeweerd and D. H. Th. Vollenhoven.[25] A great strength of this school of thought, I believe, is that it has consistently struggled to avoid the dualism, moralism, and individualism that characterizes so much evangelical scholarship and piety while retaining an attitude of trust and submission to the Scriptures. Fortunately, there are many Christians indebted to this school of thought who are already convinced of the importance of incorporating feminist concerns into their scholarship and spirituality. Some Christian feminist scholars, such as Elaine Storkey and Mary Stewart Van Leeuwen, have done valuable work drawing on the resources of this tradition in their areas of study. In addition to making some suggestions about what such an approach might look like in the area of philosophical theology, I also hope to persuade those members of this school of thought who are doubtful about the merits of "Christian feminism" that this is a valid and important avenue of exploration.

My concern to engage as many as three potentially distinct audiences can be seen most clearly in chapter 3. On the one hand, the way I introduce this discussion on feminism and the Bible reflects my desire to make as much contact as possible with Ruether's concerns, even though I end up working with the Scriptures in a very different way from her. On the other hand, the hermeneutical and exegetical suggestions that I put forward have been written partly with the reformational and evangelical communities in mind in order to alleviate fears or suspicions that Ruether's stance towards the Bible automatically invalidates her Christian feminist proposals in general.

I am well aware that attempting to write for a number of different communities carries the risk that I will end up communicating with none of them. I have taken this risk all the same because I believe that both evangelical and non-evangelical Christians need to hear each other if the Body of Christ is to wrestle successfully with what it means to be normatively male and female in God's good but fallen creation. Ruether's theology is an important contribution in this context, so I hope that this study can make her thought accessible for those who might normally dismiss her as being too close to the "liberal" end of the theological spectrum, while also offering a critical yet sympathetic assessment of her strengths and weaknesses for those who already rightly recognize her importance.

Although I am not just writing for members of the academic community, this study is still intended to be theoretical in focus. I began this introduction by raising the possibility of engaging in praxis-oriented scholarship. I believe that scholarship, which is itself a form of praxis, should (where possible) be related to the praxis of social and personal transformation—even when it includes the examination of "Sanskrit verb forms." It is therefore my hope that this piece of work, including both my summary and assessment of Ruether's theology and my own proposals, will be of some help to fellow Christians who are engaged in the vitally important task of trying to discern where the Spirit of God is leading us as women and men in our times.

Notes

1. Rosemary Radford Ruether, "Asking the Existential Questions" *The Christian Century* 97 (April 2 1980): 374-75.
2. Marx's "Theses on Feuerbach" are reproduced in Robert C. Tucker, ed., *The Marx-Engels Reader* (New York: W.W. Norton & Co., 1972), 108-109.
3. Nicholas Wolterstorff, *Until Justice and Peace Embrace* (Grand Rapids: Eerdmans, 1983), 162.
4. See chap. 2 of Rosemary Radford Ruether, *Gregory of Nazianzus: Rhetor and Philosopher* (Oxford: Clarendon Press, 1969), hereafter referred to as *GN*.

5. See Rosemary Radford Ruether, *To Change the World: Christology and Cultural Criticism* (New York: Crossroad, 1981), hereafter referred to as *TCW*.
6. William M. Ramsey, *Four Modern Prophets: Walter Rauschenbusch, Martin Luther King, Jr., Gustavo Gutierrez and Rosemary Radford Ruether*, (Atlanta: John Knox Press, 1986).
7. This quotation is transcribed from a recording of Ruether's lecture on sexism and religious language. This was the first of three lectures which she gave on the subject of "Women's Experience and Christian Thought." This and her two other lectures on theological anthropology and Christology were published soon afterwards in Rosemary Radford Ruether, *Sexism and God-Talk: Toward a Feminist Theology* (Boston: Beacon Press, 1983), hereafter referred to as *SGT*.
8. The fullest published bibliography that I am aware of can be found in Mary Hembrow Snyder, *The Christology of Rosemary Radford Ruether: A Critical Introduction* (Mystic, Connecticut: Twenty-Third Publications, 1988), 134-41.
9. Early feminist essays by Ruether include: "The Becoming of Women in Church and Society," *Cross Currents* 17 (Fall 1967): 419-26, "Male Chauvinist Theology and the Anger of Women," *Cross Currents* 21 (Spring 1971): 173-85, "Male Clericalism and the Dread of Women," *The Ecumenist* 11 (July-August 1973): 65-69, and "Sexism and the Theology of Liberation," *The Christian Century* 90 (December 12 1973): 1224-29. In her book *Disputed Questions: On Being a Christian* (Nashville: Abingdon, 1982; Maryknoll: Orbis Books, 1989), 109, hereafter referred to as *DQ*, Ruether writes, "It is hard to trace my awakening to feminism in the same way as my political awakening, because it seems to me that I was implicitly always a feminist, if by being a feminist one means a woman who fights for her full realization and accepts no special barriers to her aspirations on the basis of sexual identity." Later (p. 118) she writes, "my first feminist writings of the midsixties focused on a criticism of the Catholic views of sexuality and reproduction.... In the late sixties I began formal research on attitudes toward women in the Christian tradition." See also Rosemary Radford Ruether, "The Development of My Theology," *Religious Studies Review* 15 (January 1989): 1-4.
10. See chaps. 7 and 8 of Rosemary Radford Ruether, *Liberation Theology: Human Hope Confronts Christian History and American Power* (New York: Paulist Press, 1972), hereafter referred to as *LT*. Feminist concerns can also be seen in chap. 1.
11. See Rosemary Radford Ruether, *Gaia and God: An Ecofeminist Theology of Earth Healing* (San Francisco: HarperCollins, 1992), hereafter referred to as *GG*. This important work came to my attention too late to be integrated into the following study as fully as I would have liked. There are some comments on it in chaps. 4 and 5, however.

12. See Rosemary Radford Ruether, ed., *Religion and Sexism: Images of Woman in the Jewish and Christian Traditions* (New York: Simon and Schuster, 1974), hereafter referred to as *RS*.

13. See Rosemary Radford Ruether and Eleanor McLaughlin, eds., *Women of Spirit: Female Leadership in the Jewish and Christian Traditions* (New York: Simon and Schuster, 1979), hereafter referred to as *WS*.

14. See Rosemary Radford Ruether and Rosemary Skinner Keller, eds., *Women and Religion in America*, 3 vols (San Francisco: Harper and Row, 1981, 1983, 1986).

15. See Rosemary Radford Ruether, *Faith and Fratricide: The Theological Roots of Anti-Semitism* (New York: The Seabury Press, 1974), hereafter referred to as *FF*.

16. See Rosemary Radford Ruether, *New Woman/New Earth: Sexist Ideologies and Human Liberation* (New York: The Seabury Press, 1975) hereafter referred to as *NWNE*.

17. See Eugene C. Bianchi and Rosemary Radford Ruether, *From Machismo to Mutuality: Essays on Sexism and Woman-Man Liberation* (New York: Paulist Press, 1976), hereafter referred to as *FMM*.

18. See Rosemary Radford Ruether, *Mary—The Feminine Face of the Church* (Philadelphia: The Westminster Press, 1977), hereafter referred to as *MFFC*.

19. See Rosemary Radford Ruether, *Womanguides: Readings Toward a Feminist Theology* (Boston: Beacon Press, 1985), hereafter referred to as *WG*.

20. See Rosemary Radford Ruether, *Women-Church: Theology and Practice of Feminist Liturgical Communities* (San Francisco: Harper and Row, 1986), hereafter referred to as *WC*.

21. In addition to *GN* and *FF*, the works that contain little or no explicit attention to feminist issues are: *The Church Against Itself: An Inquiry into the Conditions of Historical Existence for the Eschatological Community* (New York: Herder and Herder, 1967), hereafter referred to as *CAI*; *The Radical Kingdom: The Western Experience of Messianic Hope* (New York: Paulist Press, 1970), hereafter referred to as *RK*; *The Wrath of Jonah: The Crisis of Religious Nationalism in the Israeli-Palestinian Conflict* (San Francisco: Harper and Row, 1989), co-authored with Herman J. Ruether, and *Beyond Occupation: American Jewish, Christian, and Palestinian Voices for Peace* (Boston: Beacon Press, 1990), co-edited with Marc H. Ellis. In addition to *LT*, *TCW*, *DQ* and *GG*, her works that contain explicitly feminist theological reflections together with other material are: *The Liberating Bond: Covenants—Biblical and Contemporary* (New York: Friendship Press, 1978), co-authored with Wolfgang Roth, hereafter referred to as *TLB*, and *Contemporary Roman Catholicism: Crises and Challenges* (Kansas: Sheed and Ward, 1987), hereafter referred to as *CRC*.

22. See Mary Daly, *The Church and the Second Sex* (New York: Harper and Row, 1968) and her "Postchristian Feminist Introduction" to the 1975 edition of that work.
23. Pamela Dickey Young, *Feminist Theology/Christian Theology: In Search of Method* (Minneapolis: Fortress Press 1990), 20.
24. This is a combination of the translations offered by the RSV and NIV. Biblical quotations in this study are taken from the NIV unless otherwise stated.
25. Two popular introductions to this academic tradition which are aimed primarily at an evangelical audience are Brian J. Walsh and J. Richard Middleton, *The Transforming Vision: Shaping a Christian World View* (Downers Grove: InterVarsity Press, 1984) and Albert M. Wolters, *Creation Regained: Biblical Basics for a Reformational Worldview* (Grand Rapids: Eerdmans, 1985). For more philosophical introductions, see Hendrik Hart, *Understanding Our World: An Integral Ontology* (Lanham: University Press of America, 1984) and Roy A. Clouser, *The Myth of Religious Neutrality: An Essay on the Hidden Role of Religious Belief in Theories* (Notre Dame: University of Notre Dame Press, 1991). On Dogmatics, see Gordon J. Spykman, *Reformational Theology: A New Paradigm for Doing Dogmatics* (Grand Rapids: Eerdmans, 1992).

Part One

WRESTLING WITH THE PAST

The Negation and Affirmation of Woman
in the Christian Tradition

Chapter 1: Ruether's Critique of the Theological Tradition

If there is one point on which feminist and anti-feminist Christians agree, it is that much of the theological tradition that we have inherited from our forefathers is clearly incompatible with feminist commitments. Whether this is a strength or a weakness of the tradition, however, is the bone of contention.

Ruether is very clear about where she stands on this issue. She writes,

> The critical principle of feminist theology is the promotion of the full humanity of women. Whatever denies, diminishes, or distorts the full humanity of women is, therefore, appraised as not redemptive. Theologically speaking, whatever diminishes or denies the full humanity of women must be presumed not to reflect the divine or an authentic relation to the divine, or to reflect the authentic nature of things, or to be the message or work of an authentic redeemer or a community of redemption.[1]

If the "full humanity" of women is appealed to as a norm by which to evaluate the tradition, Ruether argues, then a radical reappraisal becomes necessary. While much that is currently regarded as "mainstream" must now be regarded as deficient, by the same criterion, there are marginal and even "heretical" movements which "must now be seen as efforts to hold on to an authentic tradition of women's equality." In Ruether's words, "We underestimate the radical intent of women's studies in religion if we do not recognize that it aims at nothing less than this kind of radical reconstruction of the normative tradition."[2]

The task of criticizing our theological heritage is important to Ruether because she believes that religion is "undoubtedly the single most important shaper and enforcer of the image and role of women in culture and society." Even if the major cause of misogyny is taken to be economic or psychological, she argues, we should still recognize that religion has tremendous power as "the ideological reflection of this sexual domination and subjugation."[3]

This chapter will therefore summarise Ruether's assessment of the weaknesses of traditional Christian thinking in the areas of theological anthropology, evil, Mariology, ecclesiology, Christology, nature, eschatology, and God. While these eight topics have been chosen because they are the areas of traditional theology selected by Ruether herself in her most systematic work, *Sexism and God-Talk*, these summaries will draw on material found throughout her corpus.[4]

I. Theological Anthropology

"Christian theological anthropology," writes Ruether, "recognizes a dual structure in its understanding of humanity" which distinguishes our "essence" from our "existence." On the basis of this "dual structure," it is claimed that "[w]hat humanity is potentially and authentically is not the same as what humanity has been historically."[5] This essence/existence distinction is also crucial to Ruether's own theological anthropology.[6] What Ruether objects to in the theological tradition is the tendency to correlate this distinction between essence and existence or *imago dei* and fallenness with humanity as male and female. Thus, while the tradition never categorically and unambiguously denies that woman is in the image of God, it nevertheless closely identifies her with the body or passions, which are, in turn, understood as the sin-prone part of the self. In Ruether's judgment,

This ambiguous structure of Christian anthropology expresses what today might be called a "case of projection." Males, as the monopolizers of theological self-definition, project onto women their own rejection of their "lower selves." .... Woman in her essential nature is seen as having less of the higher spiritual nature and more of the lower physical nature. She is an "inferior mix" and, as such, is by nature non-normative and under subjugation.[7]

This form of subjugation corresponds to the first of the three "layers" which Ruether sees as making up the ideology of sexism: objectification, paranoia, and idealization. In this first "layer," woman is regarded as the object or tool of male power and is imaged as body or property in the same manner as other groups that are reduced to servitude.[8] In Ruether's earliest and most detailed research into Christian anthropology, which focuses on the patristic period, this assimilation of the male-female distinction into a soul-body dualism is made the focus of attention and thus provides us with a good example of the above phenomenon.[9]

The Church Fathers, Ruether claims, are caught between the competing claims of the body-affirming view of creation found in the Hebrew scriptures, and an ascetic spirituality rooted in Platonic dualism. Consequently, the patristic view of woman fell between the two stools of this ambivalence about the goodness of the body and sexuality.[10]

Of all the Latin Church Fathers, Ruether believes that Augustine is the most historically significant. As "the classical source of ... patriarchal anthropology," he functions as her *bête noire*. Not only does he make explicit the anti-woman elements that are present in earlier theologians, but he also functions as "the source of this type of anthropology for the later Western Christian tradition, both Catholic and Protestant, which looks to [him] as the font of orthodoxy."[11]

Here I will give just a few examples of what Ruether takes to be the misogynous and androcentric features of his thought. Perhaps the most important example for her is his interpretation of the image of God. According to her reading, the *imago dei* is summed up for him in the original Adam who contained both male spirit and female corporeality. Eve, who is taken from his side to be his helpmate in the task of procreation, comes to symbolize this bodiliness. Although she too is a composite of spirit and body, Ruether notes that "in relation to man she stands for body *vis-à-vis* male spirit."[12] The male alone possesses the full image of God while the woman does not unless taken together with her husband. In response to this androcentrism, Ruether writes,

> Woman is therefore defined as a *relative being*, who exists only in relationship to the male, who alone possesses full autonomous personhood. This view of woman is perhaps the ultimate core of misogynism.[13]

Although this identification of woman with body does enable him to account for her subordination in the order of nature, Augustine must also allow her the power to overcome bodiliness in order to be redeemed. Thus he is forced to distinguish what she *is*—a rational spirit equivalent to the male—and what she *symbolizes*— "the subjugation of body to spirit in nature and that debasing carnality which draws the male mind down from its heavenly heights."[14] But, as Ruether points out, Augustine, like other Church Fathers, still tends to *identify* what woman symbolizes with her true nature. Thus in his discussion of marriage, for example, a "strange schizophrenia" is created whereby the man is simultaneously exhorted to love his wife's spiritual nature while despising "all her bodily functions as woman and wife."[15]

The distortions of male perception that give rise to this definition of woman as "body" are never recognized for what they are by Augustine or by the tradition of male dominance that he exemplifies. Neither are women themselves allowed to challenge this identification of their true nature with the way they are perceived by the dominant sex. Ruether comments,

> The essence of male ideology can be said to be contained precisely in this cultural relationship, where the woman is the

one acted upon and defined by the male perception and "use," and her own self-definition and perspective are never heard or incorporated culturally. Women, as all oppressed people, live in a culture of silence, as objects, never subjects of the relationship.[16]

This definition of woman in relation to male "use" is particularly striking in Augustine's view of the sexual relationship. Unlike the Fathers in the Greek or Eastern tradition, Augustine did believe that there would have been procreation before the fall—although it would have taken place without sexual libido. In Paradise, Ruether argues, Augustine believed that man would have "used" woman as he now uses his hands or feet: dispassionately, and in full accord with the rational will. He would have sown his seed in her as a farmer now sows his seed in the furrow of a field. In other words, he would have been completely innocent of what fallen man experiences: the " 'hideous' erection of his sexual organ and that rush of sensual feeling that defies rational control in his response to the visual image of woman."[17]

Augustine's obsession with the male erection as revealing the nature of sin should not be dismissed as merely a sexual hang-up that is otherwise extrinsic to his thought, Ruether argues. It is quite integral to his whole position and cannot be adequately criticized "without finally entering into a fundamental reconstruction of this entire system of theological anthropology of which it was an expression." Ruether does not flinch from spelling out the misogyny inherent in such a view of sin. She writes,

[I]f the male erection was the essence of sin, woman, as its source, became peculiarly the cause, object and extension of it. This . . . results in an essentially depersonalized view of the relationship to woman. She becomes literally an extension of the male body, to be used either in a masturbatory way for "carnal pleasure," or, in a right ordering of the male body in relation to its "head," in an instrumental way as a mechanism under male control for impregnation and incubation of the fetus. In neither case does she appear as a true "other" or

sonalization of woman must be seen as a necessary consequence of the assimilation of the male-female relationship into
the body-soul relationship, which implies a subject-object
relationship between man and woman.[18]

This depersonalized view of sexual relations, writes Ruether,
conditions the three images of woman that we find in Augustine and
the other Church Fathers. Woman is either whore, wife or virgin.
As "whore," she "represents sinful carnality which is the essence of
the fall."[19] As ideal "wife," she is "the image of that totally submissive body, obedient to her 'head' . . . . [She] has no personal rights
over her own body . . . [but] allow[s] herself to be used solely as an
instrument of procreation."[20] In this light, Ruether challenges the
frequently made claim that Christianity elevated the position of
woman in the ancient world by noting that by means of teachings
such as these it actually lowered the status that wives had been
accorded in some of the legislation of later Roman society.[21]

It is only in the new order of the resurrection as "virgin" that
woman could rise to equality with the male. If we are sensitive to
historical context, Ruether argues, then we can appreciate that at
the time when the old Roman way of life was disintegrating, the
ascetic life was a genuinely liberating option for women as it gave
them the chance to throw off traditional roles and pursue self-
development and self-definition within the security of female-led
and female-funded communities.[22]

However there is an ambiguity to what Ruether calls "virginal
feminism" which is fully appreciated in her analysis. On the one
hand, she writes, "[T]he image of the virginal woman appear[s] as a
new cultural ideal, raising up the possibility of woman as capable of
the highest spiritual development, which could lead to the *summum
bonum* of communion with the divine, intellectual nature of the
Divine itself."[23] On the other hand, woman could achieve this "only
at the expense of crushing out of her being all vestiges of her bodily
and her female 'natures' and rising to 'unnatural manliness.' "[24] If
Ruether is sympathetic to the women who chose this path, she has
no praise for the males, like Jerome, who strongly advocated this as

the direction in which their spiritual pilgrimage should go. Thus, in a far more cynical tone she writes,

> Virginal woman was thus bound for heaven, and her male ascetic devotees would stop at nothing short of this prize for her. But they paid the price of despising all real physical women, sex and fecundity, and wholly etherealizing women into incorporeal phantasms in order to provide love objects for the sublimated libido and guard against turning back to any physical expression of love with the dangerous daughters of Eve.[25]

Although Ruether's only detailed work on anthropology focuses on the patristic period, she does offer some brief assessments of later thinkers which back up her claim that "[t]his pattern of patriarchal anthropology can be illustrated in the entire line of classical Christian theology from ancient to modern times."[26] Aquinas, for example, "continues the Augustinian tradition"[27] by strengthening the identification of woman with the inferior side of the self through the adoption of an Aristotelian biology that saw men and women in terms of a form-matter distinction. While her inferiority is deepened by sin, she is by nature a misbegotten male who is under subjection to the man due to his greater rational capacities.

The Reformation, in Ruether's judgment, brings minor modifications but no essential change. Although Luther thought that Adam and Eve would have been originally equal, he believed that woman must remain subject to man in the present dispensation as a punishment for her sin. Similarly, although the Calvinist tradition stressed that woman is as fully in the image of God as man even after the fall, it still claimed that she should be subordinate, not because of sin or inferiority, but on the basis of a difference of appointed social office that represents an original creation order that is now restored in Christ. It is this pattern of thought, Ruether observes, that is clearly present in the theology of Karl Barth.[28]

Apart from this dominant form of patriarchal anthropology, Ruether does note the presence of more egalitarian alternatives in the Christian tradition, especially among Christian Gnostics and various mystical ascetic sects and movements. In the Protestant tradition, utopian and millenarian sects such as the Rappites, the Shakers, and the Quakers are important in this respect.

Ruether discusses most of these movements under the heading of "Eschatological Feminism."[29] This tradition, she explains, "affirmed the restored equality of men and women in Christ by referring to an original transcendent anthropology that existed before the fall into the finite condition characterized by sexual dimorphism."[30] Although these movements felt that the equality that had existed between the sexes in this transcendent state should be expressed in the present age in the life of the church, they did not believe that woman's subordination in society could be altered. Women were not invited by such movements to change society, in other words, but were encouraged to leave it for a community that was preparing for the transcendent life of heaven.

Like the "virginal feminism" of the patristic period, "eschatological feminism" proves to have severe limitations. Where it fails, according to Ruether, is in its lack of affirmation of the equivalence of men and women in the order of creation and thus in society as a whole, an affirmation that is crucial if Christians are to make any decisive break with patriarchy here and now. In opposition to "virginal" and "eschatological" feminism, Ruether claims, the church must reject the identification of the order of nature with male dominance as liberal feminism realized when it adopted a secularized form of the Christian doctrine of the *imago dei*.

In Ruether's judgment, it was the impact of Enlightenment thought which allowed modern Christians, for the first time, to connect ideas of redemption and equality in Christ with social reform. This perspective is to be sharply contrasted with positions that understand salvation as "available only in heaven" or that associate it "with a sectarian, redemptive community who anticipate the eschatological order by transcending the civil and familial order." Clearly approving of this new development, Ruether writes,

[R]edemption can now be conceived as a reform of the civil and even the familial order in such a way as to vindicate the equivalence of all persons with equal access to political power and economic and cultural opportunities for self-expression. This shift in the relationship of the theology of creation and redemption is basic for all modern theologies of liberation, including feminist theology.[31]

II. Evil

The second of the three "layers" that Ruether sees in the ideology of sexism "goes beyond objectification to paranoia."[32] Women are not merely seen as body or property, but as evil. As such, they become the victims of hostile outbursts in the same way as Jews and negroes. In Ruether's words, "Genocidal campaigns, witch-hunts, and pogroms go beyond the self-interest of the powerful into a fantasy realm in which the dominant group imagines that by purging society of the 'other' it can, in some sense, eradicate 'evil.' "[33]

The identification of woman with evil is an extension of the patristic view of her dangerous carnality. Yet for all his fear of the female body, it was still possible for a Church Father such as Jerome to count female ascetics among his closest and most highly respected friends.[34] But, as Ruether notes, by the late medieval period, the bifurcation between spiritual femininity, symbolized by the Virgin Mary, and the ordinary fleshly woman became so extreme that even nuns were seen as sexually dangerous.[35]

The increasing demonization of woman, Ruether argues, can be seen in the fact that by the thirteenth century, the male demonic figure *Mundus* had been replaced in the medieval cathedral by *Frau Welt* or *Dame Nature* whom Ruether describes as "a female figure who is speciously fair from the front but behind is crawling with verminous decay," and who thus "typifies this association of the female with the sphere of corruptibility, from which male spirit must flee for its life."[36]

In her description of the late medieval world, Ruether uses all her literary skill to evoke and thus expose its paranoia. The passion of her analysis is best captured by letting her address this subject in her own words:

For the late-medieval and Puritan worlds, woman, outside the control of male authority, became the embodiment of the lurking demonic power. Woman, as the cause of the fall of man and nature in the beginning, is the hidden enemy who threatens to hurl the realm of grace and salvation back into the grip of the devil. As lustful, carnal, and naturally insubordinate, woman is the likely tool of the devil in his relentless attempt to undermine God's plan of salvation. As witch, woman is the image of deceitful nature, enticing and fair without but filled with foul corruption underneath, dragging male consciousness down into the power of sin, death, and damnation.

It was such fears of the human body, the natural world, and those at the bottom of the social hierarchy, coupled with misogyny, she claims, that fuelled the prolonged bouts of witch-hunting that occurred between the fourteenth and seventeenth centuries. For the fearful males of this period, she continues, "The old woman, her sagging breasts and wrinkled abdomen the image of the corruptible flesh of despised maternity, became the archetype of the witch as instrument of the devil."[37]

The explicit connection of woman with evil has a history that extends back far beyond the medieval and patristic periods. Ruether points out that in Western European culture, the myths of Pandora and Eve have scapegoated women as evil's primordial cause. She also notes this tendency in the intertestamental story of the Watchers and in the Lilith traditions in folk Judaism.[38] Such myths, she says, "reveal a tremendous male fear of women's suppressed power" and are repeated generation after generation as part of a strategy to "marginalize women from power roles in society." When women resist, notes Ruether, "The whole range of coercive techniques, from brute force to contempt and ridicule to artful blandishments, is necessary to keep her in her 'place.'" "Religion," she is quick to point out, "is relied upon as both the foundation and the daily aid in this project."[39]

In this context, Ruether sees the witch persecutions as the apex of a long history of suppression and control. The definitive document on witch hunting, the *Malleus Maleficarum* (written in 1486) which summed up one hundred years of official theory, reveals an unbelievable level of paranoia and woman-hatred. What is particularly sobering is Ruether's claim that it can also be read as merely an extreme expression of Thomistic thinking.[40] When this "holocaust" of persecution finally came to an end in Puritan Massachusetts, this was not just because of the triumph of Enlightenment rationality, in Ruether's judgment. It was also because "[w]omen . . . had 'learned their lesson,' at least for a time."[41]

III. Mariology
The third "layer" to the ideology of sexism, in Ruether's analysis, occurs when woman, like the "noble savage," is idealized and romanticized because "[t]he dominant class and sexual caste, feeling themselves cut off and alienated from their deeper roots, exalt the other into a mediator of that which they have lost in themselves."[42] This finds its clearest expression in Mariology.

The most interesting example that Ruether gives of this phenomenon is the relationship between the Victorian view of woman, which is probably the most striking example of the romanticizing of femininity in recent history, and the veneration of the mother of Jesus. With a wry sense of humour, she writes,

> In the Victorian ideal, marriage is fused with romantic love, and the fusion is sublimated in the mariological tradition of antisexual purity to create a model of the ideal wife and mother who is a fruitful mother yet a lifelong sexual innocent. The immaculate conception and virgin birth become everyday miracles.[43]

Although there are some potentially positive elements in the Mariological tradition such as the ability that the mother of Jesus gains, as a result of belief in her Immaculate Conception and Assumption, to "exemplif[y] the primordial potential for good of created existence undeformed by sin,"[44] these are not sufficient to convince Ruether that Pope Paul VI was right when he claimed in 1974 that Christianity had in the Virgin Mary a model of the liberated woman.[45] By contrast, Ruether stresses that, like patristic "virginal feminism," the cult of the Virgin Mother is part of the warped and alienated spirituality of male ascetics whose "repressed libidinal feelings are sublimated in mystical eroticism." It arises "not as a solution to, but as a corollary of, the denigration of fleshly maternity and sexuality." In other words, "The love of the Virgin Mary does not correct but presupposes the hatred of real women."[46]

Mary looks no more promising as a model for liberated womanhood when examined from the vantage point of gender symbolism. Ruether argues that patriarchy sets up a symbol system in which ultimate divine power and authority is imaged as male while the female is allowed to symbolize only a receptive or mediating principle in relation to male sovereignty. As the idea of even an intermediate female persona in the Godhead was eliminated in "orthodox" views of the Trinity, the female can only appear as a creature in the Christian tradition.[47] In this symbol system, "the patriarchal feminine,"[48] as Ruether calls it, "represents either the original creation, the good material shaped by the hand of God" (as noted above), or "the eschatological community reborn from the Passion of Christ. As such, the good feminine is a spiritual principle of passive receptivity to the regenerating powers of God."[49]

The two major female images in this symbol system are the church, which is both the "Bride of Christ" and the "Mother of Christians"[50] and the individual soul seen "as a female (passive-receptive) awaiting divine insemination."[51] Ruether argues that both of these become personified by the Virgin Mary who, in spite of the exalted language that is used about her, is never a female divine hypostasis but merely fulfils her "correct" role within the symbol system, either as an image of the self and the community in relation to God, or as the merciful maternal mediator between the faithful on earth and their stern, patriarchal Lord in heaven.[52]

Although the veneration of Mary disappears in the Protestant tradition, this gender symbolism continues. Ruether even goes as far as to claim that, "Protestantism strengthens the dichotomy between the transcendent masculinity of God, who alone possesses all initiative and power, and the abject passivity of the Christian, represented by the femininity of the Church." Even the humanizing of Jesus that takes place in Pietism does not result in a fundamental challenge to this gender symbolism. The femininity of the church is simply transferred to Jesus "who becomes a mariological figure in relation to the patriarchal Father God." The fact that Protestant theologians such as Luther, Calvin, and Barth have found Mariology to be an acceptable symbol of the church's dependency on God is for Ruether additional evidence that,

> [I]n Protestantism more than ever, the super- and subordination between God and creatures, Christ and the Church, is represented by a hierarchical, omnipotent "masculine" God and a passive, self-abnegating "feminine" humanity. The symbolic relations between Christ and the Father, Christ and the Church, and pastor and people continue to enshrine this rigid hierarchical complementarity of male over female.[53]

At the heart of Ruether's critique of the Mariological tradition, then, is her rejection of the splitting of activity and receptivity along hierarchical and sexist lines. She expresses this point most clearly in her book which is devoted to the topic of Mariology, *Mary—The Feminine Face of the Church*. Here she argues forcefully that authentic receptivity, which is necessary for healthy relationships, flows out of personal power and self-esteem. To identify it with powerlessness, dependence, and self-negation, by contrast, is to encourage relationships that are "sadomasochistic" in character. One is either "receptive," i. e., "fawning, servile, and suffering before superiors" or "active," that is to say "domineering, patronizing, and punishing toward subordinates." Furthermore, when this view of receptivity is identified with authentic femininity, the full humanity of women is eclipsed. As Ruether explains,

> The split between dominance and receptivity in male psychology has created a demand for the repression of the whole personhood of women as a group. By identifying powerless passivity with "femininity," women are commanded to be the specialists in self-denying and auxiliary types of life. Men then monopolize the feedback of both the male and the female types of life. This means that man, male and female, appears as a

person only in the male. Women exist as helpers and reflectors of this process of male self-becoming.[54]

Although Ruether does believe that Mary can function as a liberating symbol for women, it is clear to her that Mariology cannot fulfil this function "as long as it preserves this meaning of 'femininity' that is the complementary underside of masculine domination."[55]

IV. Ecclesiology
I have already alluded to some of Ruether's criticisms of traditional ecclesiology in the previous section, by noting her observation that the imaging of the church as female is caught up in an oppressive symbol system that reinforces male dominance and female passivity. This destructive pattern, she maintains, is also reinforced by and expressed in the typical relationship between priest and laity and helps to explain the Christian tradition's opposition to the ordination of women to the symbolically "male" role of the priest.

In her historical analysis of this phenomenon, Ruether notes that while the earliest strata of the New Testament show the considerable participation of women in church leadership, and while even "the patriarchal Church of the pastorals" ordained women deacons, subsequent church history has been far from promising.[56] To be sure, women have been allowed to preach and teach in a number of Spirit-led movements, but these roles are always deemed off limits to them once such movements become institutionalized.[57]

Ruether believes that the decisive blow against women's ordination came in the fourth century with the triumph of a "sacerdotal-caste" concept of the priesthood. When Christianity was made the official religion of the empire, ministers were made into a privileged social caste. At the same time, a cultic view of worship, ministry and liturgy encouraged the revival of Old Testament laws of cultic purity and these were applied to Christian priests. Such laws also defined women as unclean. Referring to the Canon law of the period, Ruether argues that this view of cultic purity, which was the basis for advising women to stay away from the communion table during menstruation, was a chief reason for the abolition of the office of deaconess.[58]

Ruether claims that this view of male sacral purity which "is created by rigid demarcation of the sanctuary against the 'pollution' of the female,"[59] is still operative today on an unconscious level. She cites the example of the "near hysteria" that recently broke out in the Episcopal Church when women became visible in the priestly role. "The most extreme repugnance against the idea of women in ministry," Ruether remarks, "typically is expressed in the question 'Can you imagine a pregnant woman at the altar?' "[60]

Ruether also makes the fascinating observation that maternity can simultaneously inspire both revulsion and jealousy in the male clergy. This combination of "womb envy with womb negation" finds expression in certain priestly roles in which,

> . . . the sexual and maternal roles of real women . . . [are] both sublimated and taken over into male "spiritual" power. Male headship power controls the higher conception, gestation, birth, and suckling and relates this to a transcendent sphere that negates the "carnal" maternity of women. It then becomes possible to symbolize the female life-giving role as the source of "death," while expropriating the symbols of conception, birth, and nurture to males.[61]

Arguments for excluding women from ordination today, Ruether points out, are often built on the assumption that Jesus was necessarily male—an argument which was first made by Aquinas due to his adoption of Aristotelian biology.[62] Christ, as the head and bridegroom of the church, so the argument typically goes, must be male and thus so must his representatives. Behind this, Ruether points out, lies the assumption of the maleness of God. Males within this androcentric symbol system can represent both the divine and the creaturely, while women can represent only the latter. The 1976 Vatican declaration against women's ordination sums up this "Christological masculinism" with the statement that "there must be a physical resemblance between the priest and Christ." "The possession of male genitalia," notes Ruether, "becomes the essential prerequisite for representing Christ, who is the disclosure of the male God."[63] Such an argument for an all-male priesthood based on physical resemblance, she remarks, with not a little humour, is certainly a novel way of applying the principle of the imitation of Christ![64]

Although it is mainly fundamentalist churches and those which hold to a cultic view of the priesthood that bar women from ordination today, Ruether notes that the religious symbolism of "sexist hierarchicalism," which is what lies behind the conservatives' opposition to change,[65] can still exert an influence in more liberal Protestant congregations, including those that have female clergy. In such cases, women are often too content to take on a form of ministry shaped by a patriarchal culture. In Ruether's words,

> They adopt the garb, the same titles (Reverend, if not Father), the same clerical modes of functioning in a hierarchically structured church. They too stand in the phallically designed pulpit and bring down the "seminal" word upon the passive body of the laity.[66]

Not content with such a superficial change, Ruether stresses the urgent need for more extensive reform. As she said in an interview on Canadian television recently, "I'm not simply interested in getting a few women into the clerical role. I want to go beyond that to rethinking the clerical role itself."[67] Central to this project is the development of a critique of and alternative to "clericalism" which she describes as "sexism raised to the second power."[68] As Ruether puts it,

> Clericalism is built upon and presupposes patriarchy. The symbols of clerical power duplicate on the level of ecclesiastical hierarchy the symbols of patriarchal domination of men over women, fathers over children. It is impossible to liberate the Church from patriarchy and retain a clerical definition of the ministry.[69]

Like so much of her work, Ruether's analysis of ecclesiology is not motivated by a desire to find the correct answers to abstract theoretical puzzles, but to do scholarship that flows out of a commitment to liberating those who suffer from oppression. In her words,

> Women in contemporary churches are suffering from linguistic deprivation and eucharistic famine. They can no longer nurture their souls in alienating words that ignore or systematically deny their existence. They are starved for the words of life, for symbolic forms that fully and wholeheartedly affirm their personhood and speak truth about the evils of sexism and the possibilities of a future beyond patriarchy. They desperately need primary communities that nurture their journey into wholeness, rather than constantly negating and thwarting it.[70]

These words, as well as any, express why the task of feminist ecclesiology is an urgent one.

V. Christology
Ruether begins her chapter on Christology and feminism in *To Change The World* by stating that "Christology has been the doctrine of the Christian tradition that has been most frequently used against women." The central question, therefore, that she sets out to answer is: "can Christology be liberated from its encapsulation in the structures of patriarchy and really become an expression of liberation of women? Or is it so linked with symbols of male-dominance that it is unredeemable as good news for women?" Asking whether a male saviour can save women, Ruether is quick to stress, should not be seen as merely a provocative theoretical question. "It is one on which many thousands of women have already voted with their feet by leaving the church and seeking alternative feminist communities."[71]

The fact that Ruether has not left the Christian church implies that she believes that feminism and Christology need not be incompatible. At the same time, she remains a trenchant critic of traditional thinking on this issue. I have already referred to what Ruether believes to be the clearest example of an anti-woman use of Christology: Aquinas's assertion that God had to be incarnate as a male due to woman's ontological inferiority. But the "patriarchalization" of Christology is a process that Ruether sees as beginning even before the closure of the New Testament canon.

In *Sexism and God-Talk*, Ruether claims that when Christology is de-eschatologized, as she believes that it is even in Luke's gospel,

> Christ becomes a timeless revelation of divine perfection located in a past paradigmatic moment. This disclosure of timeless perfection is closed. The Risen Lord does not live on in ecstatic utterances of Christian prophets or prophetesses; rather he ascended into heaven after forty days.[72]

Ruether levels a very serious charge against this way of thinking. She writes,

> To encapsulate Jesus himself as God's "last word" and "once-for-all" disclosure of God, located in a remote past and institutionalized in a caste of Christian teachers, is to repudiate the spirit of Jesus and to recapitulate the position against which he himself protests.[73]

As with the development of the dominant view of ministry, the decisive step in the "patriarchalization" of Christology occurs in the fourth century when Christianity becomes the official religion of the Christian Roman Empire. The millennial rule of Christ becomes identified with Christendom and in the imperial Christology of Eusebius, the Caesaro-papist adviser to Constantine at the Nicene Council, Christ as Pantocrator becomes "the founder and cosmic governor of the existing social hierarchy." Within this hierarchical chain of being, women, along with slaves, barbarians, and non-Christians are seen as the mindless ones who must be ruled by the rational male representatives of the divine Logos. Thus "Christology becomes the apex of a system of control over all those who in one way or another are 'other' than this new Christian order."[74]

With the adoption of Aristotelian views of gender in medieval scholasticism, Christological sexism became founded not just on symbol but on biology.[75] Although Ruether has significant disagreements with the post-Christian feminist theologian Mary Daly, she believes that Aquinas's masculinist view of the incarnation can be aptly described with the help of Daly's famous aphorism, "When God is male, the male is God."[76]

While this "imperial Christ" is a consistent feature of the masculinist Christologies that "dominate" the Christian tradition, Ruether does note the presence of three other images in church history. "Spirit Christologies" and images of "the prophetic iconoclastic Christ" will be considered in the context of Ruether's own proposals in chapter 4. The tradition of androgynous Christologies will be examined here, however, as she considers it to be more a part of the problem than the solution.[77]

Ruether's main criticism of this tradition, which is exemplified by the Gnostics, early modern mystics such as Jacob Boehme and Emmanuel Swedenborg and sects such as the Rappites, is that it betrays a hidden androcentrism that is reminiscent of the fatal flaw in the anthropological ideas of "eschatological feminism." In this belief system, an original androgynous Adam who contained both male and female natures is believed to have preceded the creation of woman from his side. Gender duality signals a fall into sexuality from which we are now redeemed in Christ, who is the second androgynous Adam. By transcending their sexuality, women are equal participants in the new spiritual community. Some groups are even radical enough to hold to androgynous ideas of God. But they still fail to overcome the male-centredness that characterizes the dominant tradition. As Ruether explains,

> Christ represents the male as the normative human person. Femaleness represents the lower instinctual and bodily side of "man," which was originally unified in a spiritual whole. The separation of the female out of the side of Adam represents the disintegration of this original whole, the revolt of the lower against the higher side of "man." The very existence of woman as a separate gender represents the fall of "man." Femaleness is still correlated with the lower side of human nature, which is to be abolished in Heaven.[78]

The medieval mystic Julian of Norwich represents a variation on this tradition as Jesus is not seen as transcending masculinity and femininity but is understood as both mother and father. But Ruether points out that because the divine and human persons of Jesus are clearly male in medieval thought, a bias towards the male still cannot be fully eradicated in this form of piety. Because a male Jesus is given "mothering" qualities, it is only the male mystic who is given a role model of androgynous personhood. Within the culture of that time, males were thus allowed to be nurturing, but females were not allowed to represent Christ's "masculine" qualities as priests or teachers.[79]

A similar lack of ability to sufficiently challenge social roles occurs with the feminization of Jesus in Pietism. This Christological position is the result of the identification of religion with the domestic realm. While women, at this time, became identified with spirit instead of matter in a reversal of traditional gender symbolism, they were now seen as *too* "Christlike" or altruistic to rule or exercise power in church or society![80]

Thus in the final analysis, androgynous Christologies in general fail to challenge the status quo. At the heart of the problem is their inability to allow women to represent full human potential. Ruether claims that,

> As long as Christ is still presumed to be, normatively, a male person, androgynous Christologies will carry an androcentric bias. Men gain their "feminine" side, but women contribute to the whole by specializing in the representation of the "feminine," which means exclusion from the exercise of the roles of power and leadership associated with masculinity.[81]

Christian feminists, therefore, must look elsewhere if they are to find a viable Christology that is not encapsulated in the structures of patriarchy.

VI. Nature

A central element in Ruether's analysis of the origin, character, and development of patriarchy, is the correlation she finds between dominated woman and dominated nature, or between androcentrism and anthropocentrism.[82] Thus for her, ecological concerns are intrinsic to a Christian feminist theology.

Given this important correlation, it is no surprise to Ruether that demonic nature is portrayed in medieval times by the female figure *Frau Welt*, as noted above. Neither does she believe that it is merely coincidental that highly sexual imagery is used to symbolize the domination of nature by reason at the beginning of the modern period.[83]

Like its view of woman and the body, the dominant Christian view of nature which prevailed from the patristic period until the end of Christendom, reveals the destructive influence of the Greek worldview, which regrettably proved to be a stronger influence than the creation-affirming tradition inherited from the Old Testament.[84] Ruether captures the contours of this position in these words:

> The Christian view of nature split creation into two opposite possibilities: sacramentality and demonization. Nature, restored to the sovereignty of God through Christ, was exemplified in the sacraments. Here, in the sacral sphere conquered by the Church, nature once more shone forth as the image and incarnate presence of God. But, outside this sphere of redemption, nature was demonic and alien to God, an outer darkness where Satan and his evil host abounded.[85]

The inability of this view to affirm and cherish the goodness of creation is hardly solved by the modern "exorcism" and secularization of nature as a sphere of human domination.[86] In her insistence that Christians should not be seduced by the modern worldview at this point, Ruether has more explicit criticisms of developments in twentieth-century theology on this issue than on any other topic that has been examined so far in this chapter. Thus, with considerable disapproval, she writes,

> "Crisis" and "secular" theologians such as Bultmann and Gogarten continually stress the transcendence of history over nature, defining the Gospel as the freedom of the liberated

consciousness to depart endlessly from natural and historical foundations into the contentless desert of pure possibility. Such theologians are happy to baptize modern technology as the expression of the freedom mediated by the Gospel to transcend and dominate nature.[87]

Ruether's desire to affirm nature also leads her to take distance from contemporary theologians who, like herself, are far from conservative in their social analysis. In their desire to stress the need to find new possibilities that are not found in our present historical systems, "patriarchal theologies of 'hope' or liberation," as Ruether calls them, appeal, as she does, to the God of Exodus. But unlike herself, Ruether believes that they do this in opposition to the ecologically important idea of God as "ground of our being" which they confuse with the foundation of existing social systems. Having made this false identification, their acute awareness that many of these social systems are unjust forces them to define redemption as "liberation out of or against nature into spirit." This leads to a lack of sympathy with many of the themes that are central to the kind of feminist liberation theology that Ruether wants to advocate. She writes,

> The identification of matter, nature, and being with mother makes such patriarchal theology hostile to women as symbols of all that "drags us down" from freedom. The hostility of males to any symbol of God/ess as female is rooted in this identification of mother with the negation of liberated spirit. God/ess as Matrix is thought of as "static" immanence. A static, devouring, death-dealing matter is imaged, with horror, as extinguishing the free flight of transcendent consciousness.

She goes on to add that "[t]he dualism of nature and transcendence, matter and spirit as female against male is basic to male theology."[88]

As this last sentence makes clear, it is Ruether's contention that the gender symbolism of the patristic and medieval periods is not merely a thing of the past. Nor does it only live on in conservative theologies. In this light, to challenge the dualism of spirit and matter becomes very central to feminist cultural analysis and to the construction of a theological position that is ecologically sensitive and woman-affirming.

VII. Eschatology

The highly ambiguous attitude of traditional Christian theology towards woman can be seen in the area of eschatology as clearly as anywhere. Ruether points out that some Church Fathers, out of their desire to escape bodiliness which was so closely identified with woman, actually postulated that in the resurrection all females would become male—an idea that she compares with the racist Mormon belief that negroes will one day be transformed into white people.[89]

Even Jerome and Augustine, who opposed such beliefs, argued that while women would remain female in the resurrected state, · their bodily characteristics now necessary for sexual intercourse and childbearing would nevertheless be transformed so that they would be "suited to glory rather than shame." In response to this, Ruether confesses, "What this angelic hysterectomy is supposed to mean is anyone's guess."[90] But she does stress that such eschatological ideas illustrate in a very graphic way the dilemma of patristic anthropology. As she explains,

> [The Church Fathers] wish to affirm a doctrine of redemption that coheres with the original bodily, bi-sexual nature which God had declared "very good" in the beginning; but since they have declared this to be "very bad" and define redemption as the overcoming of the body, sexual relationship and female nature, they can only affirm this continuity by peculiarly mutilating redemption or creation or both in these particular characteristics.[91]

But Ruether's critique of Christian eschatology goes beyond a rejection of what we moderns may try to dismiss as the eccentricities of patristic thought. Drawing on her ecological sensitivities, she rejects all eschatological ideas that she believes reflect a desire to deny our finitude and our roots in the earth. Three areas of eschatological thought come under fire from this vantage point.

Firstly, Ruether rejects all views of an eschaton seen as a final and literal salvific "end point" to present history. All visions of the future based on a linear view of history, whether in its original Christian form or in the secularized versions found in liberalism or Marxism, are inadequate for the same reason: they contradict the "possibilities of historical existence."[92]

This failing is manifest in different ways. The liberal and Marxist attempts to reach this end point by means of "infinitely expanding technological prosperity," for example, are profoundly anti-ecological in their disregard of "finite limits and relationships between humanity and the nonhuman environment."[93] In addition, Marxist identifications of a particular social revolution with this end point lead to an absolutization of that revolution which soon hardens into a repressive and totalitarian system that is blind to its own mistakes and limitations.[94] As Ruether argued in *The Church Against Itself*, the *church* may also falsely identify its historical existence with its eschatological essence.[95] An alternative to such ecclesiastical triumphalism takes place when the end point is seen as occurring outside of history. But such an otherworldly vision "fails to provide a point of reference for historical hope. Historical becomes eschatological hope, and history itself is reduced to 'one damn thing after another' leading nowhere."[96] Thus, in Ruether's eyes, belief in a literal eschaton is incompatible with a theology that wishes to affirm history and its limits.[97]

Secondly, Ruether criticizes the appeal made by modern theologians to an eschaton as a non-literal transcendent end point beyond history. In this way of thinking, it is openly admitted that the eschaton can never occur in time. Instead it functions as a useful myth by which we relativize our own historical achievements and criticize all false absolutizations such as those of "Marxist millennialism." Ruether's response to this is similar to her critique of theologies of hope and liberation examined in the previous section. While she admits that "[t]his desire to keep history open and able to constantly transcend itself is an important concern," she also points out that this perspective "is still based on a model of endlessly stretching forward into the future." This has some undesirable consequences:

God, the ideal humanity and ideal world, exists only in the unrealized future. [This eschatology] has no roots in an ontology of creation and in God/ess as ground of creation. There are no clues to the good in that which is natural. This endless flight into the future idolizes change and fails to respect the relational patterns of our bodies as ground of holy being.[98]

Thirdly, Ruether dismisses traditional Christian belief in personal immortality as a refusal to embrace our own finitude. The alienation from the earth that gives rise to such beliefs is evident when we bury ourselves in steel coffins. "Such a manner of burial," writes Ruether, "represents a fundamental refusal to accept earth as our home and the planets and animals of earth as our kindred."[99] She is also inclined to view belief in eternal life for the individual as an inauthentic hope that is rooted in concerns that males and not females typically have about their own self-perpetuation. In Ruether's words,

The question is not whether men and women share the same mortality; it is whether women have the same stake in denying their mortality through doctrines of life after death, or whether this is not the apogee of male individualism and egoism.[100]

Thus, for Ruether, analysis of traditional Christian beliefs about the eschaton, no less than any other subject discussed in this chapter, reveals that males have monopolized the theological tradition to the extent that it reflects and legitimates the limitations and distortions of male experience.

VIII. God

In Ruether's account of the development of patriarchal consciousness, the rise of "male monotheism" in the Judeo-Christian tradition and the subsequent "dualizing of gender metaphors" is of crucial importance.[101] Paired images of the Divine as God and Goddess are replaced by a tradition in which "God"—which is itself a male word that she prefers to replace with the neologism "God/ess"—is primarily or exclusively imaged in male language. Such a God, in

Ruether's view, becomes "the ultimate theological rationale for the hierarchical symbolism of masculinity and femininity"[102]—a symbol system that we have encountered repeatedly in previous sections of this chapter.

The image of God as Father, in particular, can have a terrible social impact as it encourages us to think of the relationship between God and humanity in terms of "a domination-subordination model [which] allow[s] ruling-class males to identify themselves with this divine fatherhood in such a way as to establish themselves in the same kind of hierarchical relationship to women and lower classes."[103]

Ruether is convinced that such a use of religious language is nothing other than idolatry. In a sermon that she preached at the "Woman Church Speaks" conference in 1983, she made this point very forcefully in the following words:

> This is the idol of masculinity, the idol of father-rule. And it claims all the earth as the creation and domain of father-rule. It monopolizes the image of God, claiming that God can only be spoken by the name of the Patriarch, can only be imaged in the image of Father-rule. God is sovereign, King, Warrior, God of Power and Might, who magnifies the rule of the powerful and abases the degradation of the lowly, who gives the scepter to the mighty and teaches the little ones of the earth to cower in fear and self-hatred. This God is not to be imaged as Mother, as Helper, as Friend, as Liberator. It cannot be imaged in the faces of women, or children, of the poor, of the timid and gentle creatures of the earth.[104]

She goes on to repudiate this view of the Divine "in the name of God, in the name of Christ, in the name of church, in the name of humanity, in the name of earth." "Our God and Goddess, who is mother and father, friend, lover, and helper," she insists, "did not create this idol and is not represented by this idol."p1051w

Another place where Ruether abandons her more formal, academic style of writing to convey a similar point, is in the feminist midrash which begins her book *Sexism and God-Talk*. In Act One of this short play entitled "The Kenosis of the Father," this male

God/idol expresses the true self-awareness that is beginning to dawn on him in the following speech:

> The angels that sing my praises, the kings of the earth that bow down before me in their temples cry that I am their only Lord and ask Me for help in their battles. Perhaps I have become more their creature than their Creator? I and the kings of earth have come to resemble each other too closely. By calling me Father, Lord, and Ruler, they claim the power to rule the earth as I rule the heavens. Beneath their feet ranks of servants bow down even as the angels bow before Me. Men teach women their place on earth, following My example. Perhaps this hierarchy of earth and heaven is a facade, a delusion, concealing other realities that we dare not know.[106]

Some Christian theologians, such as Jürgen Moltmann, have suggested that ideas of God as Trinity can help us avoid the problems of patriarchal male monotheism,[107] but Ruether is far from convinced. In fact traditional views of the Trinity actually magnify the androcentrism, she claims. In this context, she notes that the members of the Trinity in the Athanasian creed, for example, are "the triune multiplication of one single male divine identity."[108]

It has also been suggested that a more promising view of the Trinity can be found in literature such as the apocryphal gospels, the works of Clement of Alexandria, the third century church order *The Didascalia*, Syriac Christianity and later mystical writers because in these traditions the Holy Spirit is seen as female. Although some feminists have claimed that this solves the problem of all-male God-language, Ruether is sceptical to say the least, pointing out that this female member of the Trinity is outnumbered two-to-one. Furthermore, there is the ever-present danger that contemporary androcentrism will ensure that this "female side of God" is viewed as nothing more than "a subordinate principle underneath the dominant image of male divine sovereignty."[109] Such a view, in other words, will probably do little more than reinforce gender stereotypes at the divine level.

While finding alternative images for God that are not taken from the patriarchal ruling class clearly means, for Ruether, that we must challenge the exclusive use of male metaphors, this is not the most important issue for her. In a recent interview, she said, "I tend to see that the crucial issue . . . is not simply gender change but how we understand the power relationship [between us and God], because I think that's really the deeper question." By this she means that we should no longer see the God-human relationship in terms of a model of competitive power in which God, as King and Master, is seen as all-powerful, while we as his subjects and servants, are by definition impotent. Because Ruether believes that the way we image God also reflects and legitimates the way we image ourselves, she is convinced that the perpetual danger of such hierarchical God-language is that it will encourage societal patterns of domination and subjugation.[110]

When the question of changing our images of God is raised, the gulf between feminist and non-feminist Christians, to which I alluded at the beginning of this chapter, becomes very visible. On the one hand, a conservative like William Oddie can be so opposed to change that in the very title of his book on "Feminism and the Reconstruction of Christian Belief" he asks with considerable trepidation, "*What Will Happen to God?*"[111] On the other hand, a feminist theologian such as Ruether is adamant that traditional patriarchal imagery for the divine *must* be changed because it presently sanctions human evil. If we are worried that our beliefs about God, eschatology, nature, Christology, ecclesiology, Mariology, evil, and anthropology will be transformed beyond recognition if we agree that the task of reconstruction is valid and necessary, then it is imperative, Ruether would say, that we do not allow our fear of the future to prevent us from turning our backs on the evils of the past and of the present.

This does not mean that Ruether wants us to sever all ties with the past. In the next chapter I will explore her conviction that we may embrace radical change in a way that enables us, and even requires us, to maintain significant continuities with aspects of the Christian tradition. Before moving on to such considerations, however, I will first offer a brief response to those aspects of her thought that I have summarized so far.

IX. An Initial Response

While future chapters will show that Ruether's theological analysis evokes both my enthusiasm *and* my disagreement on virtually every topic, my reaction to the material summarized in this chapter is far more straightforward. I am in fundamental agreement with Ruether's analysis of the predominantly androcentric and thus unacceptable character of the dominant theological tradition. I am one with her in the conviction that we urgently need change in both our theology and our praxis. I also agree with her that fellow Christians who believe that we must defend ourselves against the impact and challenge of contemporary feminism in order to avoid falling into apostasy are not only mistaken, but also betray an alarming lack of sensitivity to the thousands of women and men, both Christian and non-Christian, who are becoming increasingly alienated from the Christian faith because of the sexism of the church.

It is always possible to quibble with Ruether on certain points of emphasis or detail,[112] but in my opinion, the basic contours of her account are sound. Particularly compelling is her analysis of the way the tradition has dualistically separated spirit and matter, soul and body, history and nature, and creation and redemption. While such dualisms have also been consistently exposed and opposed by scholars in the reformational tradition of Kuyper and Dooyeweerd,[113] what Ruether demonstrates is the way in which such polarizations reflect and reinforce an androcentric symbol system.

If I do not always find Ruether's *solutions* to the sexism of past Christian tradition to be fully satisfactory, I do believe that she consistently identifies the *problems* we need to address. Her ability to do this, I suggest, is linked to her acute awareness of the pain that so many women experience when they are confronted with the power of this tradition in our contemporary spirituality. We can only deny the problems, I contend, if we numb ourselves to this pain and thus betray the Gospel.

Fundamental agreement notwithstanding, there are a few points where Ruether and I differ which need to be mentioned, though I will not address them at this stage. In chapter 3, I will argue against Ruether's claim that Luke's portrayal of the ascension functions to locate Jesus and his spirit in a remote past. In chapter 4, I will challenge her view of the relationship between history and the eschaton and will also take issue with her attempt to dismiss belief in life after death as nothing more than the supreme manifestation of male individualism and egoism. In the concluding chapter, I will argue for a more nuanced version of her critical principle for feminist theology.

The only other criticism that I have of Ruether's analysis of the theological tradition is that she does not spend more time evaluating the work of modern and contemporary theologians. The androcentrism of patristic and medieval theology is now widely accepted, in part thanks to Ruether's work. But the male-centredness of contemporary theology is more subtle. When Ruether does subject it to her feminist hermeneutic of suspicion, her assessments are insightful. Judith Vaughan's study *Sociality, Ethics, And Change: A Critical Appraisal of Reinhold Niebuhr's Ethics in the Light of Rosemary Radford Ruether's Works*[114] demonstrates that a "Ruetherian" analysis of recent theological reflection can be developed and applied in a detailed and systematic way. A similar analysis of the work of thinkers such as Gilkey, Griffin, Lonergan, Moltmann, Pannenberg, and Rahner, for example, would strengthen Ruether's case even more. But to say this is not so much a criticism of Ruether as an acknowledgment that her theological approach is a powerful tool for uncovering the androcentric and woman-negating character of theologies that express the limitations and distortions of male experience in a fallen world.

Notes

1. *SGT*, 18-19.
2. Rosemary Radford Ruether, "The Feminist Critique in Religious Studies," in Elizabeth Langland and Walter Gove, eds., *A Feminist Perspective in the Academy: The Difference It Makes* (Chicago: University of Chicago Press, 1983), 59. This book is reprinted from *Soundings* 64 (Winter 1981).

3. Rosemary Radford Ruether, "Preface," in *RS,* 9.

4. These eight topics are addressed in *SGT* chaps. 4, 7, 6, 8, 5, 3, 10, and 2 respectively. The order in which they are presented here does not represent a ranking in terms of importance. Only two chapters from *SGT* are not represented in the summaries here. *SGT* chap. 1 concerns questions of methodology which are the focus of the next chapter. *SGT* chap. 9 contains little reflection on the theological tradition.

5. *SGT,* 93.

6. This is examined most fully on 334-38 below. Cf. 253-54 below.

7. *SGT,* 93-94.

8. See *NWNE,* 27. The two other "layers" are described in the next two sections.

9. See Rosemary Radford Ruether, "Misogynism and Virginal Feminism in the Fathers of the Church," in *RS,* 150-183. This essay is a revised version of *LT,* chap. 7.

10. See Ibid., 153.

11. *SGT,* 95. She is far more positive about the Eastern Orthodox tradition, however. See *DQ,* 37.

12. "Misogynism," 156.

13. *LT,* 100.

14. "Misogynism," 158.

15. *LT,* 101.

16. Ibid., 102.

17. "Misogynism," 162.

18. Ibid., 163.

19. *LT,* 107.

20. "Misogynism," 164.

21. See ibid., 165.

22. See Rosemary Radford Ruether, "Mothers of the Church: Ascetic Women in the Late Patristic Age," in *WS,* 73.

23. "Misogynism," 178.

24. *LT,* 109.

25. "Misogynism," 179.

26. *SGT,* 95.

27. Ibid., 96.

28. See ibid., 97-99, on which this and the following paragraph are dependent.

29. See ibid., 99-102 on which this and the following paragraph are dependent.

30. Ibid., 100.

31. Rosemary Radford Ruether, "Christianity," in Arvind Sharma, ed., *Women in World Religions* (Albany: State University of New York Press, 1987), 229.

32. *NWNE,* 27.

33. *SGT,* 163.

34. See "Mothers," 76-82 and "Misogynism," 175.

35. See *SGT*, 80-81.
36. *NWNE*, 18. Cf. *SGT*, 81.
37. *SGT*, 82.
38. See ibid., 165-68.
39. Ibid., 168-70.
40. See *NWNE*, 72.
41. *SGT*, 173.
42. *NWNE*, 28.
43. Ibid., 21.
44. *SGT*, 151.
45. See *NWNE*, 36.
46. Ibid., 18.
47. See *SGT*, 139.
48. Ibid., 149.
49. Ibid., 139.
50. Ibid.
51. Ibid., 145.
52. See ibid., 149-50 and *NWNE*, 46.
53. *NWNE*, 56.
54. *MFFC*, 79.
55. *NWNE*, 58.
56. See ibid., 67-74. See also Rosemary Radford Ruether, "Entering the Sanctuary II: The Roman Catholic Story," in *WS*, 373-83.
57. See *SGT*, 197.
58. See *NWNE*, 70-71.
59. Ibid., 71.
60. *SGT*, 195.
61. Ibid., 143-44.
62. See *NWNE*, 71-72 and *SGT*, 125.
63. *SGT*, 126.
64. She made this comment as an aside in the third of the three presentations that she gave at the Institute for Christian Studies in 1983.
65. See *NWNE*, 73 and 79.
66. *SGT*, 200.
67. This interview took place on Vision T.V.'s "The Spirit Connection" and was broadcast on January 9th, 1989.
68. *NWNE*, 80.
69. *SGT*, 207.
70. *WC*, 4-5.
71. *TCW*, 45 and 47.
72. *SGT*, 124. This argument is very reminiscent of her discussion of the perils of "undialectical incarnational ecclesiology" in her first book. See *CAI*, 28-29.

73. *SGT*, 122.
74. Ibid., 125.
75. See ibid.
76. *TCW*, 45. The quotation is from Mary Daly, *Beyond God the Father: Towards a Philosophy of Women's Liberation* (Boston: Beacon Press, 1973), 19.
77. While Ruether distinguishes between androgynous and spirit Christologies in *SGT*, 127-134, both are examined under the title of androgynous Christologies in the earlier *TCW*, 49-53.
78. *SGT*, 128.
79. See ibid., 128-29.
80. See ibid., 129.
81. Ibid., 130.
82. See *LT*, 115-26, *NWNE*, 186-214, and *SGT*, 75-79.
83. See *NWNE*, 186.
84. See ibid, 188.
85. Ibid., 190.
86. See ibid., 191.
87. *LT*, 122-123. See also Rosemary Ruether, "An Unexpected Tribute to the Theologian," *Theology Today* 27 (October 1970): 335-336.
88. *SGT*, 70.
89. See *LT*, 102-103.
90. Ibid., 103.
91. Ibid. Cf. "Misogynism," 160-61.
92. *SGT*, 253. Cf. *GG*, 258 and 273.
93. *SGT*, 253.
94. See ibid.
95. See *CAI*, 2, which in different language is echoed in *SGT*, 253.
96. *SGT*, 253.
97. See esp. *RK*, 283-88.
98. *SGT*, 253-54.
99. Ibid., 258.
100. Ibid., 235.
101. See ibid., 53-54.
102. *NWNE*, 74.
103. Ibid., 65.
104. *WC*, 69-70.
105. Ibid., 72. Cf. *WG*, 172.
106. *SGT*, 2-3. Just as Babylonian mythology sought to dethrone the Goddess in favour of a male deity, this feminist midrash aims to dethrone, relativize, and preempt the male God-construct.
107. To my knowledge, Ruether does not explicitly respond to Moltmann's view on this topic. For a brief overview of different ways in which theologians have

evaluated the doctrine of the Trinity in the light of the feminist challenge, see Reta Halteman Finger, "Your Daughters Shall Prophesy: A Christian Feminist Critiques Feminist Theology," *The Other Side* 24 (October 1988): 28-41. Her appreciation for Moltmann's position is clear on pp. 36-37. Another overview that includes a section on feminist approaches to the Trinity is Randy L. Maddox, "Toward an Inclusive Theology: The Systematic Implications of the Feminist Critique," *Christian Scholar's Review* 16 (September 1986): 7-23. See esp. pp. 12-13. The pertinent work by Moltmann is *The Trinity and the Kingdom of God* (San Francisco: Harper and Row, 1981). See esp. pp. 191-202.

108. *WG*, 22.

109. *SGT*, 60.

110. These points were all made clear in the interview mentioned in n. 67 above.

111. See William Oddie, *What Will Happen to God? Feminism and the Reconstruction of Christian Belief* (London: SPCK, 1984).

112. For example, as I have argued in the chapter on Augustine's anthropology in my book *The Troubled Marriage of Adam and Eve* (Bristol, U.K.: Regius Press, forthcoming), Augustine does not have to be read as claiming that women are not made in the image of God. In the rational contemplation of things eternal, he believed that both sexes imaged God. It is true that he thought that woman does not image God in her role as man's helper or wife, but this is because he believed that neither sex can image God in bodily and thus temporally-oriented activity. See the excellent discussion of Augustine in Genevieve Lloyd, *The Man of Reason: "Male" and "Female" in Western Philosophy* (Minneapolis: University of Minnesota Press, 1984), 28-33. To say this, however, is not to deny the androcentric nature of his theology as a whole.

113. See, for example, Walsh and Middleton, *The Transforming Vision*, Hart, *Understanding Our World*, and Herman Dooyeweerd, *Roots Of Western Culture: Pagan, Secular, and Christian Options*, trans. John Kraay (Toronto: Wedge Publishing Foundation, 1979). On the response of the Reformed tradition, which in my view should be distinguished from the "reformational" tradition, although it provided the denominational and historical context in which the latter originally developed, see Douglas J. Schuurman, "Humanity in Reformed and Feminist Perspectives: Collision or Correlation?" *Calvin Theological Journal* 26 (1991): 68-90, and *idem*, chaps. 5 and 6 in Mary Stewart Van Leeuwen, ed., *After Eden: Facing the Challenge of Gender Reconciliation* (Grand Rapids: Eerdmans, 1993).

114. Lanham, MD: University Press of America, 1983.

Chapter 2: The Methodological Foundations of Ruether's Feminist Theology

The previous chapter was concerned with clarifying why Ruether believes that an acceptance of the full humanity of women is incompatible with an adherence to many of the fundamental tenets of the dominant theological tradition. We also looked at some alternative approaches to various theological issues found outside the mainstream of Christianity, but, in the final analysis, these also proved to be inadequate. This chapter focuses on the norms that Ruether believes should guide us and the resources that she believes we can draw upon as we go about reforming the Christian tradition in the direction of a truly woman-affirming theology for our times.

I. When a Tradition Faces a Crisis
When a religious tradition faces a crisis, and the members of the tradition experience this as a call to change of some kind, Ruether argues that they have three basic options.[1] The most conservative response is to look for new ways to interpret or adapt the received tradition so that it may speak more easily to new experience. The community's method of transmitting the tradition is not challenged in this process however, thus ensuring a fundamental continuity with

the past. The introduction of minor modifications is an ongoing reality in most traditions. It therefore signifies a "business as usual" mentality rather than the genuine recognition that there is a crisis to be dealt with.

A second kind of response, which is far more radical, is classically exemplified by the Reformation. In such a case, the institutional structures that transmit the tradition are seen as corrupt and are denounced by means of a call to return to the original source of revelation. As Ruether explains,

> In the literal sense of the word, there is no possibility of return to some period of the tradition that predates the intervening history. So the myth of return to origins is a way of making a more radical interpretation of the revelatory paradigm to encompass contemporary experiences, while discarding institutions and traditions that contradict meaningful, just, and truthful life. . . . The original revelation itself, and the foundational stages of its formulation, are not challenged but held as all the more authoritative to set them as normative against later traditions.[2]

In the third position, the crisis is seen as the result of the corruption of the entire religious tradition. Marxism, for example, completely rejects religion as false consciousness. Ruether does recognize a milder version of such radical questioning in which "Ideological criticism of the truthfulness of the religion may still allow for some residue of genuine insight into the original religious experiences and foundational teachers,"[3] although these are believed to have become distorted even within the sacred writings of the faith. But in the most extreme manifestation of this position, even the foundational teachers are rejected as the critic turns to alternative sources of truth.

Ruether's own response to the crisis that she believes Christianity is facing is closest to this third position. This is not to suggest that she embraces it in its most extreme form. That would require a stance that so emphasizes change at the expense of continuity that it would be incompatible with a *Christian* feminist theology by definition. But it is accurate to say that she accepts this position in its milder form.

While it is easy to see from the summary of Ruether's extensive critique of the dominant tradition in chapter 1 why she would find the first response to be too superficial as it emphasizes continuity at the expense of change, it is not clear from the material that has been discussed so far why she rejects the second option. This is a topic worth pursuing in some detail, firstly, because feminists who work in the area of religious studies disagree about the extent to which the Bible supports their projects,[4] and secondly, because this approach, which she identifies with the Reformation, is the one I will defend as an alternative to Ruether's own position in chapter 3.

II. Ruether's Critique of the Bible

The most fundamental reason why Ruether is not convinced that a call to return to the Bible is an adequate response to the sexism of the theological tradition, is that she believes that the Bible itself is part of the problem. Just as Ruether did not flinch in her book *Faith and Fratricide* from accusing the New Testament of anti-Semitism,[5] so in her feminist works, she does not hesitate to highlight where she believes the Bible reflects and reinforces patriarchal ideology.

Perhaps the most serious example of this phenomenon, for her, is the biblical portrayal of God. It is her contention that "male monotheism" has its historical origin in the Old Testament period. Belief in a singular deity who is also male sets up a symbolic hierarchy of God-male-female in which women are not in direct relation to the Divine but are connected to him through the male. This view, she believes, is evident in the structure of Old Testament law, in which only the male heads of families are addressed directly, and in Paul's hierarchical order of headship found in 1 Cor. 11:3ff.[6]

The maleness of the Hebrew God-construct, Ruether proposes, is also evident in the creation narrative of Gen. 1. This God stands outside the world and over against him is a primal watery chaos. This is not his primal Mother or parents nor is it a womb in which both gods and humans gestate. In place of the earlier way of imaging the deity as the Primal Matrix, this God is "symbolized as a combination of male seminal and cultural power (word-act) that shapes [creation] from above."[7]

Ruether sees male monotheism as the vehicle of "a psychocultural revolution of the male ruling class in its relationship to surrounding reality."[8] This arises early in the first millennium B.C. in both Hebrew and Greek cultures as a result of males seeking to master nature by linking their essential selves to an intellectual, male principle that is seen as transcending creation.[9] Although she acknowledges that Greek philosophy goes in an even more dualistic and alienated direction by raising male consciousness to the same transcendent status as God,[10] Ruether clearly has the God of Gen. 1 in mind and not simply Greek conceptions of the divine, when she claims,

> This image of transcendent, male, spiritual deity is a projection of the ego or consciousness of ruling-class males, who envision a reality, beyond the physical processes that gave them birth, as the true source of their being. Men locate their true origins and natures in this transcendent sphere, which thereby also gives them power over the lower sphere of "female" nature.[11]

While Ruether argues that the Hebrews inherited much from the Canaanites, she claims that they repressed the role of the Goddess that was integral to the cult of their neighbours. The feminine imagery of this non-Hebrew deity, however, survives in a disguised form within Israelite faith as the covenant community, which is seen as Yahweh's bride. Unlike the Canaanite Goddess, this bride "was subordinate and dependent to the male Lord of Hosts who reigned without consort in the heavens."[12] The clearest example of this assimilation of the Goddess into Israel, Ruether argues, can be seen in the prophet Hosea's description of the community as a wayward bride playing the harlot with Baal. "To portray the covenant of God and Israel as a marriage relationship," writes Ruether, "transforms the Canaanite sacred marriage [of God and Goddess] into Hebrew patriarchy."[13]

Another way in which the suppressed female deity can still be glimpsed in the Old Testament, she suggests, is in the figure of Wisdom, which was a traditional characteristic of the Goddess. This powerful female image appears in the biblical and apocryphal literature as a secondary persona of God who mediates God's will to creation. But in this context, this Goddess "has become a dependent attribute or expression of the transcendent male God rather than an autonomous, female manifestation of the divine."[14]

Ruether does recognize the presence of female metaphors for God in the Hebrew Bible. As its root word for compassion is *rechem*, or womb, she argues that in ascribing ideas of mercy to Yahweh, "Hebrew thought suggests that God has maternal or 'womblike' qualities." But while Ruether admits that the "male patriarchal image proves too limited to represent the variety of relationships to Israel that Hebrew thought wished to express,"[15] she does not believe that this falsifies her claim that the God of the biblical tradition is essentially patriarchal. Instead, she interprets the presence of such female metaphors as revealing nothing more than " 'feminine' aspects of a male God."[16]

If Gen. 1 is a text that reveals Yahweh as a deified Patriarch, then, from Ruether's point of view, the image of Eve in Gen. 2 and 3 is scarcely any more positive for a feminist theology. Gen. 2, for example, is described by Ruether as a "patriarchal reversal myth" because Adam, as the original human prototype, is described, in direct contradiction to natural experience, "as giving birth to the woman with the help of a father God."[17] For Ruether, the narrative expresses a

> . . . male ideology which seeks to deny the original experience of dependency on the matrix of nature, and on the mother, as both one's personal origin and the symbol of the primal matrix. Male culture seeks to reverse this relationship, so the male ego can see itself as supernatural or transcendent to nature, the creator of "the world" and of woman.[18]

She also argues that the story intends to provide an etiology of and justification for woman's secondary status. While she acknow-

ledges the argument of Phyllis Trible and others that partnership
and not inferiority is implied when woman is called a "helper,"[19]
Ruether still maintains that her creation from Adam's rib implies a
derivative and auxiliary role in relation to the male who alone is
portrayed as "the essential and original autonomous human person."[20]

As a way of explaining what she sees as the androcentric nature
of the narrative, Ruether is very sympathetic to Theodor Reik's
claim that it has its origin in male puberty rites which functioned to
help males sever their relationship with their mothers on whom they
had been so dependant in infancy and transfer their identity "to a
new world where the older males are in control and the women have
been defeated and banished." In this world, woman is no longer the
powerful mother figure but the dependent wife. According to
Ruether's reading, "It is precisely this situation of the male reborn
into the male-identified world, where the woman is given to him as
auxiliary to his male identity, that is depicted in the Hebrew story of
the creation of Eve from Adam."[21]

The etiology of woman's subordinate status is continued in the
story of the fall in Gen. 3. As in the story of Pandora, the origin of
evil is traced to a woman.[22] In a psychological reading of the text
similar to her reading of Gen. 2, Ruether makes the following
suggestion:

> If [the] "original paradise" is recognized to be a mythologizing
> of early infancy, in which the mother provides the time of ease
> and plenty from her own body, then such male myths [as the
> stories of Eve and Pandora] actually scapegoat women as
> mothers for the loss of the paradise which *she* had once
> provided but which is lost to the male, wrenched from
> childhood into the adult (male) world of harsh struggle.[23]

The narrative is deliberately structured so that woman is second
in creation but the first to sin. As a result, she must face the pangs
of childbirth and the domination of her husband in a fallen world.
"This is not intended to describe patriarchal domination as unjust,"
writes Ruether. "On the contrary, it is intended to describe it as a

just punishment that defines her condition within history. To revolt against this status is to revolt against God."[24]

I have already noted Ruether's observation that the Old Testament law is only addressed to the male heads of families. There are also other aspects of the law that she mentions as evidence of woman's dependent status. "Women," she writes, "were dealt with as quasi-chattel in the sense that various laws dealt with them in terms of the property rights of the patriarch. The transfer of women to another male in marriage, the right to sell them into slavery, the violation of property rights when rape or adultery with a married woman occurred—all this was part of the framework of property rights of husband or father."[25]

Another aspect of life in Old Testament times that would have severely limited woman's autonomy were the menstrual taboos. In Ruether's words,

> These taboos ascribe demonic character to sexual fluids, primarily female. This concept of uncleanness is used to segregate adult women for most of their lives and forbid them access to male precincts of sacerdotal, political, and educational power.[26]

A further example of an anti-female bias that Ruether believes operates within this system is the fact that a woman was considered to be unclean for twice as long if she gave birth to a daughter rather than to a son (Lev. 12).[27]

Given the above arguments, it is not difficult to see why Ruether has concluded that in the majority of this legal material, God has "become simply the sanctifier of the existing social order."[28] It is not that she thinks that all the laws merely reinforce oppression. Lev. 25, for example, limits the length of time a fellow Hebrew may be kept a slave by appealing to the memory of slavery under Pharaoh. But what Ruether objects to as a feminist is that the servitude of women is never seen in need of a similar critique or rectification within the legal material.[29] As this literature functions to support patriarchy, Ruether rejects it as extremely antithetical to the cause of feminist theology.

Ruether finds further examples of androcentrism in the narrative material of the Old Testament. The exodus, for example, which
has been seen as an important text for liberation theology, is not so
obviously liberating for women, Ruether argues, because the assembly of the people before God at Sinai is actually an all-male
gathering. In addition, this group of males are told to consecrate
themselves to God by not going near a woman (Ex. 19:14-15).[30]

The story of Miriam in Num. 12 provides a particularly good
example of Ruether's feminist hermeneutic of suspicion. In this text,
she claims, we are presented with a story of God's judgment against
a woman that aims to undercut other traditions that conveyed her
power and importance as a priest and prophet during a foundational
period in Israel's history. Intent on exposing the patriarchal motiva-
tions that lie behind the narrative, Ruether writes,

> In this story both Miriam and Aaron challenge Moses' leader-
> ship by rebuking him for marrying a Cushite woman. But only
> Miriam is punished. When called forth before the tent of
> meeting, the cloud of God's presence descends over her and
> she is turned into a leper. She is then exiled from the camp for
> seven days. God's punishment is compared to a father spitting
> in his daughter's face. Healed of this expression of God's wrath,
> Miriam is then brought back into the camp, noting that the
> people did not set out on their march until she returned.
> Clearly, Miriam was seen as the formidable rival of Moses'
> leadership who must be put in her place![31]

Even less subtle in its oppressive patriarchal intentions, Ruether
claims, is a text such as Judg. 19 which portrays for us the betrayal,
rape, torture and dismemberment of an unnamed concubine.[32]

As we move into the New Testament, Ruether sees a continua-
tion of this androcentrism. Although her evaluation of the life and
message of Jesus is a very positive one, as I shall show below, and
although there is evidence that women were surprisingly prominent
among the early Christian leadership even in the Pauline epistles,
Ruether notes that there is an ambivalence towards woman in Paul's

writings which degenerates into a highly patriarchal and oppressive stance in the "Deutero-Pauline" material.[33]

Ruether accounts for the difference in tone between Gal. 3:28 and 1 Cor. 11:3ff. by suggesting that although Paul was a "theological radical," he was nevertheless a "social conservative."[34] This conservatism explains why the latter passage sets up a cosmic hierarchy of God-Christ-Man-Woman (v. 3), and makes women the source of sin (v. 10) by interpreting Gen. 6 to mean that they were responsible for seducing the angels. Thus woman must cover her head (v. 6), as a sign of her subjugation in the hierarchy and as a result of her sin.[35]

Many of Paul's more socially conservative statements, in Ruether's judgment, are rooted in his belief in Christ's imminent return. But when they are taken out of this context of eschatological expectation, they function to "absolutize the status quo of a sexist, class, and slave society."[36] And if Paul occasionally preserves something of the anti-patriarchal vision of the Jesus movement, "the Deutero-Pauline recasting of Christianity in patriarchal terms made this inclusive theology nonnormative."[37] Thus her overall impression of the writings attributed to Paul is a negative one.

Ruether's most biting criticism is aimed at the household codes (Col. 3:18ff. and Eph. 5:22ff.). Like the law codes of the Old Testament, such passages use God to sacralize the status quo. Ruether is particularly critical of the portrayal of marriage in this latter text, because it advocates the kind of hierarchical gender symbolism which is so prominent in the theological tradition, and which was referred to repeatedly in the last chapter. In her comments on this passage, Ruether does not mince her words:

> The author of the Epistle to the Ephesians, who ratified a subjection of wives to husbands modeled on the subjugation of the creature to God, established a sexist idolatry in the heart of Christian symbolism that allowed males to play God in relation to subjugated women.[38]

Such a "sanctification of patriarchal dominance,"[39] says Ruether, is nothing less than a "betrayal of the heart of the Gospel."[40]

Ruether believes that this betrayal continues in 1 Tim. 2:11ff. where we are given an argument for woman's subordination based on "[h]er secondary place in the order of creation and her primary responsibility for the fall."[41] This is the same Deutero-Pauline tradition, Ruether suggests, that was responsible for interpolating the highly restrictive command for women to be silent in 1 Cor. 14:34.[42]

Ruether's vehemence against what she takes to be the sexist nature of all these biblical passages, is most clearly expressed in a litany entitled "Exorcism of Patriarchal Texts" that she has included in her book *Women-Church*. Ruether proposes that a series of passages with "clearly oppressive intentions," such as Lev. 12:1-5, Ex. 19:1,7-9,14-15, Judg. 19, Eph. 5:21-23 and 1 Tim. 2:11-15 (all of which have featured in the above discussion) are read out while the community "cries out in unison, 'Out, demons, out!' " at the conclusion of each passage. At the end of the exorcism, Ruether suggests that someone should announce:

> These texts and all oppressive texts have lost their power over our lives. We no longer need to apologize for them or try to interpret them as words of truth, but we cast out their oppressive message as expressions of evil and justifications of evil.[43]

III. Usable Tradition

Although, as we have seen, Ruether is deeply critical of the androcentrism of biblical and post-biblical traditions, it would be a mistake to conclude that she is opposed to the importance of tradition *per se* in human life. While she stresses that all traditions are fundamentally rooted in human experience,[44] and fall into crisis when their teachings significantly contradict our experience, Ruether strongly disagrees with feminists who believe that an adequate feminist theology or worldview can be built solely on the basis of contemporary women's experience.

Such an approach is naive, she argues, because it ignores the need "to situate oneself meaningfully in history." If we think that we can even articulate our contemporary experience without making use of patterns of thought that have a history, we are deluding ourselves, she says. For while we might be right to discard large historical periods as too corrupt to be redeemed for our purposes, we still find ourselves trying "to encompass this 'fallen history' within a larger context of authentic and truthful life." "To look back to some original base of meaning and truth before corruption," she says, "is to know that truth is more basic than falsehood." Furthermore, when we find "glimmers" of this truth in traditions outside the mainstream, we are strengthened in our convictions and are less prone to thinking we are crazy to oppose majority opinion. In this light she writes,

> Only by finding an alternative historical community and tradition more deeply rooted than those that have become corrupted can one feel sure that in criticizing the dominant tradition one is not just subjectively criticizing the dominant tradition but is, rather, touching a deeper bedrock of authentic Being upon which to ground the self. One cannot wield the lever of criticism without a place to stand.[45]

Ruether's affirmation of our need for tradition does not preclude our need to discern which tradition(s) to embrace to give us guidance. Such a choice, I suggest, can only be made by appeal to a norm of some kind. To this end, Ruether points out that the "critical principle of feminist theology," which was cited at the beginning of chapter 1, can be restated positively in the following form:

> [W]hat does promote the full humanity of women is of the Holy, it does reflect true relation to the divine, it is the true nature of things, the authentic message of redemption and the mission of redemptive community.[46]

Such a principle, Ruether readily admits, is not new. To apply the notion of full humanity to women is nothing more than to see them as being in the image of God. But because the theological tradition has made males and not females normative humanity, it has never fully affirmed women in this way.[47]

Because the full humanity of women has not existed historically, the search for "an alternative historical community and tradition
more deeply rooted than those that have become corrupted" cannot
be simply a matter of embracing one particular tradition as a pure
embodiment of normativity which can guide us towards wholeness.
On the other hand, the fact that the humanity of woman has always
been denigrated in the past does not mean that history cannot help
us at all. For as Ruether also points out,

> [T]he humanity of women, although diminished, has not been
> destroyed. It has constantly affirmed itself, often in only limited
> and subversive ways, and it has been touchstone against which
> we test and criticize all that diminishes us. In the process we
> experience our larger potential that allows us to begin to
> imagine a world without sexism.[48]

Because of her conviction that the humanity of women can be
glimpsed in history, Ruether has selected five areas of cultural
tradition within which she believes we can find "usable foundations
for feminism."[49] But she does not mean that these are the only
possible areas of "usable tradition." As if anticipating the objections
of feminists from different cultural and religious backgrounds than
herself, she writes,

> While particularity is affirmed, exclusivism is rejected. God is
> not a Christian or Jew rather than a pagan, nor white rather
> than Asian or African. Theological reflections drawn from
> Judeo-Christian or even the Near-Eastern-Mediterranean-
> European traditions do not have a privileged relation to God,
> to truth, to authentic humanity over those that arise from
> Judaism, Islam, and Buddhism. Nor are they presumed to be
> the same. Exactly how a feminist theology drawn from other
> cultural syntheses would differ is not yet known. But we affirm
> at the outset the possibility of equivalence, or equal value, of
> different feminist theologies drawn from different cultural syn-
> theses.[50]

Having noted this important qualification, we can now explore the five areas of tradition with which Ruether interacts in constructing her Christian feminist theology.

A. The Bible

In spite of her negative comments about the Scriptures examined above, the biblical tradition is, arguably, Ruether's main dialogue partner.[51] For this reason, and because I will also appeal to the Scriptures as a basis for my own responses and proposals in the following chapters, this positive side of Ruether's view of the Bible will receive far more attention here than the other traditions to which she appeals.

As should be very clear from the discussion in section I above, Ruether would be the last person to claim that the whole canon should be given equal attention or weight. "Feminist readings of the Bible," she writes, "can discern a norm within Biblical faith by which the Biblical texts themselves can be criticized. To the extent to which Biblical texts reflect this normative principle, they are regarded as authoritative. On this basis many aspects of the Bible are to be frankly set aside and rejected."[52]

The "norm within Biblical faith" to which Ruether appeals is "the prophetic principle" or "prophetic-liberating tradition"; a tradition, she argues, which "can be fairly claimed, on the basis of generally accepted Biblical scholarship, to be the central tradition, the tradition by which Biblical faith constantly criticizes and renews itself and its own vision."[53]

She sees four themes as being essential to this prophetic tradition:

(1) God's defense and vindication of the oppressed; (2) the critique of the dominant systems of power and their power-holders; (3) the vision of a new age to come in which the present system of injustice is overcome and God's intended reign of peace and justice is installed in history; and (4) finally, the critique of ideology, or of religion, since ideology in this context is primarily religious. Prophetic faith denounces religious ideologies and systems that function to justify and sanctify the dominant, unjust social order.[54]

It is not hard to see, in the light of the above description, why Ruether believes that the prophetic literature is a valuable tradition for contemporary feminism. One might even suggest that Ruether's own work is prophetic, given the above criteria.

But Ruether's appeal to the prophets has not escaped criticism. In response to an earlier attempt by Ruether to advocate this part of the canon, the feminist New Testament scholar Elizabeth Schüssler Fiorenza has claimed that Ruether has selected the prophetic tradition as an "Archimedian point" or "canon within the canon" in a way that betrays a problematic neo-orthodox approach to the Bible.[55] To support her conviction that such an approach is exegetically and hermeneutically inadequate, Fiorenza says,

> Not only does [Ruether] draw a rather idealized picture of the biblical and prophetic traditions but also she overlooks the oppressive androcentric elements of these traditions. Because she does not analyze the classical prophetic tradition as a historical phenomenon, but uses it rather as an abstract critical interpretative pattern, she does not consider its patriarchal polemics and repression of the cult of the Goddess. Rather, she simply postulates that as a social-critical tradition the prophetic traditions can be used in the interest of feminism. Without question this is the case, but we are not told how and in what way feminist theology can transform this social-critical androcentric tradition into a feminist liberating tradition and use it to its own ends.[56]

If we examine Ruether's discussion of this topic in *Sexism and God-Talk*, which was published shortly after the above comments saw print, we can see that many of these criticisms miss the mark.[57] This book clarifies what Fiorenza could also have discovered from a careful reading of Ruether's previous works, namely that she does not idealize the prophets, but often points out what she sees as their limitations and distortions.[58]

She also fully recognizes the need to find a way in which "feminist theology can transform this social-critical androcentric tradition," as Fiorenza puts it, "into a feminist liberating tradition." It is to this end that Ruether writes,

[F]eminism goes beyond the letter of the prophetic message to apply the prophetic-liberating principle *to women*. Feminist theology makes explicit what was overlooked in male advocacy of the poor and oppressed: that liberation must start with the oppressed of the oppressed, namely, *women* of the oppressed. This means that the critique of hierarchy must become explicitly a critique of patriarchy. All the liberating prophetic visions must be deepened and transformed to include what was not included: women.[59]

Fiorenza's accusation that Ruether uses the prophetic tradition as "an abstract critical interpretative pattern" and reduces it to "an abstract dehistoricized critical key" is a little more plausible, as is her identification of neo-orthodox tendencies in Ruether's thought. Ruether's appeal to "the prophetic principle" or "the prophetic dialectic"[60] is an appeal to something that can be "abstracted" from, but is not fully identifiable with, the prophetic writings in which it is expressed. This is indeed reminiscent of the neo-orthodox distinction that Ruether frequently makes in her first book, *The Church Against Itself*, between "the Word of God" and "the many words about God in scripture and tradition."[61] Nevertheless, it is precisely this kind of distinction that enables her to *criticize* the biblical prophets for their historical limitations while also appealing to them for her own contemporary purposes. Thus she writes,

Prophetic critique as the norm of Biblical faith . . . is not limited to the insights of the societies that produced the biblical texts. Rather, this principle goes out ahead of us, allowing us to apply it in new ways in new contexts. Only in this way is biblical faith a living faith and not a dead letter.[62]

Whether there is an element of truth to Fiorenza's characterization of Ruether's critical key as "dehistoricized" is a matter to which I shall return in chapter 3.[63] What is important to note here is that Ruether rejects the accusation. In order to distance herself from an ahistorical position she has replied by referring to the prophetic principle as a "liberating *'dynamic'* which is expressed in

the prophetic-messianic tradition."[64] Similarly, in her review of
Fiorenza's *Bread Not Stone: The Challenge of Feminist Biblical
Interpretation* she claims,

> [Fiorenza's] accusation of an abstract archetypal "canon within
> the canon" is incorrectly attributed to this author. I do not
> speak of an *abstract archetype* of liberation, to be distinguished
> from its oppressive deformations, but of liberating *historical
> prototypes*, limited by their social and cultural contexts, which
> must be translated and recontextualized in the concerns of
> liberation communities today [my emphases].[65]

The only part of the canon which Ruether identifies with the
prophetic tradition but does not criticize in any way, is the teaching
of Jesus. In fact she even goes as far as to say,

> [T]he Jesus of the synoptic Gospels can be recognized as a
> figure remarkably compatible with feminism. This is not to say,
> in an anachronistic sense, that "Jesus was a feminist," but rather
> that the criticism of religious and social hierarchy characteristic
> of the early portrait of Jesus is remarkably parallel to feminist
> criticism.[66]

Ruether frequently appeals to Jesus' attitude towards power
as a central element of his prophetic vision. In this context, one of
her favourite biblical texts is Mt. 20:25-28,

> You know that the rulers of the Gentiles lord it over them, and
> their great men exercise authority over them. It shall not be so
> among you; but whoever shall be great among you must be your
> servant, and whoever would be first among you must be your
> slave; even as the Son of Man came not to be served but to
> serve, and to give his life as a ransom for many.[67]

Ruether is fully aware that historically, the church has often set
up lords and princes as its leaders and "has tried to baptize this
lordship by calling it 'service'." In contrast, Ruether argues that
Jesus' words should be understood as advocating

... a ministry of service [which] does not seek power for itself
... [but] uses power to empower others. It particularly supports
the empowerment of those who have been put down: women,
the poor. Only in this way do people become equals, and so a
community of service becomes a real possibility.[68]

She also emphasises, with particular reference to the story of
Mary and Martha (Lk. 10:38-42), that Jesus does not use this view
of ministry to reinforce the image of woman as a servant. While the
leadership of the community is to be modeled on the *diaconia* of
women and servants, what this story shows is that "women are freed
from exclusive identification with the service role and called to join
the circle of disciples as equal members."[69]

Jesus' vindication of Mary's right to be his student, which was
quite contrary to contemporary rabbinic practice, is just one of a
number of examples of what Ruether describes as his "iconoclasm
toward the traditional subordination of women in Jewish life."[70]
Other examples include his deliberate discarding of the taboo of
uncleanness in his interaction with the woman with a haemorrhage
(Mk. 5:25-34, Mt. 9:20-22, Lk. 8:43-48), and his violation of the law
that forbade the Jewish male to talk alone to a woman other than
his wife, when he spoke with the Samaritan woman (Jn. 4:27). She
also draws our attention to the fact that women are among Jesus'
close friends to the extent that Mary, Joanna, and Susanna (Lk.
8:1-3) accompany him and the twelve on journeys "in a way that must
have seemed highly unconventional in traditional society."[71]

Not only was Jesus open to women, Ruether argues, but women
were particularly open to him and his message. If we grant that the
oppressed are the most receptive to the Good News, she argues,
then how much more so will this be true of the "oppressed of the
oppressed." In this light, Ruether observes that Jesus' dialogue at
the well was not just with a Samaritan, although all Samaritans were
marginalized by the Jews. It was with a Samaritan woman. Similarly,
the poor and the moral outcasts who respond so quickly and positively to him are represented by the widows and prostitutes. "This is
not accidental," Ruether points out. "It means that, in the iconoclas-

tic messianic vision, it is the women of the despised and outcast people who are seen as the bottom of the present hierarchy and hence, in a special way, the last who shall be first in the kingdom."[72]

Another text that Ruether particularly likes to quote from the gospels, is Mt. 23:8-11:

> But you are not to be called rabbi, for you have one teacher, and you are all brothers (and sisters). And call no man father on earth, for you have one Father, who is in heaven. Neither be called masters, for you have one master, the Christ. He who is the greatest among you shall be your servant.[73]

Although a passage that refers to God as Father may not sound as though it will help the cause of feminist theology, but will merely buttress patriarchal gender symbolism, Ruether interprets these words as having "revolutionary implications." What she takes this text to mean is that Christians are not to encourage the setting up of hierarchical patterns of leadership by using terms and titles for their leaders that are also associated with the divine. She writes,

> If this teaching of Jesus had been maintained, the very root of sexism and clericalist hierarchicalism in Biblical religion would have been decisively undercut. The fatherhood of God could not have been understood as establishing male ruling-class power over subjugated groups in the Church or Christian society, but as that equal fatherhood that makes all Christians equals, brothers and sisters.[74]

I am personally very sympathetic to Ruether's exegesis at this point. Nevertheless, I think that the fact that she does not raise the fairly obvious feminist objection that Jesus actually *reinforces* patriarchy by transferring the rule of the father from earth to heaven[75] is significant, as it would seem to reflect a reluctance on her part to subject Jesus to feminist critique—an attitude which she neither defends nor shows towards any other part of the canon.

B. Countercultural Christianity

A second area of "usable tradition" for Ruether is what she calls "countercultural" Christianity.[76] While she believes that this has its origins in the egalitarianism of the Jesus movement, she also thinks that it was opposed by the Deutero-Pauline traditions and was not fully reflected in the official canonical framework of the New Testament. Given this opposition, she claims that it went underground to appear outside the dominant form of Christianity in various heretical movements such as Gnosticism and Montanism. In later history, this countercultural Christianity is represented by the Albigensians, the Quakers, and the Shakers.

As we have already seen in Ruether's comments about such movements in her discussion of "eschatological feminism," she does not believe that their ideas are fully adequate for a feminist theology, but she does think that they are suggestive if their strengths and weaknesses are carefully discerned. She writes,

> Where women's messianic equality was affirmed in heretical Christianity, it was generally done by asserting an eschatological order of redemption as a counterpoint to the patriarchal order of creation. Thus a paradox arises: Gnostic Christianity affirmed women's equality, but against the goodness of nature and bodily existence. Orthodox Christianity, which affirmed doctrinally (if not in its actual spirituality) the goodness of body and creation, nevertheless used its doctrine of Creation to subordinate women. Neither orthodox nor heretical Christianity brings together the wholeness of vision that feminist theology seeks. Only by correcting the defects of each with the other do we begin to glimpse another alternative Christianity.[77]

Such observations express clearly Ruether's conviction that while there are many traditions that are suggestive of the way we should go, there are none that can be embraced as fully normative.

C. The Basic Categories of Christian Theology

Although the ways in which the basic categories of Christian theology have functioned have been distorted by androcentrism, as we saw in the last chapter, Ruether claims that their meaning can be rediscovered in radically new ways.[78] Such a reinterpretation of basic Christian themes, she argues, is precisely what is going on in much feminist thought. She goes as far as to claim that even among the most post-christian of feminists, such as Mary Daly, who aim to construct a worldview based solely on women's experience, these basic Christian categories unconsciously shape their thinking. In Ruether's words,

> One continues to find the basic paradigm of classical theology which connects an original good human nature, united to the cosmos and the divine, contrasted with an alienated, fallen, historical condition of humanity (sin, evil). Revelatory, transformative experiences (conversion) disclose the original humanity and allow one to liberate oneself from the sinful distortion of existence. This new humanity is then related to a redemptive community that gathers together and announces a prophetic, critical, or transformative mission against sinful society.[79]

Although the basic paradigm of Christian systematics is not the only possible one for developing a feminist theology, Ruether is quick to add, she justifies her own use of it by pointing out that its use by various liberation movements in both the West and the Third World witnesses to "[i]ts continuing power to provide an interpretative framework for human situations of conflict and struggle for justice."[80]

D. Paganism

Ruether also wishes to draw upon pagan resources in her development of a feminist theology,[81] but she is anxious that this is not confused with the approach of the Goddess or feminist Wicca movement which is confident that paganism can provide us with a ready-made feminist religion rooted in ancient matriarchy. Ruether is highly sceptical about this movement's historical reconstructions of this early religion, and even charges it with ideological distortion due to its uncritical acceptance and use of assumptions that are rooted in nineteenth-century romanticism.[82]

In opposition to this movement, Ruether emphasizes that she has no intentions of idealizing ancient Near Eastern religions at the expense of biblical traditions, but she does suggest that a comparison between the Old Testament and Canaanite faiths, for example, in which each is allowed to speak positively to the other, can help us "discover new insights into the foundation of Western religions and cultural consciousness." Such an exercise, she believes, will shed light on the origin of patriarchy itself. Quoting Mary Wakeman, she says, "To see patriarchy coming into existence (through ancient near Eastern religions) is also to see it passing away."[83]

E. Post-Christian Thought

The fifth and final area of "usable tradition" which Ruether wishes to employ is modern post-Christian thought.[84] Here she identifies three streams of critical culture with which she wishes to interact: liberalism, romanticism, and Marxism. Of particular significance for her purposes is that all of these traditions have given rise to different ways of approaching women's liberation. But rather than championing one type of feminism, her personal goal and recommendation to other feminists is to seek a synthesis of all three of these traditions in order to build a model that appropriates the strengths of each while avoiding their respective limitations.

Ruether's strategy for moving beyond the misogyny and androcentrism of the Western theological tradition by interacting with these different streams of tradition—her "practical eclecticism" or "feminist 'ecumenism' "[85]—is captured well in the following words with which she concludes her discussion of methodology in *Sexism and God-Talk*:

> The feminist theology proposed here is based on a historical culture that includes the pre-Christian religions suppressed by Judaism and Christianity; Biblical prophetism; Christian theology, in both its majority and minority cultures; and, finally, the critical cultures through which modern Western consciousness has reflected on this heritage. It seeks, in effect, to recapitulate from a feminist, critical perspective this journey of Western consciousness.

Ruether does not claim to have sifted every aspect of Western thought for material to be incorporated into her theology. That would be an impossible undertaking. Her aim is simply to develop "a working paradigm of some main trends of our consciousness, both its dominant side and its underside." This will hopefully be sufficient, she claims, to enable us to "begin to glimpse both what has been lost to humanity through the subjugation of women and what new humanity might emerge through the affirmation of the full person-hood of women."[86]

Ruether's own vision of this "new humanity" that she hopes will emerge and her ideas about how this vision and the traditions in which it can be glimpsed should transform the way we think about theological anthropology, evil, Mariology, ecclesiology, Christology, nature, eschatology, and God will described and assessed in chapter 4. First, however, I will offer a preliminary response to those aspects of Ruether's thought that have been examined in this chapter, and suggest an alternative way of constructing a Christian feminist theology based on a different approach to fundamental questions of methodology and normativity.

Notes

1. See *SGT*, 16-18 on which the rest of section is based.

2. Ibid., 16-17.

3. Ibid., 17.

4. See *DQ*, 133 for Ruether's distinction between evangelical, liberation and counter-cultural feminists in this context. Cf. "The Feminist Critique in Religious Studies," 63-66.

5. See *FF*, 64-116. See also Rosemary Radford Ruether, "Anti-Semitism in Christian Theology," *Theology Today* 30 (January 1974): 365-81.

6. See *SGT*, 53-54.

7. *SGT*, 77. Cf. *WG*, 37-42.

8. *SGT*, 54.

9. See *NWNE*, 13.

10. See *SGT*, 78.

11. *NWNE*, 13-14. In this passage, Ruether makes no attempt to distinguish between the Hebrew and Greek worldviews. Later in the same book, however (pp. 188-189), she is more careful to differentiate between them.

12. *LT*, 120.

13. *NWNE*, 41.
14. *SGT*, 57.
15. Ibid., 56.
16. Ibid. 67.
17. *NWNE*, 15.
18. Ibid., 148.
19. See *WG*, 62 and, to a lesser extent, *FMM*, 12.
20. *FMM*, 12. Cf. *WG*, 63, *GG*, 21, 25, 179 and 277 n. 12.
21. *WG*, 63. Cf. *GG*, 295 n. 16.
22. See *NWNE*, 15.
23. *SGT*, 168.
24. *FMM*, 13.
25. Ibid., 9.
26. *NWNE*, 15-16.
27. See *WC*, 44-45.
28. *DQ*, 33.
29. See *WC*, 45.
30. See ibid., 44, *WG*, 157. Cf. *GG*, 178.
31. *WG*, 176. Cf. *WC*, 44.
32. See *WC*, 137.
33. See *NWNE*, 67-70.
34. Ibid., 67.
35. See *SGT*, 53, *NWNE*, 68. *NWNE*, 84 n. 5 reveals Ruether's dependence on Bernard P. Prusak's attempt to read this passage as exemplifying an interpretation of Gen. 6 that was popular in intertestamental literature. See his "Woman: Seductive Siren and Source of Sin? Pseudepigraphal Myth and Christian Origins," in *RS*, 98-99. Her biblical interpretation has also been strongly influenced by the chapters on the Old and New Testaments in that volume. See Phyllis Bird, "Images of Women in the Old Testament," in ibid., 41-88 and Constance F. Parvey, "The Theology and Leadership of Women in the New Testament," in ibid., 117-49.
36. *NWNE*, 68-69.
37. *SGT*, 196.
38. *FMM*, 135. Cf. *SGT*, 141-42, which is milder in tone.
39. *WG*, 160.
40. *FMM*, 135.
41. *NWNE*, 69. Cf. *SGT*, 167 and *WC*, 48.
42. See *NWNE*, 69-70 and *FMM*, 13.
43. *WC*, 137. The one other text that she refers to in this context, but which I have left out as it does not single out women, is 1 Pet. 2:18-20, which she interprets as supporting slavery.

44. See *SGT*, 16-17.

45. Ibid., 18.

46. Ibid., 19.

47. See ibid.

48. Ibid.

49. Ibid., 21.

50. Ibid.

51. However Pamela Dickey Young is correct in her observation that since *SGT*, Scripture plays a less central role in Ruether's theologizing than in her earlier work. See her *Feminist Theology/Christian Theology*, 35. The Bible does play a more prominent role in *GG*, however.

52. *SGT*, 23. Cf. *TCW*, 4-5.

53. *SGT*, 24.

54. Ibid.

55. See Elizabeth Schüssler Fiorenza, *In Memory of Her: A Feminist Theological Reconstruction of Christian Origins* (New York: Crossroad; London: SCM, 1983), 16-19.

56. Ibid., 17.

57. See *SGT*, 27-33. Cf. *WG*, 158-59 and *WC*, 42-3.

58. See *NWNE*, 41, *MFFC*, 21-22 and *DQ*, 33-34.

59. *SGT*, 32.

60. Ibid., 22 and *DQ*, 34.

61. *CAI*, 5. Cf. *CAI*, 226. The neo-orthodox tone of this book is unmistakeable, although in the review symposium which looked at Fiorenza's *In Memory of Her*, in *Horizons* 11 (Spring 1984): 147, Ruether writes, "it is so long since I thought about neo-orthodoxy that I cannot quite remember what it was all about, except that I never liked it."

62. *DQ*, 34-35.

63. See 153-55 below.

64. Ruether, "Review symposium: *In Memory of Her*," 148 (my emphasis).

65. Rosemary Radford Ruether, review of Elizabeth Schüssler Fiorenza, *Bread Not Stone: The Challenge of Feminist Biblical Interpretation*, *Journal of the American Academy of Religion* 54 (Spring 1986): 142.

66. *SGT*, 135.

67. *MFFC*, 83, *NWNE*, 65, *TCW*, 54 and *SGT*, 29. I have followed Ruether in using the RSV here.

68. *MFFC*, 83.

69. *NWNE*, 66.

70. Ibid. 63.

71. Ibid., 64.

72. *TCW*, 55.

73. *NWNE*, 66, *MFFC*, 83. She also refers to this text in *SGT*, 65, 136. I have followed Ruether in using the RSV here.
74. *NWNE*, 66.
75. Cf. Phyllis Trible's critique of Robert Hamerton-Kelly, *God the Father: Theology and Patriarchy in the Teachings of Jesus* (Philadelphia: Fortress Press, 1979) in *Theology Today* 37 (1980): 116-19. This is a book that Ruether refers to favourably in *SGT*, 271 n.23.
76. See *SGT*, 33-37 on which this paragraph is dependent.
77. Ibid., 36-37.
78. See ibid., 37-38.
79. Ibid., 38.
80. Ibid.
81. See ibid., 38-41.
82. See ibid., 40. Cf. Rosemary Radford Ruether, "Goddesses and Witches: Liberation and Countercultural Feminism," *The Christian Century* 97 (September 10-17 1980): 842-47. Cf. *GG*, 149-155.
83. *SGT*, 41.
84. See ibid., 41-45.
85. These are Ruether's own terms as cited by Young, *Feminist Theology/Christian Theology*, 33. See pp. 31-39 for her helpful discussion of Ruether's method which she calls "feminist eclecticism." She also provides helpful discussions of the theological methods of Fiorenza (pp. 24-31) and Letty Russell (pp. 40-48).
86. *SGT*, 45.

Chapter 3: Towards An Evangelical-Reformational Feminism

In the introduction, I raised the question of what it might mean to develop a feminist theology in a distinctively Christian way. Focusing on the need to take critical distance from the Christian past while also maintaining significant continuities with it, I argued that the minimal requirements for a Christian feminism involved not only a desire to purge the tradition of elements of sexism and androcentrism but also a willingness and ability to justify and ground this call to change by appealing to norms and criteria that are a part of our Christian heritage.

Chapter 1 examined ways in which Ruether has subjected the Christian tradition to a feminist hermeneutic of suspicion. Nevertheless, clear evidence that she maintains a positive relationship to aspects of the Christian tradition in her struggle for reformation can be seen in her appeal to the Bible, "countercultural Christianity," and "the basic categories of Christian theology," as examined in chapter 2. This also holds for the positive formulation of her critical principle of feminist theology, also examined in the last chapter, which she understands as nothing more than the attempt to take seriously what the tradition has usually only paid lip service to: the belief that women are made in the image of God. Taken together, therefore, chapters 1 and 2 show that Ruether easily meets the

minimal requirements for being classified as a Christian feminist
theologian.

This is not to say that Ruether's approach is necessarily the best
way to construct a feminist theology in a distinctively Christian way.
In this chapter, which concludes Part One of this study, I will outline
an alternative way of drawing on the Christian tradition in order to
challenge and reform current theology and praxis. Here the focus
will be on a particular way of reading, evaluating, and appealing to
the biblical tradition. This will provide support for the approach I
take when I respond to Ruether's attempt to construct a feminist
theology in Part Two. In contrast to my sympathetic response to
Ruether at the end of chapter 1, this chapter will reveal those areas
in which we disagree most strongly. Nevertheless even here I find a
number of very significant points of contact between our positions.

I. A Place To Stand

Not only do I accept Ruether's judgment that the theological tradition is in need of critique, but I am also happy that she stresses, in
opposition to the Enlightenment notion that our liberation lies in
purging ourselves from all the constraints of tradition, that "One
cannot wield the lever of criticism without a place to stand," or
without "situat[ing] oneself meaningfully in history." Her conviction
that we need to find a tradition which we have reason to believe is
"more deeply rooted than those that have become corrupted,"[1] is
one I share.

Of course the acceptance of this proposal does not immediately
solve the problem of *which* tradition(s) should be chosen so that we
can "ground the self" on "a deeper bedrock of authentic Being," as
Ruether puts it.[2] While she does emphasize our need for tradition,
Ruether's desire to avoid the charge of exclusivism, coupled with
the way she uses her own "lever of criticism," (i. e., the "critical
principle of feminist theology" in its negative and positive forms),
prevent her from accepting any one tradition as a privileged
authoritative guide to contemporary theory and praxis. Instead she
feels that a number of traditions must be embraced, all of which need
to be assessed so that they can be purged of distortions even as they

are being used to give support to the ongoing Christian feminist struggle. Thus she writes,

> We must be able to claim the critical principles of every tradition and also to find how to transform the tradition by applying these principles to sexism. This means that our relation to every inherited tradition must be dialectical.[3]

The biblical tradition, which is Ruether's main dialogue partner, proves, in her position at least, to be a highly unstable place to stand. While she clearly believes that a feminist can ground herself/himself in the teachings of Jesus and can appeal to the prophetic principle, little else approaches normativity for her. Furthermore, she does not consider all of the teachings of Jesus found in the gospels to be authentic.[4] And for all its value, the prophetic principle is something that is expressed in but cannot be equated with the prophetic books of the Bible. It is, after all, a principle not a tradition. Far from offering the support of bedrock—to use Ruether's own metaphor—it would seem that the biblical tradition functions more like a tightrope which can only be safely walked by those sufficiently skilled in the appropriate feminist critical techniques.

Ruether has distinguished three different approaches to the Bible that are taken by feminists who are committed to reconstruction in the area of Religious Studies.[5] "Evangelical feminists," she says, "believe that the message of Scripture is fundamentally egalitarian . . . [and] would hope to clean up the sexism of Scripture by better exegesis." "Liberationist feminists," however take "a more critical view of Scripture" that consists of appealing only to "the prophetic tradition as the norm to critique the sexism of the religious tradition." In contrast to the approach of the evangelical feminists, "[b]iblical sexism is not denied, but it loses its authority. It must be denounced as a failure to measure up to the full vision of human liberation of the prophetic and gospel messages." The third group, whom Ruether calls "countercultural feminists," believe that it is a waste of time to try and salvage any part of the canon. In Ruether's words, "What liberation feminists would call patriarchal ideology within the biblical tradition, counterculture feminists declare to be the *only* biblical tradition."[6]

I agree with Ruether that the countercultural feminists are wrong to dismiss the biblical tradition. However a fundamental difference between us is that while Ruether believes that the process of reconstruction is best carried out in terms of the liberationist paradigm, I feel closest, in the final analysis, to the evangelical feminist position—hence the title of this chapter. Let me hasten to add, however, that I do see the need to incorporate many of the liberationist concerns within my framework. And while I do believe that much can be done to "clean up the sexism of Scripture by better exegesis," as Ruether describes the position with which I am identifying, I am convinced that a better *theory of hermeneutics* is of even greater importance if such a position is to be at all plausible.

The position I wish to articulate later in this chapter is rooted in the conviction that the place to stand from which Christians can best wield the lever of criticism is the biblical tradition. This does not mean that I regard this as the only tradition in which wisdom and revelation can be found. I do not reject Ruether's claim that such wisdom may be found in pagan or post-Christian traditions. Still less do I object to her belief that much of value may be found in Christian traditions that have not been seen as "orthodox" by those in the mainstream or in positions of ecclesiastical power. Where I differ from her is on the criteria we should use to distinguish between what is revelatory of the true God in these traditions and what is revelatory of "gods" other than Yahweh. No one can avoid the question of norms or criteria here. I happily confess that I take the Christian Scriptures to be a privileged tradition which can help us distinguish between the wheat and the chaff in other traditions—be they pagan, humanist or Christian. This is a tradition, I believe, that is dependable in a unique way for the vitally important task of discerning God's Word and Spirit in our times.

In this chapter, I am not interested in defending my belief in the authority that the biblical canon can and should have for Christian cultural discernment against all possible objections. But I will spend some time defining my position to clarify where I stand in relation to Ruether. This will also help to lay a foundation for a more focused discussion on whether the Bible supports patriarchy as Ruether believes. Of course there are many theologians and non-theologians to whom I do not have to defend the notion of biblical authority, although not all of them will support the way I will use the Bible to defend a "Christian feminism." As for those readers who feel critical of the biblical tradition because of their feminist commitments, all I will attempt within these pages by way of response is a demonstration of my own approach, which struggles both to be faithful to the Scriptures and to address the issues that Ruether has raised. Thus my own proposals are intended to play an apologetic as well as a constructive role.

Ruether says "If women today are able to find any continuity with the biblical and Judaeo-Christian traditions at all (and many women feel that this is impossible) it cannot be by creating pseudo-apologia for these traditions."[7] I agree whole-heartedly. This requires the development of a hermeneutical theory and exegetical strategy that is sufficiently nuanced if the charge of pseudo-apologia is to be avoided. This will be the focus of the remaining sections of this chapter. My aim is not only to show that a theology that is sensitive to feminist concerns need not reject the Scriptures—and thus need not alienate Christians for whom the authority of the Bible is non-negotiable—but also to demonstrate that there is far more biblical support for engaging in a feminist critique and reformation of the theological tradition than Ruether imagines.

II. Experience, Faith, and Revelation

No matter how much some Christians may stress the need to submit to biblical authority, it is important to note that this can only be done in terms of the particular beliefs one has of the Bible's nature and normative function. As James Olthuis puts it, "Our submission to the Scriptures as the Word of God never takes place apart from concrete embodiment in a view of biblical authority through which and in which we articulate our submission."[8] Because the assumptions we make here have a profound effect on how the Scriptures function in our cultural discernment, it is important that I clarify my own beliefs in this area.

Ruether tells us that in her own interaction with the biblical tradition she has "never assumed that it dropped out of heaven undefiled by historical gestation." "Rather," she says, "I understand it as a product of a human quest for meaning that moved through many different stages and contexts."[9] I am not unhappy with this description and will use this as a starting point for outlining my own position. Ruether is clearly articulating her own position here in sharp opposition to views of the Bible that characterize the theological Right. Because I have indicated that my own position lies in the "evangelical" tradition, which is a tradition many tend to identify exclusively with the attitudes and beliefs of its more reactionary members, I should stress that I too see much that is undesirable in theological conservatism.

What I find particularly helpful about Ruether's description is that it functions as a helpful safeguard against "romanticized" views of inspiration. Like romanticized views of women by means of which males place females on a pedestal in order to keep them in their place, romanticized views of biblical inspiration piously minimize the full creatureliness of the Bible with the result that—good intentions notwithstanding—its true nature is not honoured and the full implications of its message are missed or misconstrued. As Calvin Seerveld rightly says,

> The Bible was not written by a poet in a garret living on bread and water or by a scribe like Ezra who sat down one night, quill in hand, with half a dozen secretaries, while God dictated stream of consciousness for hours and hours, forty days (Cf. the apocryphal book II Esdras 14), which then got published. . . . The point is that God's Word got booked in all kinds of time-consuming ways, in the moil of human life and blood and language, and the fact that God used copying scribes and editors to get it in script and canon formation is no embarrassment for the holy Scripture's having final authority (any more than that Jesus Christ should blush as less divine because he had an umbilical cord).[10]

To examine the biblical tradition in the light of its origin in the "human quest for meaning" (Ruether) is to focus on "the moil of human life and blood and language" (Seerveld). It is to acknowledge with Ruether that the Scriptures, like all traditions, are deeply rooted in *human experience*.[11] One need only read the Psalms to see how true this is.

Human quests for the meaning of life, in which we respond to God's call to find certainty and develop a vibrant worldview and an authentic way of life,[12] are often set in motion by certain life-transforming experiences. While not every type of experience has the same power to set people off on such a religious quest, such questing often has its origin in *limit experiences*,[13] by which I mean experiences such as joy, angst and hope in which the ultimate questions of life come to the fore of our consciousness.

Limit experiences always have a certain intensity. They force us to question the limits of and for our lives and will often do so in an urgent, existential way. They need not be particularly out of the ordinary, however. While near death experiences, giving birth, visiting a sweat lodge, viewing the earth from a space shuttle, and witnessing a miracle may well be the kinds of experiences which many of us need before we allow ourselves to be confronted with such questions, others may find themselves in touch with the limits of and for their lives in the context of relatively "mundane" activities such as attending a funeral of a distant relative, watching children playing, reading a moving novel or biography, or turning forty.

It is out of experiences such as these that the Psalms were written. Their ability to articulate and wrestle with these limit situations which are part of the warp and woof of human life is what gives this literature its power across the generations. Perhaps more clearly than any other part of the Bible, the Psalter reveals the impact of limit experience on the Hebrew worldview. For this reason, it provides a good entrée into the canon as a whole.

In his insightful commentary, Walter Brueggemann suggests that we can distinguish between psalms of orientation, disorientation, and new orientation.[14] One particular strength of this typology, he argues, is that "the flow of human life characteristically is located either in the actual experience of one of these settings or is in movement from one to another."[15] This typology, I will suggest, can help us see the close relationship between life experience and the overall contours of the biblical worldview.

Psalms of orientation, says Brueggemann, reflect seasons of well-being, joy, blessing and security.[16] They are expressions of "creation faith" in which "[l]ife is experienced as protected space. Chaos is not present to us and is not permitted a hearing in this well-ordered world." Borrowing a phrase from sociologist Peter Berger, Brueggemann claims that these psalms "maintain a 'sacred canopy' under which the community of faith can live out its life with freedom from anxiety. . . . Whenever we use these psalms, they continue to assure us of such a canopy of certitude—despite all the incongruities of life."[17]

But human life also consists of "anguished seasons of hurt, alienation, suffering, and death [which] evoke rage, resentment, self-pity, and hatred." Psalms of disorientation match this season "in its ragged, painful disarray."[18] In the Psalter, such experiences of darkness are honestly voiced and wrestled with before a God who clearly "does not have protected sensitivities."[19] Brueggemann is surely right when he comments,

> The community that uses these psalms of disorientation is not easily linked with civil religion, which goes "from strength to strength." It is, rather, faith in a very different God, one who is present in, participating in, and attentive to the darkness, weakness, and displacement of life.[20]

But if these psalms recognize a move "from an ordered, reliable life to an existence that somehow has run amok,"[21] others testify to the fact that in the midst of the darkness we can experience new orientation, the gift and surprise of new life and hope and the resolution of brokenness and despair. At such times, "a new coherence [is] made present to us just when we thought all was lost."[22]

Taken together, psalms of orientation, disorientation and new orientation capture something of the breadth and depth of human experience and give us a sense of the "moil of human life and blood and language" out of which Israel's faith arose and developed. This three-fold typology also suggests that we can distinguish between three fundamental types of limit-experience, which I will call *connection*, *disconnection* and *reconnection*.

Such profound experiences provoked Israel—and provoke us—to face the ultimate questions of life. They set in motion the quest for ultimate meaning, which Ruether correctly sees as giving rise to the Scriptures.[23] Quest-ions such as How can we find security? Why do we suffer? What is the basis of our hope? Who or what is the ultimate author of the blessings of life? How can we find healing and liberation? inevitably arise for those who are open to experience. In this context it is important to realise that these questions are not posed for theoretical entertainment but are urgent matters which must be wrestled with long and hard and in the light of our ultimate commitments. When all is said and done, such limit-questions can only be answered in faith, in the context of our surrender to what we believe is ultimately trustworthy.

In our search for a "place to stand," what we need is not just a tradition, as Ruether stresses, but a *faith* tradition which answers these ultimate questions to our satisfaction. Although embracing such a tradition involves a fundamental act of trust, we do not surrender our lives to the tradition itself but to the God/idol of the tradition—be that Yahweh, Progress, Reason, Nature or some other confessed Ultimate.[24] At the same time, humans cannot give themselves to God or to an idol without ascribing some level of religious or revelatory authority to those traditions, histories and processes in which they find their deity revealed—hence the reverence that different communities have had for the Bible, the Book of Mormon, the history of the Class Struggle, the lives of the Saints, evolutionistic reconstructions of the birth and growth of the universe, the annual cycle, and the accomplishments of the Scientific Method. These provide a wide variety of people with the myths or founding stories of and for their lives.

When we finally arrive at answers to questions of ultimate meaning, what was previously so unclear becomes "unveiled." Our eyes are opened to what was once invisible to us. Truth is experienced as a *revelation*, as a gift that comes from beyond ourselves, even though we were fully involved in the process of discovery. Even in our culture, which is so religiously committed to the myth that human reason can ground itself, we often find ourselves speaking of a moment when the truth finally "dawns on us." For those who believe that God is a partner with us in the joys and struggles of life (as the psalmists did), the human process of arriving at ultimate answers in the surrender of faith can be experienced and interpreted as *receiving revelation from God.*

If we grant that it makes sense for theists to speak this way about the experience of revelation, we are in a position to see why Christians came to see the biblical canon, which has functioned as the occasion for this kind of experience for many of its readers, as the *Word of God.* Similarly, belief in the phenomenon of revelation can also help us understand why Christians have viewed biblical authors as *inspired.* Yet, as I hope to show, to speak in this way does not mean that we have to minimize the deep roots that the Scriptures have in human experience. What I want to suggest is that revelation and inspiration can be seen as phenomena in which both God and humanity are fully involved. It is possible to subscribe to the belief that the biblical writings are both inspired and revelatory without asserting that they have "dropped out of heaven." Agency does not have to be ascribed to God *in opposition to* humanity or *vice-versa.* Instead of such an either-or perspective, we need to speak of the partnership or covenant between God and humanity that marks all authentic human action, and which is only absent to the extent to which we engage in evil.

Even for those with a vibrant theistic worldview, this co-partnership with God is undoubtedly easier to experience than it is to explain. At the heart of our conceptual difficulty with this way of speaking, I believe, is the fact that the relationship between God and creation is fundamentally different from all other relationships—which are *intra*-creational. Even metaphors that try to capture one type of intra-creational (or creature-creature) relationship in terms of another have limitations which must be respected if communication is not to break down. To try and capture the Creator-creation relationship itself in terms of one of these intra-creational relationships, (such as Self-body or King-subject), is not possible without greatly stretching the metaphors that are employed.[25] In this context, we should not judge attempts to describe God's role in the phenomena of revelation and inspiration by using the same criteria by which we evaluate the sense or non-sense of our everyday language about the world.

I have used the metaphor of "partnership" to talk about the God-human relationship in this context. But because it is not an intra-creational relationship, the God-human relationship is a "partnership" unlike all others. While the fullest human partnership that we can imagine consists of two people who each contribute fifty percent, so to speak, to a shared task, such language of equality does not get at what is unique about the God-human relationship. In this relationship, I am proposing, both "partners" may contribute a full one hundred percent, which is what I mean by the prefix in *co*-partnership.[26] Therefore what can be viewed from one direction as a human quest for and subsequent confession of life's ultimate meaning can at one and the same time be viewed as revelation and inspiration given by God. In the same way, I believe that it is both meaningful and helpful to speak of the Christian Scriptures as simultaneously the Word of God and the words of human faith.[27]

This view of co-partnership may seem very strange if we tend to think of the relationship between God and humanity as basically heteronomous and competitive rather than covenantal. If that is the case, we will see Divine and human agency as more or less mutually exclusive, by definition. I am convinced, however, that the co-partnership that I am emphasizing is implicit in the biblical worldview. This is why the psalmist can say, "Unless the Lord builds the house, its builders labour in vain" (Ps. 127:1). This is also why Paul can transcend the limitations of our Arminian and Calvinist categories when he says, "continue to work out your salvation with fear and trembling, for it is God who works in you to will and to act according to his good purpose" (Phil. 2:12,13).

Another way of explaining how the Bible can be viewed as simultaneously the Word of God and the words of human faith involves an appeal to a Christian anthropology. As creatures made in the image of God, human beings inescapably either image the true God or we image the false gods/idols that we trust. When we confess our faith or articulate our ultimate commitments, beliefs, and hopes, we make present in our words the God or gods to which we have given ourselves. To listen discerningly to a speech of Hitler, for example, is to hear not only a human dictator, but also the voice of a (false) deity that we call German Nationalism. To listen in faith to the words of Moses, Jeremiah, Jesus or Paul, by contrast and by analogy, is to hear the voice of the God of Jews and Christians addressing us.

III. Tradition, Story, and the Language of Faith
However we may decide to analyze the experience of revelation, finding answers to the ultimate questions of life is not like solving a crossword puzzle and then putting it aside to move on to something else. What a community takes to be revelatory is often preserved, at least in part, in the form a canon (such as the Bible) and will play an important role in giving direction to its way of life. As Ruether herself writes,

> A collection of [sacred] texts is the accumulated heritage of a people's reflection on its experience in the light of questions of ultimate meaning and value. The texts provide norms for judging good and evil, truth and falsehood, for judging what is of God/ess and what is spurious and demonic.[28]

One important way in which the Bible played this role for the communities that first preserved various collections of its books at the different stages of the growth of the canon, was by helping to provide a coherent worldview for those communities.[29] Worldviews, it is important to note, not only function to bind together members of a community, but they also link the generations. In other words, they are traditions. The vision *of* life and *for* life that a community passes on (*traditum*) can be received by the next generation as a gift (or curse) that it did not work for. Yet it is also experienced as an assignment or call to preserve, modify and expand what is received in the light of new circumstances and experiences before handing it on to the next generation.

The biblical canon in its written form was developed and passed on for perhaps twenty-five generations.[30] Such a traditioning process (*tradendum*) is not like handing over a baton in a relay race. What is passed on changes. Indeed a living tradition must change and develop if it is to stay alive in history. Yet this process is not like playing children's games such as "chinese whispers" or "operator." Continuity is as important as change if it is to remain the "same" tradition (*traditio*).[31] Commenting on the nature of tradition in general, Olthuis writes,

> We must modify tradition in order to keep tradition and we must keep tradition in order to modify it. We change in order to retain our identity, but we need to retain our identity in order to change. To maintain the continuity of a tradition we need to modify its contours appropriate to the changing conditions. In order to modify the contours of a tradition we need to maintain the continuity and constancy of a tradition. Constancy requires modification, as modification requires constancy.[32]

Those who helped form the biblical tradition were faced with the same challenge. Constancy and change, unity and diversity are as much features of the biblical canon as they are of any tradition and must be recognized and honoured if we are to develop an adequate hermeneutic.

I propose that we approach the question of the unity of the Bible in terms of its overarching narrative coherence. One of the major ways in which worldviews are transmitted across the generations is by means of stories—and not primarily by propositions, doctrines and creeds. There is good evidence within the biblical tradition that story was very important in the transmission of the faith of the Hebrews (cf. Ex. 12:26,27; 13:14,15; Deut. 6:20-25; Josh. 4:6,7,21-24).[33] Yet the Bible is far more than just a collection of stories. The Scriptures can also be read as providing an overarching Story in the light of which all its individual narratives, and indeed all the life stories of all its readers down the ages, can be placed and interpreted.[34]

Out of their own particular stories and experiences of key events such as the Exodus, the Exile, the life, death and resurrection of Jesus, Pentecost and so on, biblical writers searched for the meaning of their communities' present existence by placing their times within the larger story of Israel and the church which was passed on to and appropriated by them. In the canonical process, the story of the covenant people was in turn placed within the wider context of the origin and destiny of the whole creation. In the light of the dialectic between the faith in which they were nurtured and the numerous limit-experiences of their own generations, biblical authors wrestled to find the meaning of and for history as a whole. Their combined answer was the unfolding Story of God's covenantal relationship with creation that the Bible tells.

The process by which the overarching Narrative of the canon took shape is far too complex for us to reconstruct in any detail. Nevertheless, I think we can assume that it was out of their experiences of connection, disconnection and reconnection as interpreted in the light of their conviction that goodness is more primordial than evil,[35] that the biblical authors wrote of a beginning to history when the creation was as it ought to be: "very good" (Gen. 1)—a time of orientation, connection, security and communion between God, humanity (male and female), the earth and all creatures. They also wrote of a time of disorientation, disconnection and the rupturing of relationships (Gen. 3)—usually referred to as the Fall. As the story progresses, it is clear that life is no longer as it ought to be. But the experience of God's redemptive and liberating action in history (which for the New Testament writers climaxed in the life, death and resurrection of Jesus) inspired them to imagine a future eschatological fulfilment of history when evil, oppression and brokenness would be fully overcome and purged from the earth. This is portrayed as a time when the goodness of creation will be fully restored, not in the repristinated form of a garden but as a New Jerusalem (Rev. 21 building on Isa. 60)—a city into which all the fruits of human culture will be brought.[36] The beginning and the end of the Story therefore fit together as these human cultural products are themselves the response to God's call to subdue the earth (Gen. 1:28). At this time, God's loving rule over and intimacy with creation will be restored and the God who walked in the garden in the beginning (Gen. 2) and called humanity to fill the earth (Gen. 1:28) will be "all in all" (1 Cor. 15:24-28).[37]

All readings of the biblical drama are shaped by post-biblical traditions of interpretation. My brief summary above is clearly indebted to a tradition of interpretation that is common in Kuyperian Calvinism but is not fully shared by all Christians. But at this stage I am more concerned to argue that the Bible, viewed as a canonic whole, can be legitimately read as a unified Story than I am to defend the particular *details* of how I read it. I do, however, wish to highlight some significant ways in which I disagree with Ruether in this area.

Like many theologians, Ruether does reflect the influence of (what I am calling) the overarching narrative coherence of the Scriptures when she speaks of creation, fall and redemption.[38] Unlike myself, however, Ruether is convinced that a belief in a literal historical eschaton is in sharp contradiction with an affirmation of present historical existence.[39] Creation and eschaton are important biblical themes for her, but her writings suggest that she sees them as "supratemporal" rather than historical realities, as ways of talking about the "essence" or "true nature" of life which stands in judgment over our historical and "fallen" existence.[40]

Such a view, I believe, severely limits the power of the biblical worldview and, in the final analysis, undermines its message of liberation. When Gen. 1 speaks of the formation of the world that God has created into a place that can be inhabited by the creatures of the earth, when Gen. 3 speaks of the subsequent alienation of human beings from God, one other, the earth and other creatures, and when Rev. 21 speaks of the full arrival of the eschaton, these texts are referring to events in the history of our universe. Such texts intend to direct our present praxis by revealing, in the language of faith, what has happened in the past and what will happen in the future.[41] They speak of facts, events and processes as they appear to the eyes of Hebrew and Christian faith, not as they would be described by positivistic historians (whose own faith functions to drastically close down the richness of human experience to the point where there is little left to see).

There are a number of legitimate ways to write history. In this context, a brief discussion of James Olthuis's notion of "certitudinal history" will be helpful for understanding how I believe the biblical authors are addressing us.[42] In *The Church Against Itself*, Ruether correctly writes,

> [T]he gospels . . . are essentially confessional documents whose *sitz im leben* is the faith, worship, and exigencies of the early church. Any tradition about Jesus which survived, survived only because it was relevant to the faith, worship, and needs of the Church.[43]

Claiming on this basis that "the gospels do not furnish us with materials for a life of Jesus," she goes on to argue,

> It is not true that the historical Jesus is unrecoverable through the texts; but it is true that he is unrecoverable through the *proper intentionality* of the sources, and through the *proper intentionality* of the church, the intentionality of *faith*. The historical Jesus is always destroyed by faith which desires to know him only *kerygmatically*, only as the Risen Lord, only in his saving significance *pro nobis* [my emphases].[44]

The question I want to raise here is: What is "the proper intentionality" of the gospels in particular and of the Bible in general? This is closely related to our understanding of the nature of kerygmatic or confessional literature. I would claim that the gospel writers intend to provide an account of Jesus' life, death and resurrection not as an exercise in writing general cultural history but in order to give an account that focuses on historical events in terms of their ultimate significance, or, to use Ruether's own language, their "ultimate meaning and value."[45]

While the faith of the author is present at least in an implicit way in every historical account that has ever been written, in some literature—and this is certainly true of "sacred texts" such as the Bible—ultimate commitments and convictions are made more explicit as they are central to the message of such texts. Ruether is right to focus on the kerygmatic nature of the gospels, but there is no need to resort to a myth/fact or fact/value dualism to account for the unique nature of confessional literature.[46] When a baby is born, to confess "God has given us a child" is not to refer to a realm of meaning above impregnation, gestation, and the activities of the delivery room. Neither is this confession a bad rival to a biological explanation that functions like the story of the stork. Furthermore, it is not analogous to the individual, subjective reading of ink blots in a Rorschach personality test. What is being referred to is a publically accessible reality. It is there for all to see—but is seen only by those with the eyes of faith.

Confessional statements attempt to capture the depth-level or ultimate meaning of concrete historical events. When Neil Armstrong stepped onto the moon in 1969, he uttered the words "That's one small step for man, one giant leap for mankind." I understand this statement to be saying the same thing twice. The second half of this statement, however, translates the first half into the language of faith in the attempt to capture the ultimate significance of the event. To the eyes of faith—faith in the false god of Progress—the small step taken was nothing less than a giant leap. For those committed to this vision of life, this giant leap forward has to be recognized if we are to fully grasp what really happened.

Historical events such as landing on the moon and giving birth to a child may be captured and assessed in terms of their ethical, economic, biotic, certitudinal (or confessional), legal, aesthetic or other dimensions because history is *multi-modal* or *multi-aspectual* in character.[47] It is important to recognize this if we are not to misconstrue the intentionality of biblical authors in their approach to historiography. As Olthuis argues,

> History in the Scriptures is certitudinally qualified history. It is no more or less historical than economic, political, or general cultural histories. But just as these kinds of history have their own distinct focus, as do histories of music and art, sport and recreation, certitudinal history is written from a distinct focus: ultimate realities, ultimate questions and ultimate certainty.[48]

Certitudinally qualified history writing may use a variety of literary genres.[49] It may also include details and information found in other types of history writing, but when it does, such details find their primary meaning in the context of the account's macro-purpose, which is to evoke, strengthen and challenge the faith response of its readers. A confessionally qualified account of the birth of a healthy child, for example, may include details about the baby's weight and response to stimuli that could appear in a not dissimilar form in the doctor's report, but given the overriding purpose of certitudinal literature they will function to support and express the conviction that this birth is, at bottom, a sign of God's blessing.

We should also note that an author may be quite ignorant of such details but still be able to capture the ultimate significance of a birth. By the same token, it is quite possible, in principle, to speak of the depth-meaning of the creation of the world, the fall into sin and the eschatological fulfilment of history without relying on information gained through eye-witness reports. In other words, we do not have to resort to theories of inspiration in which information that is otherwise completely extrinsic to the experience of the human authors is "supernaturally" supplied by God. One may conclude, on the basis of a rival faith, that the biblical authors do not reveal to us the true meaning of past and future events. But to demythologize these accounts (as Ruether often does) is to misconstrue the nature of such writings.

When it is taken as a canonic whole,[50] and viewed in terms of its overarching Story (which I have summarized in terms of the themes of creation, fall, redemption and eschaton), the Bible intends to give us a way of reading the depth-meaning of history from the vantage point of faith in God's covenant with creation. As such it answers the most ultimate questions that humans have about life such as: Who am I? Where am I? What is wrong with the world? What is the remedy? and Where is history ultimately going?[51] In the light of the biblical Story, we are encouraged to answer such questions by confessing that we are human beings made in the image of God, living in God's good but fallen creation which is in need of reconciliation with its Creator. We are also called to be disciples of Jesus Christ, co-partners with God in the healing and liberation of all creation in the power of the Holy Spirit. We live in the expectation of the final defeat of sin and oppression, already anticipated in Christ's resurrection from the dead, when all creation will be healed and when the eschatological fulfilment of history will take place.

To relate the discussion more explicitly to the issue of the relationship between the biblical message and the patriarchal nature of traditional theology, it is my contention that the overarching Story of the Scriptures, which I have attempted to outline above, is not sexist. While some feminists (and non-feminists) may reject it because they choose to see ultimate questions in the light of a different religious vision (such as neo-paganism, or humanism in its liberal or radical forms), I am convinced that there is nothing inherently patriarchal in this vision of and for life. Ruether appears to have no explicitly feminist criticisms of the biblical drama at this level, with the exception of the role that belief in the resurrection of the dead plays within it. (Whether this aspect of biblical hope can be dismissed simply by claiming that it is the manifestation of the alienated male ego will be explored in chapter 4.)

Nevertheless, I am aware that it is not enough to defend the Bible in terms of its general *Weltanschauung*. When people assert that the Bible rightly or wrongly defends patriarchy, they usually have specific passages in mind (as Ruether does). An apologist for "biblical feminism" must defend not just the biblical *Story* but biblical *stories*, not just the basic contours of the biblical *worldview* but the *specific* ways in which the Scriptures give guidance to a *way of life*. These matters will be addressed in section VI, below.

IV. The Relationship Between Bible, Word, and Spirit
In order to justify the way I approach the exegesis of particular biblical texts, it is important that I further clarify some of my fundamental hermeneutical assumptions. The two diagrams on the next page attempt to distinguish my own perspective (B) from the position that I am most eager to avoid (A).

Although I firmly believe that the Scriptures have the capacity to sensitize us to God's presence in our times, I want to sharply distinguish my position from that of biblicism (which is portrayed in diagram A) as this makes the serious error of assuming that we have

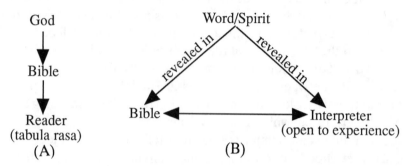

no reliable access to God's guidance apart from the Scriptures. Such a position wrongly mistrusts our ability, and that of the millions of charismatics and mystics within the Christian tradition, to experience God's presence and direction in other ways.[52] To feel safe only with a Bible that is reduced to a system of timeless propositions and which is to be read only when we suspend our subjectivity and allow its truths to imprint themselves on our tabula rasa-like minds, is a stance that no biblical author would recognize as his or her own. In my position, by contrast, I want to affirm the importance of human subjectivity in the act of interpretation. In diagram B, the Bible is not portrayed as our only access to God. God as Word and Spirit can be intimately known in our experience because life itself reveals God to all creatures.[53]

Although our awareness of God is certainly blunted in a fallen world, this is because of our sin and alienation, not because of our creatureliness *per se.* Thus it is only because of our evil, and not because of any limitations inherent in our structural make-up as humans, that we need revelation in its biblical form. (I shall return to the topic of the revelatory power of life experience at the end of this chapter.)

The Bible, I am proposing, is a reliable tradition of the presence of Word and Spirit in a segment of human history. When received as revelation, it not only provides us with an overarching Narrative in which to situate our own stories, but it also functions to sensitize us so that we can recognize God as Word and Spirit in the specific challenges and concerns of our generation. This awareness, in turn, opens up our biblical interpretation. Thus not only can the text increase our awareness of how the Spirit is moving today, but a sensitivity to how the Spirit is moving today can help us discern the way the Spirit was moving when the various biblical books were written.

A good hermeneutical theory, then, must not advocate the suppression of human subjectivity but should emphasize that reading the Bible involves a complex interaction between the two horizons of text and interpreters in which the experience of the readers can be enlarged and the way they interpret their experience (either tacitly or reflectively) can be confirmed or challenged. As diagram B suggests, the process has as its goal a deepened awareness of a third "horizon"—God as Word and Spirit—which is present *both* in the world of the biblical text *and* in that of the interpreter, thus making a vital and life-transforming communion with an ancient text possible.

What I am suggesting may be clarified further by the analogy of seeing the Bible as the Spirit's "passport."[54] Just as Canadian officials may check a person's passport when she enters the country to make sure that she is who she says that she is, so we may read the Bible to discern whether the various courses of action that Christians and non-Christians currently claim will lead to increased normativity and/or healing are, in fact, recognizable as ways of the Spirit.

In addition to arguing that the Bible is a reliable inscripturation of and witness to God's Word and Spirit, I also want to stress that no approach to the biblical canon is adequate as a *Christian* approach unless it gives a central place to Jesus. The fact that Jesus took very seriously what was the biblical tradition of his day should be of great significance to all Christians. But this should not be divorced from paying careful attention to the distinctive way in which Jesus worked with the Scriptures, and related the biblical tradition to himself (cf. Jn. 5:39; Lk. 24:44).[55] If the Scriptures are believed to inscripturate God's Word and Spirit, then it is only appropriate that Jesus is viewed as the focal point of the canon as he is described in the New Testament as the One who *incarnates* Word and Spirit.[56]

Having made some comments about what I see as the normative function of the Bible, it is now possible to highlight where my position differs from that of Ruether with respect to the nature and shape of the canon and its relationship to the Spirit. For Ruether, the formation of the New Testament canon was not one of the high points of church history. The picture she paints of the early Christian community is one in which Christian prophets played a prominent role by speaking out of the "spirit" or iconoclastic and prophetic vision of Jesus. This charismatic period did not last, however. Ruether proposes that by the end of the first century "a developing institutional ministry (bishops) felt the need to cut off this ongoing speaking in the name of Christ."[57] She implies that the same impulse is behind the writing and collection of the gospels which come to function as the definitive texts of the sayings of Jesus. By contrast, those who continued to prophecy in Jesus' name, such as the Montanists, are judged as heretics. Clearly disapproving of these developments, she comments,

> Revelation is said to be closed and located in the past in a historical Christ and a past apostolic community. The ongoing power of the Spirit sent by Christ to the community is no longer to "blow where it will" but is institutionalized in the authority of the bishops. They received the original "deposit of faith" from the apostles and they pass it down unaltered in their official teaching traditions. Both the interpretation of the words of Christ and the power of reconciliation with God is to be wrested from the hands of charismatics, prophets, and martyrs and placed in the hands of the episcopacy, which takes over the claims of apostolic authority.[58]

There may be a great deal of truth to the scenario that Ruether paints. But I do not think that we need to ascribe a motive to the gospel writers any more sinister than the pastoral desire to preserve narratives about Jesus for the next generation. Tensions between charismatics and anti-charismatics may well have existed at this stage of the church's history but we do not have to equate this with a necessary, ontological tension between the oral and the written. Neither do we have to assume that those who initially formed collections of the writings that were later accepted as the New

Testament were anti-charismatic or opposed to prophecy or martyrdom for the simple reason that the very writings which they gathered
support the legitimacy of such activities.

In chapter 1 I noted Ruether's claim that Luke's view of the
ascension served an anti-charismatic purpose because it aimed to
encapsulate Jesus as God's "last word," thus delegitimating ongoing
prophecy in the Christian community.[59] This is a bizarre claim to
make. It is Luke who tells us that Jesus' last words to the disciples
before the ascension are: "I am going to send you what my Father
has promised; but stay in the city until you have been clothed with
power from on high" (Lk. 24:49). This promise is reiterated at the
beginning of Luke's second book which we know as Acts. Luke
clearly sees this promise fulfilled in the outpouring of the Spirit at
Pentecost in Acts 2 and in the numerous charismatic phenomena
that occur in the rest of this book. That his account of the ascension
was in conflict with the ongoing prophetic activity of the early church
is something that would have come to Luke as a great surprise! In
fact it is quite possible that he sees the ascension of Jesus as a
necessary prerequisite for the outpouring of the Spirit. At least this
is how John understands it. Although he does not have an explicit
ascension narrative, he tells us that before his death Jesus says to
his disciples, "Now I am going to him who sent me . . . I tell you the
truth: it is for your good that I am going away. Unless I go away, the
Counsellor will not come to you; but if I go, I will send him to you"
(Jn. 16:5-7). For John, and arguably for Luke, Jesus must ascend so
that the Spirit may descend.

While the writings that make up the New Testament fully
support the legitimacy of charismatic activities, and thus cannot be
opposed to the importance of the ongoing work of the Spirit in and
through the church, it is still the case that the canon may well have
functioned as a tool of oppression and repression in the hands of an
increasingly patriarchal clerical caste. On this point Ruether is
probably correct. But to say this is quite different from saying that
a respect for the canon is by nature opposed to notions of the Spirit
"blowing where it will." If the Scriptures reliably witness to the
movement of the Spirit, as I am suggesting, then there is no need to
oppose Spirit and canon. The role of the canon, I am proposing, is

precisely to help us become sensitized to where the Spirit is "blowing" in our times. This is an approach to the canon that I hope to
illustrate in sections V and VI below.

If the initial *formation* of the canon is suspect for Ruether, the
closure of the canon is even more problematic. In the final chapter
of her book *Womanguides*, she writes,

> Neither revelation nor the telling of stories is closed. Every new
> upsurge of the liberating spirit must challenge the efforts of
> fossilized religious authority to "close the canon," to declare
> that God has spoken once and for all in a past time and "his"
> words are enshrined in a final and definitive form in a past
> collection of texts, and therefore, that all true theology is
> confined to circumscribed commentaries on these past texts.[60]

The approach that she is opposing here is comparable, she suggests,
to that of the scribes and Pharisees. The Gospel writers were correct
to note that unlike them Jesus spoke "with authority."

If the church is to speak with authority today it will certainly
have to do more than to confine itself to commenting on past texts.
But if we are to be prophetic in the way Jesus was, then, like him,
we must be steeped in the biblical tradition. Jesus shows that there
is a way to relate to Scripture as authoritative that is very different
from the approach taken by the scribes and Pharisees. To follow in
Jesus' footsteps does not mean viewing the Bible as containing all
that God has ever said and will ever say.

If we view the Bible as a "canon," we are not thereby obliged
to see it as containing the only writings in existence that are inspired
by God. This would only follow if we viewed it as analogous to the
"literary canon" which is sometimes regarded as a body of writings
that includes all the truly great works of literature. By contrast, I
understand the Bible to be a "canon" in the sense of a standard or
criterion by which we can judge as inspired or uninspired what is
said and done outside its pages. As the Spirit's "passport," it hardly
contains a record of all that the Spirit has done or will do. A
relationship with it is no substitute for a relationship with the Spirit.
But if we are to recognize the difference between the voice of the

Spirit and the voice of idols in our day, then to ignore this "passport" is both arrogant and foolish.

Ruether continues her argument against the closure of the canon by saying that once we reject a view of theology as nothing more than commenting on past texts,

> [W]e are also free to generate new stories from our own experience that may, through community use, become more than personal or individual. They may become authoritative stories, for it is precisely through community use in a historical movement of liberation, which finds in them paradigms of redemptive experience, that stories become authoritative. Woman-Church, too, as church may, through its use of stories and parables generated through its struggles, raises [sic] some of these stories to the level of authoritative texts.

She then closes the book with these words:

> The Spirit blows where it will. The Spirit is not confined to past institutions and their texts. It leads us into new futures. We don't know the path, for we make the path as we go. But it is through generating stories of our own crisis and hope and telling them to one another that we light the path.[61]

I would like to stress that I feel very comfortable with Ruether's emphasis on the Spirit. I couldn't agree more with her assertion that "The Spirit is not confined to past institutions and their texts. It leads us into new futures." She is also right to stress that a Christian community should encourage its members to share their stories, for stories can certainly have authority as vehicles for the Spirit. Actually, this is not a particularly radical claim. Even the most reactionary of evangelicals recognize this, in their own way, when they stress the power of personal testimony in evangelism.

Does this emphasis on the potential inspiration of our stories mean that those that repeatedly function to reveal the presence of God should be added to the canon? And is belief in the closure of the biblical canon necessarily a stance that is closed to the ongoing work of the Spirit? It is ironic that although Ruether sees the initial formation of the New Testament canon to have been in opposition to the work of the Spirit, she now wants to see the emergence of "a new canon" that can serve as the textual base for feminist theology.[62] (Presumably, this will be a canon that will be revised from generation to generation, and may even differ from community to community. But Ruether is less concerned about answering such questions than she is about getting the process under way.)

I have already argued that there is no need to oppose the blowing of the Spirit to the formation of the New Testament. I will now argue that, far from minimizing the ongoing work of the Spirit, it is possible to believe in the "closure" of the canon on the basis of the *importance* of the role of the Spirit in our times.

If we try to evaluate the closure of the canon by viewing it as an event that we can plot within the Story that the Bible itself tells, then we must take into account the fact that most, if not all, of the books that make up what we call the New Testament were written within a generation of Pentecost.[63] Its writings mark the closure of an old era, while facilitating the transition to a new age characterized by different challenges and responsibilities. Viewed in the light of Pentecost, the fundamental reason why we should not keep adding material to the biblical canon, I suggest, is because *we do not need to* as we now live in an era in which God's Spirit can be poured out on all people (cf. Joel 2:28,29, Acts 2:16-18 and Jer. 31:33). The New Testament announces this new era, made possible by the coming of Christ, and gives some introductory guidance about how to live in it. But it is precisely because of the pouring out of the Spirit that its authors do not feel compelled to give directives for life in the detailed manner of the Old Testament. With the gift of the Spirit comes increased responsibility to work out our salvation in fear and trembling.[64] Thus our desire to keep adding to the Scriptures rather than simply sharing our stories can, ironically, be the result of our inability to trust the Spirit as our guide.

This is not to deny what I have already argued, namely that the Scriptures are an important way in which we can get in touch with the Word and Spirit in our times. But we must not use the Bible (or any writings that we take to be inspired) in a way that seeks to deny our responsibility as believers who live in the age of the New

Covenant. The Story of the Bible, I have argued, speaks of human history from creation to eschaton. Its narrative scope, therefore, goes well beyond the time period in which it was written. If we look at the canon in terms of the metaphor of a play, then, from the vantage point of the biblical Story, the closure of the canon (by which I mean the time when its last book was written) occurred at the end of the first scene of the final Act of history. All Christians since the time of Pentecost are, to continue the metaphor, called to act out the rest of the story in the power of the Spirit as co-partners with God in the redemption of creation.[65]

Although we have some hints as to how the story will end, the script between the first and last scenes of this final Act is fundamentally open. There is truth in Ruether's words when she says that "we make the path as we go." Yet not only do we do this as a community, as she rightly suggests, but we are also called to travel as a community in covenant with God with whom we are co-authors of the story. It is not as though one way to "act" is as good as any other. If we are to have wisdom, if we are to be in touch with the Spirit, then we not only need to see our stories in the light of the overall biblical Story, but like a seasoned jazz musician who only improvises once she has the feel of the structure and flow of the music her band is playing, we need to be steeped in the plot and details of "the story so far," by which I mean the biblical account of how God has been redemptively at work up until the beginning of this age of the Spirit. Viewed in this way, the authority of the Bible is not seen as something that heteronomously controls and dominates us but is to be accepted as a normative resource that can empower us in our task by shaping our communal memory, vision and ethos. As Brueggemann rightly says, the Christian community that embraces the biblical tradition will be a community "rooted in energizing memories and summoned by radical hopes."[66]

V. Towards a Redemptively-Sensitive Hermeneutic

If we are called to be co-partners with God in the redemption of creation, then we need a hermeneutic that will allow the Scriptures to empower us in that task. A good test of any such theory will be whether it can shed any light on a way to go as we wrestle with what it means to be normatively and redemptively male and female. This section will therefore make some general suggestions about method, laying the foundation for section VI, which will address Ruether's claim that parts of the Bible are little more than a capitulation to patriarchal ideology.

As we have seen, Ruether speaks of the ability that stories have to "light the path" that we are on. Such "journeying" language is an appropriate way to speak about spiritual discernment because life and history never "stand still." The Bible frequently speaks of living in covenant with God by using directional metaphors.[67]

Doing God's will, for example, is often described as knowing God's ways and walking in God's paths (cf. Ex. 33:13; Deut. 10:12; 26:17; Job 21:14; Ps. 1; Isa. 2:3; 35:8; Hos. 14:9). Walking in God's ways is also described as doing the truth (Ps. 25:4,5; 86:11). Thus in Jn. 14:6, Jesus is described as the one who incarnates and reveals what it means to be on the Way, to do the Truth, and to live Life. It is also significant that in Acts, Christianity itself is referred to simply as "The Way" (9:2; 19:9,23; 22:4).

In connecting "the Way" and "the Life," Jesus' words in Jn. 14:6 allude to Deut. 30:11-30, where to follow God's ways is described as leading to life and blessing while covenantal disobedience is said to lead to death and curse. When viewed from the vantage point of breaking or keeping the covenant, human existence can therefore be seen as a choice between two ways or directions (Prov. 4:18,19; 5:6; Mt. 7:13,14).

Given such language, it is not surprising to find that God is often spoken of as a guide who directs our steps (Ps. 23; 25:9; 32:8; Isa. 48:17) and as the One without whom we will lose our way (Isa. 53:6; Zec. 10:2). Indeed even the word *Torah*, which is misleadingly translated as "Law," is best rendered as instruction, guidance or signpost. Furthermore, Ruether's own language about "lighting the path" is, in spite of its apparent stress on human autonomy, reminiscent of the famous words of Psalm 119:105, "Your word is a lamp to my feet and a light for my path."

We can further explore such directional metaphors and make some connections with the earlier discussion about limit experiences and the Psalms by speaking of the function of specific biblical texts in terms of their power to either *orient* or *reorient* our way of life.

A. Orientation Texts

One of the most basic assumptions in Ruether's work is that there is a vital distinction to be made between the way life *is* and the way it *ought* to be. What I am calling orientation texts highlight this difference. They speak of normativity and of creational paths that bring blessing because they reflect God's original intentions for human life. They speak of the normative development of creation from its origin to its destiny. They put us in touch with the perduring calls of God to all peoples in all times and in all cultures and thus help us live our lives in a way that does not go "against the grain" of how our world has been made. Orientation texts include the call to be stewards of the earth (Gen. 1:28), to accept life as a gift and not a possession (Deut. 8), to engage in leadership as a servant and empowerer of others (Mt. 20:25-28), to practise mutual submission between all people (Eph. 5:21), to live all of life to God's glory (Rom. 12:1), and to entrust our lives to Yahweh and not idols (Ex. 20:3).

It is relatively easy to see how texts of orientation address us in our times, especially when then they take the form of general statements, as they do in the examples that I have given. Sometimes such biblical texts take the form of very specific commands which are not applicable in our culture in their original form. In such cases we have to translate such texts into general principles in order to get in touch with the normative call embodied in them. Thus Deut. 22:8, in which the Israelites are told, "When you build a new house, make a parapet around your roof so that you may not bring the guilt of bloodshed on your house if someone falls from the roof," can be read as challenging us to have safety regulations for buildings.[68]

We also need to judge what is the appropriate level of generality when we try to re-articulate such specific directives. Read in the light of the overarching "certitudinal thrust"[69] of Deuteronomy which calls us to recognize the true nature of life in terms of the all-embracing nature of the covenant, Deut. 22:8 challenges us to see that responsibility for the safety of buildings is part of what it means to love God, neighbour and self. We may ask whether this text only has relevance to houses that resemble the ones the Hebrews built in the Mosaic period, or whether it applies to all buildings or even to all possessions? (Paul, after all, feels free to apply a text about not muzzling oxen from Deut. 25:4 to the rights that preachers have to be fed in 1 Cor. 9:9 and 1 Tim. 5:18). This question cannot be answered by appealing to authorial intention. Neither is it primarily an academic problem. While similar problems are faced by those in the legal profession when they attempt to abstract principles from case law, the hermeneutical decisions that we face with this biblical text cannot be solved merely by applying principles from a field such as jurisprudence.

If we see this problem in the light of diagram B in section IV, then texts that function to orient life by means of very specific directives can be seen as expressions of the Word of God which transcends them. The text has value for us as a faithful witness to something beyond itself. God's Word or normative call to creation embodied in Deut. 22:8 is not exhausted by that text but holds for us also. It is this call that we are trying to get in touch with when we move from the specifics of the text to a general statement which attempts to capture, from our situation, what is common to the particular ways in which Yahweh led Israel and the particular ways in which we are called today.[70]

This still leaves the question of the specific ways in which we are to reappropriate a text such as Deut. 22:8 unanswered. Diagram B highlights the fact that the Word of God to which the text is a response also impinges on our experience. If the text awakens us to the need for safety regulations of some kind, then we have to struggle to get in touch with that "same" call of God as it comes to us in our culture. Subjective responsibility and responsible subjectivity are indispensable here. It is only in this way that we can decide whether we should respond to this text as mediating a call to clear the snow and ice from the sidewalk in front of our houses, insist on stricter safety regulations in the workplace, or campaign for laws that protect those who live in boarding houses from landlords who allow their properties to become dangerous and rundown.

There are many other examples that could be given. The crucial point here is that our context will affect the way a text is heard. It may also sensitize us to the original implications of the text. Those concerned about the rights of women in our culture may draw attention to the fact that the roof which should be made safe according to Deut. 22:8 was the place where Israelite women did many of the household chores.[71] In re-articulating what God is saying in this law for today, Christian feminists and single women may be particularly sensitive to the way Deut. 22:8 calls us to ensure that women who live in apartment buildings do not have to come home to badly lit underground garages. The message of Deuteronomy is that a concern such as this is nothing less than what it means to love your neighbour and thus love God. Texts that obviously or explicitly address issues of sex and gender are not the only ones that may give guidance to a biblically informed Christian feminism.

Texts of orientation, then, highlight how life ought to be. If life is seen as a journey to the north pole, we can say that they give direction to life by pointing the way north. As I will argue below, passages of this kind that specifically address our nature as male and female do not advocate patriarchy as normative. Yet it is important to realize that not all biblical texts that speak to this or any issue should be seen as texts of orientation or else we will be misled.

B. Reorientation Texts

What I am calling reorientation texts address us with a special awareness of human fallenness. Unlike orientation texts, their primary concern is not to confront us with creational norms as this can be redemptively insensitive in many situations. Missionaries who try to uphold the norm of monogamy by persuading males in polygamous cultures to divorce all but their first wife, for example, often find that the ex-wives are forced into becoming prostitutes. By contrast, recognizing that we are not heading north but are travelling in quite the wrong direction, these texts attempt to redirect our steps from where we are—even if, to continue the metaphor, that means pointing us "north-west" or "north-east" for the time being.

I find it helpful to distinguish between at least three different kinds of reorientation text. What I call *prohibitive reorientation texts* are particularly concerned to reveal that some forms of behaviour, such as idolatry, are the way of death. Texts such as Ex. 23:19b; Lev. 18:6-24; Deut. 18:9-12 and 27:14-26 aimed to prevent Israel from travelling down "dead ends" and getting more lost than they already were. They alerted Israel's attention not to what was normative or healing but to what was *anti*-normative and destructive. Such texts can guide us also, but we need to exercise care in applying such prohibitions to our times. Caution can be justified here by pointing to the fact that some prohibitions do not stay in force even throughout the biblical period (compare Deut. 23:1 with Isa. 56:4,5), while others, such as Lev. 18:19, are no longer seen as binding by most Christians.

Limiting/limited reorientation texts highlight God's patience and mercy towards our brokenness and limitations. They exhibit a pastoral sensitivity by refusing to burden human life with a tyranny of impossible expectations. The gospels stress that this is very important to Jesus (see Lk. 11:46 and Mt. 11:30). This is also a concern that can be found in Ruether's writings (though she doesn't connect it with biblical directives of this kind).[72]

In her early book *Liberation Theology*, for example, while she stresses the need to "resist the age-old temptation to dogmatize and eternalize [our] human historical works," she also warns that we must not "make of the Revolution a Molech which devours each present generation for the sake of that future 'new man' who is never here, but always 'on the way'." In this context she makes use of a very helpful biblical illustration. She writes,

> Like the people of the Exodus we must learn to live by faith, gathering manna from day to day, pressing on to the Promised Land, neither hoarding yesterday's accomplishments, nor looking back to Egypt, nor yet becoming unable to rejoice in God's daily grace in the name of those future kingdoms which are not yet here.[73]

If prohibitive reorientation texts are incompatible with permissiveness in either the "private" or "public" areas of life, limiting/limited reorientation texts also challenge both social and moral absolutism.[74] Divorce is allowed—though there are limits placed upon it (Deut. 22:13-19; 24:1-4); warfare is permitted—though many are exempt from fighting (Deut. 20:2-8); slavery is allowed—though for a limited time (Deut. 15:12-18); land can be sold—but must be returned in the Jubilee year (Lev. 25:8-55); polygamy is tolerated—but kings must not acquire harems (Deut. 17:17), and a man must not marry two sisters (Lev. 18:18); kingship is permitted (1 Sam. 8[75])—but its meaning is radically redefined (Deut. 17:14-20).

The purpose of these texts may be clarified by a few analogies. Raising children successfully, I would contend, is not possible without some level of compromise with the brokenness of the culture in which we raise them. Some parents who are in principle strongly opposed to violence, nevertheless decide to allow their children to use force in self-defense. In the same way, instead of trying to prevent them from playing with toy guns, they may decide to limit and redirect their behaviour by allowing them to "shoot" only at imaginary targets or only at people who have agreed to join their game. When the child is older, it is hoped, he will come to see that his parents' compromise with his unhealthy interest in violence contained a critique of his behaviour. Similarly, missionaries who wish to successfully reorient a culture away from polygamy will often have to tolerate existing polygamous marriages for the time being and exhort the males to love all of their wives. This later directive is a compromise with polygamy, yet it also criticizes and subverts this distorted form of marriage without imposing a norm in an absolutist way which burdens rather than liberates. Another example of limiting/limited reorientation would be the case of the school principal who disapproves of teenage sex but who still argues for condom vending machines to be located in the school washrooms in the hope that they will promote some degree of sexual responsibility in the context of the ongoing threat of the AIDS virus.

Viewed from the vantage point of orientation, limiting/limited reorientation texts compromise with evil. Yet these texts must not be seen as deficient orientation texts. For this reason, we cannot apply the relatively straightforward hermeneutical strategy, discussed above, of moving from the textual specifics to general principles here or else we will end up saying on the basis of Lev. 25:39-43, for example, "It is perfectly acceptable to own slaves in any age or culture provided they are well treated and set free periodically." Such an appropriation is at best conservatistic and misses the redemptive intentions of this kind of text which does not intend to describe a creation norm but tries to limit and redirect our fallenness in a way that accepts the reality of certain cultural and historical restraints.[76]

These texts not only limit but can also redirect our steps in our times if we get in touch with their deepest redemptive intentions. These are not to be fully identified with the conscious intent of the original author. What we are after here is the spirit/Spirit of the text. As diagram B illustrates, the text is an inscripturation of and witness to the way the Spirit was moving at a certain time. The ultimate aim of reading the Bible for us is not to figure out how the Spirit was moving *then*, but through the text to become aware of how the Spirit is moving *now*. Where the Spirit *was* and where the Spirit *is* are related but not identical. Hermeneutically, we often need to go *beyond the Bible in the spirit/Spirit of the Bible.*

Although this last statement may sound very strange to "orthodox" ears, I believe that this is often the way Jesus himself works with the Scriptures. In Mt. 5:43-48, for example, Jesus takes Lev. 19:18, which calls the people to love and not seek revenge against fellow Israelites, and "deepens" its meaning so that it is made to explicitly include the love of non-Israelite enemies. Thus a critique of Jewish tribalism in Leviticus is recontextualized as a challenge to Jewish nationalism. Similarly, in Mt. 5:38-42, the redemptive redirection of the *lex talonis* (Ex. 21:24; Lev. 24:20; Deut. 19:21) which in its Old Testament contexts laid out a principle of proportion for legal justice and functioned to limit personal revenge, is radicalized so that its redemptive intentions (the spirit/Spirit of the law) can be seen to go beyond the original formulation (the letter of the law).[77]

Limiting/limited reorientation texts complement and serve a different purpose from orientation texts. They should be evaluated, interpreted and applied in a different way. Their primary aim is not to highlight the gulf that exists between "is" and "ought," creation norm and fallenness. Instead, they are concerned to make contact with our brokenness and are geared to the healing that can be achieved in their time.

Before we judge their "limitations" too harshly from the vantage point of whatever norms we prize in our times (such as monogamy, vegetarianism, non-violence or equality), we should remember that for us as well as for those living in the biblical period, there are limits to: a) the degree of redemption that is possible in any generation; b) the degree of redemption that is even imaginable in any generation; and c) the extent to which any generation is aware of its own brokenness. Judged either in contrast to our present accomplishments or in the light of the Bible's own orientation and eschatological reorientation texts, the vision of redirection offered by some biblical authors may well seem limited. Our judgments need to be historically sensitive, however, if we are not to engage in a "modernocentric" dismissal of the biblical writers. As Ruether herself says,

> [C]onsciousness is more a product of social relations than we like to admit. Individual consciousness is not merely passive; it is critical as well. *But it can only leap a little way ahead of the available social options* [my emphasis].[78]

Similarly, one does not have to accept Marx's view of historical progress to recognize the truth in his famous words,

> [M]ankind always sets itself only such tasks as it can solve; since, looking at the matter more closely, it will always be found that the task itself arises only when the material conditions for its solution already exist or are at least in the process of formation.[79]

Not only should we realise that the Spirit of such biblical texts goes beyond the letter, but we also need to remember that what these authors were trying to do was to sense how a God who does not burden people with impossible expectations was calling them *in their time.* In that respect I believe they were successful. Their writings can be valued as the occasion for our "deepened" redemptive appropriations. But when we go "beyond the Bible in the Spirit of the Bible," we should not condemn those who came up with the original form of such biblical directives, for our "more radical" appropriations would not have been germane in their times.[80]

Eschatological/prophetic reorientation texts have a different character yet again. In a way that complements what I have just said about limiting/limited reorientation texts, these scriptures *do* have the capacity to go some way beyond what was normally imaginable as possible in their time. They point to the future—sometimes the eschaton itself—as a time when the trajectories of orientation and reorientation will come back together again. To work with the metaphor we have been using, texts such as Isa. 2:1-4; 60; 65:17-25; Zec. 14:20-21; Joel 3:18-21; and Rev. 21 give us a glimpse of the "North pole"—which we have to imagine as an inviting place for the purpose of the analogy!—but they don't tell us how to get there. Their main purpose is to nurture what Brueggemann has called a "prophetic imagination"[81] by building hope and discouraging us from "normalizing" present brokenness and compromise.

If we summarize this typology of how different types of biblical texts function to (re)direct our way of life in terms of the "gap" that presently exists between how life *is* and how it *ought* to be, then this should clarify how these different types complement each other. Orientation texts tell us how life *ought* to be. Prohibitive reorientation texts describe what *ought not* to be. Limiting/limited reorientation texts limit what *ought not* to be and help us begin to move from *is* to *ought*. Eschatological or prophetic reorientation texts describe what *ought* to be and *will* one day be a full reality. They invite us to live in anticipation of that reality now.

Although such a four-fold typology is a simplification (many texts, for example function *both* to orient *and* reorient), I contend that it can help us honour and work with the *diversity* of the canon. I also believe that it fits well with my discussion of the *unity* of the Bible in terms of an overarching Story of God's covenant with history which I summarized in terms of the four themes of creation (cf. orientation), fall (cf. prohibitive reorientation), redemption (cf. limiting/limited reorientation) and eschaton (cf. eschatological/prophetic reorientation). Thus, the way in which any given directive relates to the overall contours of the biblical drama as captured by these four themes serves as an important indication of what kind of orientation or reorientation text it is in this schema.

The typology also connects well with my proposal that the formation of the canon has its roots in the dialectic between faith and the limit-experiences of connection, disconnection and reconnection so clearly expressed in psalms of orientation, disorientation and new orientation. It is my hope that this model can help form a hermeneutic that is sensitive to the different ways in which God guides human life through the Scriptures. In the next section, I will explore whether such a hermeneutic can help us formulate a biblical view of what it means to be normatively and redemptively male and female in our times.

VI. Male and Female in the Scriptures
Given the limited scope of this work, the exegetical comments in this section will be brief and will interact primarily with comments that Ruether herself has made about various biblical texts (as summarized in chapter 2), rather than with the considerable amount of scholarly and popular material that has been produced on this subject in recent years.

A. Genesis 1-3[82]
Gen. 1 is a good example of an orientation text. It addresses the question of what it means to be normatively human and puts us in touch with God's original intentions for life on Earth. In a way that challenges the androcentric bias of the dominant theological tradition that Ruether has so clearly exposed in her writings, this text declares unambiguously that both men and women are made in the image of God (v. 27). Both are called to fill and subdue the earth and thus continue the creational forming that God has begun. Both are called to lead creation from its origin to its destiny. The equality of men and women in the *imago dei* was not only crucial—albeit in a secularized form—to the development of liberal feminism, as Ruether argues, but is also an important basis for any Christian feminist position as it means that the restoration of male-female equality does not entail a reform "against nature." Liberation, it can be argued on this basis, puts us in touch with our authentic nature. Contrary to eschatological feminism, about which I fully share

Ruether's misgivings, liberation need not and should not be opposed to an affirmation of creation.

While, to the best of my knowledge, Ruether has not criticised the portrayal of woman in Gen. 1, she has accused Gen. 2 of considerable androcentric bias. Adam, she claims, is portrayed as "the essential and original autonomous person" while Eve's secondary status is implicit is her being fashioned from his rib. Furthermore, the whole narrative functions as a "patriarchal reversal myth" as Adam takes over the female birthing role.[83]

While this chapter does orient us to what is creationally normative, it should also be read as a reorientation text. It is my belief that the narrative is deliberately constructed to function as a polemic against the androcentric assumptions of its first audience(s). While Adam is created first and thus exists for a period of time without the woman, the function that this performs in the way the narrative is constructed is one of allowing God to say, in sharp contradiction to Ruether's accusation of androcentrism, "It is not good for the man to be alone" (v. 18). Inadequate to fill and subdue the earth on his own, and faced with the prohibition concerning the tree of the knowledge of good and evil (v. 17), he clearly needs help.[84]

The call to mutuality between the sexes and the poignant observation that the first male is incapable of fulfilling the cultural mandate or imaging God on his own is underscored in a number of ways within the narrative. The reference to the woman as man's *ēzer*—is striking. Clearly this Hebrew term is not fully conveyed by the English term "helper" as it usually refers to a superior elsewhere in the Old Testament and is commonly used of God.[85] While the fact that this helper is described as "suitable" for the man implies mutuality between Adam and Eve and thus precludes a gynocentric interpretation, the strength of this Hebrew term makes it impossible in any responsible reading to ascribe a secondary status to her. Instead it re-emphasizes Adam's inadequacy without her.

Mutuality is also highlighted in the portrayal of Eve's creation. As the man is in a deep sleep when this occurs (v. 21— which indicates that it is God not man who forms the woman), it is hard to interpret this as a birthing process. Neither does the fact that Eve is taken from Adam's side imply that she is subordinate or inferior to him, unless we want to make the same inference in the case of Adam's derivation from the earth (v. 7)! James Olthuis captures the significance of the narrative well when he comments, "That woman came from man's rib simply and beautifully declares that man and woman together constitute humanity. They came to each other from each other; they belong together."[86]

Adam's poem (v. 23) also emphasizes mutuality by punning with the words woman (*issa*) and man (*is*). The phrase "This is now bone of my bone, flesh of my flesh" is a covenantal formula that expresses abiding loyalty between two parties. The terms explore the two extremes of human life with flesh suggesting vulnerability and bone referring to power. Thus man and woman are to complement each other in their "bone-power" and "flesh-weakness."[87]

The polemic against an androcentric view of life is underscored in v. 24 in which we are told that the *man* will leave his parents and cleave to the woman. This is a striking reversal of patriarchal practice, as it was the woman who normally left her family when entering marriage. There is no need to speculate, as von Rad does, that this text comes from a matrifocal culture.[88] The reversal is deliberate as it points to man's need of woman. Without her, he is literally helpless. That he is described as "cleaving" to his wife makes the same point as the Hebrew verb here usually connotes a weaker cleaving to a stronger.[89] Thus to conclude that the woman is given an auxiliary role in Gen. 2 is highly insensitive to the textual givens.

This narrative, then, orients us towards the norm of mutuality and reorients us away from the androcentric bias that would see the male as normative humanity. The text functions to criticize what Ruether claims it defends, namely the erroneous belief that man is "the essential and original autonomous person." Gen. 2 is not a "patriarchal reversal myth" as she claims. In fact it is a "reversal of patriarchy myth"!

Although Ruether claims that Eve is scapegoated for the origin of evil because she is portrayed as the first to sin, we should not take Gen. 3 as implying that it is the woman who is primarily responsible for the Fall. The text does not support the assumption made by Milton and others that she is alone with the serpent when she yields to temptation.[90] Neither is there evidence for von Rad's claim that

"The one who has been led astray now becomes a temptress."[91]
Robert Alter has noted that, in reporting dialogue, "the fixed
practice of biblical narrative, with only a few rather marginal exceptions, limits scenes to two characters at a time—or sometimes, to the
exchange between one character and a group speaking in a single
voice as a collective interlocutor."[92] That this latter technique is
being used here is supported by v. 6b which tells us that Adam "was
with her." The serpent thus tempts both the man and the woman
together, while the woman acts as the spokesperson for the human
couple.

Recognizing that the narrative of Gen. 3:1-19 is chiastically
arranged in the form of inverse parallelism greatly helps exegesis. In
the temptation scene, the serpent (A) addresses the spokesperson
Eve (B), who eats and gives to Adam (C). When God questions the
man (C'), he promptly blames the woman (B') who, in turn, blames
the snake (A'). In the judgment scene, the serpent (A") is cursed and
will now experience enmity with the woman (B") who will now
experience "enmity" with the man (C") from whom she was formed
(cf. 2:21). Similarly the man will now experience "enmity" with the
earth from which he came (cf. 2:7). This literary structure clearly
highlights how both the man and the woman "pass the buck"—an
action that the narrative does not condone. Verse 12 ("The woman
you put here with me—she gave me some fruit from the tree and I
ate it") can be read, therefore, as an exposé and critique of what
Ruether believes the narrative defends: man's sinful tendency to
scapegoat woman.

It should also be pointed out that Ruether is mistaken when
she claims that v. 16 "is not intended to describe patriarchal
dominion as unjust . . . [but] is intended . . . as a just punishment."[93]
Quite the opposite is the case. Although some of the Church Fathers
took these words as prescriptive,[94] the vast majority of comment-
ators have now rejected this interpretation. Gen. 3:16-19 describe
what is the case in a fallen world, not what ought to be. The man will
now rule over the woman (v. 16). The disorder of the Fall replaces
the order of creation as partnership gives way to patriarchy and
"machismo" replaces "mutuality."

In contrast to Ruether's tendency to project her (understandable) frustration with the theological tradition onto the biblical text, Phyllis Trible has captured how the opening chapters of the Bible can speak to us in our times when she writes,

> Visiting the Garden of Eden in the days of the Women's Movement, we need no longer accept the traditional exegesis of Genesis 2-3. Rather than legitimating the patriarchal culture from which it comes, the myth places that culture under judgment. And it functions to liberate, not to enslave. This function we can recover and appropriate. The ... narrative tells us who we are (creatures of equality and mutuality); it tells us who we have become (creatures of oppression); and so it opens possibilities for change, for a return to our true liberation under God. In other words, the story calls female and male to repent.[95]

B. The Old Testament Law

In *Faith and Fratricide*, Ruether countered what she saw as anti-Semitic tendencies in Paul's attitude to the Torah by asserting,

> Judaism was never a religion of "legalism," but a religion of revealed commandments which seeks thereby to concretize God's presence in everyday life. For Judaism, there can be no such antithesis of law and grace, letter and spirit, for the Torah is itself God's gift and mediates the presence of the Spirit.[96]

While any human tradition which is a vehicle for the Spirit, such as the Torah or the Bible as a whole, can be made to function by a community in such a way that it no longer mediates the Spirit (which is precisely Paul's problem with his Jewish contemporaries), Ruether's description captures well how the Law was meant to function. But in spite of this apologetic outburst on behalf of Judaism, Ruether rarely, if ever, appeals to the Torah in a positive way in her writings. When it comes to the question of whether it mediates the presence of the Spirit on issues of gender, Ruether is quite sure that it doesn't.

In chapter 2, I noted Ruether's observation about the patriarchal structure of the Law. This is undeniable (although this does not make the various laws unusable for Christian feminists as I will illustrate below). Ruether is right that laws are usually addressed to the male heads of families. This can even be seen in the phrasing of some of the Ten Commandments in Ex. 20, (see vv. 10, 17). Nevertheless it should be noted that Deut. 31:12 makes it very clear that the Law is to be read not only to the males of the community, but also to women, children and aliens. Furthermore, there seems to be no solid textual basis for Ruether's claim that the assembly at Sinai was all male. English translations typically understand both sexes to be present in this part of the narrative. It is true that some translations understand Ex. 19:15 as a command to the males to shun sexual contact with women.[97] If this was a command specifically given to the males this may simply reflect the androcentric nature of that culture. The more important issue is whether the motive behind this command is misogynistic as Ruether implies. In other words, are the men to avoid sexual contact with women because females are seen as inherently polluting and unholy,[98] or is there a different rationale for the prohibition? That the text does not engage in a sacralization of gynophobia becomes clear when we place this command within the wider context of Ex. 19-32.

In Ex. 19: 10, Yahweh says to Moses, "Go to the people and consecrate them today and tomorrow. Have them wash their clothes and be ready by the third day, because on that day the Lord will come down on Mount Sinai in the sight of all the people." In vv. 14, 15 Moses repeats this to the people and *adds* the command about abstaining from sexual relations. This alone should cast doubt on Ruether's charge of misogyny here. If this command presupposes the inherent impurity of women and thus functions to legitimate a male fear of the opposite sex, then it is odd that the males responsible for committing this tradition to writing do not put this command in the mouth of God. I think that it is far more plausible to interpret Moses here as trying to ensure that the Israelites are not tempted to consecrate themselves to Yahweh by engaging in the kind of orgiastic rituals common in the fertility religions of that time. As they prepare to hear the voice of their God at a crucial time in their history, Moses is anxious that the people do not confuse Yahweh with the idols worshipped by their neighbours.

If we examine how the story unfolds, we can see that Moses was not erring on the side of caution. When Yahweh does manifest himself to the people, they are afraid. Moses tells them that they need not be terrified because, "God has come to test you, so that the fear of God will be with you *to keep you from sinning*" (20:20). Israel need not fear God once they know the "fear of the Lord." Commenting on this technical biblical term, Brevard Childs observes that it "is not a subjective emotion of terror, but the obedience of God's law."[99] Now that the people have heard the Ten Commandments (20:1-17), Moses concedes to the people's request that he and not God speak to them (20:19), and thus spends the better part of Ex. 20:21-31:18 away from the people talking with Yahweh. When he finally comes down from the mountain, the people have clearly forgotten the significance of his earlier command in 19:15 to abstain from sexual relations. Instead they have held a "festival to the Lord" complete with burnt offerings and an idol in the shape of a calf, which was a common symbol of fertility. When the Israelites "rise to play" as the Revised Standard Version euphemistically interprets 32:6, it is clear that "[a] religious orgy has begun" (cf. 1 Cor. 10: 7).[100] Taken as a whole, the story is not a reflection and legitimation of the Israelite male's fear of woman. It is about what it means for the covenant people to "fear the Lord."

While it can be strongly argued that Ruether's statement that the women were viewed as "quasi-chattel" needs to be far more nuanced,[101] there is no doubt about the considerable legal power of the patriarch presupposed by the Old Testament legal material. Yet it is only if we misread these texts as orientation literature that we have to agree with Ruether that the biblical God sanctions such a social structure. Legal material, however, is not primarily concerned with describing the best of all possible worlds but "arises out of actually existing conditions and situations which it seeks to guide and control."[102] Legislation, in other words, provides limiting/limited reorientation and should be judged in that light.

Katherine Bushnell, an evangelical feminist writing in the 1920s, has provided a very helpful illustration in this context. She asks us to imagine a heavy cart (representing human progress) being pulled up a hill by a man (who represents moral and religious instruction). Because moral progress has many interruptions, the man has to pause frequently. When he does, a boy (representing law makers such as Moses) greatly helps the man in front by pushing a stone (legislation) behind the back wheel to act as a brake. In answering those of her contemporaries who were troubled by the fact that the Mosaic law fell so short of Christian standards in its treatment of women, Bushnell writes,

> Those who imagine that moral elevation can be accomplished by means of ideal legislation, may be likened to a boy thinking that his stone brake alone is sufficient to push the cart to the top of the hill. Those who advocate "no law" are generally hoping to see the cart plunge to the bottom. And those who imagine that our legislative measures should always correspond to the ideal set forth in the N.T., might put the brake high up the hill, far ahead of the cart.

While Bushnell is happy to admit that the Mosaic legislation "is not altogether suited to our needs" in those areas in which we are further up the hill of moral progress, she nevertheless points out that it "was precisely suited to a people just emerging from slavery."[103] Implicit in her argument is the claim that while such legislation bears the marks of a patriarchal culture it nevertheless functioned to help the Old Testament people of God move in a religious direction which Christians today, who are much further along on the same journey, can now recognize as a movement away from patriarchy.

Not only did these ancient laws function in their own limited way to point Israel in the right direction, but they can also give us guidance that is relevant to the stage we have reached in the exodus from patriarchy if they are approached in a hermeneutically sensitive way. The patriarchal form of the Old Testament laws is to be expected because reorientation texts have to make contact with human brokenness. Yet they are not confined by that brokenness. In order to recognize this, we must look at the deepest redemptive intentions of these laws and ask whether they are patriarchal in form but *counter*-patriarchal in spirit/Spirit. If this is the case, as I believe it is, then the God of the Torah need not be seen as a sanctioner of patriarchy any more than the culturally and redemptively sensitive missionaries I described above need be accused of sanctioning polygamy.

What I am proposing is that we need to go beyond the letter of these laws to the Spirit expressed in them (the position of diagram B). This will take us beyond what the original biblical authors would have thought. There is no need to argue (anachronistically) that the Old Testament authors were Christian or Jewish feminists ahead of their time. They would not have interpreted the way the Spirit was moving in exactly the same way as we do. That does not necessarily mean that they got it wrong or that we are bending the texts to our own ends. We are to interpret the movement of the Spirit in biblical times out of our situation and in order to get in touch with the movement of the "same" Spirit in our situation. Thus we may legitimately discern and describe the Spirit as reorienting a past culture "in a counter-patriarchal direction" even if that culture would not have been able to either conceive of or make sense of such a characterization in its time.

Let me offer some examples. The legislation on rape in Deut. 22:25-9 read alongside the numerous Old Testament narratives that involve sexual assault against women (such as Judg. 19), leave us in little doubt that this is a violent patriarchal world. This piece of legislation is often accused of being primarily concerned with the property rights of the virgin's father. A closer examination reveals a genuine desire to protect the woman coupled with a sharp critique of some patriarchal attitudes that are still with us.

V. 26 states that the woman must not be put to death for she has not sinned. Presumably the Israelites were inclined to stone her for what they saw as an evil she had committed, or else such a statement would be completely superfluous. Viewed in its cultural context, this text clearly opposes such a mentality by asserting her innocence. It also functions as a protest against the opinion held by many of our contemporaries that women are probably "asking for it" when they are sexually violated and assaulted. Similarly, it is significant that v. 27 gives the woman who claims that she has been raped in the countryside the benefit of the doubt, even though it is her word against that of her male attacker. This is in striking contrast to the attitude exhibited by many a judge and policeman in our day.[104]

The financial punishment stipulated in v. 29 for a man who rapes an unpledged virgin is that he must pay the equivalent of the bride price to the woman's father. Although this is a penalty that operates within the existing patriarchal system, there is also concern here for the woman's future. V. 29b says that the rapist "must marry the girl, for he has violated her. He can never divorce her for as long as he lives." While this sounds very bizarre to modern ears, in its original context this functioned to protect the woman and any child that might be born as a result of the assault.[105] It is also important to add that this law does not require that the rapist should live in the same house as his victim, only that he should be legally married to her for the rest of his life. Although it is far removed from our experience, taking away the threat of divorce was a major way of giving security to a woman in that society. By contrast, our legal system provides no compensation of any kind to the victims of male sexual violence—thus opposing the spirit/Spirit of the Torah.

Deut. 24:1-4 is also patriarchal in form but counter-patriarchal in spirit/Spirit. It is addressed only to males because only they could initiate a divorce. This situation is not condoned but is the reality that is to be reoriented (though not in absolutistic fashion). That the man must go through the motions of issuing his wife with a bill of divorce can be read as providing some measure of protection for the woman as it helped curb a purely arbitrary use of male power.[106] Possession of the bill would also serve to protect her from further action.[107] In addition v. 4, which is the heart of this law, curbs male power further by stipulating that once a man divorces his wife, he cannot make her his wife again. In our culture, remarriage of a couple who have previously divorced each other often signals a redemptive move. This is not the kind of situation being addressed here. Instead the law opposes those males who would exploit their power to initiate divorce and marriage by passing women from pillar to post and back again.[108]

Jesus' discussion with the Pharisees in Mk. 10:1-9 focuses on Deut. 24:1. It is clear from Jesus' reply to what the Pharisees say in

v. 4 that they take what I would call a text of limited/limiting reorientation as an orientation text. They assume that Moses teaches that it is perfectly acceptable to divorce your wife provided you write a certificate of divorce. In v. 5, Jesus explains that the law presupposes the hardness of men's hearts. In his eyes this is a reorientation text, we might say. Then he quotes Gen. 2:24 as a true orientation text that highlights what is creationally normative, thus undercutting the attempt of the Pharisees to "normalize" divorce.

Jesus' words should not be read as a rejection of the Law. Nor should we understand this as a "moral absolute" which now prohibits divorce under all circumstances. Jesus' words, also spoken to a culture in which only the males could initiate divorce,[109] re-articulates the law's desire to protect the women from the economic and social hardship that such divorce would bring. As Ruether herself correctly argues,

> Jesus' pronouncements on divorce must be seen in the context of a society where a woman, who had no means of support, could be cast out by her husband on the slightest pretext. The stricter attitude toward divorce in Jesus' time had the purpose of providing women with greater respect and security in marriage.[110]

If we bear this desire to protect the woman in mind, then one way of applying Deut. 24:1ff. and Mk. 10:1ff. today, which operates with the hermeneutical principle of going "beyond the Bible in the spirit/Spirit of the Bible," would be to say that a woman who is currently suffering at the hands of a violent husband can, with a good conscience, seriously consider divorce.

Num. 30 presupposes that husbands and fathers have the authority to revoke vows made by wives and daughters. Read as an orientation text, this passage sounds as though it fully justifies this patriarchal social system. Read as a reorientation text however, vv. 5b, 12b and 15 become the focal points of the legislation. Here the woman is released from her vow for her own protection. As Faith Martin has observed, "Without the law, if a woman made a legal contract and her guardian, who held the family property, prevented her from honouring the terms of the sale or purchase, she herself could be sold into slavery."[111] Thus, given the reality of a staunchly patriarchal culture in which women were legal minors, this law is sensitive to their vulnerable position. Rather than advocating male power, it sets out to curb it, even to the extent that a husband who nullifies a wife's vow without doing so immediately is said to be responsible for her guilt!

Another area of the law on which Ruether has commented is the legislation concerning a mother's uncleanness after childbirth (Lev. 12) and a woman's uncleanness due to menstruation (Lev. 15:19-24). While Ruether assumes that menstrual taboos ascribe a demonic quality to female sexual fluids, this fails to account for why no sacrifice is required to atone for them. Care should be taken to understand this legislation within the wider context of uncleanness attributed to the discharges of *both sexes* (see Lev. 15:1-18). Accusations of patriarchal paranoia are at best premature when they do not take proper note of the careful work that has been done by scholars such as Mary Douglas and William Countryman on the nature and purpose of the clean/unclean distinction as a whole.[112]

We must also be careful to honour the distance between this ancient culture and our own. While it might seem to us as though a Jewish woman in the Old Testament period would be unclean for much of her life due to menstruation, this is doubtful. As Gordon Wenham has pointed out, early marriage, late weaning and a desire for large families would have made menstruation much rarer for most Jewish women at this time.[113]

Uncleanness following childbirth is probably due to the *discharge* that follows rather than to the baby, male or female. Why the mother is unclean for twice as long if she gives birth to a daughter rather than a son is a mystery. Perhaps it is due to the ancient belief that postnatal discharges lasted longer when a girl was born.[114] Whatever the reason, the charge of misogynistic androcentrism fails to account for why the sacrifice to be offered after the birth of a baby of either sex is the same (Lev. 12:6-8).

One final comment that should be made on the Old Testament Law is that comparison with other ancient Near Eastern legal systems helps us recognize the uniqueness of Ex. 21:15, which stipulates a severe penalty for a son who strikes either his father *or mother*, and Ex. 20:12 (the fifth commandment), which calls for children to honour *both* parents. Even the feminist historian Gerda Lerner, who is generally not impressed with the effect that she believes the Old Testament Law would have had on women, makes the important observation that when compared with the attitudes of surrounding cultures such texts indicate a strong upgrading of the role of woman as mother in Israel.[115]

C. Old Testament Narrative
The questionable way in which Ruether handles Gen. 2-3 is analogous to the way she handles other Old Testament narratives. Her reading of Num. 12 is a clear example of an overly suspicious argument from silence.[116] Once one has decided *a priori* that Old Testament stories have the negation of woman as part of their agenda, then it is easy to find "evidence" for such a position. But if a primary objective of this narrative is to "put Miriam in her place" then we must ask, Why does it do such a poor job? The fact that the people do not set off on their journey until Miriam is healed reflects her high standing in the community, as Ruether admits. Why does the writer not extirpate this aspect of the tradition? And why, if the narrator is so keen to find fault with Miriam, does Aaron confess his own guilt in v. 11? Why is he also summoned to the Tent of Meeting if she is being singled out for the blame? To claim that the tradition was too firmly established to be recast at these points (which is the only counter-argument that I can imagine) strikes me as special pleading.

Miriam is punished for doubting Moses's calling by being briefly afflicted with the same disease with which Moses himself is struck when he doubts his own calling in Ex. 4:6. Aaron's exemption from punishment may seem to lend support to Ruether's interpretation, but here the question we should ask is not: Why was Miriam punished?, so much as Why was Aaron *not* punished? The simplest answer, I suggest, is that the requirements of purity were so strict for priests (cf. Lev. 21) that if Aaron had also been struck with leprosy, he would not have been able to function as high priest for a long time thus unfairly penalizing the whole community.[117] Thus Aaron's escape from punishment, in this reading, is to be seen as an example of God's mercy. It is not the result of a Hebrew narrator projecting his misogyny onto Yahweh.

Ruether's claim that Judg. 19 is oppressive is also based on a less than careful analysis of the narrative. It is undeniable that what happens to the unnamed concubine is *horrific*. This story and the other "Texts of Terror" that Phyllis Trible has analyzed leave us in no doubt that this is a brutally patriarchal culture.[118] But the *portrayal* of violence against women need not itself be patriarchal or oppressive—or else we would have to insist that films such as *The Accused* and novels such as Alice Walker's *The Color Purple* no longer enjoy our feminist approval. Admittedly, the text does not explore the inner life of the unnamed concubine, as a modern storyteller might, in order to affirm her personhood in the face of the male violence that seeks to reduce her to an object. But Hebrew narrative from this period has other often subtle and sophisticated ways of getting its point across. In order to understand the way the narrator passes judgment on this brutal episode, we need to be sensitive to the overall literary structure of the book which as modern readers we are apt to overlook.

Judges tells the story of how the people repeatedly do evil in the sight of God (2:11; 3:7; 3:12; 4:1; 6:1; 10:6) and thus bring suffering and oppression upon themselves. Nevertheless they are periodically delivered because Yahweh hears their cries. But while this deliverance is attributed to God's mercy, it would be a mistake to see the judges through whom Yahweh saves Israel from its enemies as heroes of the faith. Lillian Klein has argued persuasively that not only Abimelech and Samson but all of the judges in the main body of the narrative (3:1-16:31) display significant character faults.[119] We should not assume that the narrator's voice can be easily identified with any of the protagonists in the story he tells.

The literary structure of 3:1-16:31 is chiastically arranged to centre on a juxtaposition between Abimelech, the anti-judge, and his father Gideon, whose leadership at times demonstrates what the people of Israel can expect if they are faithful to Yahweh.[120] But even he is no ideal judge. Abimelech's name, which means "my father is king," raises questions about Gideon's aspirations to the throne in spite of his obedience to Yahweh in other respects.[121]

While he refuses to become king in 8:23, he nevertheless makes an idol out of the people's gold earrings which Israel then worships. Even when he obeys Yahweh by reducing his army to just 300 men (7:1-8), an act of faith that results in the routing of the Midianites (7:15-22), he immediately disobeys Yahweh by calling in reserve forces (7:23-25), thus forgetting that the reason Yahweh called for the reduction of the army by over 32,000 men was to ensure that Israel would not boast that their own strength had saved them (7:2). It is no coincidence that the voice of Yahweh is not heard for the rest of the Gideon narrative.

The leadership of Deborah is no less ambiguous. While there is military success, we must not assume that the narrator necessarily approves of all that she says and does. In the song of Judg. 5, Deborah, a *"mother* in Israel" (v. 7), would appear to revel in the brutal murder of Sisera and take great delight in callously describing Sisera's *mother* worrying about her son when he is "late" returning from battle (vv. 28-30). Does the narrator mistake what seems to be a clear example of sadistic nationalism for something honourable and praiseworthy? Not if the account is read sensitively. As Kikawada and Quinn have argued on literary grounds, the glaring inconsistencies between the prose account of the murder of Sisera and the account of the same event in Deborah's song are deliberate, and not to be explained away as the conflation of diverse traditions by a careless editor. The narrator is subtly pointing out that Deborah's perspective is not the same as his and is thus not to be trusted.[122]

They also argue that the portrayal of violence throughout the book, including the repeated attention to gory details (see 3:22; 4:21) is deliberately excessive because the narrator wishes to evoke disgust from those among his contemporaries who have "ears to hear" in order to counteract any nationalistic pride they may otherwise be tempted to feel. Kikawada and Quinn write,

> The Book of Judges, therefore, can be seen as a moral test for its readers. Those who are like the sinning Israelites will enjoy the story of Deborah as a victory of "us" over "them"—and will be indifferent to the truth or to the sentiments of common

humanity, as long as this indifference is to "our" advantage. Those, in contrast, who do see the ironies, see the parallel between the mother of Sisera and the daughter of Jephthah, the treachery of Jael and that of Delilah, will find Judges an excruciating experience, a wrenching call to humanity and repentance.[123]

What Kikawada and Quinn are suggesting is that the narrator employs considerable irony in the way he tells his story. That this is the case has been demonstrated in considerable detail by Klein. This has major implications for the way we interpret and evaluate both the overall message of the book and the account of the rape and murder of the unnamed concubine. We would do well to heed Klein's warning and follow her example when she writes,

> The narrator's is practically the only reliable voice in the book, verified by the narrator's function as spokesman. I do not therefore assume Yahweh's sanction when unprincipled and undependable characters claim divine support, even when they act on behalf of Israel.[124]

Judg. 19-21, which includes the account of the cruel fate of the unnamed concubine, is the final narrative in the book and forms the second part of an epilogue that begins in chap. 17. A refrain that is repeated four times in this epilogue tells us that "In those days Israel had no king" (17:6; 18:1; 19:1; 21:25). The first and last occurrences of the refrain also tell us that "everyone did as he saw fit." It is significant that the last two of these four occurrences closely frame this final narrative. This factor alone is sufficient evidence for us to conclude that the violence to which the concubine is subjected is condemned.

The point of the refrain is not simply to remind us that these events occurred before the rise of Saul and David or to tell us that the problems being described demonstrate the need Israel has for the monarchy. Read in the light of the theocratic perspective of the preceding narratives and in the light of the important statement of Gideon in 8:23, the king who is absent in the epilogue is none other than Yahweh. This is not the world of covenantal obedience. It is not even the ambiguous world of the judges. They too are absent.[125] The fate of the concubine must be seen in this light.

It could be argued, however, that while the preceding argument is sufficient to show that the narrator does not support what happens to this woman, it still is not enough to get him off the hook. As Phyllis Trible has written, "If the storyteller advocates neither pornography nor sensationalism, he cares little about the woman's fate." Later she writes, "Truly, to speak for this woman is to interpret against the narrator, plot, other characters, and the biblical tradition because they have shown her neither compassion nor attention."[126] The narrator's sin, in other words, is one of omission not commission. I do not believe that compassion and attention are as absent from the narrative as Trible claims, however.

Evidence for the narrator's alleged lack of sympathy might include the fact that the concubine is not even named. If we employ a feminist hermeneutic of suspicion without serious attention to the book's literary contours, this seems to be an unavoidable conclusion. But the concubine is not the only nameless character in this section of the narrative. Her Levite husband and her father are also anonymous. Speaking of the characters that appear in the epilogue as a whole, Klein writes,

> [T]hey are inappropriately and ironically named, or even name-less, and full of talk and action which unfold with diminishing reference to time (tradition, history) and, in a certain sense, place (city, geography). The resolution of the book of Judges, then, projects the utter namelessness of the individual cut off from the tradition of the covenant.[127]

The concubine is nameless and thus rootless not only because she too is an Israelite alive at this time of general covenantal dis-obedience but also, as I will argue below, because she symbolizes Israel as a whole.

That Judg. 19:25b tells us not only that the rapists "knew" the concubine and "sent her away" but also explicitly states that they "abused her" is significant in a story in which the narrator usually conveys his own perspective in ironic and allusive ways. Klein notes that "The narration of the multiple rape of the young woman is one of the rare passages in Judges where the narrator's objectivity is sufficiently abridged so that a narrative attitude may be discerned. Condemnation is conveyed in [this] central verb."[128]

The Levite's response to her death results in a civil war and in the capture of wives for the tribe of Benjamin. In Trible's words, "the rape of one has become the rape of 400."[129] The subtle way in which the narrator conveys his perspective on this final episode of Judges can be seen if we compare it with the opening episode of the book. This will also shed further light on his view of the concubine's murder.

The deliberate contrasts in these two episodes become clear when we place them side by side, as we see on the next page.

The way the opening and closing sections of the book have been structured highlights the difference between the blessings of covenantal obedience and the curse of covenantal disobedience. Whether or not Israel is faithful to Yahweh has major implications for the way women are treated. While numerous Israelite women are abducted against their will to become wives for the Benjamites in the period of cultic and societal disintegration portrayed in the epilogue, the narrator places this in sharp opposition to the way Caleb's daughter Acsah is treated. She shares in the blessings of covenantal faithfulness. In her request for land and water, she is portrayed as one who initiates and receives. In Klein's judgment she is presented as "an image of ideal Yahwist womanhood."[130]

Not only does the narrator contrast Acsah with the women who are captured for the Benjamites by means of the thematic parallelism outlined above, but he also provides a subtle but important verbal clue that suggests a contrast between the Acsah episode and the events surrounding the death of the concubine. In 1:14, we are told that Acsah gets down off her donkey to literally prostrate herself on the ground before speaking with her father. The mention of the donkey here is not a superfluous detail for it is a catchword that establishes a contrast with the donkey in 19:28 onto which the concubine who lies dead on the ground outside her father's house has to be lifted by the levite.[131] Both episodes also involve a woman,

Judges 1:1-2:6

(1:1) The Israelites ask of Yahweh, "Who will be the first to go up and fight for us against the Canaanites?"

(1:2) Yahweh replies, "Judah is to go: I have given the land into their hands."

(1:3) The men of Judah suggest teaming up with the Simeonites—"their brothers"—against the Canaanites.

(1:4-11) Resounding victory of Judah against the Canaanites. Jerusalem put to the sword and set on fire.

(1:12) Caleb promises, "I will give my daughter Acsah in marriage to the man who attacks and captures Kiriath Sepher."

(1:13-18) Caleb freely gives his daughter to Othniel. Acsah is given both land and springs. Judah continues to be victorious. Zephath is destroyed.

(1:19-36) The victories come to an end. Cohabitation with the Canaanites.

(2:1-6) Israel's true king—Yahweh—brings a covenant court case against Israel.

Judges 20:18-21:25

(20:18a) The Israelites ask of Yahweh, "Who of us shall go first to fight against the Benjamites?"

(20:18b) Yahweh replies, "Judah shall go first." [No promise of victory until v. 28!]

(20:19-20) Not only Judah but all the other tribes team up against the Benjamites—"their brothers."

(20:20-48) Heavy loses to both sides in the civil war. Towns of Benjamin put to the sword and set on fire.

(21:1) The Israelites promise, "Not one of us will give his daughter in marriage to a Benjamite."

(21:2-12) Wives taken by force from their part of the land for the Benjamites. Civil war continues. All in Jabesh Gilead are killed except 400 virgins who are taken from their land and given to the Benjamites.

(21:13-24) The civil war comes to an end. Peace with the Benjamites who are encouraged to abduct wives at Shiloh.

(21:25) "In those days Israel had no king. Everyone did as he saw fit."

her husband, and her father. Acsah, Othniel the model judge and warrior, and Caleb the generous and responsive father, are thus contrasted with the unnamed concubine, and the unnamed husband and father who betray her.

It is also very likely that both Acsah and the unnamed concubine symbolize Israel as the bride of Yahweh. Acsah like faithful Israel is blessed with fertile land. The concubine, however, symbolizes a people who break the covenant. That is why we are told that she has been unfaithful in 19:2. The fact that the tribe of Benjamin is almost "cut off" thus functions as warning to later generations of God's people. Just as the concubine is cut up into twelve pieces so will the twelve tribes of Israel be divided up if they continue to do what is "right in their own eyes."

Yet it would be a mistake to emphasise the symbolic roles of Acsah and the concubine to the extent that we ignore the fact that they are individual characters in their own right. As flesh and blood women within Israel whose gender makes them especially vulnerable in a potentially savage patriarchal culture, the way they are dealt with corresponds very closely to the spiritual health or sickness of the nation as a whole. What the narrative of Judges suggests is that the treatment of women reflects, and thus can function as a kind of gauge or litmus test for, a society's standing before God. To cite just one example, the high incidence of wife abuse that has recently come to light within the evangelical world[132] should provoke members of that community who are sensitive to the message of Judges to look beyond the apparent success of church growth, orthodox preaching, and inspiring worship music, and even beyond current evangelical teaching on marriage, to the way in which the dualistic and otherworldly spirituality characteristic of that community leads to a complete disregard of the covenant in most areas of human life. In the areas of ecological sensitivity, political discernment, artistic expression, scholarship, recreation, business, and popular culture, we have no King. We simply do what is right in our own eyes. Although the connection is not immediately obvious to us, the book of Judges—as I read it—says that the way women in the evangelical community suffer, which itself is a terrible evil in its own right, is related to yet wider forms of covenantal disobedience.

D. The Prophets

Of all the prophets, Ruether is the most critical of Hosea because she believes that the imagery that he uses for the relationship between God and sinful Israel sacralizes a patriarchal form of marriage. Hosea's portrayal of Yahweh as faithful husband and Israel as an adulterous wife is certainly patriarchal in form. But if we pay attention to the way in which the patriarchal metaphor actually functions to reorient our perceptions, we can see that it is also counter-patriarchal in spirit. In this context, the insightful argument of Sandra Sneiders deserves our attention. While admitting that in Hosea's marital metaphor, "The male is assimilated to God and the female to sinful humanity," she goes on to argue that the significance of this imagery has to be judged in a way that is sensitive to Hosea's cultural context. At this time, she argues, marital fidelity was not required of a husband in the way that it was of a wife. Thus,

> To make the point that God took the free initiative in choosing Israel, that God entered into a relationship of intimate love with Israel, and that Israel was unfaithful to that covenant, God had to be imaged as the husband who alone could act this way. However, in the husband role God acts not as a patriarch would have acted but as a wife would have acted. A husband who had been betrayed by his wife would at least have divorced her if he had not had her executed. A wife who had been betrayed would be expected, nevertheless, to be faithful and loving. God, in the marital metaphor, is a faithful lover who continually seeks reconciliation through the offer of forgiveness. In other words, *the patriarchy of the metaphor is assumed because of the culture, but the message of the metaphor subverts patriarchy* [my emphasis].[133]

This beautifully illustrates the way in which texts of reorientation make contact with our brokenness in order to challenge and redirect it. The com-promise with sin that can be levelled at the patriarchal form of the imagery thus comes with the promise of healing.

In the light of Peter's sermon in Acts 2:14-40, Pentecost can and should be seen as fulfilling Joel 2:28-29, a passage in which the prophet proclaims the inclusion of the maidservants, who were right at the bottom of the social hierarchy, as among those on whom the Spirit would be poured out. This overcoming of sexism by the Spirit anticipated in the Older Testament, promised by Jesus, and experienced by the first generation of his followers is a vital element in God's gift and call to the Christian community. It is a sad fact that, with notable exceptions, so many churches in the charismatic movement, while rightly recognizing that the Pentecost event should have direct relevance to the churches of our day, have not grasped its full implications for issues of gender justice.

Other future realities imagined by the prophets are equally counter-patriarchal. Jer. 31:22, which Ruether herself quotes right at the beginning of *New Woman/New Earth* and right at the end of *Sexism and God-Talk*, reads "For the Lord has created a new thing on the earth: the female overcomes the warrior." Other translations speak here of the woman surrounding and protecting the man, and even changing places with him.[134] For the crushed male ego of the exilic period, says Jeremiah, there is the promise of comfort. The patriarchal order is to be overturned. There is the opportunity for woman to surround and protect man and for man to let go of his posturing and accept his deep need for her to be his helper (cf. Gen. 2).[135]

No less striking in its imagery is Isa. 60:16 which transforms the nature of kingship by conflating it with the powerful maternal image of the young child at the breast. The Israelites of the exile are told "You will suck the milk of nations, you will suck the breast of kings."[136] Prophets such as Joel, Jeremiah, and Isaiah highlight the need we have today to nurture imaginations that challenge and subvert the patriarchal view of life that surrounds us.

E. Wisdom Literature
Jer. 18:18 may be taken as evidence that alongside the offices of prophet, priest and king we may also have to add that of the wiseperson. This important teaching role or office may be traced as far back as the time of Joseph (Gen. 41:39) and was sometimes held

by women (see 2 Sam. 14:1-24; 20:16-22). This evidence is relevant to the debate about whether a consistent biblical case can be made for women preaching and teaching in the church.

Of all the biblical material that is classified as or grouped with wisdom literature by modern scholars, the Song of Songs is particularly pertinent to the issue of the relationship between the biblical writings and patriarchy. Ruether understands this book as the celebration of love between Solomon and a maiden of Jerusalem. In reading its "frankly sensual imagery and delight in the pleasures of sexual love . . . ," she says, "[w]e are flooded with light and untouched by judgmental words."[137] While Ruether is right to point to the uninhibited celebration of sexuality, there is far more to be said about this particular love story.

I am personally convinced by Seerveld's argument that the song has a coherent dramatic unity.[138] Contrary to Ruether's reading, the story that it tells is of the faithful love between a country maiden and a shepherd who are separated when the woman is brought, against her will, to Solomon's court to become yet one more of his wives. The story concludes when the lovers are reunited. The book is skilfully constructed, Seerveld argues, to function as both a celebration of love and as a critique of Solomon.

Seerveld's analysis suggests that we should carefully distinguish between those speeches in which the lovers celebrate their passion and those in which Solomon expresses his patriarchal and pornographic perception of female sexuality. As Seerveld explains,

> The lover's song . . . and profession of love (4:9-15) is fervent, gentle, sensuous and reticent, inherently playful and intimate. By contrast, Solomon's speeches to the Shulammite are a finely characterized expression of lust, not love. He catalogues her charms anatomically to her face (4:1-5); and while the artful comparisons (7:2-8) would be inoffensive, simply unhandy, if they were not so fastidious, through it all hangs an insinuating air . . . that kills the natural simplicity of love. Unlike the lover, who is indeed fascinated by his beloved's loveliness, King Solomon is interested in gauging her delights for himself. And

this calculating forwardness is what perverts any movement toward love. . . .

Solomon's authoritative, heavy-handed coveting of the Shulammite girl is artistically, empathetically portrayed in the Song, but judged. The rapacious, egomanic climax of his attempted self-gratification [7:8-9a] is diametrically opposed in spirit to the quiet, tender approaches of the lover (5:1)—there is no temptation in the lover's advances, only warm expectation. And the Shulammite's exulting description of her lover (5:10-16) exuberates the kind of chaste bodily passion that Solomon's panegyrics miss.[139]

The contrast between Solomon's possessive and controlling view of "love" and the striking mutuality that is expressed by the lovers is nowhere sharper than when the woman, in Seerveld's reading, interrupts Solomon when at his most "rapacious" and "egomanic" to assert in 7:10: "I belong to my lover, and his desire is for me"—which redemptively nullifies the curse of Gen. 3:16— "Your desire will be for your husband and he will rule over you." Here the woman's desire for the man does not provide the occasion for him to dominate her. Instead it is reciprocated. In opposition to Solomonic sexism, patriarchy gives way to partnership.

Ruether's claim that the female personification of wisdom in the book of Proverbs can be seen as a suppressed goddess figure is one of her more plausible suggestions—though this "suppression" need not be attributed to a patriarchal motive. Von Rad has argued that there are parallels between the powerful female figure in Prov. 8 and *Ma'at*, the Egyptian goddess of law, justice and primeval order. Yet he also stresses that she has been transformed by the Hebrew worldview. Wisdom here is not divine but is clearly *created* (thus she is not an attribute of God) and unlike *Ma'at*, she calls out to humanity, leading von Rad to conclude that we should understand her as "the self-revelation of creation."[140]

While appreciative of von Rad's proposal, Roland Murphy has suggested the following modification. He writes,

The call of Lady Wisdom is the voice of the Lord. She is, then, the revelation of God, not merely the self-revelation of creation. She is the divine summons issued in and through creation, sounding through the vast realm of the created world and heard on the level of human experience.[141]

We can accept the thrust of Murphy's suggestion and maintain von Rad's emphasis on the creatureliness rather than the divinity of Wisdom if we understand her to be a personification of the creation's capacity to reveal the presence of God.

Murphy is also correct, I believe, to resist von Rad's tendency to identify Wisdom too narrowly with a mysterious kind of creation "order." While noting that "One need not deny that the presumption of regularity underlies the observations of the sages," Murphy rightly points out that the metaphors used hardly suggest an understanding of Lady Wisdom as *Ordnung*. "Who has ever sued for, or been pursued by, order," he asks, "even in the surrogate form of a woman?"[142] But if von Rad's notion of order is problematic, his emphasis on mystery is insightful.[143] Wisdom is not just a personification of creation's capacity to reveal God's presence in general. What she specifically reveals to us from our Creator, I suggest, is the key to abundant life, a mystery which remains hidden except to those who "fear the Lord" (Prov. 1:7, 9:10, 31:30).[144]

If we grant that an interpretation of Wisdom as a created reality is on the right lines, then Ruether's claim still does not necessarily follow. The fact that Wisdom is no longer a goddess, so to speak, need not be seen as the result of an androcentric antipathy to linking the female and the divine. It is entirely plausible that the biblical wisdom tradition, in as much as it is aware of or concerned with *Ma'at* (or some other goddess), rejects her divine status not because of a belief that divinity and femininity can't go together, but simply because *Ma'at* is perceived as an idolization of something creaturely.[145] The Hebrew worldview thus seeks to relativize her to her valuable yet creational position just as it seeks to relativize fertility, which the Canaanites worshipped as the *male* god Baal, to its true place in life as a gift of God.

Wisdom, understood as the voice of creation or as creational revelation, can still be seen as a powerful female figure within the biblical symbol system. Ruether would not be impressed with this as she is unhappy with female symbols—such as the Virgin Mary—that do no more than mediate between a male God and his world. In the next chapter, I will challenge her contention that the biblical God is male.[146] If my argument is accepted, then Wisdom need not be seen as a female symbol that is contained within an androcentric symbol system. Female metaphors, I will argue, are used within the biblical canon to refer to both the Creator and to her/his good creation.

Another powerful female figure in the book of Proverbs who deserves Christian feminist attention is the woman of 31:10-31. In the context of the book as a whole, she should probably be viewed as incarnating wisdom. Albert Wolters has argued on form critical grounds that "the song of the valiant woman" should be seen as an example of a genre he calls the "heroic panegyric."[147] Wolters highlights how numerous words that are used to describe her have powerful, aggressive and even military connotations. He also notes (with some surprise?) how the verb in the final verse, *(wi) haleluha*, is a call to praise the woman that deliberately alludes to *halelu-yah[weh]*. As a woman who embodies wisdom, I suggest the writer is telling us, she may be praised as one who incarnates the very presence of God in her humanity and in her womanhood.

Wolters also contrasts this song with contemporary Ancient Near Eastern literature that only praised women for their sex appeal. Read today, the earthiness and power of this woman functions as a critique of the contemporary attempts to romanticize woman that Ruether exposes so well,[148] while the wide range of activity ascribed to her clearly contradicts the narrow sphere that many conservative Christians map out for her.

F. The Gospels

Except for some minor details,[149] Ruether's arguments for seeing Jesus as a figure who is remarkably compatible with feminism are ones with which I can agree enthusiastically. There is one area in particular, however, where Ruether's own presuppositions prevent her from making her case even stronger than it is. This is the way that she deals with the resurrection narratives.

That Jesus appeared first to women after his resurrection is very remarkable given the cultural context. Ruether captures this well in the midrash that opens *Sexism and God-Talk*. When Mary runs quickly to bring the news to the male disciples, Ruether appropriately has them reply, " 'Would Jesus have appeared first to her and not to us? . . . . Would the Lord have preferred a woman to us men? Women by Mosaic law are not even allowed to be witnesses. Surely the Lord would not have entrusted such a message to a woman!' "[150]

The resurrection of Jesus of Nazareth is portrayed by the New Testament as *the* most significant event in the whole of history. At a time when a woman's word was not trusted in a Jewish court of law, the narrative tells us that the risen Jesus deliberately chose to appear to women at the dawn of the New Age to entrust them with the most important news that any human being would ever hear! This is *extremely* powerful biblical evidence that God affirms woman in spite of the patriarchal nature of fallen history. Yet Ruether is unable to stress the true significance of this event because she does not believe in a historical bodily resurrection. All that she can say, given her worldview, is that Mary Magdalene "was the first to grasp the Easter faith and tell it to the others."[151] I agree that the resurrection narratives witness to Mary's faith, without which the most she would have seen would have been a person who looked like a gardener (cf. Jn. 20:15). What I miss in Ruether's position is an acknowledgment that these narratives also witness to something beyond Mary which her faith enables her to perceive: a deliberate counter-patriarchal action of the risen Jesus himself.

All the Gospel writers mention that Jesus first appeared to believing women rather than to the unbelieving men, yet John chooses to single out Mary Magdalene in his account (20:10-18). His redactional and story-telling skills serve to highlight yet another aspect to this event's ultimate significance which is important for a Christian feminist theology. As Hendrik Hart rightly argues,

> Human beginnings and the fall are told in a garden story. So John tells of new beginnings and restoration also in a garden story that has its parallel in the Genesis account. John tells the story of the resurrection in terms of the restoration of the woman.[152]

Thus Eve is restored to her true place in creation right at the beginning of the New Age. It is therefore no surprise that when the Age of the Spirit is powerfully manifest at Pentecost, the Spirit that Jesus promised falls on male and female alike.

G. Paul's Writings[153]

Although Ruether generally sees a profound discontinuity between Paul and Jesus, her assessment of the prominent role played by women in Paul's churches and in his own ministry rightly stresses how Paul and the early church continue Jesus' counter-patriarchal praxis.[154] She mentions Paul's description of Euodia and Syntyche (Phil. 4:2,3), his habit of mentioning Priscilla before her husband (Rom. 16:3; 2 Tim. 4:19) and the number of women greeted in Rom. 16, although she could have made more of Phoebe's role as a *prostasis* of many (v. 2[155]) and fails to mention that Junia is considered to be "outstanding among the apostles" (v. 7).

Yet Ruether is mistaken, I believe, to see a basic inconsistency between Paul's woman-affirming practice, to which these references point, and his allegedly misogynistic pastoral advice found elsewhere in his writings. While correctly noting that 1 Cor. 11:3-16 assumes that women have a significant role in the community as prophetesses, Ruether is (ironically) far too uncritical of the traditional conservative exegesis of this passage.

A great deal depends on how we reconstruct the situation Paul is dealing with. While most translations imply that the main issue is whether or not women should wear veils, the only verse that clearly refers to a veil is v. 15, the Greek of which could be understood as saying that a woman is given long hair *instead of* a veil. The other terms used are much vaguer and suggest that the issue may be one of hair length. The alternative translation offered in the NIV margin sees the whole of Paul's discussion in this light. This has the merit of highlighting the coherence between vv. 4-7 and vv. 14-15 that other translations miss.[156]

This suggests that Paul is not dealing with a group of insubordinate women so much as some kind of gender confusion that was expressed in the way both the men and the women wore their hair. There are a number of factors that could have adversely influenced the Corinthians in this respect. Acts 18:18 tells us that after he had spent some time in Corinth and just before setting sail for Syria, Paul had his hair cut off because he ended a vow. This is probably a reference to a Nazirite vow which involved letting the hair grow very long. Corinthian males could easily have been confused by this and may well have tried to imitate their favourite apostle. Corinthian women may have imitated the hairstyle of males because of the common belief—found in Gnostic and early "orthodox" Christian writings—that to be truly spiritual, women must become male.[157] In addition, both sexes could have continued to hold on to pagan cultic beliefs that made a virtue out of gender confusion after their conversion to Christianity. Members of the cult of Dionysus, for example, imitated the sexual ambiguity of their god (god/dess?) by practising transvestism. Highly significant for our purposes is the fact that the men would wear their hair at a length that was considered normal for women and *vice-versa.*[158] Thus Paul patiently argues on the basis on Gen. 2 that true spirituality does not require the transcending or blurring of the gender distinction because to be male and female is a feature of God's good creation.

While v. 3 has frequently been taken as setting up a cosmic hierarchy, a closer look at the text reveals that Paul does not start with God and then move down "the great chain of being" until he gets to woman. This is not Paul's order at all. In addition the word translated as head, *kephalē,* only rarely carries hierarchical or leadership connotations in the LXX (Septuagint), and never does so in the everyday Greek of the day, or in Pauline usage elsewhere. This word is best translated as origin or source.[159]

In saying that "man is the origin of woman" in v. 3, Paul appeals to the Genesis account in which Eve is formed from Adam (a point he repeats in v. 12). This is to highlight that in creation, man and woman are distinct yet connected or interdependent. Thus, emphasising the creational distinction, Paul argues in v. 4 that males who wear their hair long in imitation of females dishonour their created nature as males. Similarly, by either alluding to a cultural practice of shaving the head of a disgraced woman or by evoking an image that all would find offensive, Paul says in v. 5 that women who tried to appear male by cutting their hair short depreciated their nature as women. Therefore they should let their hair grow again (v. 6, NIV margin), or perhaps wear a covering of some kind in the meantime.

V. 7 should not be read to imply that women are excluded from the *imago dei*. As Fiorenza correctly notes, "the midrashic argument in vv. 7-9 does not deny woman the 'image of God' status but focuses on 'glory'."[160] Paul expresses himself this way to highlight the difference between man and woman. Woman, he is saying, is the glory of man in a way that man is not the glory of woman. This is Paul's way of translating what Gen. 2 means when it refers to Eve as Adam's "helper." Like the use of the Hebrew term *ēzer* in Gen. 2, the description of woman as the glory of man is clearly no put down. *Doxa*, for those familiar with the LXX at this time, probably carried connotations of the Hebrew *kabod*, a word that conveys power, dignity and honour.[161] Thus God is sometimes called the glory of Israel in the Old Testament.[162] In the same way that calling man the origin of woman speaks simultaneously of interdependence and distinction between the sexes, so to refer to woman as the glory of man is to highlight, at one and the same time, both the creational difference and communion between men and women. As Olthuis has put it, "She is the glory of man because only with him can she be really woman and because only with her can he be fully man."[163]

Maleness and femaleness are correlates. If he can only be fully male if she is fully female and *vice-versa*, then it is important that the gender distinction not be deliberately blurred. This and not the subordination of woman is what concerns Paul in vv. 8-9, where he says, "For man did not come from woman, but woman from man; neither was man created for woman, but woman for man." The thrust of his argument is that, according to Genesis, woman is formed from man *and not vice-versa*. She is made to be his helper *and not vice-versa.* In other words, men and women, just like Adam and Eve, are not interchangeable.

An important implication of this argument is that woman does not have to imitate man in order to be fully acceptable to God. The male is not to be seen as the normative human. Woman too is fully human. That is why Paul says in v. 10 that she should have a sign of authority on her head. This sign should probably be seen as her own long hair which, in that culture, expressed her nature as a woman. That is why it is referred to as her glory in v. 15. This is not to be interpreted as a sign that she is under the authority of a male, as traditionally understood. The text simply does not say this. Instead Paul is talking about her own authority as a partner with man in ruling over creation. The angels are not to be seen in the light of the intertestamental Watcher myth as Ruether suggests. They are probably mentioned because they are guardians of the creation order. Perhaps Paul is also suggesting that they too need to recognize that woman in Christ is being restored to her rightful place in creation, for according to 1 Cor. 6:3, the angels will one day be judged by women and men.

In vv. 11,12, having so far stressed the *bi*-unity of men and women, Paul now emphasizes their bi-*unity*. Then in vv. 13-15 he recapitulates his earlier argument that was based on Genesis by appealing to the Corinthians' own awareness of creational normativity in their own experience.

Taken as a whole, Paul should not be heard as insisting that men in all times and in all cultures must have short hair or that women must wear it long. What Paul tells us, I suggest, is that women and men should not deliberately imitate one another's appearance to further their spiritual status, whatever cultural form that might take. God created us as male and female and this difference is *good*. Women *as women* are full partners with men—not inferior to them and not subordinate to them.

Although Ruether's suggestion that 1 Cor. 14:34-36 is a misogynous interpolation is not strong on text-critical grounds,[164] it does have the merit of recognizing that, taken in their most straightforward meaning, these verses do not sound authentically

Pauline. There are a number of other more plausible interpretations
however.

It is quite possible that vv. 34-35 should be understood as a
quotation in which Paul cites the misogynous view of his opponents.
V. 36, in which the Greek word translated as "you" is masculine
plural in both cases, could then be see as a sarcastic reply to those
male Christians who wish to restrict woman's activities in a way that
is, according to Paul, opposed to the Spirit.

Another possibility is that we should read Paul as dealing with
a particularly chaotic situation. Stressing the need for order (vv.
33,40), he sets out to address those whose behaviour is at fault. Thus
he not only addresses the women but also the tongue speakers (v.
28ff.) and prophets (v. 30ff.). All three groups were responsible for
speaking at the same time as others and so are requested to be quiet
(vv. 28, 29, 34). On this reading, v. 36 is taken generically to refer to
all who were contributing to the chaos. The verb in v. 34b does not
call for submission of women to men but is in the middle voice and
should be translated as "let them exercise self-control."

The "law" mentioned in v. 34 could be an appeal to current
Roman legislation that attempted to limit female cultic excesses.
This latter suggestion gains support if we see *lalein* in vv. 34, 35 as
referring to the noisy chanting or ululating that was common in
ecstatic pagan cults and which often drowned out the males.[165]
Alternatively, the "Law" could mean the Hebrew Scriptures as a
whole rather than the Torah in particular. (This is how Paul uses the
term just thirteen verses earlier where he cites a passage from
Isaiah.) In v. 34, Paul may be appealing to a general Old Testament
principle that worship should not be chaotic. The possibility that he
does not have a specific text in mind is supported by the fact that,
unlike in v. 21, he does not cite one. But it is also possible that the
reference to drunken prophets immediately before the Isaiah text
which he quotes in this earlier verse, is the kind of chaos he is
thinking of (see Isa. 28:7).

The disorderly behaviour of the women is connected in some
way to Paul's comments about husbands and wives in v. 35. It is
possible that the women found their husbands' prophecies or tongue
speaking to be so meaningless or wrong that they were verbally

challenging the authenticity of their gifts and thus initiating open conflict about such matters. This kind of speaking in the context of a public worship meeting is disgraceful, Paul says. In this light, v. 35 can be read as an attempt to keep such behaviour, if it must go on, outside of church gatherings. It can thus be seen as a parallel to 11:22 where Paul says to those gorge themselves and get drunk at the Lord's Supper, "Don't you have homes to eat and drink in?"

Another possibility is that the women were chattering among themselves or were calling out to their husbands to explain ideas with which they were unfamiliar because they were not used to being taught from the Scriptures. Thus rather than asking their husbands questions *in church* in this way (v. 34), Paul simply recommends that they ask their husbands *at home* (v. 35). In this reading Paul's aim is to minimize the disorder of a particular without denying a woman's need or right to learn.

These two latter considerations are also a priority for Paul in 1 Tim. 2:11-15.[166] In fact the phrase translated by the NIV as "a woman should learn" is actually an imperative in the Greek—the only one in this passage. It is important to recognize that this is a positive statement because women did not learn the Law in the synagogue at this time. Needless to say, education is very important for liberation and has often been denied to women for this reason. Paul says that women should learn in quietness (not silence) for this is the best way to learn. The submission that they should show is not to men *per se*, but is an attitude of respect that they should show for the Scriptures and towards those currently able to build up the community with their teaching gifts.

To translate v. 12 as "I do not permit a woman to teach or have authority over a man" (NIV) is very misleading. The word rendered "have authority," (*authentein*), is actually a slang term in the Greek which could even carry connotations of murder. This would imply that Paul is not referring to the ordinary exercising of authority but an extreme form of domineering behaviour.[167]

In her book of readings *Womanguides*, Ruether includes this passage in her chapter on the origins on evil under the title "Adam Exonerated: A Patriarchalizing Commentary."[168] This reflects a traditional reading of v. 14 which I think is erroneous. Ironically, the passage that she reproduces just before this one is the Gnostic re-reading (or re-writing) of Genesis 2 and 3 found in "The Hypostasis of the Archons."[169] Ruether fails to see the connection between the two passages but if, following the work of Catherine Kroeger, we read this 1 Timothy passage as a reply to false Gnostic beliefs about the role of Eve, the meaning of vv. 13-14 changes dramatically.[170]

In some Gnostic cosmologies, Eve found an important place among the Powers. Sometimes she was believed to have pre-existed Adam. She was also believed to have possessed special knowledge which she would later impart to man. In one text she even brings Adam to life.[171] It seems to me to be highly plausible, therefore, that a group of women (who can perhaps be identified with the women who Paul says have been taken in by false teaching in 2 Tim. 3:6), may have become influenced by Gnostic ideas which suggested that Eve was the source of Adam's being and became his Gnostic instructor through eating from the tree of "knowledge."[172] They may then have believed that they had the right to dominate the males with their superior wisdom.

Vv. 13 and 14 can then be read as Paul's appeal to Genesis to debunk such Gnostic distortions. Eve, he argues, was not the source of Adam's being for the simple reason that he was formed first. Neither was she an enlightened Gnostic teacher who had to liberate Adam with her wisdom. She was deceived. This argument is strengthened if we follow Kroeger's suggestion that v. 12 is best translated as "I do not allow a woman to teach nor to represent herself as the originator or source of man."[173]

Space prohibits a detailed discussion of v. 15 here except to say that the claim that women will be saved or kept safe through childbearing can also be read as a critique of the Gnostic teaching which forbade childbirth because of the belief that it kept the soul tied to the body.[174] The thrust of Paul's argument is that women are fully acceptable to God within their childbearing function and need not transcend or negate their sexual identity to find salvation or to share in the promise to Eve that the fruit of her womb will one day crush the serpent's head (cf. Gen. 3:15). Thus it complements my reading of 1 Cor. 11.

Finally we turn to Eph. 5:22-33, a passage which Ruether claims exemplifies a "sexist idolatry" which betrays the heart of the Gospel. Such a conclusion is based on the erroneous assumption that this is a straightforward orientation text. It can, however, be seen in a different light. Our exegesis should begin at least as early as v. 18, where Paul begins to describe some characteristics of being filled with the Spirit. Such a life, he says, should lead members of the Christian community to sing to one another and to the Lord (v. 19), to give thanks to God (v. 20), and to *submit to one another* (v. 21). This is orientation language. Life in the Body of Christ should involve mutual submission between all its members. In other words, there should be mutual submission between parents and children, slaves and masters, and husbands and wives. When Paul goes on to address these relationships in v. 22ff., he should be read as trying to *reorient* these relationships, which were very hierarchical and non-reciprocal in that culture, in the light of the call to mutual submission.[175]

Wives, slaves, and children are called to serve and show love to those who have illegitimate power over them. Paul, unlike the Stoic teaching to which this passage is often falsely compared,[176] addresses them as full moral agents who have the hard task of translating the universal call to mutual submission into their own difficult situations.

That Paul is not trying to consecrate the social order but challenge it in a way he felt was rooted in the Gospel can be seen from his advice to husbands, masters and fathers. All are called to use the illegitimate power invested in them by their culture to *empower* those who had been placed under them. This is why it is the fathers who are singled out in 6:4 because they, not mothers, were given so much illegitimate power over the family within the Roman Empire. Husbands are called to love their wives as Christ loved the church. The analogy here is with his sacrificial love not with his divinity. (In v. 23 Paul connects Christ as the church's head or source of life with his role as Saviour not Lord.) Husbands are not being told to practise a patronising attitude of "love" which maintains the existing hierarchical structure of marriage. Instead by using this analogy, Paul is advocating a dynamic model in which husbands use their power to give power to their wives.

This can be seen if we look at how Paul talks about the end result of Christ's love for the church—of which there are many references in this very letter. Christ's love for the church, he says, meant that he left his Father (Eph. 5:31,2) and his position of (legitimate) power to take on the form of a servant (cf. Phil. 2:6,7). But now that he is raised to God's right hand (Eph. 1:20), the church is not below him once more but is *raised to rule with him* (Eph. 2:6). If husbands took Paul's metaphor seriously as a way to move from hierarchy to mutual submission then patriarchy would not just be modified but subverted in an ongoing dynamic process that pushes towards full partnership. (Mis)read as an orientation text, it is hard to deny Ruether's accusation of "sexist idolatry." Read as a reorientation text, what Paul is advocating is best described in one of her own phrases: "the *kenosis* of patriarchy."[177]

This reading of Paul suggests that the liberating message of Gal. 3:28, which has been described by one theologian as the "Magna Charta of humanity,"[178] is not an anomaly in his thought, or merely an expression of the more progressive and truly Christian way he thought on the rare occasions when he managed to free himself from his predominantly repressive rabbinic view of women. Neither need we polarize Paul and Jesus. While Jesus' remarkable counter-patriarchal praxis in particular and his life, death, and resurrection in general should remain very much the focal point of the canon, they serve to highlight in a concentrated way an affirmation of woman that has a broadly based foundation in the Scriptures.

VII. Some Concluding Hermeneutical Comments

Although my hermeneutical approach clearly differs from that of Ruether in a number of ways and results in some quite different exegetical conclusions, in this final section I would like to highlight a number of points of contact that I believe exist between Ruether's work and the approach that I am advocating.

Central to my hermeneutic has been my four-fold distinction between texts of orientation, prophetic-eschatological reorientation, prohibitive reorientation and limiting/limited reorientation.

The first two types of texts, as I have explained above, focus on what "ought" to be as that differs from what "is." While prohibitive reorientation texts point indirectly to what ought to be by defining what is anti-normative and unredemptive, limiting/limited reorientation texts pay far more attention to how life is with little interest in ideals that cannot be realized by those whose sinful ways they seek to modify. Thus if the first two types of text become stressed in isolation, absolutism and utopianism could result. The last type taken alone, however, might function to encourage an overly conservative, pragmatic or relativistic attitude. In contrast to these two forms of extremism, I believe that all four types should be held together in a complex dialectic if the Scriptures are to best help us find our way in life in partnership with God.[179]

This broad distinction between texts that are more "utopian" (such as Gen. 1:27, Jer. 31:22, Gal. 3:28) and those that are more "pragmatic" in the way they address life (such as Num. 30, Eph. 5:22-33, 1 Tim. 2:11-15) clarifies a major difference between Ruether and myself. For while Ruether is quite positive about the role that this former kind of text can play in her feminist theology, it is this latter type of text towards which she is most dismissive—to the point of literally ex(or)cising them from the canon. I have argued above that what I call limiting/limited reorientation texts try to reorient patriarchal praxis in a way that is geared to the redemptive possibilities and limitations of a particular era. Because they are more "pragmatic" than "idealistic," in the eyes of the prophetic visionary they can look as though they do nothing more than support patriarchy. While Ruether has no use for such texts in her theology, there are places in her thought (where she is not reflecting on the Bible) where she can be seen to argue persuasively for the maintenance of a dialectical relationship between pragmatic and utopian considerations in a way that I find to be close to what I am advocating here.

This is most clearly expressed in a chapter entitled "The Dilemma of the White Left in the Mother Country," in her book *Liberation Theology*, where she discusses the best way to bring about political change in the U.S.A. As Ruether sees it, the problem revolves around not only distinguishing, but also finding a way to bridge the gap between "is" and "ought." To this end she proposes a synthesis between radical and liberal creative forces. She begins her argument by noting that

> [E]very period of profound crisis and demand for a "better world" opens up a vision of ultimate good as its final horizon and point of reference. And so every particular crisis becomes a moment for glimpsing a vision of absolute transformation of the "is" into the "ought" which is the standard of meaningfulness in human life. This utopian horizon is essential to the creativity and fertility of particular occasions of change. It is the grace that gives men power to strive for real change rather than one-dimensional alterations. Without this transcendent horizon men lack the imagination and vital spirit to seek really new possibilities.

> Of course, this utopian horizon is fecund with self-delusions when applied literally. Yet without some element of hope that an ultimately better world can be built, no significant improvement in social life can take place. Though never completely incarnated in history (as we have known it), this hope is the ultimate meaning of every struggle for change, and no relative change comes about except through its mediating power.[180]

To achieve necessary political change, she argues, we need the cooperation of two types of people who relate to this utopian horizon in a different way. First there is the "liberal," who is "sufficiently established in the present social system to have some power and influence within it, and yet is sufficiently open to the validity of the injustices being revealed to respond to the demand for change." Although in his focus on the "is" rather than the "ought," he can minimize both the need for and possibility of change, nevertheless, if he is responsible he can "create the mediating connection between the present system and the changes that actually lie within his grasp."[181] In my terminology, his is the job of limiting/limited reorientation.

The "radical" has a very different approach. As Ruether explains, unlike the "liberal,"

[H]e becomes a spokesman for the cutting edge of crisis and the need for historical transcendence. The radical is therefore the one who becomes most acutely conscious of the absolute horizon of the "ought" that is revealed in times of crisis, and he particularly becomes dissatisfied with partial solutions and struggles for the radically adequate way of incarnating this "ought." This involves him in some delusion, because this ultimate "ought" escapes the limits of historical finitude. But it also causes him to unmask any too-limited recognition of the "possibilities" and the tendency of those in power to create ideological blinders.[182]

In my terminology, he has been gripped by a vision of orientation and/or prophetic-eschatological reorientation.

I have argued that both the "pragmatic" and "visionary" sides of my four-fold typology of biblical texts should be held together if we are to find the best way to live in the tension between how life is, how it can be, how it should have been, and how it will be. I find Ruether's argument for a liberal-radical synthesis in the political arena to reflect a very similar concern. She writes,

The emergence of new creative forces hinges on the formation of a mediating group combining sensitivity to injustice, an access to power, and the political and organizational expertise to turn demands into realities. In short, the ability to create effective movements and parties of "radical-liberals" is the crucial test of whether or not a society is capable of creative change from within.

Radical-liberalism is simply a synthesis of the anger and hopes of the radical with the practicality and political understanding of a good organizer. Only this synthesis can bring together transcendent hopes and historical possibilities in such a way as to incarnate a new social order that can temporarily correct some of the evils of past situations.[183]

To use Ruether's own language, we can say that some biblical texts focus on "transcendent hopes" while others are geared to more immediate "historical possibilities." If the Scriptures are to guide us in our struggle to bring about significant change in our time, then we will do well, it seems to me, to listen to both emphases within the biblical Story. We need to be visionaries who know how to be redemptively effective. While we need a strong sense of normativity that will not allow us to fully tolerate or "normalize" anything less than full mutuality and equality between the sexes, we also need to be acutely aware that there is a limit to how much redemption can be achieved in any situation. Thus when Ruether claims that "what . . . promote[s] the full humanity of women is of the Holy,"[184] she has to be careful that her "critical principle of feminist theology"— important as it is for giving us a sense of orientation—is not used in such a way that it functions to disqualify all texts that don't explicitly articulate feminist transcendent hopes from being possible vehicles for the Spirit. Room must be made for the more limited, pragmatic ways of promoting and working towards the full humanity of women that previous generations engaged in. If, in addition to being a "visionary," God was not also a "pragmatist" who was prepared to work with and through our limitations, then it would be hard to imagine what the history of the covenant would look like!

In other words, absolutism or normativism must be rejected, even if it assumes a feminist form. This is a danger that I see in my own work as well as in Ruether's. In order to indicate the direction that I am recommending, it might be helpful for me to relativize one of my own arguments. In my exegesis of Eph. 5:22-33, I argued that this text should be heard as a call to full mutuality in marriage. I am not now denying this. Yet I also believe that previous generations were not wrong to hear in this text a call to practise a form of marriage that we would describe as a "compassionate hierarchy." If we grant that the role of the biblical text is to reveal God as Word and Spirit to its readers *in their time*, then we must also grant that because redemptive possibilities change over time (either by increasing or decreasing) the message of the text will itself change. There is no *one* correct reading that holds for all time. There are some people even today for whom a compassionate yet hierarchical form of marriage may be the most redemptive way to go. This is not to say that a "benign" form of patriarchy is creationally normative or that any form of marriage is as good as any other. I am not recommending relativism or permissiveness. All I am saying is that we need to distinguish between what is (creationally) *normative or anti-normative* and what is (redemptively) *right and wrong*. In other words, while divorce, warfare, polygamy, abortion and patriarchal social structures are always anti-normative, they may not always be wrong.

I have been led to the above argument because of my belief that what I have called limiting/limited reorientation texts are vehicles for the Spirit. At the same time, my desire to take seriously what I have called texts of orientation and eschatological-prophetic reorientation leads me to agree with Ruether that such texts of limiting/limited reorientation, as I have already argued, do indeed have limitations. Given the greater redemptive possibilities of our times, I also agree with her that we should not be content to remain within the limitations of these past texts. While the patriarchal assumptions of their original writers will only be highlighted in a hermeneutic theory that has as its final goal the recovery of authorial intention, I have advocated an approach that I have called going "beyond the Bible in the spirit/Spirit of the Bible." Although Ruether has no interest in rescuing or renovating these texts in this fashion, nevertheless this kind of hermeneutical strategy can also be found in her work.

In order to explain how this functions in her theology, I will first explore another area of her thought in which I find significant similarities to my own. This concerns her distinction between Scripture and the Word (or Spirit) of God. Because of my belief that the Scriptures reliably reveal the Word, I do not wish to disconnect the two in the way that Ruether often does (especially in her earlier more explicitly neo-orthodox writings[185]). Nevertheless, as diagram B in section IV attempts to illustrate, the Bible is not its own norm. While the Bible can put us in touch with the Word of God, it also distinguishes itself from the Word (see Ps. 147:15-18; Jn. 1).

What Ruether tries to get at by appealing to the "utopian horizon" or "the absolute horizon of the 'ought' " in the above quotations, I would rather speak of in terms of the call of the Word of God to creation. God, by his/her Word calls creation to respond in certain ways that promote life, troth, justice, style, health, partnership, faith, and so forth. God's covenantal calls to life in our fallen world are what make it possible for us to distinguish "is" and "ought." Individuals and communities which struggle to live life in covenant with God can learn to sense not only those aspects of their own cultures and eras that were not intended by God from the beginning but they may also discern aspects of past cultures which should not have been. While God's will for any area of human life always has a specificity that relates to a particular time and place, this is present in a correlation with features that are constant, perduring and relevant beyond that context. Our ability to conceptually isolate and grasp these universal features does not give us the power to spell out in any detail what would constitute a normative response to the Word for those living in the distant past or in the distant future. But it does make it possible for us to infer that certain social relationships, even when they occur in cultures vastly different form our own, are not an obedient response to the Word "from the beginning" and are at best only valid as a strategy for minimizing evil. We know that like warfare, pollution, and child abuse, and unlike families, friendships, and meaningful work, the very existence of patriarchy in human life, even when it is a relatively "benign" form that serves a redemptive purpose by replacing a more oppressive form, could never have come into being without human evil. We know that it is something that ultimately we, and not God, have brought into existence. Thus, we can say with confidence "Patriarchy is, always has been, and always will be anti-normative."[186]

While it would be a mistake to see the perduring or universal side to God's calls as atemporal in nature ("perduring" is itself a thoroughly temporal word), an important way that we try and get in touch with such norms is by means of humanly constructed standards and principles, and these ways of *formulating* certain constant features of God's Word or calls do have a general, *trans*-temporal character. When our language or our understanding lack philosophical precision, perduring realities are often misunderstood as *a*-temporal in nature. This may explain what Fiorenza is getting at when she claims that Ruether's attempt to capture the heart of the prophetic tradition reduces this collection of writings to "an abstract dehistoricized critical key."[187]

Yet there is another way we can get in touch with this "utopian horizon," to which biblical texts such as the ones found in the prophets point, other than by talking about principles or standards. That is by talking about vision or hope. This connects us with God's presence as Spirit for which we need more dynamic language.[188] It is this approach, I believe, that Ruether takes when, in her response to Fiorenza, she says that what she was trying to appeal to was "a certain liberating 'dynamic' which is expressed in the prophetic-messianic tradition" the common elements of which are "prototypical" rather than "archetypal."[189] Even before her exchange with Fiorenza on this issue, she wrote,

> [The] expansion of the Biblical message to include the unincluded [women] rests on the assumption that the point of reference for Biblical faith is not past texts, with their sociological limitations, but rather the liberated future. We appropriate the past not to remain in its limits, but to point to new futures. In applying the prophetic principle to the critique of sexism and the liberation of women, we deepen our understanding of social sin and its religious justifications and expand the vision of messianic expectation. By applying prophetic faith to sexism we reveal in new fullness its revolutionary meaning.[190]

This sounds to me to be very close to what I mean by going "beyond the Bible in the spirit/Spirit of the Bible."

Thus even though there are significant differences between our theologies, I take these points of contact as evidence that a dialogue between our two approaches is possible. As an important way in which people with different beliefs can often communicate is by appealing to experience, I would like to close by stressing how comfortable I feel with the strong emphasis and high value that Ruether places on human subjectivity. Instead of formulating a belief in the authority of the Bible that encourages or reflects an attempt to escape from human subjectivity (which is the way submitting to biblical authority functions for many Christians), I see the proposals that I have made earlier in this chapter to be fully compatible with her belief that Scripture, like other forms of tradition, is "codified collective human experience."[191]

In diagram B in section IV, I tried to illustrate my conviction that both the Bible and our experience reveal God's presence as Word and Spirit. In principle, life itself is no less reliable at doing this than the Bible. Thus the attempt by contemporary women to construct a feminist theology based on their experience is by no means an inevitably God-less, subjectivistic enterprise, in my view. But human experience is no more self-interpreting than the Bible. To find God's presence and guidance in our life experience involves the authentic naming and interpretation of our experience.[192] It could be claimed that our experience of life is trustworthy, but our interpretation of our experience is fallible. But even this is far too simplistic as interpretation is itself a way of experiencing the world, and constitutes a moment in even the most unreflective of experiences. It is more accurate to say that the "experienceability" of life is trustworthy, but our experience is fallible. This means that we only have access to the authority of life—as we only have access to the authority of the Bible—via our fallible interpretations.

It is well worth stressing in this context that acts of interpretation are greatly influenced by our ultimate commitments, by the way we answer the limit-questions of life. The way we name and evaluate our life experience will be guided by that dimension of experience we call faith. For me, the Bible is a book of authentically interpreted faith experience that can be trusted to answer such ultimate questions. Thus the Scriptures should never be opposed to life experience. By contrast, in nurturing our faith and thus our worldview and our whole way of experiencing the world, they open our eyes to otherwise hidden features of life around and within us, and help us interpret that experience with sensitivity, coherence, and discernment.

In conclusion, the kind of theology that I am proposing is one in which the Bible, human experience, and God's presence and guidance are not played off against each other. We need to be sensitively open to our experience to be able to find God's presence in and through the Scriptures. Yet we need to be deeply steeped in the Bible's overarching narrative and faith vision in order to be able to find God's presence and guidance in and through our life experience.

To put this more concretely, the experience of a "Take Back The Night" march can provide a fruitful way to engage a biblical text such as Jn. 1:5, in which we are told that the Light shines in the darkness and will never be overcome by it. At the same time, the ultimate significance of such a demonstration against the darkness of male violence will be more fully visible to us when seen in the light of Jn. 1:5, and in relation to the One who incarnates the Light in his humanity, that we may do the same as sons and daughters of God (vv. 12-13).

In the next chapter, which opens Part Two of this study, the focus will shift from the problems of the past to the promise of the future. Yet the way we respond to the Christian tradition we have inherited will influence the way we set about constructing a theology that is sensitive to feminist concerns. Ruether's emphasis on "usable tradition" echoes Andrew Greeley's observation that "the future is built *in* the present and built *on* the past."[193] Where I differ with Ruether is in my belief that it is possible to ground a Christian feminist reformation of the dominant theological tradition more firmly and consistently in the biblical tradition than she believes is possible. Rather than seeing the Scriptures as part of the problem—a stance which functions as a stumbling block to many Christians—the position I am advocating turns to the Bible as a privileged faith tradition in which (to use Ruether's own language) "a deeper bedrock of authentic Being" can be found in which to "ground the self" and on which to wield the "lever of criticism." Thus in the following chapters I will continue to draw on the biblical tradition, and on what I see as its implications for a contemporary Christian worldview, cosmology, and way of life, as I assess and respond to the various proposals that Ruether has put forward in her attempt to construct a Christian feminist theology for our times.

Notes

1. *SGT*, 18 as cited more fully on 61 above. On the Enlightenment attitude towards tradition, see Edward Shils, *Tradition* (Chicago: University of Chicago Press, 1981), 4-7.

2. *SGT*, 18 as cited more fully on 61 above.

3. Ruether, "Asking the Existential Questions," 378.

4. In *FF*, 64-116, for example, Ruether argues that the portrayal of Jesus' attitude towards Jewish opponents in the gospels has been shaped by the anti-Semitic attitude of the early church.

5. See Ruether, "The Feminist Critique In Religious Studies," 63-66 upon which the rest of this section is dependent and from which all quotations have been taken unless otherwise noted.

6. *DQ*, 133.

7. *FMM*, 14.

8. James H. Olthuis (with Donald G. Bloesch, Clark H. Pinnock and Gerald T. Sheppard), *A Hermeneutics of Ultimacy: Peril or Promise?* (Lanham: University Press of America, 1987), 11.

9. *DQ*, 31.

10. Calvin G. Seerveld, *Balaam's Apocalyptic Prophecies: A Study in Reading Scripture* (Toronto: Wedge Publishing Foundation, 1980), 37-38.

11. See *SGT*, 12.

12. See James H. Olthuis, "Visions of Life and Ways of Life: The Nature of Religion," in Arnold H. De Graaff and James H. Olthuis, eds., *Towards A Biblical View of Man: Some Readings* (Toronto: ICS, 1978), 162-90.

13. See ibid., 169-70 and David Tracy, *Blessed Rage for Order: The New Pluralism in Theology* (Minneapolis: The Seabury Press, 1975), 93, 105ff. and 131ff.

14. See Walter Brueggemann, *The Message of the Psalms: A Theological Commentary* (Minneapolis: Augsburg Publishing House, 1984), 15-23.

15. Ibid., 19.

16. Ibid. See pp. 28-49 for his discussion of Pss. 145, 104, 33, 8, 1, 119, 15, 24, 37, 14, 112, 133, 131 as examples of psalms of orientation.

17. Ibid., 26.

18. Ibid., 19.

19. Ibid., 53.

20. Ibid., 52. See pp. 58-121 for his discussion of Pss. 13, 86, 35, 74, 79, 137, 88, 109, 50, 81, 32, 51, 143, 130, 49, 90, 73 as psalms of disorientation.

21. Ibid., 123.

22. Ibid., 20. See pp. 126-167 for his discussion of Pss. 30, 40, 138, 34, 65, 66, 124, 114, 29, 96, 93, 97, 98, 99, 47, 27, 23, 91, 117, 135, 103, 113, 146, 147, 148, 100, 149, 150 as psalms of new orientation.

23. I take this to be implicit in the quotation from *DQ*, 31, which is cited above, about the Bible being a product of the "human quest for meaning" and in the quotation from *WG*, ix on sacred texts in general, which is cited below.

24. On the nature of idolatry, see Bob Goudzwaard, *Idols of Our Time*, trans. Mark Vander Vennen (Downers Grove: InterVarsity Press, 1984).

25. The two examples given—Self-body and King-subject—represent the model championed by Sallie McFague and the "monarchical" model that she opposes in her fine book on metaphor *Models of God: Theology for an Ecological, Nuclear Age* (Philadelphia: Fortress Press, 1987). My point about the stretching of such metaphors relates far less to the way we speak of God's presence with us *in specific contexts* via the metaphors of e. g., friend, king or mother than it does to our attempts to talk about the God-world relationship *in general*. This is done via our *privileged* metaphors.

26. Here I am only talking about the normative relationship between divine and human agency within the covenant. Such language should not be used to describe God's supposed role in human evil. When human life is lived in obedience to idols, the true God becomes absent—an absence which the Bible often speaks of as God's judgment or wrath.

27. Evangelical theologians often speak of inspiration in terms of the "concursive" action of God and humanity. See, e. g., I. Howard Marshall, *Biblical Inspiration* (London: Hodder and Stoughton, 1982), 40-45. Because they rarely, if ever, have a view of existence in which divine-human co-partnership characterizes the way we are called to live the whole of life, however, they invariably end up seeing biblical inspiration as a peculiar phenomenon that is analogous to the incarnation but is otherwise without parallel. I would rather see the concursive action of God and humanity in the inspiration of the Bible as one instance of life in covenant with our creator. It is no more and no less mysterious than the nature of life, which is life *with* God.

28. *WG*, ix.

29. For a discussion of the nature of worldviews, see Walsh and Middleton, *The Transforming Vision* (Downers Grove, IL: InterVarsity, 1984), 15-39 and James H. Olthuis, "On Worldviews," *Christian Scholar's Review* 14/2 (1985): 153-64.

30. This calculation, which may well be too conservative, is based on the assumption that the biblical people considered a generation to be forty years in length.

31. Here I am indebted to Calvin Seerveld's three-fold distinction between *traditum* ("a deposit of sorts"), *tradendum* ("a fixed pattern, the needing to be handed on further, the activity of transmitting") and *traditio* ("the whole structured, configured course whose identity is recognizable") in his "Footprints in the Snow," *Philosophia Reformata* 56 (1991): 5.

32. James H. Olthuis, "Finding and Forming Stories that Give Life: The Narrative Character of Interpretation," (unpublished paper, Toronto, 1990), 11. A revised version of this paper may be published in the future under the title, "Self-identity, Tradition, and the Narrative Character of Interpretation: Towards a Hermeneutics of Connection."

33. See Walter Brueggemann, *The Creative Word: Canon as a Model for Biblical Education* (Philadelphia: Fortress Press, 1982), 15-27.

34. On the recent rediscovery of story in narrative theology, see Michael Goldberg, *Theology and Narrative: A Critical Introduction* (Nashville: Abingdon, 1982), Stanley Hauerwas, *A Community of Character: Toward a Constructive Christian Social Ethic* (Notre Dame: University of Notre Dame Press, 1981) and the important collection of essays in Stanley Hauerwas and L. Gregory Jones, eds., *Why Narrative? Readings in Narrative Theology* (Grand Rapids: Eerdmans, 1989).

35. As Paul Ricoeur writes in *The Symbolism of Evil*, trans. Emerson Buchanan (Boston: Beacon Press, 1967), 233, "The etiological myth of Adam is the most extreme attempt to separate the origin of evil from the origin of the good; its intention is to set up a *radical* origin of evil distinct from the more *primordial* origin of the goodness of things."

36. See Richard Mouw, *When the Kings Come Marching In: Isaiah and the New Jerusalem* (Grand Rapids: Eerdmans, 1983).

37. For an excellent discussion of the "all in all" theme in the New Testament, see Hendrik Hart, *Setting our Sights by the Morning Star: Reflections on the Role of the Bible in Post-Modern Times* (Toronto: The Patmos Press, 1989), 189-97.

38. See *CAI*, 187 where she speaks of "the biblical dynamic of creation, fall, and redemption." Cf. *RK*, 2 and her adoption of the basic categories of Christian theology as discussed in section III C in the previous chapter.

39. See the discussions of her eschatology in chaps 1 and 4.

40. See *CAI*, 30, 56, 60, 90, 188-189, 210, *RK*, 287 and *SGT*, 159. See also 338-40 below.

41. I am aware that many theologians deny that this is the case with the early chapters of Genesis. For a good example of an interpretation of Gen. 1-3 as myth, see Ricoeur, *Symbolism of Evil*, 232-278. Even the conservative theologian Bernard Ramm argues for a generic interpretation of Adam and Eve, the temptation, and the Fall in his *Offense to Reason: The Theology of Sin* (San Francisco: Harper and Row, 1985), 62-75. While space prohibits a detailed discussion, I would like to point out that the *toledoth* structure of the book—the tenfold refrain found in 2:4, 5:1, 6:9, 10:1, 11:10, 11:27, 25:12, 25:19, 36:1, 37:2, which may be translated "these are the generations of"—strongly suggests that we are supposed to understand the narrative, at least from 2:4 onwards, as referring to sequential historical time.

42. See Olthuis, *A Hermeneutic of Ultimacy*, 42-43.
43. *CAI*, 37.
44. Ibid., 48.
45. *WG*, ix as cited above.
46. Thus I reject Ruether's dualistic distinction between *historisch* and *geschichtlich* in *CAI*, 40. For a brief but lucid critique of the fact/value dualism, see Hart, *Morning Star* 118-19. Cf. idem, *Understanding Our World*, 305-12. Ruether's rejection of fact-value dualism in *GG*, 6 and chap. 2 is far less incisive.
47. See Donald Sinnema, "The Uniqueness of the Language of Faith—With Special Reference to the Language of Scripture" (Toronto: Institute for Christian Studies, 1975), 14. My appeal to the multi-modal or multi-dimensional nature of reality presupposes the ontology that was developed by Herman Dooyeweerd, especially as modified and articulated by Hendrik Hart in *Understanding Our World*. See esp. chap. 4.
48. Olthuis, *A Hermeneutics of Ultimacy*, 42.
49. To say that Gen. 1-3, for example, is historical does not mean that it isn't predominantly figurative or symbolic. In his insightful article, "Thoughts on Genesis," *Calvinist Contact* (December 14, 1990): 4, Al Wolters compares the way the opening chapters of Genesis describe the early history of the world to a famous cartoon in a 1914 edition of *Punch* magazine. This cartoon portrayed the attitude of the Belgian people towards the German forces that were about to invade their country by showing a defiant farmboy, symbolizing the courageous Belgian resistance, defending the gate of his farm, on which is written "No Thoroughfare," armed with nothing more than a stick. He is facing a large menacing bully brandishing a huge cudgel, who represents the German forces. Wolters argues that the cartoon accurately portrayed a very specific historical event. It was not an allegory for military aggression in all times and in all places. To those who are inclined to dismiss symbolic representations as second-best, Wolters points out that the cartoon succinctly captures the overall dynamics of the situation for all to see. An aerial photograph would not only have been hard to decipher for anyone who was not a military expert, but would have completely failed to highlight at least one very crucial element: the Belgian border, graphically symbolized here by the farm gate.

    A certitudinally qualified piece of history writing, if it employs figurative elements, will do so to highlight ultimate questions and concerns. Figurative language is especially prevalent in protology and eschatology as they explore realities beyond our ordinary experience.
50. For the importance of viewing sources and books within the wider canonical context, see Brevard S. Childs, *Introduction to the Old Testament as Scripture* (Philadelphia: Fortress Press, 1979).

51. See Walsh and Middleton, *The Transforming Vision*, 35, though they omit this last question.

52. For a clear example of "orthodox" mistrust of Christian charismatics and mystics, see the otherwise helpful book by Harvie M. Conn, *Contemporary World Theology: A Layman's Guidebook* (Phillipsburg: Presbyterian and Reformed Publishing Co., 1973), 93-99.

53. It may be asked what I mean by speaking of God as "Word" and "Spirit" here. This relates to my view of God as Trinity (Creator, Word, and Spirit). While a detailed account of my beliefs on this topic would be out of place in this context, the basic distinction that I am making is related to the difference between our discernment of God's presence with us and direction for us as mediated by the structural contours of creation/history—when (in my terminology) we know God as *Word*—and our awareness of God's presence and direction in the dynamic, unfolding development of creation/history—when we know God as *Spirit*. To know God as *Creator*, in my terminology, is to sense the presence of God in the way in which our world reveals its dependence on God as its Origin. Some may wonder if this is a modalist view of the Trinity. If modalism means belief in a God who is essentially "one" but who in relation to creation is experienced in "three" fundamental ways, then I am not a modalist. For me, it makes no sense to talk of God's unity or God's diversity apart from His/Her relationship with creation. In covenant with creation, God's unity is no more basic than God's diversity and *vice-versa*. The same can be said of the unity and diversity of the structural, directional, and historical dimensions of creation that reveal God to us as Trinity.

54. I owe this analogy to Hendrik Hart.

55. Of course it is possible for Christians to be prepared to accept as authoritative Jesus' view of the biblical tradition of his day while distrusting the way his attitude towards this tradition is portrayed in the New Testament. It is logically possible to distinguish what it means to trust that Jesus is the Messiah sent from God from what it means to trust the writings that make Jesus known to us. Nevertheless it hardly occurs to me to trust one but not the other. That is because in the web of our beliefs our trust or distrust of one will be very closely tied to our trust or distrust of the other. The fundamental tenets in any worldview tend to come in a cluster of mutually supporting beliefs. The defense of such basic beliefs will, sooner or later, sound like circular thinking to someone with a different worldview.

56. This is a welcome emphasis in Hart, *Morning Star*. See esp. pp. 181-215, where he develops a Christocentric approach that does not fall into Christomonism.

57. *SGT*, 123.

58. Ibid., 124.

59. See 34 above.

60. *WG*, 247.

61. Ibid., 247-248.

62. See ibid., ix.

63. Even if a letter such as 2 Peter is dated in the second-century (which it need not be), this is a moot point that does not alter the thrust of my argument here. Similarly the difference between the Protestant and Roman Catholic canons is not relevant. An argument for a "closed" canon that accepts the Apocrypha still has to make an argument for including the Protestant canon. Such an argument could presumably supplement mine and would have no need to negate it as it concerns intertestamental (i. e., pre-Pentecost) material. Although I reject the Apocrypha as canonical, what I am interested in arguing for here is the legitimacy of the notion of a "closed" canon *per se,* rather than debating which books should be included in it. On this secondary issue, see Roger Beckwith, *The Old Testament Canon of the New Testament Church* (London: SPCK, 1985; Grand Rapids: Eerdmans, 1986) and Herman N. Ridderbos, *Redemptive History and the New Testament Scriptures* (formerly *The Authority of the New Testament Scriptures*) trans. H. De Jongste, revised by Richard B. Gaffin, Jr. (Phillipsburg: Presbyterian and Reformed Publishing Co., 1963, 1988).

64. See Hendrik Hart, "New Testament People Are Responsible People: A Verbatim Transcript of a Sermon on 1 Corinthians 7," *Vanguard* 10 (March/ April 1980): 10-12. I am indebted to Hart for the thrust of the argument in this paragraph.

65. For the Bible's own talk of partnership with God, see 1 Cor. 3:9, 2 Cor. 6:1 and 2 Pet. 1:4. On this latter passage, see Al Wolters, "'Partners of the Deity': A Covenantal Reading of 2 Peter 1:4," *Calvin Theological Journal* 25 (April 1990): 28-44.

66. Walter Brueggemann, *The Prophetic Imagination* (Philadelphia: Fortress Press, 1978), 11. I owe the metaphor of the Bible as an a play to N. T. Wright who suggested it in a lecture on biblical authority presented at Institute for Christian Studies on 13th December 1989. Cf. his paper "How Can The Bible Be Authoritative?" *Vox Evangelica* 21 (1991): 7-32. I owe the improvisational side of the mixed metaphor to Brian Walsh.

67. Here I am using a particular metaphor to explore how the Bible functions. Cf. Hart, *Morning Star*, who uses the related metaphor of light for the same purpose.

68. Similarly Deut. 23:12-14 can be heard as addressing the need for hygiene.

69. See Olthuis, *A Hermeneutics of Ultimacy*, 41.

70. I do not want to be heard as saying that the Word of God is universal and the responses to it are individual. The Word and our responses display both universality and individuality. I have addressed this matter in some detail in "The

Trouble With Normative. . . Creation Order, Hermeneutics, and Homosexuality" (Unpublished paper, Toronto, 1991).

71. This is noted by Peter C. Craigie in *The Book of Deuteronomy* (Grand Rapids: Eerdmans, 1976), 289.

72. She uses the phrase "tyranny of impossible expectations" in *TCW*, 69. For a biblical case for avoiding this kind of tyranny, see Hendrik Hart, "Those Who Have Ears . . .," *Vanguard* (July-August 1975): 27-28.

73. *LT*, 190-91.

74. On the need to avoid the moral permissiveness and social absolutism of the Left and the social permissiveness and moral absolutism of the Right, see Hart, *Morning Star*, 44-47.

75. For a striking re-reading of this text, see ibid., 47-53.

76. For a helpful summary and analysis of the nineteenth-century debate about the Bible and slavery, see the discussion in Willard M. Swartley's fine book, *Slavery, Sabbath, War, and Women: Case Issues in Biblical Interpretation* (Scottdale: Herald Press, 1983), 31-64. Swartley gets at the nature of what I am calling limiting/limited reorientation texts when, in his comments on the Old Testament practice of slavery, he writes on pp. 59-60, "we must emphasize the way God *regulated* those practices *in the direction of* justice and mercy" [my emphasis].

77. I am arguing here for a spirit/letter correlation (distinction) not a schism of letter and spirit. Ruether rightly rejects the latter in *FF*, 239-45.

78. *DQ*, 129.

79. From the preface to Marx's *A Contribution to the Critique of Political Economy*, reprinted in Tucker, ed., *The Marx-Engels Reader*, 5

80. I am not defending a progressivistic view of history. While the church may go beyond the limitations of previous generations in its redemptive redirection of evil and brokenness to the point of recognizing features of our lives that require change that previous generations would not have seen as problematic, this is only the case if the church is faithful to its calling. Such progress is not an inevitable law of history.

81. See Brueggemann, *The Prophetic Imagination*.

82. The ideas in this subsection have been expressed more fully in the chapter on Gen. 1-3 in my *The Troubled Marriage Of Adam And Eve* (forthcoming).

83. See 55-56 above.

84. My argument that the man is portrayed as inadequate to fill and subdue the earth on his own presupposes the legitimacy of reading Gen. 1 and 2 together. That they may well have been separate narratives before being placed within the Genesis narrative does not mean that they cannot be read as parts of a single unfolding drama. Biblical passages and sources cannot be reduced to the meaning they had in their pre-canonical forms any more than the current meanings of words in a living language can be reduced to their etymologies.

85. See Phyllis Trible, *God and the Rhetoric of Sexuality* (Philadelphia: Fortress Press, 1978), 90 and Mary J. Evans, *Woman in the Bible* (Exeter: Paternoster Press, 1983), 16.

86. James H. Olthuis, *I Pledge You My Troth: A Christian View of Marriage, Family, Friendship* (New York: Harper and Row, 1975), 5.

87. See Susan Bower, "Imaging God as Woman and Man Together: A Study of Genesis Two" (Toronto: ICS, n.d.), 7-8 and Walter Brueggemann, "Of the Same Flesh and Bone (Gen. 2:23)," *Catholic Biblical Quarterly* 32/4 (1970): 532-542.

88. See Gerhard von Rad, *Genesis: A Commentary*, rev. ed. (Philadelphia: The Westminster Press, 1972), 85.

89. See Evans, *Woman in the Bible*, 17.

90. See *Paradise Lost* Bk. IX lines 997-99.

91. Von Rad, *Genesis*, 90.

92. Robert Alter, *The Art of Biblical Narrative* (New York: Basic Books, 1981), 72.

93. *FMM*, 13.

94. See Elizabeth A. Clark, *Women in the Early Church* (Wilmington: Michael Glazier, Inc., 1983), 27-76.

95. Phyllis Trible, "Eve and Adam: Genesis 2-3 Reread," in Carol P. Christ and Judith Plaskow, eds., *Womanspirit Rising: A Feminist Reader in Religion* (San Francisco: Harper and Row, 1979), 81. On whether the narrative is best read as "myth"—if that is defined in opposition to history—see nn. 41 and 49 above.

96. *FF*, 241.

97. See the translations of Ex. 19:15 in the New Revised Standard Version and the New Jerusalem Bible. The New International Version interprets even this verse as a command to both sexes.

98. This is claimed by L. William Countryman in his otherwise fine book *Dirt, Greed and Sex: Sexual Ethics in the New Testament and their Implications for Today* (Philadelphia: Fortress Press, 1988), 29.

99. Brevard S. Childs, *The Book of Exodus: A Critical, Theological Commentary* (Louisville: The Westminster Press, 1974), 373.

100. Ibid., 566.

101. Mary Evans in *Woman in the Bible*, 23, argues that the Old Testament concept of corporate personality helps explain why there is no clear distinction made between a man, his wife, his possessions and his animals. She writes, "This leads to the concept of the man worshipping on behalf of the whole family and also explains the references where the wife appears to be linked with possessions. It was not so much that the wife was seen as a possession, but rather that, in one sense, the possessions were, like the wife, part of the man himself." As a corrective to anachronistic interpretations of property in the OT, see the fine discussion in Christopher J. H. Wright, *God's People in God's Land: Family, Land, and Property in the Old Testament* (Grand Rapids: Eerdmans; Exeter: The Paternoster Press, 1990), chap. 6.

102. J. M. Powis Smith, *The Origin and History of Hebrew Law* (Chicago, 1931), 3; cited in Gerda Lerner, *The Creation of Patriarchy* (New York: Oxford University Press, 1986), 102.

103. Katherine C. Bushnell, *God's Word to Women* (Oakland, California: privately printed, 1923), lesson 71 paragraph 571.

104. It is also worth contrasting with MAL (Middle Assyrian Law) 55 and 56, which are briefly discussed in Lerner, *The Creation of Patriarchy*, 116-17, in which we are told that the rapist's wife is to be dishonoured for what her husband has done to another woman—unless the rapist swears that the other woman seduced him.

105. See Craigie, *The Book of Deuteronomy* (n.71), 295.

106. As Roland de Vaux points out in his *Ancient Israel*, vol. 1, *Social Institutions* (New York: McGraw-Hill Book Co., 1961), 35, no such restriction on the male existed in Assyria.

107. See Craigie, *The Book of Deuteronomy* (n.71), 305.

108. I understand that this "pillar to post" approach to (re)marriage is still prevalent in the Middle East.

109. Evidence from textual criticism suggests that Mk. 10:12 is not a reference to women initiating divorce, but separating from their husbands and then getting "remarried." See William L. Lane, *The Gospel of Mark* (Grand Rapids: Eerdmans, 1974), 352 n.5, 358. Lane asserts that divorce could not be initiated by a Jewish woman according to the Jewish law of the time. He suggests that this verse, which is peculiar to Mk., is a reference to the adulterous behaviour of Herodias. Ben Witherington III argues that only males could initiate divorce "[w]ith rare exceptions." See his *Women in the Ministry of Jesus: A Study of Jesus' Attitudes to Women and their Roles as Reflected in His Earthly Life* (Cambridge: Cambridge University Press, 1984), 5. See also de Vaux, *Ancient Israel*, vol. 1, 35. On the exception clause in Mt. 5:32 and 19:9, see Olthuis, *I Pledge You My Troth* (n.86), 69-70.

110. *NWNE*, 64-65.

111. Faith McBurney Martin, *Call Me Blessed: The Emerging Christian Woman* (Grand Rapids: Eerdmans, 1988), 38.

112. See Mary Douglas, *Purity and Danger: An Analysis of the Concepts of Pollution and Taboo* (London: Ark Paperbacks, 1966) and L. William Countryman, *Dirt, Greed and Sex (n.98)*.

113. See Gordon J. Wenham, *The Book of Leviticus* (Grand Rapids: Eerdmans, 1979), 223-24. This judgment is echoed by Countryman, *Dirt, Greed and Sex*, 26.

114. See Wenham, *The Book of Leviticus*, 188.

115. See Lerner, *The Creation of Patriarchy*, 106, 171.

116. See 58 above.

117. See Dennis T. Olson, "Numbers," in James L. Mays, ed., *Harper's Bible Commentary* (San Francisco: Harper and Row, 1988), 191.

118. See Phyllis Trible, *Texts of Terror: Literary-Feminist Readings of Biblical Narratives* (Philadelphia: Fortress Press, 1984).

119. See Lillian R. Klein, *The Triumph of Irony in the Book of Judges* (Sheffield: The Almond Press, 1988), 17-18, 37-139.

120. For a brief but lucid analysis of the book's literary structure that supplements the fine analysis of Klein, see John J. Davis and Herbert Wolff, "Judges: Introduction," in Kenneth L. Barker, ed., *The NIV Study Bible* (Grand Rapids: Zondervan, 1985), 326-27.

121. See Klein, *The Triumph of Irony in the Book of Judges*, 70-71.

122. See Isaac M. Kikawada and Arthur Quinn, *Before Abraham Was: The Unity of Genesis 1-11* (Nashville: Abingdon, 1985), 131.

123. Ibid., 134.

124. Klein, *The Triumph of Irony in the Book of Judges*, 12.

125. Klein interprets the refrain to mean "in those days Israel had no judge." See *The Triumph of Irony in the Book of Judges*, 141.

126. Trible, *Texts of Terror*, 76 and 86.

127. Klein, *The Triumph of Irony in the Book of Judges*, 142.

128. Ibid., 170. Klein's discussion of the narrative artistry of this episode contains a number of important observations that are missed in Trible's account.

129. Trible, *Texts of Terror*, 83.

130. Klein, *The Triumph of Irony in the Book of Judges*, 26. See also her discussion on pp. 172-73.

131. It is surprising that Klein misses this verbal clue as this is the kind of observation that she is usually quick to make. In *The Triumph of Irony in the Book of Judges*, 25, she notes the emphasis on Acsah's prostration of herself, but comments, "That she gets down from her donkey is unimportant." The contrast between Acsah boldly talking to her husband in 1:14 (wrongly "corrected" by the LXX) and the inability of the concubine to answer her husband in 19:28 should also be noted.

132. See James Alsdurf and Phyllis Alsdurf, *Battered into Submission: The Tragedy of Wife Abuse in the Christian Home* (Downers Grove: InterVarsity Press, 1989).

133. Sandra M. Sneiders, *Women and the Word: The Gender of God in the New Testament and the Spirituality of Women* (New York: Paulist Press, 1986), 33-34.

134. For a brief comment on this passage and on Joel 2:17-18, see Alice L. Laffey, *An Introduction to the Old Testament: A Feminist Perspective* (Philadelphia:

Fortress Press, 1988), 174-77. On the Jeremiah passage, see also Trible, *God and the Rhetoric of Sexuality*, 47-50, and J. A. Thompson, *The Book Of Jeremiah* (Grand Rapids: Eerdmans, 1980), 575-76.

135. I am indebted here to an unpublished sermon entitled "Surrounded by Women" by Hendrik Hart.

136. See Mouw, *When The Kings Come Marching In*, 36.

137. *MFFC*, 22.

138. Calvin G. Seerveld, *The Greatest Song: In Critique of Solomon* (Toronto: Tuppence Press, 1963, 1988), 86-88. Seerveld argues that the title verse is best translated as "The Song of Songs which is about Solomon" (93). It is thus not an ascription of authorship to Solomon. His three-character interpretation is supported by Hill in Andrew E. Hill and John H. Walton, *A Survey of the Old Testament* (Grand Rapids: Zondervan, 1991), 299-306.

139. Seerveld, *The Greatest Song*, 71-72.

140. Hence the title of chap. 9 of Gerhard von Rad, *Wisdom in Israel,* trans. James D. Martin (London: SCM, 1972). His discussion of the parallels with *Ma'at* can be found in this chapter on pp. 152-55.

141. Roland E. Murphy, "Wisdom and Creation" *Journal of Biblical Literature* 104/1 (1985): 9-10.

142. Ibid., 9.

143. Ironically the mystery is reinforced by the fact that a number of key words in Prov. 8 are very hard to translate! The problems are succinctly summarized by Kathleen A. Farmer in her *Who Knows What is Good? A Commentary on the Books of Proverbs and Ecclesiastes* (Grand Rapids: Eerdmans, 1991), 53-56.

144. That this life is seen incarnated in Jesus may be the reason Paul refers to Christ as the "wisdom of God" (1 Cor. 1:30).

145. Perhaps *Ma'at* is, in part, a non-intellectualistic absolutization of the "orderliness" of life (its capacity to be conceptually grasped). If Prov. 8 is, at least in part, a polemic against such idolatry, this has negative implications for much of the reformed tradition's understanding of an abiding creation order. I have reflected on this latter topic in "The Trouble with Normative . . . Creation Order, Hermeneutics and Homosexuality."

146. See the section on God in chap. 4.

147. See Al Wolters, "Proverbs 31:10-31 as Heroic Hymn: A Form-Critical Analysis," *Vetus Testamentum* 38 (1988): 446-57.

148. See, eg., *FMM*, 39-53.

149. For example, Jesus' "discarding" of the taboo of uncleanness in the case of the woman with the haemorrhage need not be seen as a permissive approach to the Law as Ruether argues. I would rather understand this as an example of Jesus' self-understanding as the temple (the place of purification). See N. T. Wright, *The Quest for the Historical Kingdom*: lecture 1, unpublished ms.

presented on Jan. 31, 1989 at the Institute for Christian Studies as the "Christ-ianity and Learning Lectures" of that year.

150. *SGT*, 9.

151. *MFFC*, 87.

152. Hart, *Morning Star*, 89. To expand on this line of thought, the fact that Mary initially sees Jesus as a gardener may be an allusion to Adam as the one originally put in the garden to take care of it (Gen. 2:15). Are Jesus' words in Jn. 20:17a related to Gen. 2:24?

153. I have explored this topic at greater length in my chapter on Paul in my *The Troubled Marriage Of Adam And Eve*. My comments on 1 Cor. 11 there and here find support in the detailed exegesis of Gordon D. Fee in his *The First Epistle to the Corinthians* (Grand Rapids: Eerdmans, 1987), 491-530.

154. See *NWNE*, 67 where she gives the examples that follow.

155. On the leadership connotations of this word, see Fiorenza, *In Memory of Her*, (New York: Crosssroad; London: SCM, 1983), 181-82. A very helpful book on the women Paul mentions in his letters is Florence M. Gillman, *Women Who Knew Paul* (Collegeville, Minnesota: The Liturgical Press, 1992).

156. For some strange reason, the NIV does not offer an alternative translation of v. 13 along these lines, even though *akatakalupto* is the same word that is used in v. 5.

157. See, e. g., *The Gospel of Thomas*, 114:24-25 reproduced in James M. Robinson, ed., *The Nag Hammadi Library* (San Francisco: Harper and Row, 1978), 130, *The Acts of Paul and Thecla* 40 and *The Martyrdom of Perpetua and Felicitas*, 10, both reproduced in Clark, *Women in the Early Church*, 87, 101.

158. See Richard and Catherine Clark Kroeger, "Sexual Identity in Corinth: Paul Faces a Crisis," *Reformed Journal* 28 (December 1978): 11-15 and Catherine Kroeger, "The Apostle Paul and the Greco-Roman Cults of Women," *Journal of the Evangelical Theological Society* 30 (March 1987): 36-38. If it is concluded that veils rather than hair length are in view in this passage, this does not affect the thrust of my argument as the Kroegers note that members of the Dionysus cult also expressed their desire to invert the male-female distinction by having males and not females wear a head covering.

159. See Fee, *I Corinthians*, 502-503, C. Clark Kroeger, "The Classical Concept of 'Head' as 'Source' " in Gretchen Gaebelein Hull, *Equal To Serve: Women and Men in the Church and Home* (Old Tappan: Fleming H. Revell Co., 1987), Appendix III, 267-83, Berkeley and Alvera Mickelsen, "What Does *Kephalē* Mean in the New Testament?," in Alvera Mickelsen, ed., *Women, Authority and the Bible* (Downers Grove: InterVarsity Press, 1986), 97-110 and the response by Philip Barton Payne on pp. 118-32 of that volume.

The translation of *kephalē* as origin or source fits very well indeed in Col. 2:19 and Eph. 4:15. It also makes sense of the close connection between Christ's as *kephalē* and *archē* (origin) in Col. 1:18. This is also a plausible translation in Col. 2:10. Contextual support for this translation in 1 Cor. 11:3ff. and Eph. 5:23ff. will be offered below.

The only other metaphorical use of *kephalē* by Paul—Eph. 1:22b—is more complex. Often *kephalē* is taken with *huper panta* and understood as ruler over all. This supposed meaning of *kephalē* is then read into its occurances elsewhere. Christ clearly has a position of authority in this passage, but this is not conveyed simply by the meaning of *kephalē*, but by the wider context. In no other passage is *kephalē* followed by *huper* plus an accusative. (Gilbert Bilezikian in his *Beyond Sex Roles: What the Bible says about a Woman's Place in Church and Family*, second edition [Grand Rapids: Baker Book House, 1989], 244, claims that such a construction seems not to exist in Greek literature.) Elsewhere in the NT, when translated "head of," it is always followed by a noun or pronoun in the genitive.

Thus even if the word does connote leadership here, the difference in phrasing means that we can't simply read this meaning into other grammatically dissimilar contexts. Furthermore, it is quite legitimate to take the phrase "He (God) appointed him (Christ) to be head" most directly with *te ekklesia*, i. e., to the church. The point would then be that the church's head—the source of its life and the one who brought it into being—is also above all things. This fits very well with the fact that the church of which Christ is the "head" is not classified with the "all things" which he is "over." The phrase *huper ta panta* refers back to v. 22a in which we are told that God placed all things (*panta*) under Christ's feet. This is taken from Ps. 8 which originally applied to the authority of humanity as a whole. Here it is applied to Christ and to his body. We too are over all things.

160. Elizabeth Schüssler Fiorenza, "1 Corinthians," In Mays, ed., *Harper's Bible Commentary*, 1183.

161. See Olthuis, *I Pledge You My Troth* (n.86), 139, and the articles on *doxa* by Kittel and von Rad, in Gerhard Kittel, ed., *Theological Dictionary of the New Testament*, vol. 1 (Grand Rapids: Eerdamns, 1965), 232-55.

162. See 1 Sam. 15:29 and Mic. 1:15. Cf. 1 Sam. 4:21,2; Ps. 106:20; Jer. 2:11 and Hos. 4:7. The LXX translates "glory" with *doxa* in all but the first two of these examples.

163. Olthuis, *I Pledge You My Troth* (n.86), 139.

164. The Western text places vv. 34-35 after v. 40, presumably to give a smoother reading, but no significant ms. leaves these verses out. See the discussion in Evans, *Woman in the Bible*, 95-96. For a different view, see Fee, *1 Corinthians* (n.153), 699-708.

165. See Kroeger, "The Apostle Paul and the Greco-Roman Cults of Women," 29-30 and Catherine and Richard Clark Kroeger, "Pandemonium and Silence at Corinth," *Reformed Journal* 28 (June 1978): 10-11.

166. I am aware that many scholars do not believe that Paul is the author of this epistle. That it is possible to make a coherent case that departs from the current consensus can be seen in John A. T. Robinson, *Redating the New Testament*

(London: SCM, 1976), 82-84 and Donald Guthrie, *The Pastoral Epistles: An Introduction and Commentary* rev. ed. (Grand Rapids: Eerdmans, 1990), 17-62 and 224-40. As Evans has noted, in *Woman and the Bible*, 152 n. 2, "The discussion of Pauline authorship for the Pastorals is complicated by the fact that a major argument used is the contrast seen between the attitude to women found in the Pastorals and that found elsewhere in the Pauline corpus." My rejection of this contrast is an indirect argument for Pauline authorship, but one does not have to accept that Paul wrote 1 Timothy in order to accept the exegesis I am proposing.

167. See Catherine Kroeger, "1 Timothy 2:12—A Classicist's View," in Alvera Mickelsen, ed., *Women, Authority and the Bible* (n.159), 229-32 and Richard Clark Kroeger and Catherine Clark Kroeger, *I Suffer Not a Woman: Rethinking 1 Timothy 2:11-15 in the Light of Ancient Evidence* (Grand Rapids: Baker Book House, 1992), Appendix 1 and chap. 7.

168. *WG*, 97.

169. Ibid., 95-97.

170. See Kroeger, "1 Timothy 2:12—A Classicist's View" (n.167), the basic argument of which has been expanded in great detail in Kroeger and Kroeger, *I Suffer Not a Woman (n.167)*.

171. See Kroeger, "1 Timothy 2:12—A Classicist's View" (n.167), 232-44 and Kroeger and Kroeger, *I Suffer Not a Woman* (n.167), Appendix 7.

172. While the Gnostic texts that we possess which display the aforementioned features are dated no earlier than in the second century A. D., it is not unlikely that such thinking was present in the first century. Even as cautious a work as *The NIV Study Bible* takes it for granted that there were problems with Gnosticism for the Ephesian church to which 1 Timothy is addressed (pp. 1833 and *passim*).

173. Kroeger, "1 Timothy 2:12—A Classicist's View" (n.167), 232 and Kroeger and Kroeger, *I Suffer Not a Woman* (n.167), chap. 8.

174. See ibid., 243 and Kroeger and Kroeger, *I Suffer Not A Woman* (n.167), chap 16.

175. See Patricia Gundrey, *Heirs Together: Mutual Submission in Marriage* (Grand Rapids: Zondervan Publishing House, 1980), 93-98.

176. See John Howard Yoder, *The Politics of Jesus: Vicit Agnus Noster* (Grand Rapids: Eerdmans, 1972), 163-92 for a critique of this assumption.

177. See *SGT*, 137. In *SGT*, 157, not realizing that Eph. 5 supports her position, she writes as follows about her understanding of Mariology as symbolic ecclesiology,

We need to move beyond the typology of Christ and the Church as dominant male and submissive female. Rather, what we see here is an ongoing process of *kenosis* and transformation. God's power no longer remains in Heaven where it can be used as a model of the "thrones of the mighty." In the iconoclastic and messianic prophet, it has been emptied out into the human situation of suffering and hope.

178. See Paul K. Jewett, *Man as Male and Female: A Study in Sexual Relationships from a Theological Point of View* (Grand Rapids: Eerdmans, 1975), 142.
179. While he does not work with a four-fold typology, the need to hold together both visionary and pragmatic emphases in the canon is stressed by Paul D. Hanson in his *The Diversity of Scripture: A Theological Interpretation* (Philadelphia: Fortress Press, 1982).
180. *LT*, 167. Cf. *RK*, 286-87.
181. Ibid., 167-68.
182. Ibid., 168.
183. Ibid., 172.
184. *SGT*, 19.
185. See esp. *CAI*.
186. Nevertheless, being (creationally) anti-normative is not the same in my terminology as being (redemptively) wrong.
187. See the discussion on pp. 00-00 above.
188. On my distinction between our experience of God as Word and as Spirit, see n.53 above.
189. See Ruether, "Review symposium: *In Memory of Her*," 148.
190. *SGT*, 32-33.
191. Ibid. 12.
192. Ruether seems to recognize this in *SGT*, 18.
193. Andrew M. Greeley, *A Future to Hope In: Socio-Religious Speculations* (Garden City: Doubleday and Co., 1968), 19 (my emphases).

Part Two

GIVING BIRTH TO THE FUTURE

Towards a Christian Feminist Theology

Chapter Four: Ruether's Proposals for a Feminist Theology

So far in this study, the discussion has centred on the Christian tradition which we have inherited from the past, and on the problems much of it poses for us as Christians if we want to affirm the full humanity of women. In this part of the study, the main focus of attention will move from critique to construction, from problems to potential solutions, and from what we have inherited from our forefathers and foremothers to the kind of Christian theology that needs to be developed today if the challenge of contemporary feminism is to be met.

In this chapter, I will examine Ruether's positive proposals for a feminist alternative to the androcentric theology that we saw her anxious to expose in chapter 1. This summary of her position will cover the same areas of theology examined in that chapter, and will illustrate how she employs the different types of "usable tradition" that were identified in chapter 2.[1] Towards the end of each section, I will also offer a response both to highlight areas of agreement and to point out how my alternative way of "wrestling with the past" outlined in chapter 3 may lead to a different way of "giving birth to the future."

I. Theological Anthropology

Perhaps the easiest way to capture the basic character of the theological anthropology Ruether wishes to propose is to examine her ideas in the light of her stated desire to go beyond liberalism and romanticism—the two traditions which have most influenced contemporary feminism—while incorporating their best insights into a new creative synthesis.[2]

Liberal feminism, as we saw Ruether argue in chapter 1, was the first movement that asserted the full equality of women in a way that was directly relevant to the organization of society as a whole, thus opposing the dominant anthropology of the Christian tradition in a way that eschatological feminism had been unable to do. She argues that this outlook was achieved by secularizing the *imago dei* and establishing the equal rights of the sexes on the basis of their common possession of reason or moral conscience. The Fall, therefore, comes to be seen as the distorting of the original equivalence of all humans and the setting up of hierarchies and patterns of domination. Redemption is seen as the overthrowing of an unjust order and the reform of social institutions that subjugate women. Ruether also discusses Marxist feminism in this context by noting that it builds on the liberal tradition, but goes beyond it by proposing not just *legal* reform, but also the eradication of *economic* discrimination against women.

Historically, Christians who have understood the *imago dei* in the light of liberal feminism have stressed the need for the church to undergo reform so that it may honour the equality of men and women in its institutional life. But ecclesiastical reform is not to be pursued by turning one's back on the wider culture. The church, in this view, is seen "as a paradigm of what all social institutions should become, not as a representative of an eschatological humanity outside of and beyond history."[3] This clearly highlights the departure of this position from that of eschatological feminism—a departure of which Ruether fully approves.

While liberal feminism opposes the traditional correlation of the *imago dei* and fallenness with spiritual maleness and carnal femaleness by asserting that both sexes are equally in the image of God, Ruether observes that anthropologies which draw on the ideas of romanticism oppose the patriarchal tradition by *reversing* this traditional correlation so that it is now woman who comes to represent the original goodness of humanity most fully. This gives rise to all kinds of alternative ideas about what it means to be male and female with which Ruether wishes to interact.

In order to make sense of the wide and bewildering variety of social reform strategies inspired by such thinking, Ruether believes that it is helpful to distinguish between *conservative, reformist,* and *radical* forms of romanticism. Conservative romanticism is actually an anti-feminist position. Like all forms of romanticism, woman is seen as an exponent of a higher nature than man, but because the home is so exclusively identified with the values of purity and altruism while the public sphere is seen as the realm of egoism and sin, conservative romanticists are convinced that woman can only hold on to this higher nature by staying within the private sphere. Furthermore, they insist that this is where she must remain if she is to have any positive influence on her husband when he comes home to retreat from the struggles of the workplace. Morally uplifted by his wife, he can take something of her higher goodness into the public realm, for his nature is more suited to bear such an environment, while she would soon lose her important feminine qualities in such a world.

By contrast, reformist romanticism has far more confidence in woman's ability to hold on to her spiritual qualities outside the home. Because it shares liberal feminism's desire for the reform of social institutions, it believes that women should not confine their influence to the domestic realm. As Ruether puts it, "For reformist feminism, the bourgeois ideal of the family is seen as a launching pad for a mission into the world to uplift and transform it to the higher standards of goodness, peace, and loving service of womanhood and the home."[4]

Such a vision was expressed in a wide range of programmes for social reform in late-nineteenth-century America, especially in the areas of temperance and education, and in crusades against immorality and political corruption. Ruether captures the idealism of this form of feminism when she writes,

In its most visionary moments, reformist-romantic feminism glimpses the contours of a new society characterized not only by honesty, purity, and cleanliness but, above all, by peace. The nature of woman is incompatible with war. Not only have women historically been noncombatants, but the nature of woman is particularly related to all that brings peace and love rather than egoism, strife, and violence. Thus a new era of world peace, the abolition of strife, and the dawning of the reign of peace on earth represent the millennial vision of reformist-romantic feminism at its highest.[5]

It becomes clear from Ruether's later comments that "the most strenuous belief in the innate superiority of women"[6] that she finds in this movement is too optimistic for her tastes. By contrast, if we read between the lines of her account of radical romanticism (or radical feminism as it is more commonly called) and pay attention to her description of its characteristic *lack* of hope about the possibility of reforming either male institutions or even male individuals, we can see that this is far more *pessimistic* than she would like. Highlighting where it differs from reformist romanticism, Ruether writes,

> Radical romanticism despairs of reforming ambiguous and evil male institutions. By implication it also is more pessimistic about the possibilities of converting male nature to female goodness. Rather, it repudiates male culture (including patriarchal religion) and withdraws into the female sphere as a separatist enclave of female values. It seeks to convert this female sphere from a dependent appendage to the male world of politics, war, and work into a self-sufficient utopian community. Here the higher female qualities of love, relatedness, and mutuality can reign unimpeded by ambiguous male institutions.[7]

As later comments will reveal, Ruether finds this confidence in innate female goodness to be a faith that she cannot fully share. When she goes on to tell us that "Separatist feminist utopianism dreams of an alternative world where women have learned to reproduce without men, to produce only female children, and to give their love only to women,"[8] I think that it is possible to detect a certain amount of cynicism in her voice.

Her lack of enthusiasm for this position is especially clear in her earlier work, *From Machismo to Mutuality*. While she is happy to recognize that the community that oppressed people experience with one another is a legitimate stage in the process of liberation, she is adamant that it cannot be its final goal. The community of the oppressed, she argues, must make way for a fuller community of reconciliation within which *both* oppressor *and* oppressed can be set free from their previous pathologies in relation to each other. Thus she writes,

> Separatism cannot be presented as the goal of the women's movement, nor can we speak as though males alone are capable of oppressive relations while relations between "sisters" will automatically be loving. Such a view retains remnants of that Victorian feminism that regarded women as intrinsically more moral than men. To redeem humanity, therefore, one does not have to struggle against the demon in oneself. One only has to reject "evil" males and join the natural community of human goodness, namely a community of women. Such a view of women is really premoral. If women are to grow up and take responsibility for the world they must recognize that they too are capable of sin, not just as victims but as aggressors as well.[9]

Ruether believes that while both liberal and romanticist feminism offer some helpful insights, they also have significant limitations. Liberal feminism, she argues, "too readily identifies normative human nature with those capacities for reason and rule identified with men and the public sphere."[10] Although giving women the opportunity to develop these capacities through education and allowing them to express such gifts by granting them equal political rights is an important part of liberation, she is convinced that this alone does not constitute a fully adequate solution. "Liberalism," she notes "assumes the traditional male sphere as normative and believes it is wrong to deny people access to it on the basis of gender. But once women are allowed to enter the public sphere, liberalism offers no critique of the modes of functioning within it."[11]

In the light of this shortcoming, Ruether does appreciate romanticism's recognition of the moral ambiguity of the roles of the public world, even if it tends to idealize the home to the extent that it often overlooks the violence that can occur there too. She captures something of its strength and weakness when she writes,

> Romanticism is not entirely wrong in believing there are clues to a better humanity in the virtues relegated to women and the home in bourgeois society. But these virtues exist in deformed and deforming ways within the institutionalization of "woman's sphere." Moreover, the capacities traditionally associated with men and with public life also contain some important human virtues that women should not be forbidden to cultivate.[12]

While this quotation exemplifies Ruether's belief that both liberalism and romanticism have something to teach us, her very next paragraph shows that she is just as convinced that both traditions need to be relativized. She writes,

> Thus neither masculinity traditionally defined nor femininity traditionally defined discloses an innately good human nature, and neither is simply an expression of evil. Both represent different types of alienation of humanity from its original potential. Socially, both home and work represent realms of corruption. If women will not be automatically redeemed by being incorporated into male political power and business in its present form, men will not automatically be redeemed by learning to nurture infants and keep house.[13]

What Ruether is saying, in other words, is that we will not find a good model for authentic humanity by locating the norm in either the traditional male and his role, as liberalism does, or in the traditional female and her role, as romanticism is in the habit of doing.

The above argument illustrates Ruether's aim to form a feminist anthropology that goes beyond liberalism and romanticism. It would be a mistake, however, to assume that she succeeds in breaking with both of these traditions in an equally decisive manner. Ruether defines liberalism as an outlook that is "based on a unitary essence of humanness, modeled on pragmatic rationality" in contrast to romanticism which "stresse[s] the differences of 'natures' according to race, class, and sex."[14] In this light, I want to suggest that her rejection of romanticism is far more decisive than the break she makes with liberalism. Although, as I have already noted, she wishes to reject liberalism's privileging of rationality above other human capacities,[15] her own tendency to understand the authentic humanity of men and women in terms of a "unitary essence of humanness" can be inferred, in part, from the fact that she devotes a disproportionate amount of her energy to attacking the romanticist notion that there are essential differences between the sexes.

One place where Ruether can be seen to be far more eager to attack the ideas of romanticism than she is to criticize liberalism, is in her discussion of whether "androgyny" is a good term for describing the "holistic psychic capacities" which men and women need to recover if they are to realize their "lost full human potential."[16] Ruether rejects the term because she believes that it falsely implies that a normative psychic capacity for men and women would consist of the integration of two sides that could be legitimately labelled "masculine" and "feminine." In her characteristically forthright style, Ruether writes,

> There is no valid biological basis for labelling certain psychic capacities, such as reason, "masculine" and others, such as intuition, "feminine." To put it bluntly, there is no biological connection between male gonads and the capacity to reason. Likewise, there is no biological connection between female sexual organs and the capacity to be intuitive, caring, or nurturing. . . . We need to affirm not the confusing concept of androgyny but rather that all humans possess a full and equivalent human nature and personhood, *as male and female.*[17]

This last statement is highly ambiguous if it is taken in isolation. It could mean that both men and women possess the full range of *human*—i. e., not "masculine" and "feminine"—capacities, but nevertheless express them in relatively distinctive ways depending on their sex and gender. But she could simply mean that this "equivalent human nature" is essentially the same in all humans, who in addition to a common personhood also possess male or female bodies. In this latter position, differences between the sexes would be confined to a biological level which is believed to be more or less *extrinsic* to personality. If this is all Ruether means, then her position is merely a non-rationalist variation on that of liberalism. As Ruether continues her argument, it becomes clear that it is this latter meaning she has in mind, for she says,

> Maleness and femaleness exist as reproductive role specializations. There is no necessary (biological) connection between reproductive complementarity and either psychological or social role differentiation. These are the work of culture and socialization, not of "nature."[18]

As an alternative to this sharp distinction between nature and nurture, it is theoretically possible to argue that while cultural stereotypes are indeed largely the result of unhealthy patterns of socialization, and do not derive purely from biological differences, it is still the case that sexual differences do have some influence on post-biological levels of human functioning to the extent that male and female behaviour can never be fully explained in terms of socialization. But this is an option that Ruether seems very reluctant to explore.

There is one place in her writings where she *appears* to accept the fact that biological differences do have an undeniable cultural impact. This can be found in her discussion of male and female brain lateralization. On the basis of recent research, Ruether claims that "the right brain specializes in intuitive, musical, relational, and spatial capacities and the left brain in linguistic and mathematical thinking."[19] What is particularly significant is that one-sided left brain development, which leads to ecologically dysfunctional ways of thinking, seems more dominant in males, perhaps due to their later verbal development.[20] Furthermore, she also suggests that this research "discloses a possible biological basis of men's cultural tendency to identify their ego with left-brain characteristics and to see right-brain characteristics as the 'repressed' part of themselves, which they in turn project upon and identify with women."[21]

Further investigation of what she has written on this subject, however, reveals that even here, Ruether shies away from saying that sexual differences inevitably affect human behaviour. She argues against this conclusion in two ways. Firstly, she states that the biological evidence is not as unambiguous as it may first appear. Thus she writes,

It is important to note that the evidence for gender difference in brain lateralization cannot be construed as invariable. At most, one can say there is evidence of a statistical tendency for women to integrate the functions of the brain across left and right hemispheres and males to separate brain functions between the hemispheres and to create left-brain dominance. But there is greater difference between females and between males on brain lateralization than between males and females.[22]

Secondly, she cautions against concluding that this brain research reveals a biological root cause behind certain types of behaviour by suggesting that differences even at this biological level may well be the result of socialization. Thus she continues her argument,

Moreover, there has been insufficient cross-cultural research to determine whether this tendency [to left-brain dominance in males] is more pronounced among white Western Europeans, while cultures that encourage males to develop intuitive and artistic capacities might differ. At most, we can say that the human brain has a capacity to develop either in more balanced and integrated modes of functioning between the two hemispheres or more lateralized modes and that, among white Westerners, there is some evidence that females tend more toward the first type of brain development and males more toward the second.[23]

The caution that Ruether exercises in this area does not necessarily imply that she prefers the "unitary human essence" of
liberalism to the "essential differences" of romanticism. What does
lead me to this conclusion is the fact that even when Ruether does
recognize that biological phenomena do affect us at a post-biological
level *in practice*, this in no way inspires her to explore the possibility
that, *normatively speaking*, males and females *should* express what it
means to be authentically human, or to be made in the image of God,
in different ways due to differences at the level of sex and gender.

If we explore the typology of historically recurring theories
about the degree of differentiation and equality between the sexes
that has been suggested by Prudence Allen in her important book
The Concept of Woman, I believe that we will gain a more precise
understanding of Ruether's anthropological proposals.

Allen has identified three distinct positions on these issues: sex
unity, sex complementarity, and sex polarity. Sex unity, she proposes,
is a position that stresses equality by devaluing materiality. This is a
tendency she sees in a tradition that stretches from Plato to
Shulamith Firestone. In sex-polarity theories, by contrast, an "isolated aspect of the body is used as the fundamental philosophical
basis for the evaluation of one sex as superior to the other." Thus
male superiority has been argued on the basis of the ability to
concoct seed (Aristotle), the male sexual anatomy (Freud), and the
hormone testosterone (Goldberg). Reverse sex-polarity theorists, as
Allen calls them, argue for female superiority in the same way. To
this end, Ashley Montague has based his arguments on the female
chromosomal structure, while the ability to give birth has been
chosen by Jill Johnson. The sex-complementarity position, which
Allen favours, tries to avoid both the exaggeration and denial of
bodily differences. It is, in Allen's opinion, the only position based
on "a belief in the equality of dignity and worth of women and men
that at the same time recognizes significant differences between the
two sexes."[24]

How does Ruether's position relate to this typology? It seems
very clear from the above discussion that she rejects the sex-polarity
theory in both its masculinist and feminist forms. While the
androcentric version of this position is opposed by all feminists,

Ruether's rejection of the gynocentric form of such thinking is implicit in her critique of radical romanticism and in her insistence that "neither masculinity traditionally defined nor femininity traditionally defined discloses an innately good human nature, and neither is simply an expression of evil."[25]

I believe that an opposition to the sex-complementarity theory can be inferred from her reluctance to see biological or psychic differences as in any way indicative of what it means to be normatively human as a bi-unity of male and female. At one point in an essay in *From Machismo to Mutuality*, she even goes as far as to claim the "concept of complementarity must be recognized as a false biologism that attempts to totalize on the level of the whole human existence a limited functional complementarity that exists on the level of procreative systems."[26] Now it should be noted that this statement occurs within an argument against a view of "complementarity" that is based on destructive societal stereotypes. But the fact that Ruether nowhere shows any desire to explore other more *nuanced* forms of sex-complementarity is, I believe, very revealing.

Ruether firmly believes that recovering aspects of our "full psychic potential" which have been suppressed by cultural gender stereotypes is part of what it means to be reconnected to the *imago dei*.[27] Her vision of a healthy society, however, does not seem to include the recovery and celebration of genuine differences between men and women. In the title chapter of *New Woman/New Earth*, she writes,

> Without sex-role stereotyping, sex-personality stereotyping would disappear, allowing for genuine individuation of personality. Instead of being forced into a mold of masculine or feminine "types," each individual could shape a complex whole from the full range of human psychic potential for intellect and feeling, activity and receptivity.[28]

Patricia Wilson-Kastner has suggested that the most fundamental point of departure for an inclusive theological anthropology is the question: "How does one think about persons? Primarily as humans, or first as male or female?"[29] Ontologically, this is a question about whether we choose to emphasize universality and unity or particularity and diversity. Ruether seems to opt for the first answer. Her vision for a world beyond gender *stereotypes* sounds as though it is also a vision for a world beyond gender *differences*. In other words, this is a world of persons who would experience themselves and others first and foremost as human beings. Of course such humans would have male or female bodies, but sex and gender would not be seen as expressions of our *essential* humanity.

The fact that Ruether holds to, or at least leans towards, a sex-unity position fits well, I believe, with some of her most basic ontological assumptions. While it is true that she is a vocal critic of cosmological dualism, this should not blind us to what I will later refer to as her own "soft dualism"—by which I mean the adoption of a position that, for all its stress on the unity of reality, has not fully overcome the dualistic tendencies that are present in a more blatant form in anthropologies and cosmologies most commonly labelled as dualistic. When attention is paid to the way her categories actually function, I will argue below, the correlation of the inside and the outside, spirit and matter, essence and existence, that Ruether posits in her own view of reality cannot be consistently explained as simply a distinction or bifurcation within a more primordial unity (monism). (A complex form of monism does characterize her most recent book, *Gaia and God*, but this represents a shift in her cosmology that I will discuss towards the end of this chapter.) I realise that this is not a very common way of reading Ruether, but further explorations into the basic structure of her thought in the sections on nature and eschatology below, will support this claim in some detail.

I will also argue that, despite Ruether's best intentions, she ascribes ontological priority to essence rather than existence, and values universality, unity, and spirit above individuality, diversity, and matter. This connects with the above discussion, because from these ontological assumptions it follows that our common humanity is somehow more important, fundamental or "real" than our male-ness and femaleness.[30]

These comments anticipate some misgivings that I have about Ruether's theology which will become apparent in later sections.

Nevertheless, I can agree with much of what Ruether says in the area of anthropology. Her typology and description of the different feminist positions is very insightful (and would be especially fruitful if it was applied to the work of leading *contemporary* feminists). Her desire to move beyond the liberal and romanticist paradigms is also admirable. Because I believe that this entails a move beyond both a sex unity and a sex polarity position, however, I do not think that she fully succeeds in this attempt. Thus while Ruether tends towards a sex unity position, I agree with Prudence Allen that sex complementarity represents the best anthropological option. As Allen argues,

> It seems to me to be the only theory that presents an integrated view of the place of materiality in human identity and for this reason it also seems to offer the greatest possibility for fertile and creative relations between women and men. I also believe that it is not a mere coincidence that this theory was first articulated by Christian philosophers. Sex complementarity is perfectly compatible with fundamental Christian theological beliefs in the creation and the resurrection of the body.[31]

It is clear to me, on the basis of Gen. 1, that all humans—men, women and children—share the fundamental status and calling of being made in the image of God. Humankind is a bi-*unity* of male and female. Thus, with Ruether, I want to oppose androcentrism and insist that both sexes are fully human. But, unlike Ruether, I also want to insist that the *common humanity* that we share as men and women is not more fundamental to our nature than the *particular* sex to which we each belong, or *vice-versa*. There are no parents who are not *either* mothers *or* fathers because there are no *persons* who are not *gendered*. At the same time, a *man* or *woman* cannot exist without being either a male or female *person*. We experience a necessary correlation between our individuality and universality. Ontologically, I suggest, neither side of this correlation is more fundamental than the other. Thus while it may be very helpful when stressing the equality of the sexes to say that we are all fully human and made in God's image, this should not blind us from recognizing that men image God as males and women image God as females. (We also image God as, e. g., Westerners, black people, moderns, etc.)

I also agree with Ruether's rejection of androgyny on the grounds that there are no inherently masculine or feminine capacities. All humans are called to be, e. g., energetic, emotionally sensitive, clear thinking, just and trothful. The Scriptures do not divide the fruits of the Spirit (love, joy, peace, longsuffering, kindness, goodness, faithfulness, meekness, self-control, tenderheartedness, forgiveness, compassion and humility) along gender lines.[32] Nevertheless, it is important to note that a man will function intuitively as a male and a woman will make ethical decisions as a female.

An integrated, holistic anthropology, in other words, should not ignore or minimize sex and gender difference. My reading of 1 Cor. 11 in chapter 3 suggests that we should honour the fact that the sexes are a *bi*-unity as well as a bi-*unity*. This does not mean that any difference that is observed between men and women is necessarily normative. It is always possible that it is the result of harmful patterns of socialization. Sex unity theorists, in particular, are keen to attribute differences between the sexes to "nurture" rather than "nature," and their arguments are often valid. Nevertheless, it would be impossible to doubt that men and women are by nature different at least *biologically*. While a dualistic anthropology (such as Ruether's) will, in the final analysis, tend to suggest that biological processes are not fully intrinsic to us as humans and have no significant impact on post-biotic levels of functioning, a holistic anthropology must resist this. Biological processes are foundational to and thus affect the way we feel, imagine, analyze, and trust. If there is a difference between males and females at the level of genes, hormones and brain anatomy, then these differences will have an impact on the entire range of male and female behaviour. In other words, while present gender differences are not normative, it is still normative that there should be a difference between the way men and women think and feel, for example.

This line of thought should not be confused with the crass reductionism of the sociobiologists (or other sex polarity thinkers)

Biology influences but does not determine our feelings. As Mary Stewart Van Leeuwen puts it,

> Like the quarter in the juke box, which is necessary for getting a tune but does not determine which tune gets selected, so our hormones—sex-related and otherwise—produce certain tangible, physiological effects but do not "make" us act in rigidly-prescribed ways.[33]

It is also extremely important to recognize that the environment and our own "higher," or less foundational, levels of functioning can profoundly influence our biological processes. Ruether is right to stress this in her analysis of the bicameral brain.

One very legitimate objection that Ruether has to feminists who opt for romanticist forms of anthropology also serves as an important warning for all feminists who are interested in developing a non-patriarchal anthropology along the lines of sex-complementarity. Ruether rightly argues that "Women should not identify themselves with those repressed parts of the male psyche that males have projected upon them as 'feminine'."[34] In fact this concern is one of the reasons why she is even more wary of Jungian ideas in psychology than she is of the Freudian tradition.[35] I do not want to be heard as suggesting that in a perfect world women and men would be exemplars of the complementary opposites of romanticism. Normative gender differences, I believe, are real but elusive, especially when we focus on individuals rather than groups. Because there is always more to us as men and women than our sex and gender (even though no part of our existence is unaffected by our sex and gender), it is often far from clear when the differences that we observe between male and female behaviour are attributable to facets of our being other than our gender (such as our nationality, class, or sexual orientation). Even when we are confident that we have identified genuine gender differences, the fact that we live in a fallen world means that we cannot automatically assume that these differences are normative. These difficulties notwithstanding, gender differences should not be minimized or ignored in our struggle to recover what it means to be authentically male and female. The tendency of the dominant theological tradition to mis-identify good and evil, *imago dei* and fallenness, with the spiritual male and the carnal female will be most strongly opposed when we affirm that women image God with the totality of their being including their distinct bodily nature. In other words, women need to be affirmed not only as human but also as women.

II. Evil

This argument presupposes that it is still legitimate to distinguish sharply between good and evil. Although Ruether is the first to admit that "Much of the understanding of sin in patriarchal religion is inauthentic"[36] for reasons that were explored in chapter 1, she strongly disagrees with those feminists who feel that the good-evil distinction is itself an expression of patriarchal thinking.

For Ruether, the human capacity to name certain types of behaviour as "evil" or "sinful" is rooted in our capacity to distinguish between what "is" and what "ought" to be. We have the capacity to stand out against the environment and "imagine alternative images of the authentic and good self." Thus, she claims, "the very concept of evil and good is generated as the extreme polarities of the perception of an inadequate present over better possibilities."[37] In this way, we become conscious of evil in the process of disaffiliating ourselves from it, and the ideals which we project in opposition to experienced evil give rise to a particular etiology of evil.[38]

This is how Christian ideas of a "Fall" originated as a story which is symbolically constructed and mythologized as a historical "event." Stories about a primordial time when evil began (whether through the temptation of the serpent or the defeat of matriarchy by patriarchy) are human constructions. But this should not be taken to imply that evil has no historical reality outside our stories. As Ruether explains, "It simply means that we can't lose sight of the fact that the center of the drama is the human person situating itself in opposition to perceived falsifications of its own being in the name of a transcendent possibility of a good self."[39]

From this vantage point, Ruether claims that feminism no less than patriarchal forms of Christianity, clearly presupposes a radical concept of "sin" which is implicit in its own claim to judge patriarchy as evil.[40] In fact many of Ruether's most creative ideas about human evil have been worked out in relation to her perceptions of the origin and nature of patriarchy. As this area of her thought will be the special focus of chapter 5, I will limit my observations here to her more general reflections about evil.

Ruether's preferred way of talking about sin throughout her corpus is in terms of broken relationships. Thus in *The Church Against Itself*, published in 1967, she writes,

> Man's fall is summed up in the concept of "broken com-
> munity"—community broken with himself, with God, with crea-
> tion, and with his fellow man. In this self-grasping mode of
> being, he loses God and his fellow man as persons, as a "thou."
> The "thou" of the other now becomes an "it," an object to be
> manipulated by his egoistic will.[41]

In *Sexism and God-Talk*, published sixteen years later in 1983, she uses very similar language when she writes,

> [Feminism] claims that a most basic expression of human com-
> munity, the I-Thou relationship as the relationship of men and
> women, has been distorted through all known history into an
> oppressive relationship that has victimized one-half of the
> human race and turned the other half into tyrants. The primary
> alienation and distortion of human relationality is reflected in
> all dimensions of alienation: from one's self as body, from the
> other as different from oneself, from nonhuman nature, and
> from God/ess.[42]

The perception that sin "is not simply individual but refers to a fallen state of humanity"[43] is one that Ruether believes is shared by feminism and Christianity. That sin is social and not just personal is an emphasis she particularly likes in liberation theology, to which she often turns when discussing evil. Thus she writes,

> Social sin is of a different order from the sum of all the sins of
> individual sinners. It becomes a world which we inherit and
> which biases our opportunities, either as oppressed people or

as privileged people, even before we have been able to make personal choices. This means that even people of good will do evil and profit by evil because of their privileged location in this system. This sense of social sin gives liberation theology a new understanding of the Christian doctrine of inherited sin, not as sin inherited through biology, but as sin inherited through society.[44]

In this light, Ruether claims that the biblical writers were right to speak of the malevolent influence of "powers and principalities" on human life. Although she thinks that it is wrong to abstract evil into demonic powers that are beyond humanity, which she suspects is what they did, she does believe this kind of language is very meaningful as a way of referring to "the heritage of systemic social evil, which conditions our personal choices before we choose. . . ." It is therefore particularly helpful to a feminist theological perspective because "Sexism is one of these powers and principalities of historical, systematic, social evil that conditions our choices as males and females before our birth."[45]

Liberation theology again proves to be a source of inspiration for Ruether on the issues of redemptive suffering, theodicy and the cross. Noting that the meaning of the cross is very different for those who have suffered in the struggle for justice than it is for theologians living in a more comfortable environment, she appeals to the convictions and intuitions of "liberation Christians" in order to find an alternative to the substitutionary model of the atonement that is so precious to Catholic and Protestant orthodoxy. She writes,

> Too often Christians have treated the sufferings of Christ as some kind of cosmic legal transaction with God to pay for the sins of humanity, as though anyone's sufferings and death could actually "pay for" others' sins! Christ's cross is used to inculcate a sense of masochistic guilt, unworthiness and passivity in Christians. To accept and endure evil is regarded as redemptive. Liberation Christians say that God does not desire anyone's sufferings, least of all Jesus', any more than God desires or blesses poverty. Suffering, death and poverty are evils. God comes not to sanctify, but to deliver us from these

evils. Solidarity with the poor and with those who suffer does not mean justifying these evils, but struggling to overcome them.[46]

Continuing her polemic against traditional Christian thinking, Ruether argues that we should not allow ideas about the resurrection to deny "the stark meaning of the cry of Jesus from the cross: 'My God, my God, why hast thou forsaken me?' "[47] Neither should the resurrection "blind us to the unresolved evils of history." Therefore she argues,

> We forget that the cross is not initially a symbol of the victory of God, but a victory for the powers and principalities. We transform it into a symbol of the victory of God only if we deny this victory of evil by continuing Jesus' struggle against it. We should not stifle the cry of Jesus by spiritualizing this victory over death, but, instead, let it continue to ring out from the cross, from all the crosses of unjust suffering throughout history, as a question mark about the nature of present reality.[48]

The mention of unjust suffering brings us to the issue of theodicy. In typical debates among philosophers of religion, the problem of evil is usually posed in terms of the logical incongruity of there being a loving and all-powerful God who allows human suffering. In answer to this perennial Western theological question, Ruether suggests that we only see God as an omnipotent sovereign because we have made the mistake of modelling "Him" after emperors and despots to whom subjects relate as mere dependents. That this is not how God relates to the world, however, should be clear from Christ's death and from the martyrdom of the innocent. Ruether argues that the cross points towards an alternative model of God than the omnipotent deity of classical theism. She writes,

> The God revealed in Jesus has identified with the victims of history and has abandoned the thrones of the mighty. In Jesus' cross God abandons God's power into the human condition utterly and completely so that we might not abandon each other. God has become a part of the struggle of life against

death. This is perhaps why those who struggle for justice do not ask the question of theodicy. They know that the true God does not support the thrones of the mighty, but is one of them.[49]

Ruether is right to insist on the good/evil distinction. Rather than simply relating it to the human capacity to choose between relatively desirable and undesirable possibilities, however, I would prefer to root it ontologically in the spirituality of life itself, in which we are constantly confronted with the antithetical ways of Life or Death, Wisdom or Folly, the Truth of God or the Lie of the Devil. And while Ruether follows modern theology's tendency to equate the Fall with an ontological "gap" between essence and existence, I am convinced, as I will argue in the next chapter, that her desire to delegitimate patriarchy would have a firmer foundation if she saw the origin of evil as a historical rupture that occurred within an originally good creation.

On a more positive note, I like Ruether's definition of evil as broken relationship. This fits well with my discussion in chapter 3 of the limit experience of disconnection. It is an important question how relationships between men and women, humanity and the earth, and humanity and God became broken. The next chapter will explore whether the rupturing of the relationship between the sexes is more "primordial" than the others as Ruether often seems to suggest.

I also appreciate Ruether's comments on social sin as an environment which we all inherit. As I have argued elsewhere, we are all simultaneously victims and agents of sin.[50] The evil that we commit (and for which we are responsible) is always related to the evil from which we have suffered. As Ruether rightly recognizes, individualistic views of sin cannot capture the complexity of the way evil is transmitted between people and across the generations.

She is also right to connect talk of powers and principalities to the social power of evil. It is unfortunate that she doesn't integrate this important biblical topic in a more detailed way into her cultural analysis.[51] It is also regrettable that she does not connect her comments on the powers and principalities to a view of the atonement. As is clear from some of her comments above, she strongly opposes the substitutionary model (which is so popular with conservative Christians). She would seem to see the significance of the cross in terms of the moral influence model (for which most liberal Christian opt).[52] Yet as Gustaf Aulén recognized in the 1930s, the Christus Victor model of the atonement is a viable alternative even though it has been ignored by theologians for centuries.[53] What is particularly significant here is that this model sees the cross as the place where Jesus takes on and defeats the powers and principalities. Reta Halteman Finger, building on the work of Thomas Finger, has rightly argued that this model not only has extremely strong biblical support, but also has rich implications for a feminist view of the cross as it highlights how Jesus' death and resurrection function to "unmask" the powers and principalities for those who are willing to continue Jesus' struggle against them in our generation.[54]

While this important topic cannot be explored in this study in any detail, I will return to it briefly in the concluding chapter. The conclusion will also contain some comments on God's "omnipotence," understood not in the metaphysical language of classical theism, which Ruether is right to reject, but in terms of the confessional language of the Scriptures. What is at stake here is the biblical hope that God ultimately has the power to overcome evil, and thus patriarchy, once and for all.

III. Mariology

While the relevance of the category of evil to a feminist theology is immediately obvious, Mariology is one area of traditional theology that would seem, at first glance, to be beyond redemption. To many Protestants, such as myself, this strikes us as no great loss, and we are not likely to be sufficiently motivated to see if this is something that can be successfully re-thought. In this respect, Mariology appears much like the "infamous" Pauline material on women does to non-evangelicals. The idea that this is something that we can wrest back from the conservatives is viewed as literally incredible because it so clearly epitomizes all that is wrong with the Christian tradition. Many simply assume that it is not worth investing the time to prove otherwise to others, or even to themselves.

Ruether's Roman Catholic background no doubt has a lot to do with why she has not been content to dismiss Mariology without further ado. In fact, some of her most original ideas, in my opinion, address the possibility of formulating an alternative Mariology, or doctrine of the church as symbolically female, "that would allow us to name sexism itself as sin and point toward the liberation of women and men from the dualisms of carnal femaleness and spiritual femininity."[55]

In her book *Mary—The Feminine Face of the Church*, she presents a few suggestions along these lines, although her tendency is to suggest that as Jesus' disciple and friend and as the first person to understand the resurrection faith, Mary Magdalene is a far more positive female symbol for the church than the Virgin Mary who has come to overshadow her.[56] But in *Sexism and God-Talk*, Ruether's ideas have developed to the point where she can argue for a "liberation Mariology" that draws strongly on the biblical tradition and makes Luke's portrayal of the mother of Jesus the central focus.[57]

According to Ruether, Luke "goes out of his way to stress that Mary's motherhood is a free choice."[58] This is why she does not even consult Joseph after her conversation with the angel, but makes her own decision (Lk. 1:38). Ruether suggests that this act of faith has major implications for how we see the relationship between God and humanity. She writes,

> In contrast to the patriarchal theories of divine grace ex-
> emplified in Augustine and Calvin, Lucan Mariology suggests
> a real co-creatorship between God and humanity, or, in this
> case, woman. The free act of faith is possible only when we can
> recognize the genuine unity between response to God and our
> own liberation. Faith ceases to be heteronomous submission to
> external authorities and becomes a free act.[59]

As Ruether continues her argument, the extent to which she is breaking with traditional ideas that conceive of God's presence with us in terms of a relationship between master and slave or king and subject becomes even more clear. She writes,

Only through that free human responsiveness to God is God enabled to become the transformer of history. Without such faith, no miracles can happen. When such faith is absent, Christ can do nothing. This is the radical dependence of God on humanity, the other side of our dependence on God, which patriarchal theology has generally denied. Mary's faith makes possible God's entrance into history.[60]

Mary is also an important figure for modern spirituality and theology, Ruether suggests, because she personifies those who will be exalted by God. It is particularly significant that a woman like her is identified with the New Israel in the Magnificat for Ruether, because,

As a woman, specifically a woman from among the poorer classes of a colonized people under the mighty empire of Rome, she represents the oppressed community that is to be lifted up and filled with good things in the messianic revolution. Mary as Church represents God's "preferential option for the poor," to use the language of Latin-American liberation theology.[61]

If we view the female personification of the church with a focus on woman as the oppressed of oppressed, as Mary was, then, in contrast to reinforcing a view of carnal femaleness, such imagery can encourage us to see such women as models of faith in such a way that "their liberation becomes the special locus of the believing and liberated community."[62]

Ruether also believes that this perspective enables us to transform the view of power implicit in the traditional gender imagery of Christ and the church conceived as a static hierarchical relationship between a dominant male and a submissive female. Seen in the light of a liberation Mariology, Ruether proposes that,

[W]hat we see here is an ongoing process of *kenosis* and transformation. God's power no longer remains in Heaven where it can be used as a model of the "thrones of the mighty."

In the iconoclastic and messianic prophet, it has been emptied
out into the human situation of suffering and hope.[63]

We will see this view of power echoed in Ruether's proposals in the
areas of ecclesiology and Christology.

Ruether has convinced me that the idea of a feminist Mariology
is not an oxymoron. There is much in her approach with which I can
agree enthusiastically. Ruether's comments about power and
kenosis, for example, resonate well with the exegesis of Eph. 5 that
I offered in chapter 3. Her description of Mary's "co-creatorship"
with God fits closely, I believe, with my own ideas about "co-partnership" also presented in the previous chapter.[64]

Mary has always been held up as an outstanding exemplar of
the "heteronomous submission" that Ruether rightly finds so offensive. I particularly like the fact that she uses the Scriptures to
challenge the tradition rather than merely assuming that they are
also part of the problem.[65] Her ideas on this topic would have been
even more valuable if she had anticipated and defended herself
against some of the criticisms many Christians will no doubt have
against a view that sees our relationship to God as one of co-
creativity or co-partnership. As she does not, and as the same
criticisms could be aimed at my own position, I will offer a few
suggestions.

It might be argued that both Ruether and I both play down the
necessary hierarchy involved in what is a central biblical concern:
that we should *obey* God. I am happy to admit that submission to
God's will is all-important. What I take exception to, as Ruether
does, is the assumption that what God requires of us is in any way
heteronomous. It is the presence of sin and alienation that makes
submission to God appear this way. In his reflection on the command
not to eat of the tree of good and evil in Gen. 2, Paul Ricoeur
captures this when he writes,

For an innocent freedom, this limitation would not be felt as
an interdiction; but we no longer know what that primordial
authority, contemporaneous with the birth of finite freedom,
is; in particular, we no longer know what a *limit* that does not

repress, but orients and guards freedom, could be like; we no longer have access to that creative limit. We are acquainted only with the limit that constrains; authority becomes interdiction under the regime of fallen freedom.[66]

The call to obedience is the call to turn from our alienated stance of autonomy back to partnership with, *responsi*bility to, and dependence on God, who is the Ground of our being. As Hendrik Hart argues,

We may characterize the dependence relation as a tuning of wills. It is important to realize that it's never a contest of wills, but a relating of our will to God's. . . . If what we want is a way of life, we must go The Way of The Life, that is, seek The Truth, that is, let the Word come into our flesh, let *God's will* become what we experience as *our life.*[67]

To follow Jesus is to internalize and thus incarnate the will of God. Because of our sin, this is a struggle. Yet if we believe that we can be restored to partnership with our Creator, then we can trust that there will not be a tension between God's will and the will of our "authentic selves." It is interesting that Jam. 1:25 opposes both our humanistic notions of autonomy and our "Christian" views of heteronomous obedience when it refers to the internalization of God's perfect law as leading to blessing and giving *freedom.*[68]

The Spanish liberation theologian Pedro Trigo has made some helpful observations about the non-heteronomic implications of Yahweh's promise to Jeremiah and Ezekiel that the law shall be written on our hearts. He writes,

Religious relationships and moral norms are no longer to be something external and foreign to us. In the covenant to come, God will place the divine law in our very hearts. The law of our heart is the very law of God. When we obey our deepest inner pulsations, we shall be obeying God, as well: Morality is naturalized and religion humanized.[69]

Wolfhart Pannenberg has also reflected on this topic at some length. He argues persuasively that to obey God is not to disregard our selves, but involves relating to our true selfhood and proper destiny. He writes,

> Human beings owe it to themselves—that is, to the true self of their as yet unrealized destiny—to correspond to this destiny of theirs and so to themselves. To that extent all responsibility is responsibility to the self. A responsibility that was not a responsibility to the self could have only a heteronomic basis; it could be based only on a norm that is forced upon human beings and has no relation to their selfhood. And in fact agents can feel responsible in relation to a truly heteronomic norm only as long as they (mistakenly) regard this norm as a condition for their true selfhood. It must not be said, therefore, that human responsibility to God is opposed to responsibility to the self. Responsibility to God can be meaningfully asserted only as a particular form of responsibility to the self, on the ground that the true selfhood, the destiny, of human beings is grounded in God and can be achieved only by his power.[70]

I am confident that Ruether would be as sympathetic as I am to the way Trigo and Pannenberg have attempted to develop a non-heteronomic understanding of what it means to obey God. Such an approach does raise some interesting anthropological questions, however. Where exactly in reality do we locate that "selfhood," which Pannenberg says "is not yet completely possessed"? If we can't point to this "authentic" self and do not (yet) fully experience it, then what is it that we are talking about? Whether Ruether's anthropology or cosmology can adequately handle such questions is a topic to which I shall return in the concluding chapter.

IV. Ecclesiology

As Ruether approaches the issue of Mariology in *Sexism and God-Talk* primarily in terms of its function as symbolic ecclesiology, it is fitting that the church should be the next topic of discussion. Like all Christian feminists, Ruether is concerned to promote the ordination of women. For her, however, this is not to be pursued in isolation, but is part of a wider concern to reorient our whole understanding of ministry within the church away from clericalism.

As an alternative she advocates "the Gospel concept of ministry as *diaconia* or service." "*Diaconia*," Ruether explains, "is *kenotic* or self-emptying of power as domination. Ministry transforms leadership from power over others to empowerment of others . . . . Ministry overcomes competitive one-up, one-down relationships and generates relations of mutual empowerment."[71]

It would be a mistake to see these ideas about power and service as applicable only to those who hold official positions of church leadership. It is her contention that the whole community, and not some sacerdotal caste, should be seen as "the agents of the ministry and mission of the Church."[72] A typical faith community, Ruether argues, is inevitably made up of people who posses a wide variety of gifts. Different people should therefore be allowed to function as administrators, teachers, liturgical poets, social analysts and so forth in accordance with their natural abilities. Diversity of talent is good and all should be encouraged to use their gifts for the sake of empowering other members of the community. The role of the teacher, for example, is far from authoritarian or paternalistic in this perspective. In sharp contrast to the kind of "teaching" that merely perpetrates the gap between the "experts" and the "ignorant"—an exercise which she says "is not real teaching, but the clericalization of learning"—Ruether envisions a style of teaching that "gradually creates fellow teachers who can teach others." In this way "[t]he community as a whole becomes empowered to articulate the faith and to speak the Word to each other."[73]

Ruether also opposes the monopolization of the sacraments and the liturgy by a priestly caste. Following the example of the Italian Basic Community Movement, she refers to the process of declericalizing these aspects of the church's life as an exercise in "reappropriation theology." As she explains, the "[r]eappropriation of the sacraments means that not only the exercise but also the interpretation of the sacraments arises from the community's collective experience of its life in grace." Thus when someone is baptized, all members of the community "midwife [his or her] rebirth from alienated to authentic life." Penance is no longer "the disciplinary tool of any elite," for it now means members of the community forgiving one another. Likewise, the "Eucharist is not an objectified piece of bread or cup of wine that is magically transformed into the body and blood of Christ. Rather, it is the people, the ecclesia, who are being transformed into the new humanity, infused with the blood of new life. The symbols stand in the midst of and represent that communal reality."[74]

Ruether proposes that rites such as baptism and the Eucharist could be led by a variety of people at different times. To represent the community in this way, she believes, is not something that only a trained priest can do as it does not require specialized skills or learning. "It is significant," she writes, "that the New Testament contains many words for special charisms and skills, but that they are not identified with special offices responsible for the sacraments of baptism or Eucharist."[75] To declericalize such roles need not mean that these tasks will be performed carelessly. If the example of European basic communities is followed, small study groups could be set up to reflect on Scripture and tradition to prepare members for leading the worship and liturgical life of the community.

But in the final analysis, Ruether is not very optimistic about reforming the institutional churches as their present hierarchical structures mean that movement in the direction of de-clericalization has to be clergy-led. Such reform has occurred, as in the case of the Italian Basic Christian Community of St. Paul's Outside the Walls in Rome which began with the vision of the Benedictine abbot, Giovanni Franzoni. But before we become too enthusiastic about the possibilities of reforming institutional churches on the basis of this story, Ruether would say, we should also note that all official ties between this community and the Roman Catholic church were severed after Franzoni was eventually stripped of his priest's orders by the Roman hierarchy.

There are many base communities which succeed in maintaining a closer relationship with the institutional church, as is the case in Latin America. While many carry out their own agenda quite apart from the objectives of the hierarchy, Ruether points out that they do not confront clericalism and seldom address the feminist issue. This is a pattern that also tends to recur with churches that stay within the old institutional frameworks.[76]

"The feminist issue" is clearly not something that Ruether is prepared to sacrifice. She even goes as far as to say that "Without a community committed to liberation from sexism, all questions such as the forms of ministry or mission are meaningless."[77] The only alternative to the limited opportunities for change that exist within the institutional churches, she suggests, is the creation of autonomous feminist base communities. The kind of community that she has in mind is one that "takes responsibility for reflecting on, celebrating, and acting on the understanding of redemption as liberation from patriarchy."[78]

Ruether is quick to add that this strategy "does not necessarily imply a sectarian rejection of institutional churches"[79]—a stance that would not be compatible with Ruether's rejection of feminist separatism.[80] Instead she envisions the possibility of people being members of traditional congregations while also being involved in this kind of alternative support community. If this was the case, there is also the possibility that some could draw on their experiences within their base community to communicate new options to their institutional church. For those who maintain this dual membership, says Ruether, "[t]he relationship between the two becomes a creative dialectic rather than a schismatic impasse."[81]

Ruether's reflections on the possibility of a feminist base community movement in *Sexism and God-Talk* proved to be quite prophetic, for in the same year that this book was published a conference called "Woman Church Speaks" took place in Chicago. In Ruether's words,

> It was the first effort to define and to collectively experience a new stance toward being feminists in exodus within the church. It defined a new theological and practical standpoint that intends to claim the authentic theological ground of being church, and no longer to be defined by the *ecclesia* of patriarchy nor to ask for inclusion to ministry or for the right to experience sacramental life in its terms.[82]

This conference has proved to be a key event in the rise of a movement of feminist liturgical communities which has come to be known as "Women-Church" and Ruether's book of the same title charts the history and nature of this movement in a way that suggests that it is remarkably compatible with her earlier ecclesiological suggestions.[83] The 140 pages of liturgies that Ruether has collected for publication in this book, together with her own commentary, make it clear that an explicit focus on liberation from patriarchy is for her not just one of many concerns, but *the* defining feature of the authentic church.[84] But, as Ruether continues to insist, the rejection of patriarchy does not entail the rejection of males. Separatism, as we have already noted, is not to be embraced as a total ideology. It is merely a necessary stage in a larger process which has as its goal "the formation of a critical culture and community of women *and men* in exodus from patriarchy."[85]

That does not mean this can happen overnight, or even in the foreseeable future. "Patriarchy," warns Ruether, "is too old and too deeply rooted both in our psyches and in our culture and collective life to be quickly analyzed, rejected, and then overcome in [a] new unity of men and women."[86] But this does not mean that the situation is hopeless, just that we must not be tempted to take short-cuts. What is crucial is that males desire genuine change, and explore how they too might become liberated from the de-humanizing impact that patriarchy has had on them. They must thus form their own critical culture of liberation in a way that "truly complements the feminist exodus and allows the formation of real dialogue." Only then can a genuine cohumanity of men and women develop. Reflecting on this future possibility, Ruether writes.

> I assume the name for this liberated humanity would then no longer be "Women-Church," but simply "Church"; that is, the authentic community of exodus from oppression that has been heralded by the traditions of religious and social liberation but, until now, [has been] corrupted by reversion to new forms of the *ecclesia* of patriarchy.[87]

At the climax to the sermon that she preached at the Chicago conference, Ruether affirmed her desire for this new cohumanity by saying,

> We call our brothers to join us in exodus from the land of patriarchy, to join us in our common quest for that promised land where there will be no more war, no more burning children, no more violated women, no more discarded elderly, no more rape of the earth. Together, let us break up that great idol and grind it into powder; dismantle the great Leviathan of violence and misery who threatens to destroy the earth, plow it back into the soil, and transform it back into the means of peace and plenty, so that all the children of earth can sit down together at the banquet of life.[88]

The passion of these words serves to emphasize the commitment and sense of urgency that underlies her ecclesiology, and her theology in general.

I fully share Ruether's misgivings about clericalism and am very much in favour of her views of power and authentic leadership. I am more ambivalent, however, about the "reappropriation theology" she advocates. I like the fact that she stresses that the interpretation of the sacraments should arise out of the whole community's experience of grace. What troubles me is the fact that she then proceeds to tell us in the same paragraph precisely how certain sacraments should now be interpreted![89] I am sure that the last thing that Ruether would want to be seen as doing is replacing traditional clericalism with a new leadership made up of an elite group of feminist theologians! The way she expresses herself, however, does make her vulnerable to this accusation.

I trust that Ruether's interpretation of the significance of baptism, penance, and Eucharist is itself a reflection of the ideas and practices of a community or communities with which she has been involved. But other communities that are attempting to move beyond clericalism could interpret these sacraments quite differently, and it is a shame that Ruether does not explicitly acknowledge this.

Her emphasis on the responsibility and involvement of the whole community in these sacraments is vital if *de facto* forms of clericalism are to be avoided in communities that no longer ordain clergy. Here all non-clericalist Christians would agree, I suggest. Yet Ruether's reinterpretation of baptism, penance, and the Eucharist is not just a reiteration of this point. She not only replaces the role of the priest with that of the faith community but also seems to focus on the symbolizing of the *community's* life in such a way that *God's* presence and activity is nowhere to be seen.

Her reinterpretation of "penance," for example, speaks of fellow Christians forgiving each other (as indeed it should) but makes no attempt to connect this to our reconciliation with God. Likewise in her description of our role as "midwives" for those who are baptized into new life, she make no reference to the role of the Spirit who gives birth to us in this context (cf. the *ek tou pneumatos* of Jn. 3:8). Either the fact that she comes across as emphasising the sacraments' power to symbolize the authenticity and new life of the *ecclesia* in a way that ignores the community's covenant with, dependence on, and embodiment of *God* is accidental and unintended, or this reflects "reappropriation theology" done by a community with "humanistic" rather than theistic leanings.[90]

Either way, extreme conservatives who tend to see any attempt to take power away from the clergy as an expression of an anarchistic desire to abolish all hierarchies including the hierarchy of God over humanity will find their worst fears confirmed in Ruether's discussion of reappropriation theology. This makes the task of reformation unnecessarily difficult in my opinion.

The problem of insufficient continuity with traditional faith and piety also occurs in her liturgical and ecclesiastical suggestions and reflections in *Women-Church* where there is so little emphasis on *worshipping* God/ess.[91] Ruether's ecclesiology would be greatly strengthened, I believe, if she reflected on how worship of God/ess is intrinsic to being authentically and fully human, and on how such worship functions to delegitimize the idols and powers and principalities that grip our imaginations.[92] When the early Christians confessed Jesus as Lord, to cite one example, they were also articulating and strengthening their conviction that Caesar was *not*

Lord (cf. Acts 17:7). In this context, Ruether might also broaden her welcome emphasis on the Spirit[93] to explore what we can learn from the charismatic movement about styles of worship that involve the "reappropriation" of dimensions of our humanity that are depreciated in our rationalistic culture.

Ruether's comments in *Sexism and God-Talk*,[94] give the impression that she does not think that a church needs a particular group of leaders who are responsible for overseeing the life of the community to ensure that there is a *coherence* to the many other forms of ministry which she recommends. One way I would like to supplement her suggestions is by pointing out the need for this form of discernment. Given the fact that we need to work redemptively within the present system where possible, present leaders who are ordained and employed by the church could play this role, while making it a priority to use such a position to encourage the development of other forms of ministry from other members of the community.[95]

The problem of clericalism is compounded by the tendency many Christians have to reduce the Church, in the New Testament sense of *ecclesia*, to the activities of churches, denominations, and other organizations that are "ecclesiastical" in the modern sense of the term. Clergy, along with missionaries and those in holy orders, thus come to be seen as the only Christians engaged in "full-time" Christian service. Ruether appeals to the communal notion of *ecclesia* to undercut clericalism, but does not use it to correct this "ecclesiastical" narrowing of its meaning. I find it more helpful to distinguish between the Church, or the Body of Christ, which is called to be communally active in distinctive and redemptive ways in all areas of culture, and the church, which is one particular institutional expression of the Church that has the special task of nurturing the faith of Christians so that they are empowered to live out the Gospel in the rest of their lives.

This distinction is one of the strengths of the Kuyperian tradition well worth incorporating into a Christian feminist theology.[96] With this broader view of the Church, which firmly rejects a division of life into sacred and secular spheres, we can combat clericalism in the knowledge that even before we start, the present role of clergy is greatly relativized. At the same time, such a perspective also highlights the fact that we cannot criticize hierarchical and anti-communitarian patterns of relating in ecclesiastical organizations without also opposing them in all the other expressions of the Body of Christ. The relevance of this to the way Christian theologians should exercise their power in the wider Christian community is something to which I shall return later in this chapter.

V. Christology
Ecclesiology and Christology are clearly treated as separate categories in most theologies. The fact that Ruether blurs the distinction between Christ and the Church by rejecting the idea that Jesus was the *unique* incarnation of God who atoned for our sins on the cross will be seen as a serious departure from biblical orthodoxy by many Christians. It is nevertheless the case that in the area of Christology in particular, Ruether supports her proposals by appealing to the Scriptures.

As an alternative to the imperial and androcentric Christologies of the Christian tradition, Ruether appeals to the model of "the prophetic iconoclastic Christ" of the gospels, who opposes hierarchy and oppression and affirms women. It is important to note that in this model of Christ, "His ability to be liberator does not reside in his maleness, but, on the contrary, in the fact that he has renounced this system of domination and seeks to embody in his person the new humanity of service and mutual empowerment."[97]

But while Ruether claims Jesus' maleness has no ontological significance theologically speaking, she does interpret the fact that Jesus was historically a male in an interesting counter-patriarchal way by suggesting that his gender "has social symbolic significance in the framework of patriarchal privilege." Thus she writes,

In this sense Jesus as the Christ, the representative of liberated humanity and the liberating Word of God, manifests the *kenosis of patriarchy*, the announcement of the new humanity through a lifestyle that discards hierarchical caste privilege and speaks on behalf of the lowly. In a similar way, the femaleness of the social and religiously outcast who respond to him has social symbolic significance as a witness against the same idolatrous system of patriarchal privilege.[98]

Ruether is well aware that arguments such as the ones summarized above may not solve all the problems a contemporary Christian woman may face because, in the final analysis, she "is still taught to believe in a male Christ as the sole and unique expression of redeeming grace" with the consequence that this "maleness of Christ still distances the woman from full representation in the new humanity."[99] In other words, what she needs for the affirmation of her own personhood as a woman is a redemptrix or female redeeming figure.

In response to this problem, Ruether reiterates a conviction that she expressed at least as early as *Faith and Fratricide* (1974) by asserting that "Christ . . . is not to be encapsulated once-for-all in the historical Jesus."[100] While she fully believes that Jesus can be affirmed by feminist theology as "a positive model of redemptive humanity," we must also recognize that

> [T]his model must be seen as partial and fragmentary, disclosing from the perspective of one person, circumscribed in time, culture, and gender, something of the fullness we seek. We need other clues and models as well, models drawn from women's experience, from many times and cultures.[101]

To this end, Ruether appeals to the way Christ has been seen by those who have held to what she calls "Spirit Christologies."[102] This tradition sees women and men as spokespersons of the risen Christ who are sometimes encountered as exemplars of Christ. Thus when *The Acts of the Martyrs of Lyons and Vienne* describes the martyrdom of Blandina, the witnesses, so the story goes, saw "the One who was crucified for them . . . in the form of their sister." Similarly, one of the Montanist prophetesses claimed that she had a vision of Christ "in the likeness of a woman."[103]

In these examples of early Christian prophetism, Christ is not seen as what Ruether calls a "past perfect historical Christ" who has become separated from the ongoing Spirit. Instead Christ is seen in terms of a power that continues to be revealed in women and men in the present. When the institutionalized church opposes this way of thinking, Ruether observes that Spirit Christologies take on an anti-establishment character by proclaiming a coming Third Age when the limitations of orthodox theology will be overcome.

This new stage in the history of redemption often included the coming of a female redemptrix. In the thirteenth and fourteenth centuries, two women, Prous Boneta and Guglielma, were hailed as the incarnation of the Holy Spirit, while the eighteenth-century Shakers looked to the arrival of a female Christ to disclose the final stage of redemption.

Such a tradition, especially in its early examples, is highly suggestive for a feminist theology, Ruether believes, as it supplements the prophetic iconoclastic image of Jesus that we find in the gospels. Within this framework, Ruether can continue to affirm Jesus as a paradigm of the Christ in a non-exclusive way. Thus she writes,

> Christ, as redemptive person and Word of God, is not to be encapsulated "once-for-all" in the historical Jesus. The Christian community continues Christ's identity. As vine and branches Christic personhood continues in our sisters and brothers. In the language of early Christian prophetism, we can encounter Christ *in the form of our sister.* Christ, the liberated humanity, is not confined to a static perfection of one person two thousand years ago. Rather, redemptive humanity goes ahead of us, calling us to yet incompleted dimensions of human liberation.[104]

Ruether will probably find less support from conservative Christians for her proposed reconstruction of Christology than she will for her suggestions in any other area of theology. Evangelical feminists will no doubt share these reservations, although they will appreciate her comments on the prophetic iconoclastic Christ and her ideas about seeing Jesus' maleness as the *kenosis* of patriarchy.

These relatively uncontroversial aspects of her Christology are certainly insightful. Her assertion that God's incarnation as a man does not imply the ontological superiority of males can be strengthened, however, if we note the importance of beginning our reflections on gender in the light of a robust doctrine of creation. Once we affirm that both sexes were made in the image of God, it becomes far easier to see that God's incarnation as a human *male* was necessary for purely historical reasons. If we understand the incarnation in the light of redemption without sufficient attention to creational concerns, we are more likely to overemphasize the ontological significance of Christ's specific gender. Perhaps some of the groups who have opted for a Spirit Christology approached this subject from such a perspective and, unable to relativize the maleness of Jesus in the light of a strong creation theology, felt compelled to speak of a female redemptrix as the only way to hold to an egalitarian position.[105]

The most controversial aspect of Ruether's Christology for most evangelical feminists will be her claim that Jesus was/is not the unique incarnation of God. Most will part company with her at this point. Although I have described myself as an evangelical feminist, I have a lot of sympathy for Ruether's Christological position as a whole, although I would not express myself in exactly the same way.

In my view, Jesus is clearly a *unique* incarnation of God but is not the *only* incarnation of God. While Jesus fully incarnates God as a male Jew living in the first century A.D., God can not be fully or exhaustively incarnated by one human (or even one type of creature such as *homo sapiens*—a topic to which I will return in the next section).

It makes no sense, I contend, to say that the man Jesus was God. According to the biblical worldview, as I understand it, this would be the ultimate "category mistake" for God is not a creature and a creature cannot become God.[106] What creatures can do, however, is *incarnate* God. *As creatures*, they can reveal/embody/incarnate the presence of God. Thus Jesus as a Jewish male incarnated God. This is what John means when he talks about the Word becoming flesh (Jn. 1:14). As a human being who embodied/obeyed/expressed the Word of God for life, he was "the Way, the Truth and the Life" (14:6).

What is unique about Jesus is that he is sinless (Heb. 4:15). It is crucial to realize that it is our sin and not our creatureliness that prevents us from incarnating God with the totality of who we are, as Jesus did. Thus Jesus differs from us by successfully revealing what all humans are called to be and do. This is why Luke, after telling us about the voice from heaven which says to Jesus "You are my son" after his baptism (3:22), gives us a long genealogy (vv. 23-37) in which Jesus is shown to be a descendent of Adam—and he too is called "son of God" (v. 37). Similarly, Matthew, in 2:15, quotes Hos. 11:1 in which God says, "Out of Egypt I called my son." By means of a verse that originally referred to Israel, Matthew is saying that Jesus is the true Israel; that is, he reveals what Israel was called to be.

An essential part of the Good News is that in Christ we can now be who we are called to be. Thus John, in his Christologically focused prologue, does not just focus on Jesus but connects his significance to the status and calling of his followers. He writes, "Yet to all who received him to those who believed in his name, he gave them the right to become children of God—children born not of natural decision or a husband's will, but born of God." (1:12,13 cf. 1 Jn. 3:1-2). Thus a high Christology can lead to a high ecclesiology. Perhaps Paul's phrase in Rom. 8:29, which also echoes this theme, best captures both what is unique and what is not unique about Jesus. While this is usually read as claiming that "he is the *firstborn* among many brothers and sisters," we must also hear this as saying that "he is the firstborn *among many brothers and sisters.*"

Ruether uses the image of the vine and the branches to say something quite similar in the final quotation in my summary of her position offered above. What Jesus means by this phrase in Jn. 15:5 is, I believe, very close to what Paul wishes to convey with his image of Christ as the head of the body.[107] An important biblical passage in this context is Eph. 1:18-23, which concludes with a reference to what I interpret as a *corporate* Christology. Christ who has been raised above all rule and authority, says Paul, is the head of the church, which as his body is nothing less than "the fullness of him who fills everything in every way" (v. 23).[108]

For Paul, to be in Christ is to follow Jesus in his mission of redemption. This includes taking up our cross, to use the language that Jesus himself used to his followers (Mk. 8:34; Lk. 9:23; 14:27), and bearing the consequences of the sins of others.[109] Thus in Rom. 8:17, Paul articulates his own "Spirit Christology" by connecting what it means to be a co-heir with Christ to sharing in his suffering. Thus in Col. 1:24, he can even say "I fill up in my flesh what is still lacking in regard to Christ's afflictions." In this sense, in the present age we are all called to "Christic personhood," to borrow one of Ruether's phrases. Thus I can believe that the early Christians who witnessed the martyrdom of Blandina saw Christ in the form of their sister. What this means is that the call to follow Jesus, which is the call to incarnate God, to be Christ to the world, is not a call to hubris or worldly self-glorification.

In the New Testament, the healing of creation is often connected to the theme of God becoming "all in all." The overcoming of the divisions in the Church mentioned in Gal. 3:28 and elsewhere is connected by Paul to this theme in Col. 3:11 (cf. Col. 1:15-20). I take this to mean that in the eschaton, when Christ hands over the kingdom to the Father, when all evil has been purged from the earth, and when God is finally "all in all" (see 1 Cor. 15:20-28),[110] we will all incarnate God, as male and female, Jew and Gentile, slave and free, as fully as Jesus already has. The implications of such an approach to Christology for the way we understand the calling of the Church in this age cannot be underestimated. Hendrik Hart asks some excellent questions when he writes,

> Could it be that we are not prepared to let Jesus' incarnation continue in our lives? Is that why God is hidden to modern people or is not perceived among the suffering? Because we keep God hidden in Christian churches? Is that why [a contemporary atheistic] philosopher [such as] Kai Nielsen does not recognize the God of the church as a suitable God for modern people? Because to that church God is allowed to be incarnate only in Jesus? And because in Jesus, the Son-of-man, we see only God and not ourselves? And therefore not ourselves as sons-and-daughters of God?[111]

These brief comments cannot begin to do justice to the complex topic of Christology. In a more detailed discussion, I would attempt to complement this proposed "high Christology from below" by also approaching the topic in terms of a "low Christology from above." I would also discuss how both approaches relate to the spirit, if not the letter, of the famous Chalcedonian formulation. That would go beyond the scope of this study, however. But hopefully enough has been said to show why I think Ruether's Christological position, which begins to move in the same direction as the suggestions I have offered above, should be taken seriously on biblical grounds, and should not be dismissed too quickly simply because it sounds so different from the safe familiarity of our various "orthodoxies."

VI. Nature
Ruether's proposals for the way we should view nature, and her concern that we develop a profound sense of "eco-justice" are very significant aspects of her theology. Her awareness that the quest for ecological shalom must play an integral role in any viable liberation theology, and her realization that the domination and hence liberation of woman and nature are interconnected can be seen relatively early in her corpus.[112] The following discussion will focus on the fairly systematic reflections on "an ecological-feminist theology of nature" which occur in a section under this title in *Sexism and God-Talk*.[113]

This material, which is crucial for grasping the contours of her cosmology, presents more difficulties of interpretation than anything else in her corpus that I have examined so far. The reading that I will propose here is a rather "unorthodox" one, at least to the extent that I can find virtually no support for it in the work of other Ruether interpreters. What I consider to be some of the best evidence for my interpretation will be presented in the following discussion of Ruether's view of eschatology and God. So it is important to take the argument of this and the next two sections together.

In her discussion of "an ecological-feminist theology of nature," Ruether rejects the dominant Western view that has been modelled on the great chain of being, the highest point of which is seen as non-material spirit while the lowest and most inferior part is believed to consist of non-spiritual matter. As an alternative, she proposes that we do not dichotomize spirit and matter in this fashion but conceive of them as "the inside and outside of the same thing."[114] Two years earlier she used similar terms in addressing a different topic when she argued that in opposition to the dualistic interpretations of New Testament scholars as diverse as Brandon, Cullmann and Hengel,

> [T]he messianic idea [of the Bible] . . . is *both* religious and political, both transcendent and this-worldly, both *inward and outward* [my emphasis]. The kingdom of God is a holistic vision of this world, the created world as it is supposed to be, as when Jesus said, "God's will is done on earth." It means both reconciliation with God, when people obey God from the heart, *and* justice on earth and harmony between humanity and nature. These are not two different things, but, in fact, two sides of the same thing.[115]

Here, the inward and outward, like the "inside" and "outside," identify two sides of reality which Ruether believes are distinguishable but intimately related. They do not refer to two things, she assures us, but to two sides of the same thing. Such a duality, we are being told, should not be read as a dua*lism* because the distinction that is being made is less basic or fundamental than the unity within which it occurs. This is clearly "monistic" talk.[116]

In the following summary and analysis of Ruether's arguments in this and the next two sections, I will contend that while Ruether may at times use monistic language, her basic cosmological distinctions such as the "inside" and the "outside" nevertheless *function* dualistically. It is here that I part company with other Ruether interpreters.

Ruether's dualism is subtle. In the section on theological anthropology, I defined it as a "soft" dualism. I am certainly not claiming that Ruether advocates the harsh dichotomies of many of her opponents. But I do believe that there is a fundamental "two-ness" to reality in her position that cannot be accurately described as simply a bifurcation or distinction within a more fundamental unity. With the exception of the "theocosmology" that she proposes in *Gaia and God*, which will be examined at the end of this chapter, the "monizing" thrust to her thought is, in my judgment, best understood as the result of her attempt to either resist, hide, or overcome the basic duality—or rather dualism—in her picture of the world.[117]

To return to the aforementioned passage in *Sexism and God-Talk*, Ruether defends her claim that spirit is to be viewed as the "inside" of matter by noting that when we probe beneath the surface of visible reality we do not find stifling immanence or some kind of base matter devoid of all the qualities attributed to spirit. Instead we find that matter "dissolves into energy." Indeed it is "energy, organized in patterns and relationships, [that] is the basis for what we experience as visible things." At this point, she says, we reach the limit of our ability to distinguish between spirit and matter or the inside and the outside because "It becomes impossible anymore to dichotomize material and spiritual energy."[118]

This last statement could be taken to mean that Ruether believes in two distinct yet intimately related types of energy, one spiritual and the other material. Or she could be saying that there is only one fundamental kind of energy which underlies the two ways it is manifested. This would imply that the (energetic) unity of reality is shown to be more ontologically basic than its (material-spiritual) duality.[119] This latter interpretation would appear to best reflect the way Ruether wishes to be read. In my judgment, however, it is not possible to offer a consistent interpretation of Ruether's cosmology as a whole along these lines. Rather than functioning as the point of bifurcation in a monistic picture of the world, energy, as I read Ruether, is a term that identifies that part of the "realm" of Spirit that is closest to matter.[120] While the strongest evidence for this interpretation is to be found in other parts of her corpus, the passage that is under discussion from *Sexism and God-Talk* can also be plausibly read in this light.

As I read her, Ruether claims that the energy-matter correlation is so close that the former is manifested in the latter as "material energy," by which she means the energy that is perceived by physicists. It is this side of energy that Ruether seems to equate with that reality, referred to above, which is "organized in patterns and relationships" thus forming "the basis for what we experience as visible things." But while this material energy forms the "inside" of matter, it is not sufficient to explain the phenomenon of consciousness, (or anything else in our world that is invisible to us except in its effects). Ruether seems to explain consciousness in terms of "spiritual energy," which she equates with "the inwardness of material energy itself." If I read her correctly, spiritual energy is the inside of the inside of matter, so to speak.

While this reading does not uncover any blatant dualistic assumptions, it is sufficient, I believe, to raise the question of whether, unlike "material energy," this "spiritual energy" is *one step removed from matter* in Ruether's cosmology. (The same goes for all the terms that appear to function as synonyms for spiritual energy in this passage: life energy, spirit, and radial energy.[121]) If it could be shown that she believes that "spiritual energy" and matter can actually be separated—a topic which I shall address in the following section—then the suspicion of dualism raised here will prove to be well founded.

Another dichotomy Ruether wishes to avoid (and does so more successfully in my opinion) is that between nature and history. In her earlier writings, she insists, on the basis of Isa. 24, that the natural world has its place in the one covenant that exists between God and creation and has the capacity to mediate God's presence just as much as "history" or human culture.[122] Here she attacks the dichotomy by suggesting that "Nature itself is historical. The universe is a great being that is born, grows, and presumably will die." It grows by means of an evolutionary process that brings "qualitatively new dimension[s] of life . . . into being." Although these new possibilities were latent in what existed before them, they nevertheless "represent something new, something that could not simply be expected from the preexisting forms of being." This "newness" is possible because "Nature contains transcendence and freedom, as well as necessity."[123] By this remark, Ruether means that nature too must be seen in terms of an inside and an outside of spirit (transcendence, freedom) and matter (necessity).[124] From this perspective, if we take into account the non-determined energy that underlies or transcends visible nature, then the emergence of evolutionary novelties appears less incredible. In an appeal to Teilhard de Chardin's interpretation of evolution, Ruether explains the origin of qualitatively new types of creatures by proposing that "At certain 'boiling points' of life energy, there is a critical leap to a new stage of being. . . ."[125]

Although Ruether finds Teilhard's work to be very helpful for her purposes, she also feels the need to distance herself from the hierarchicalism implicit in his tendency to see the evolution of nature in terms of a horizontalized version of the great chain of being. This perspective still presupposes an inflated view of the place of humanity, which is precisely what Ruether intends to avoid.

Our view of human intelligence, in particular, needs to be relativized by seeing it in relationship to the radial energy expressed in matter. Although it is "a special, intense form," Ruether stresses that "it is not without continuity with other forms." In fact it can be seen as "the self-conscious or 'thinking dimension' of the radial energy of matter."[126]

It is on the basis of this energy dimension, and not on the basis of the possession of intelligence, that all creatures should be valued. From this vantage point, there is no hierarchy of worth. In Ruether's words,

> We must respond to a "thou-ness" in all beings. This is not romanticism or anthropomorphic animism that sees "dryads in trees," although there is truth in the animist view. The spirit in plants or animals is not anthropomorphic but biomorphic to its own forms of life. We respond not just as "I to it," but as "I to thou" to the spirit, the life energy that lies in every being in its own form of existence. The "brotherhood of man" needs to be widened to embrace not only women but also the whole community of life.[127]

A second way in which Ruether believes that her view of nature can correct our tendency to value more complex forms of life above those which emerged earlier is based on her contention that while more highly evolved creatures may have "qualitatively more mobility and freedom for response," they are also "radically dependent on all the stages of life that go before them and that continue to underlie their own existence." This point is easily grasped when we note that a "plant can happily carry out its processes of photosynthesis without human beings, but we cannot exist without the photosynthesis of plants."[128] In other words humans, as the most complex of all creatures, are also the most dependent on the support of the whole ecological community.

Ruether's notion of our dependency as humans on the eco-system is perhaps the most significant point of departure from the dominant Western model of nature. On this basis, she can claim:

> The notion of dominating the universe from a position of autonomy is an illusion of alienated consciousness. We have only two real options: either to learn to use our intelligence to become *servants* of the survival and cultivation of nature or to lose our own life-support system in an increasingly poisoned earth.[129]

A key feature of the move to a more ecologically sensitive stance, for Ruether, involves the cultivation of a new form of intelligence that does not suppress the spatial and relational thinking of the right brain. True left brain/right brain integration, she believes, would lead to a very different way of perceiving the earth compared to the dominant white, Western, male forms of rationality. As she explains,

> One has to disrupt the linear concept of order to create a different kind of order that is truly the way nature "orders," that is, balances and harmonizes, but that appears very "disorderly" to the linear, rational mind. One observes a meadow with many kinds of plants and insects balancing each other, each with their ecological niches, and then one learns to plant for human use in a way that imitates these same principles, in a more simplified and selective fashion. Converting our minds to the earth means understanding the more diffuse and relational logic of natural harmony. We learn to fit human ecology into

its relation to nonhuman ecology in a way that maximizes the welfare of the whole rather than undermining and subverting (polluting) the life system.[130]

Ruether's notion of nature's power to order is best understood if we note that she uses the term "nature" in at least three ways. Firstly, it is used as a global term that approximates what I mean by the term "creation." As I have already noted, nature, in this sense, has an inside that coincides with its transcendence and freedom, and an outside, which coincides with its necessity. What complicates matters is that Ruether's second and third usages of "nature"— which I will designate nature-2 and nature-3—are equivalent to the inside and outside, respectively, of nature-1. It is helpful to note that nature-3 corresponds to the way we often speak of "nature" in distinction from "culture." By contrast, nature-2 signifies something similar to what we mean when we refer to certain cultural activities as "natural" or "unnatural," by which we mean that they are normative or anti-normative.

The difference between nature-3 and nature-2 is clear in the following passage, where Ruether argues against Sherry Ortner's reductionistic view of the way nature has been viewed historically. She writes,

> Nonhuman nature can be seen as that which is beneath the human, the realm to be controlled, reduced to domination, fought against as font of chaos and regression. Nature can also be seen as cosmos, as the encompassing matrix of all things, supported by or infused with divine order and harmony, within which gods and humans stand and in which they have their being.[131]

When Ruether speaks of her own view of nature, she sometimes means nature-1, which I believe incorporates the two conceptions in the above quotation as its outside and inside respectively. Sometimes she has what I have called nature-3 in mind, as in *Liberation Theology*, when she speaks of the human need for "liberation from untamed nature."[132] Nature-2, or nature as cosmos, is what she means by the term in the passage quoted above in which she speaks of nature's power to order and balance in accord with its own logic of ecological harmony. This is somewhat reminiscent of the Egyptian idea of *Ma'at*, and even the reformed notion of a creation order. This view of "nature" as "encompassing matrix" will be explored further in the next two sections.

Before offering a response to Ruether's ideas on this topic, the diagram below may help to summarise and clarify how I understand the basic contours of her model of nature. (The horizontal line represents what I believe is a dualistic split and not simply a distinction between the inside and the outside. This anticipates the discussion of the next section.)

```
        SPIRIT          INSIDE      COSMOS        INVISIBLE
        Transcendence
        Freedom
N       Nature-2   M        P         A         H
A
T       spiritual/radial/life energy-spirit- "Thou-ness in all beings"  Thou —I
_ _ _ _ _ _ _ _ _ material _ _ _ _ _ _ _ _ _ _ _ _ energy _ _ _ _ _ _ |
U                 in-      la-       ni-       um-    increased          |
R                 eral-    nt-       mal-      an-    — mobility/ —► it
E                 s        s         s         s      dependency

        Nature-3
        necessity
        MATTER          OUTSIDE      CHAOS         VISIBLE
```

Ruether's proposals for an eco-feminist view of nature include important insights to which I am very sympathetic, provocative suggestions with which I am in partial agreement, and also material about which I am less than enthusiastic. On a positive note, I fully share her ecological concern and her desire to see an integration of left and right brain thinking. Most important, however, is her rejection of the nature/history distinction and her insistence that the natural world does not need the mediation of humans to be in covenant with Yahweh.[133]

If we connect this with some of her ideas about divine/human co-creativity, which were explored in the section on Mariology, this opens up the possibility of talking about a co-partnership between God and the natural world. I believe that this could be particularly fruitful in an area which, to my knowledge, Ruether never explores in her writings: the miraculous. In the biblical miracles, I suggest, we can see either concentrated expressions of God's everyday providence (such as in the feeding of the five thousand), or the restoration of true order to creation (as in Jesus' healing of the demon-possessed and in his walking on the water).[134] This latter type in particular concerns the liberation of creation from bondage, and I see no reason, apart from our tendency to be over-impressed by the naturalism of the modern worldview, why this kind of phenomenon should not receive significant attention from thinkers who are concerned to develop a biblically sensitive liberation theology. Because nature, and not just human society, stands in covenant with Yahweh, I think that it is well worth entertaining the possibility that when the land is described as vomiting out its pre-Hebrew inhabitants in Lev. 18:28, and when the Red Sea parts in Ex. 14, the land, wind and sea should be understood as acting in partnership with (or being actively obedient to) their Creator so that justice and liberation may occur.[135]

Such a view is diametrically opposed to the Western view of nature as inert matter. Ruether, in her own way, is also trying to break with this tradition which has depreciated nature in this fashion for so long. Another way in which she attempts to affirm the value and integrity of the natural world is by developing a non-hierarchical cosmology. As I have noted above, she undercuts our notion that we can dominate nature from a position of autonomy by stressing our radical dependence on the very creatures that we assume we have the right to rule over. The natural world is quite literally our life-support system. "The plant can happily carry out its processes of photosynthesis without human beings," she notes, "but we cannot exist without the photosynthesis of plants."[136]

I am sympathetic to Ruether's argument here, but would articulate my own position differently. "Hierarchy" as a term is, I believe, beyond redemption for our generation. The connotations of oppression are unavoidable for us. Nevertheless, I do believe that we need notions of nurture, guidance, and leadership. Some dimensions of life are more foundational than others. Our capacity to breath is foundational to our ability to think. Our ability to feel is foundational to our ability to trust. By analogy, plants and insects do play a more foundational role in the eco-system than humans in this sense.

We may look at power, influence, and value in this foundational, bottom-up, direction as Ruether does, but we may also look at life in its transcendental, guiding, or top-down direction.[137] Our faith can guide and open up our thinking, while our emotional state can affect our energy level and our vulnerability to disease. By analogy, humans can use their imaginations and conceptual powers to care for and protect other creatures and enhance their chances of flourishing.

Because of the influence of the Great Chain of Being on our thinking, we have made the mistake of assuming that the higher, or less foundational aspects of life are more divine, or closer to God than the lower, or more foundational. Creatures who are characterized by higher or lower types of functioning have thus been seen as closer to or further from God. For similar reasons, we have tended to emphasise the top-down direction of power, value, and influence. Ruether is reacting against this, but in a one-sided way. It would be more helpful to speak of power and importance in both the foundational and nurturing directions, simultaneously.

It is misleading to say, as Ruether does, that plants can exist quite happily without humans, but that, given our need for oxygen, we cannot exist without them. This removes autonomy from humans but then gives it to plants, thus masking the interrelatedness and mutual dependence that exists between all creatures in the one covenant of creation. If, instead of contemplating the consequences of the sudden disappearance of humans or plants, we imagine a world in which one or the other no longer carries out its God-given task as it should, this mutual dependence is more immediately visible. Ruether is correct that we would indeed be in danger if plants no longer engaged in oxygen production. But the present ecology crisis shows that plants are in danger when humans no longer care wisely for the rest of creation. It is not inconceivable that even the plant's ability "to happily carry out its process of photosynthesis" might become totally undermined.

I am glad that Ruether argues forcefully against the notion of matterless spirit and spiritless matter found in the cosmology of the Great Chain of Being. I am less than enthusiastic about the energy/matter correlation with which she replaces it. The following objections will be clarified further in the following sections on eschatology and God.

As I have already argued, I think that it is crucial that Christian theology affirms the goodness of creation in general (and thus of "nature" in particular).[138] Creation is good *as creation* and therefore does not need to be divinized. It is also inherent to the true nature of all creatures—trees, rocks, feelings, institutions, concepts, rainbows, events, relationships, parts, wholes, computers, humans, and elephants—to reveal God, though this is presently marred by human sin. To build on what I argued in the section on Christology, when God is all in all, then all creatures, not just humans, will incarnate God.[139]

In my view, energy is a foundational dimension, mode, or way-of-being-in-the-world for all creatures. It is no further from and no closer to God than, say, the biotic, psychic, logical, juridical or fiduciary dimensions of our experience. It is one of the many aspects of creaturely functioning through which we can reveal and experience God's presence. Ruether makes the mistake of elevating energy in general and "spiritual energy" in particular to semi-transcendent, semi-divine status.[140] One unfortunate (though no doubt unintended) consequence of this position is that it conveys the impression that, in comparison with "Energy," all other modes of our existence are "merely" creaturely and thus second rate. What starts as an elevation of one aspect of creation results in the depreciation of the rest of reality.

Ruether believes that all creatures stand in an I-Thou relationship to us (and presumably to each other) because this Energy flows through them too. I would rather say that all creatures stand in an I-Thou relationship to each other simply because they are creatures. Furthermore, it is as creatures functioning as they are called to function in *all* their dimensions that they reveal the Word and Spirit of God—both via their "inside" and via their "outside," to use Ruether's terms, though I would want to talk about many more "sides" of existence than these.

In Ruether's "energistic" ontology, nature is infused with grace and matter manifests rather than hides spirit. But, in the final analysis, I am not convinced that her schema will allow her to say that "matter" is good in its own right, even though it may bask in the reflected glory of the spirit which it makes visible. For Ruether, there is no hierarchy of value *between* creatures, as if only certain kinds of beings (i. e., humans) can stand in an I-Thou relationship, while the rest can only be the objects in an I-it relationship. Nevertheless, there is a hierarchy of value *within* each creature. The outside or visible material form of each being is valued as a necessary vehicle for the spirit or inside. But matter is still seen as inferior to spirit just as the I-it side of a relationship is inferior to its I-Thou side, in the final analysis. While Ruether may well not wish to say anything of the kind, this does seem to be a necessary implication of her cosmology.

Finally, it is important to note, Ruether's spirit/matter distinction is related to a unity/diversity and universality/particularity distinction. The way Ruether rejects a hierarchy of value among the different inhabitants of the earth in favour of a democracy of being is by stressing the energy or spirit that all creatures have in common. This is the ontological basis for her ethical claim that "The 'brotherhood of man' needs to be widened to embrace not only women but also the whole community of life."[141] Differences between creatures and individuality within phyla, classes and species would appear to be due to diverse material expressions of that common spirit/energy. Ethically as well as ontologically universality and spirit are valued over particularity and matter.

This helps to explain why our unisexual human nature is emphasized at the expense of male and female bodily differences, as I suggested in the section on anthropology. It also fits with a "partial universalism" in her view of the nature of our humanity, in which our inside or ego (in distinction from our outside or body), somehow partakes of the universal reality of the divine. This feature of her thought will be explored in the next two sections.

VII. Eschatology

The most fundamental assumption of Ruether's approach to nature, in contrast to so much of Western spirituality, is that we need to embrace the earth as our true home. This radical rejection of the worldflight mentality of the dominant theological tradition is also an important feature of Ruether's ideas about eschatology.

As Ruether subdivides her proposals on this topic into the areas of historical and personal eschatology, I will organize my discussion in the same way. It is this former aspect of this topic which is of primary concern to Ruether, in contrast to many Christians who only talk about eschatology in terms of the plight of the individual soul after death. Indeed, it can be safely assumed that Ruether is also expressing her own opinion when she writes that "Liberal Christianity has grown embarrassed with this popular view of Christianity as the 'medicine of immortality.' "[142] This rejection of the religion of personal salvation, says Ruether, is rooted in a conviction that the earth is where we belong, a conviction which was first asserted during the Renaissance, and which has been supported by the subsequent rediscovery of the basic theme of biblical hope. Ruether clearly approves of such developments and backs up her own position by saying,

> Most major theologians from the beginnings of liberalism in the nineteenth century, and including the Neo-Orthodox writers of the middle of the twentieth century, have taken for granted this shift of consciousness. Preoccupation with assuring one's personal immortality came to be seen almost as a perversion of the Christian message. From Schleiermacher to Tillich one speaks of the communion of the finite with the infinite, the temporal with the eternal, not in terms of a literal eschatology of the soul after death, but as a quality of life in relationship to the eternal here and now.[143]

This focus on our present reality and experience is a feature of Ruether's own thoughts in the area of historical eschatology, as we shall see. In chapter 1, I noted her dissatisfaction with models of future hope based on a linear view of history that culminates in a final salvific endpoint.[144] The tension that she sees between history and a literal eschaton, to which she often refers in her early thought,[145] is succinctly summarized in *The Radical Kingdom* when she says "The struggle for salvation must have an ultimate goal, but it is impossible because it contradicts man's historical nature."[146]

Ruether's proposed solution to this dilemma is that we do not attempt to achieve an "ultimate goal" once-and-for-all. This does not mean that we should support or accept the status quo. Change is needed and we should strive for it. But the model of social change that she suggests is one of "conversion" or "metanoia" based on the biblical idea of the Jubilee (Lev. 25) that she describes as "conversion back to the centre, rather than to a beginning or end-point in history."[147]

Such a model, she argues, rejects all attempts to return to a paradise of the past and is suspicious of all efforts to bring about a future utopia through infinite growth or a final revolution. Thus we are released from the "tyranny of impossible expectations." Yet at the same time, she points out, "the Jubilee teaches that there are certain basic elements that make for life as God intended it on earth." Thus Ruether too proposes certain basic elements that we need in our day to make up a just and liveable society:

> These include the human scale of habitats and communities; an ability of people to participate in the decisions that govern their lives; work in which everyone is able to integrate intelligence and creativity with manual labour; a certain just sharing of the profits and benefits of production; a balance of leisure and work, rural and urban environments.[148]

She also likes the recognition within the Jubilee system of the need for a revolutionary conversion to redress the imbalances when human sin causes a drift away from the desired state. Yet this is not attempted as a once-and-for-all project but as something that needs to be done on a periodic basis. Very helpful about this approach, says Ruether, is its acceptance of the reality and limits of our historical existence. This suggests that we should see our own attempts to establish "harmony within the covenant of creation" as "a historical project that has to be undertaken again and again in changing circumstances."[149]

A further argument that Ruether puts forward in order to persuade us to reconsider the "Hebrew sense of the mortal limits of covenantal existence" that she sees embodied in the Jubilee, is based on the observation that such a vision is at the heart of Jesus' view of the Kingdom. Thus she concludes *To Change the World* by saying,

> I suggest we think of the messianic hope to which Jesus points us, not as the eschatological end-point of history or as transcendence of death, but rather as the Shalom of God which remains the true connecting point of all our existences, even when we violate and forget it. Redemptive hope is the constant quest for that Shalom of God which holds us all together, as the operative principle of our collective lives. God's Shalom is the nexus of authentic creational life that has to be reincarnated again and again in new ways and new contexts in each new generation.[150]

It is not possible to fully understand Ruether's theology without a good grasp of her view of the nature of history. It is neither strictly linear nor cyclical but is best pictured as an ongoing spiral. In the previous section, I argued that she sees Nature as containing both an outside of chaos and an inside of cosmos. History, for her, seems to have a similar structure. In a striking passage from her early essay "Mother Earth and the Megamachine," she calls for a new "salvation myth" which "combin[es] the values of the world-transcending Yahweh with those of the world-renewing Ba'al in a post-technological religion of reconciliation with the body, the woman and the world."[151] In her subsequent theologizing, what she takes from Canaanite religion, I believe, is the view of world-renewal as a repetitive cycle of cosmos and chaos, which under the influence of Yahwism she cuts loose from the annual cycle of the seasons, but which in opposition to Yahwism, she sees as an ongoing historical spiral that has no end-point in which there is a final victory of cosmos over chaos, although the loops in the spiral can presumably be smaller rather than bigger if we turn our backs on evil. The way she sees the "return to the centre" may be illustrated as follows:

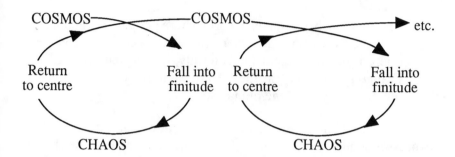

The "return to the centre" parallels the traditional category of redemption. Similarly, the move from cosmos to chaos seems to parallel certain aspects of what traditional theology has understood as the move from Creation to the Fall, except that for Ruether this is clearly an ongoing process. Ruether does not understand what I have called the "fall into finitude" as evil. This is most clearly expressed In *Gaia and God*, where she emphasizes that sin and oppression involve the attempt to overcome the self-correcting limits of the natural world (which non-human creatures cannot avoid) and the limits that are required in societal life if justice is to prevail.[152] In terms of this diagram, this is the refusal to return to the centre and thus complete the spiral. The downward movement of the spiral—in itself—is thus not identified with human evil, but it does relate to what she refers to in her recent thinking as the "tragedy" of our finitude.[153] The "fall into finitude" and "return to the centre" respectively parallel Ruether's notion of *kenosis* and reabsorption back into God/ess, which will be discussed below.

Ruether's ecologically sensitive respect for the limits of creation and her desire to embrace both the earth and our finitude has also profoundly shaped her approach to personal eschatology. But there is an interesting development that takes place in her approach to this topic. It is my contention that, with the exception of the more monistic outlook that is present in *Gaia and God*, the rest of her more recent thinking about death clearly reveals the dualism that has been present in her anthropology and cosmology for many years.

In her 1971 essay "Mother Earth and the Megamachine," to which I have just referred, she argues that,

> The new earth ... will be a world where people are reconciled with their own finitude; where the last enemy, death, is conquered, not by a flight into eternity, but in that spirit of St. Francis that greets "Brother Death" as a friend that completes the proper cycle of the human soul.[154]

There is clearly no evidence of a spirit/ matter dualism here. She expresses similar sentiments in 1975 in the conclusion to her book *New Woman/New Earth*. Her tone, however, is far more tentative. After arguing that we should cultivate an I-Thou relationship with all creatures and become sensitive to our mother, the earth, as the ground of our being, she writes,

> *Perhaps* this also demands a letting-go of that self-infinitizing view of the self that culminates in the wish for personal immortality [my emphasis]. One accepts the fact that it is the whole, not the individual, which is that "infinite" out of whose womb we arise at birth and into whose womb we are content to return at death, using the human capacity for consciousness, not to alienate ourselves from nature, but rather, to nurture, perfect, and renew her natural harmonies, so that the earth might be fair, not only for us and our children, but for all generations of living things still to come.[155]

By 1985, in her book *Womanguides*, she is even prepared to say, "Perhaps immortal life, if it is possible, can be safely left in the hands of God/ess from which all reality comes forth in the beginning?"[156] Clearly we cannot assume that she has continued to believe that death is simply a "dust to dust" process.

Her discussion of this topic in *Sexism and God-Talk*, published two years earlier, illustrates the ontological assumptions of her more recent thought that make this shift possible. This will therefore be the focus of attention for the rest of this section.

Ruether begins her discussion by admitting that death raises many questions for us, especially when it is premature or the result of oppression. Even when people live full and worthy lives, we are still left wondering "Do their achievements live on only in our fading memories, or *is there some larger realm where the meaning of their lives is preserved?*"[my emphasis].[157] Although Ruether claims that "The appropriate response to these questions is an agnosticism," it is the latter of the above suggestions that best reflects her own position. In fact in the closing words of this section, she says "Our agnosticism . . . is . . . the expression of our faith, our trust that Holy Wisdom will give transcendent meaning to our work, which is bounded by space and time."[158]

As Ruether begins her argument, it is hard to see how she can possibly reach the above conclusion, because she insists that in the area of personal eschatology we must not postulate anything that is incompatible with what we know of our finite nature. Thus she writes,

> What we know is that death is the cessation of the life process that holds our organism together. Consciousness ceases and the organism itself gradually disintegrates. This consciousness is the interiority of that life process that holds the organism together. There is no reason to think of the two as separable, in the sense that one can exist without the other.[159]

As she continues her argument, it becomes even more clear that we do not survive death as *individuals.* In answer to the rhetorical question: What will happen to "me" in this disintegration process? she writes,

> In effect, our existence ceases as individuated ego/organism and dissolves back into the cosmic matrix of matter/energy, from which new centers of the individuation arise. It is this matrix, rather than our individuated centers of being, that is "everlasting," that subsists underneath the coming to be and passing away of individuated beings and even planetary worlds.[160]

It is this cosmic matrix, I suggest, which turns out to be the key to understanding the "larger realm" mentioned earlier in which the meaning of our lives is preserved even as our individual existence comes to an end. In fact what Ruether is proposing, I believe, is that recognition of its existence can take away the dread we have of our own mortality. Thus she writes,

> Acceptance of death, then, is acceptance of the finitude of our individuated centers of being, but also our identification with the larger matrix as our total self that contains us all. In this sense, the problem of personal immortality is created by an effort to absolutize personal or individual ego as itself everlasting, over against the total community of being. To the extent to which we have transcended egoism for relation to community, we can also accept death as the final relinquishment of individuated ego into the great matrix of being.[161]

To make this proposal even more palatable to our Western ways of thinking, she stresses that the "cosmic matrix" or "total self that contains us all" should not be viewed as impersonal. Drawing an analogy between the human (or microcosm) and the universe (or macrocosm) she argues,

> If the interiority of our organism is a personal center, how much more so is the great organism of the universe itself? That great matrix that supports the energy-matter of our individuated beings is itself the ground of all personhood as well. That great collective personhood is the Holy Being in which our achievements and failures are gathered up, assimilated into the fabric of being, and carried forward into new possibilities.[162]

Although Ruether goes on to add "We do not know what this means. It is beyond our power and our imagination,"[163] and although her discussion is neither systematic nor strictly philosophical in nature, nevertheless an examination of her basic ontological assumptions should clarify why she puts forward the kind of argument that she does. Building on what I have already said about her ontology, I propose that we should interpret her view of death in the light of her belief that reality has two distinct but intimately related sides: an "outside" of matter, immanence, individuality, finitude and temporality on the one hand, and an "inside" of spirit, transcendence, universality, the infinite and the eternal on the other.

This should not be seen as a harsh form of dualism or else it would be impossible for Ruether to propose that our work which is "bounded by space and time"—a characteristic of matter—can have "eternal" or "transcendent meaning"—a characteristic of spirit. It would also be difficult to see how finite beings could in any sense be taken up at death into the universality of "the great collective personhood," which/who is the Holy Being or God/ess.

I believe that the reason Ruether can entertain such ideas is partly due to the fact that she believes that human beings exist in both of these "realms."[164] We possess both an "inside" and an "outside." We are both spirit and matter. The "inside," or what she here calls the "interiority of our organism" and which she identifies with consciousness and ego, has something in common with the Holy Being: it is personal. But what is different about us as personal centres is that we are individual while God/ess is a *"collective* personhood."[165]

This difference between our individuality and the Holy Being's universality also accounts for the relationship between us (and the relationship between the two sides of "nature"). In this respect, it is extremely significant that in many of the quotations cited in this section, Ruether does not speak of *individual* human selves/beings/egos, but of the *individuated* self, the *individuated* ego, and *individuated* beings.[166] The human self—the spirit or "inside" of the organism—is an individuated form or expression of the Holy Being. This is why God/ess can be called our "total self" or our "collective personhood."

The two "realms" fuse at the point where the universal (God/ess) takes on individuated form in human selves. One word that Ruether uses for the process of individuation seems to be *kenosis*. Thus, the "incarnation" of God in Jesus is understood in the three act drama that begins *Sexism and God-Talk* as "The Kenosis of the Father," to cite the title of Act 1 in which this takes place.[167]

The close relationship between the two "realms" can also be seen in her view of death. When we die, no longer tied down to individuality and finitude, our personal centres are reabsorbed back into the Universal, i. e., the cosmic matrix which is a part of God/ess. This is not the survival of the individual soul after the death of the body. Such a belief is the result of the dualism—what I would call *harsh* dualism—that Ruether wants to avoid and which she believes is the result of our alienated desire to absolutize the individual ego. The only kind of "survival" that Ruether envisions is our reabsorption back into the Holy Being which occurs when we surrender our individuality at death. This fits well with the sympathetic summary of Native Indian beliefs that she provides a few pages earlier in which she tells us that at death, "the Indian lives on, not as an isolated individual but in the collective soul of the tribe."[168] Ruether has simply identified this collective soul with God/ess. In this prizing of the communal over the individual there is an interesting correlation with collectivistic tendencies in Ruether's social ontology, for she says that "To the extent to which we have transcended egoism for relation to community, we can also accept death as the final relinquishment of individuated ego into the great matrix of being."[169]

I believe that the contours of the ontology that lies behind Ruether's personal eschatology here can be represented in the diagram on the next page. The triangular shape, viewed from top to bottom, represents the gradual slide from the One to the many, and from Universality to individuality, while the wavy line at the bottom of this triangle attempts to illustrate the fluid nature of this relationship between finite matter and infinite Spirit. (The movements in the direction of kenosis and reabsorption respectively parallel the "fall into finitude" and "return to the centre" illustrated in the previous diagram.)

The "larger realm where the meaning of [our] lives is preserved" turns out to be nothing less than God/ess. It is in this "realm" that the significance of our lives somehow lives on. In Ruether's words, to which I have added some interpretative comments,

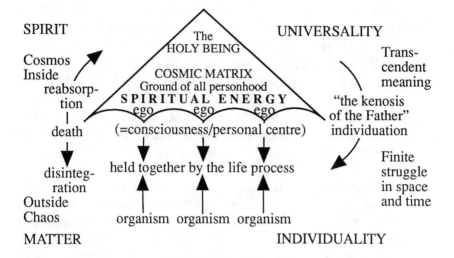

It is in the hands of Holy Wisdom to forge out of our finite struggle [lower "realm"] truth and being for everlasting life [higher "realm"]. Our agnosticism about what this means is then the expression of our faith, our trust that Holy Wisdom will give transcendent meaning [higher "realm"] to our work, which is bounded by space and time [lower "realm"].[170]

Ruether expresses the same sentiments in her later book, *Women-Church*. During a vigil with a dying person, she suggests that after friends have reflected on her life's accomplishments, the following words may be read:

All this goodness of doing and being of your life is gathered here together into *one*, brought together into a *single whole* and offered up to the Mother-Spirit, the source of all life, who will *take it back into herself and make it immortal and everlasting* [my emphases].[171]

Here she speaks of a movement from the finite back into the infinite which sounds as though it is also a move from multiplicity back to unity.

The dualistic nature of Ruether's thought is not something that other interpreters have pointed out,[172] and I am well aware that my analysis is likely to be challenged at this point. The section on personal eschatology in *Sexism and God-Talk*, which has been the focus of my argument (with the exception of this final quotation), does appear at first reading to be amenable to a different interpretation. It is not possible to read Ruether as advocating any kind dualism, it could be argued, because in the section under consideration she explicitly states that at death,

> All the component parts of matter/energy that coalesced to make up our individuated self are not lost. Rather, they change their form and become food for new beings to arise from our bones. To bury ourselves in steel coffins, so that we cannot disintegrate into the earth, is to refuse to accept this process of entering back into the matrix of renewed life.[173]

This is a thoroughly "monistic" picture, some may claim, that does not allow the continued existence of the human spirit in any higher realm. We merely dissolve into the "cosmic matrix," or nature which, in Ruether's pantheism, is identified with Deity. In this reading, Ruether's talk of "the *transcendent* meaning of our lives" and her hope that "Holy Wisdom [will] . . . forge out of our finite struggle truth and being for *everlasting* life," do not point to the presence of a realm of eternity in addition to a realm of temporality in her thinking. All she is saying is that the meaning of our lives must be seen in the light of the ongoing process of life (which is the ongoing life of God/ess) that continues long after our finite lives have run their course.

Such a reading has a certain amount of credibility, especially if we focus on this isolated passage, but it cannot help us make coherent sense of Ruether's position as a whole. *Firstly*, as I will argue in the next section, Ruether has never been a pantheist and has only adopted a panentheistic position, in the strict sense of the term, in her most recent book, *Gaia and God*. Thus whatever she means here by the assimilation of our achievements into the Holy Being, this cannot be understood merely in terms of the ongoing "geneticistic" flow of nature/history/God/ess.[174] *Secondly*, such an anti-dualistic reading cannot explain why Ruether would risk obscuring her own argument by using such language as *"transcendent meaning," "finite* struggle," *"everlasting* life," and "the *'immortal'* dimension of our lives." Such language is certainly open to being interpreted as proposing a dualistic temporal/eternal distinction. Why does Ruether take no steps to guard herself from such an interpretation if the monistic reading is correct? *Thirdly,* such an interpretation sees Ruether's view of death as very straightforward. Why then, after talking about our assimilation into the fabric of being at death, does Ruether say "We do not know what this means. It is beyond our power and our imagination"?[175] If this monistic reading is correct, why is there so much *mystery*?

To read Ruether's comments about the disintegration of the component parts of matter/energy as a sophisticated way of saying that there is nothing more to death than becoming fertilizer in the ongoing dynamic of the eco-system is to fail to take into account that this is a description that focuses only on what she would call the "outside" of life. It does not exhaust what she believes happens to humans at death. Awareness of Ruether's inside-outside distinction is crucial for a correct interpretation at this point. Having looked at death from the point of view of "matter" in the quotation with which I introduced the attempted monistic reading, Ruether is so aware that this description of the "outside" does not answer our (her) important existential questions, that *in the very next paragraph* she raises the question of lasting meaning and the role of God/ess— which requires an examination from the vantage point of "spirit." Given the overall contours of her thought, this leads her quite naturally to focus on "the interiority of our organism."[176]

This "interiority of our organism," which I interpret as the human spirit or ego, does not disintegrate back into the soil. Its destiny is "the cosmic matrix." Like, "nature," "matrix" is a very ambiguous word in Ruether's writings, and probably has the same range of meanings.[177] The cosmic matrix that is the destiny of the human spirit seems to be another way of talking about what I identified in the above section as nature-2.[178] At one point, she describes nature in this sense "as *cosmos*, as the encompassing *matrix* of all things, supported by or infused with divine order and harmony, within which gods and humans stand and in which they have their being [my emphasis]." She seems to have the same idea in mind when she speaks of "the regrounding of ourselves in the primordial matrix, the original harmony."[179] In the passage we have been examining, she says, "It is this [cosmic] matrix... that is 'everlasting,' that subsists underneath the coming to be and passing away of individuated beings and even planetary worlds."[180] Given such language, this "matrix" cannot simply be taken as a synonym for the universe as she explicitly states earlier in the same work that the latter "is a great being that is born, grows, and presumably will die."[181]

As I have attempted to illustrate in the diagram above, the cosmic matrix as the "inside" of nature is where God/ess and creation overlap. This matrix is contained within God/ess, who Ruether elsewhere calls "the *primal* Matrix."[182] This is why she can move so easily from talking about the cosmic matrix as "the ground of all personhood" to talking about the Holy Being who is "[t]hat great collective personhood . . . in which our achievements and failures are gathered up, assimilated into the fabric of being, and carried forward into new possibilities."[183] By contrast with this supra-temporal matrix, the "universe" which she describes as growing and possibly dying, would seem to be equivalent to the "outside" of nature.

Precisely what Ruether is saying about the ultimate abiding meaning of our lives is far from clear—as she herself seems to admit. Her very next words, (which I have already quoted above), are: "We do not know what this means. It is beyond our power and our imagination."[184] But perhaps what she is trying to get at can be clarified by an analogy. Let us imagine the relationship between spirit and matter in terms of the relationship between water and waves. If we look at the surface of the sea, we notice the manifestation of individuality and diversity in the form of waves (various life forms, correlations of spirit and matter). Eventually the waves break against the coast and the waters begin to retreat back into the sea (death). Although the waves lose their shape and individuality (the human organism decays), the water itself (spirit) is not lost but is reabsorbed back into the deep. New waves are formed and thus the whole process continues.

When Ruether speaks of God/ess as "That great collective personhood . . . in which our achievements and failures are gathered up, assimilated into the fabric of being, and carried forward into new possibilities," we can begin to understand this within the imagery I have been using if we imagine that God/ess is the entire ocean that contains all the water and in which all waves find their origin and destiny. Yet the ocean does not remain unchanged after the tide goes out again. Somehow the meaning of our lives is assimilated back into the ocean of life ("the fabric of being") enriching it and creating new possibilities for blessing life on our planet in future generations.

All analogies have their limitations. While I trust that this one clarifies the relationship between God/ess and the inside of nature in Ruether's thought, it may obscure the spirit-matter distinction, which I have been claiming remains dualistic in her cosmology until *Gaia and God*. While a wave stands in a part-whole relationship with the ocean, Ruether as I interpret her believes at this stage that strictly speaking only the human spirit and not the body is ultimately a part of God/ess. The separation that takes place at death between spirit and matter, or our universal and individual "sides," is harder to grasp in the above analogy than the process of individuation and reabsorption. For while a wave can leave a trace of the shape it once had on a sandy beach, it does not leave anything as dramatic as a corpse behind when it discards its individual form and is reabsorbed back into the ocean.

After coming to the conclusion that the section from *Sexism and God-Talk* that has been the focus of this exposition and discussion should be interpreted as I have been arguing, I was encouraged to find what I take to be unambiguous evidence for her assumption that spirit and matter are separable at death in the funeral service that she proposes in her later book *Women-Church*. This portrayal of death makes it clear that, for Ruether, the two "sides" to our humanity are seen in terms of a fundamental two-ness and not as a bifurcation within a monistic view of the human person. Our spirit, heart, or essence is clearly reabsorbed into God/ess leaving our material body behind.

In her introductory comments, Ruether suggests that "The prayers at the grave should indicate both an acceptance of the *mortal aspects* of our human being, *as well as a trust in the mystery of the transcendence of mortality* [my emphasis]." This dual focus can be seen in the words that are suggested for the interment. First the focus is entirely on the finite side of our being:

> Now the *body* of (name) returns to the earth, becomes again earth, earth to earth returning, the *matter* of the body dissolving back into the great source of all life and becoming compost for the nourishment of new living things. Just as leaves fall from trees and decay into the ground so that the new plants may arise in spring, so too our bodies must disintegrate into the earth to become matter for the next generation of living things. [my emphases]

But this is not the whole story. Having addressed the material or outside of our nature, she then turns her attention to the inside. After quoting verses from Paul's famous words in 1 Cor.15: 36-44, she continues:

> Unless a seed falls into the earth and dies, it does not raise again. *So our human spirits must let go of their perishable form to be transformed into imperishable spirit* This is a great mystery which we do not pretend to understand. But we trust with that faith of little children who put their hand into the hand of a loving parent, knowing they will be led aright. So we trust, even without knowledge, in that great Creator-Spirit from which all life comes, and to which it returns, *to raise this human spirit to immortal life.* Take back now our sister into your bosom, O Wisdom-Spirit. In faith we entrust her into your arms. [my emphases][185]

It might be objected that this is liturgical or confessional language which cannot be read as an exercise in philosophical anthropology. While this is true, the most fundamental distinctions of one's pre-theoretical worldview, which later come to play a guiding role in one's philosophising, are usually most clearly visible in one's confessional language. The language of faith may not be the language of ontology, but it is not to be distrusted as flowery equivocation or private emoting. Academic language often functions to hide what we really believe. By contrast, the language of faith is the blatant articulation of our most fundamental commitments, convictions, hopes and beliefs about God and the world. The above passages from *Women-Church*, therefore, provide good evidence for my claim that Ruether's cosmology betrays dualistic tendencies at least until that stage of her development.

There is one other place in which her more recent work sheds light on her ideas of personal eschatology in the section from *Sexism and God-Talk* which has formed the basis of my exposition. In the quotation which I suggested might be appealed to by those who read Ruether as a consistently non-dualistic thinker, she says that at death, "All the component parts of matter/energy that coalesced to make up our individuated self are not lost . . . [but] become food for new beings. . . ." I have argued that, when viewed in context, the paragraph from which this comes focuses only on the outside of our humanity and not on the destiny of the spirit. A serious objection that could be raised against this, however, is that she speaks here of the "individuated *self*" and not the "individuated *organism*," which is what would be expected if my view were correct.

I have long assumed that Ruether has not written exactly what she meant at this point. But I have also been aware of how unconvincing this would sound to those who would wish to challenge my reading. In the final stages of editing this manuscript, however, I discovered Ruether's more recent essay "Eschatology and Feminism." Before finally concluding her paper by quoting the same passage from *Women-Church* that I have examined above, she spends the previous two pages reproducing the section on personal eschatology published seven years earlier in *Sexism and God-Talk*. Yet she also introduces a number of small changes throughout, most of which appear to be intended to clarify rather than modify this earlier articulation of her position. In this version, she says, "The component parts of matter-energy that coalesced to make up our individuated *organisms* are not lost . . . [but] become food for new beings. . . ."[186]

There is no doubt that Ruether's cosmology draws a great deal of its inspiration and terminology from the thought of Teilhard de

Chardin.[187] If he is seen as a good example of a consistently non-dualistic theologian, then his influence on her thinking might even be used by some as an argument for interpreting her monistically. Actually Teilhard's own view of death as the reabsorption of our individual centres into the "Hyper-Personal Future-Universal," which is identified with God as the "Omega" and "centre of centres," is strikingly similar to Ruether's position.[188] While his description of reabsorption discriminates between humans and other beings in a way Ruether may well reject, he holds to a similar kind of dualism. Teilhard writes,

> To outward appearance, admittedly, man disintegrate[s] just like any animal. But here and there we find an inverse function of the phenomenon. By death, in the animal, the radial is reabsorbed into the tangential [material energy], while in man it escapes and is liberated from it. It escapes from entropy by turning back to Omega: the *hominisation* of death itself.[189]

In a discussion of his eschatology in her early book, *The Radical Kingdom*, Ruether says, "one might criticize Teilhard's system for finally rejecting its own presuppositions at the point where the radial energy effecting the complexification of matter finally takes off from this material substratum and exists by itself."[190] The same criticism can be levelled at Ruether herself. The dualism of matter and spiritual energy, which can be hard to recognize in much of her theologizing, finally becomes fully visible in her view of death.

Ruether's eschatological proposals create, in my opinion, difficulties of interpretation even greater than her reflections on nature. But even when what she is saying is relatively clear, I have least sympathy for her ideas in this area than in any other. I will present my misgivings about her proposals for historical eschatology, first. Then I will respond to her view of death.

Ruether often claims that a belief in a literal eschaton is untenable as a source of hope because it would bring history to an end (rather like the full stop which marks the end of this sentence). While I share her dislike of the tyranny imposed by impossible expectations, and have some sympathy for her comments on the

Jubilee as they echo the Reformation's motto of *Semper Reforman-da*, the task of ongoing reformation is a calling that I believe is intimately tied to the promise that our covenant Partner will eventually bring about the defeat and eradication of evil once and for all.

Although I see the full inauguration of the eschaton as a future event—and not merely as a normative call to wholeness in the present—I do not see this event as heralding the end of time. As I understand the Scriptures, our future hope is an anticipation of a time when God's redemptive struggles culminate in the final eradication of all evil and brokenness from creation and when the fruits of human culture are purged and purified and brought into the New Jerusalem (Rev. 21:24). While this does mark the end of *evil* (including the end of *patriarchy*) in a way that can be compared to a full stop, this is the "end" of *history* only if we understand "end" here as *fulfilment*. The birth of a baby signals the end/culmination/goal/fulfilment of the gestation period, but it is at the same time the inauguration of a new phase of human life and development. Similarly, to use the image of eschatological hope that occurs in the Book of Revelation, no bride is prevented from looking forward to her wedding day because she knows that from that day forward she will no longer be engaged or betrothed to her lover. Ideally, wedding vows signal the end or goal of courtship, not the end or termination of romance or commitment.

While Ruether is concerned about the enduring significance of human life, she has no interest in the kind of *speculation* on such matters that diverts our attention away from what we are called to do in the present. "It is not our calling to be concerned about the eternal meaning of our lives," she writes, "and religion should not make this the focus of its message. Our responsibility is to use our temporal life span to create a just and good community for our generation and for our children."[191]

Like Ruether, I too do not support any speculation on such matters that fosters an escapist or world-flight mentality. The Scriptures give us some insights into the continuities and discontinuities that we can expect, but there are limits to what we can know about the life that lies beyond both the "womb" and "birth pangs" of present existence. Yet we are called to live now in the light of a hope which (re)orients present praxis. Authentic eschatological hope, I contend, is not like that of the escapist teenager who wastes time daydreaming about the ideal romance that he hopes will come his way. It is, rather, the hope of engaged lovers, to use my earlier metaphor, who live in anticipation of their marriage and allow that future reality to shape their present relationship. It is also trusting in the promise that God will finally overcome evil in such a way that present evil is delegitimated and thus never accepted as how life ought to be. Thus the creation itself groans as in the pains of childbirth (Rom. 8:22) and both the Spirit and the bride say "Come!" (Rev. 22:17).

Earlier, I referred to Ruether's observation that Teilhard's prediction that energy will finally transcend matter is problematic. Commenting on the fact that he presents us with no basis by which this could occur, she writes,

> In partial reply to this criticism we can note, however, that this gap in logic is true of every projection of man's aspirations to the ultimate point. *The inner contradiction of man's historical nature* is that it presses toward a consummation that annihilates man as a historical being. Man's nature, pressed to its ultimate conclusion, reaches a point where, in order to realize himself, he must cease to be himself, and there is always a gap in logic as one tries to conceptualize the relation and transition from one to the other. The gap in logic at this point is not peculiar to Teilhard but rather *to the human condition itself*, and, if one would resolve it on the other side by taking man as a totally historical being that will perish with the perishable dimension of nature, then one has to explain this thirst for the eternal which the world cannot quench. Either way *man is partially an alien in the universe*, or, to put it in Teilhard's perspective, the universe has a dimension that can finally fulfill itself only by negating its final temporal being. [My emphases][192]

This is a very revealing passage, not least because it is further evidence of Ruether's own dualism. The alienation we feel in this life and our thirst for an eternity beyond temporality, Ruether is saying, is an inescapable part of the very structure of our humanity.

I strongly disagree. Normatively speaking, our experience of alienation has nothing to do with our finitude or temporality. As Christians, we should feel fully at home in God's creation. It is only the
presence of *evil* that should make us aliens and sojourners in this
present age. But evil should not be ontologized. It is not something
that God has built into the structure of creation or history from the
beginning. We can pray for God's will to be done on earth as it is in
heaven knowing in faith that the Kingdom of God will come. When
that day comes, we will no longer be aliens for the meek will inherit
the earth.[193]

Ruether's proposals in the area of personal eschatology are no
more promising, in my opinion. In fact, there are a number of
comments and observations already within Ruether's writings that
serve to highlight the weakness of her thought on this topic. The
opening paragraph in the relevant section of *Sexism and God-Talk*
raises some perennial existential concerns. Here she writes,

> But what of the sad insufficiencies of human finitude and the
> consequences of social evils that take the lives of little children
> and cut off adults in the prime of life before they can make their
> contribution? What of the vast toiling masses of human beings
> who have had so little chance to fulfill themselves? What of the
> whole tragic drama of human history, where so few have been
> able to snatch moments of happiness and fulfillment in the
> midst of toil and misery? What even of those worthies who have
> made good contributions and lived a full life? Do their achieve-
> ments live on only in our fading memories, or is there some
> larger realm where the meaning of their lives is preserved?[194]

These are good questions, and I have already summarized and
analyzed her attempted answer at some length. Reabsorption back
into a supra-individual Spirit is, I believe, an existentially disappoint-
ing answer for anyone who wishes to affirm creation and history
while protesting the presence of evil and suffering. If there is no final
eschatological liberation from oppression, but merely release from
the trials and tribulations of our bodily finitude, evil will continue to
have the last word.

The Bible, as I have already suggested, points us to a different solution that is seriously concerned with the question of justice, and must not be confused with the worldflight mentality of the Greek worldview (which has so permeated post-biblical Christian thought). As Ruether herself puts it in her B.A. thesis,

> It was apparently not difficult for the Jew to believe that man is mortal, but it was difficult for him to believe that God does not exact the full measure of justice. Thus his eschatology was aimed at demonstrating that the good and the bad would get all that was coming to them, rather than at satisfying the "human soul's craving for eternity."[195]

There are some hints that Ruether would like to overcome the limitations of her own position. In the "Liturgy of martyrs for justice, in solidarity with El Salvador," which she includes in her book *Women-Church*, Ruether quotes the following powerful words of Sister Maura Clarke who has said,

> My fear of death is being challenged constantly as children, lovely young girls, old people are being shot and some cut up with machetes and bodies thrown by the road and people prohibited from burying them. A loving father must have a new life of unimaginable joy and peace prepared for these precious unknown, uncelebrated martyrs. . . .[196]

The resurrection of the dead to life on a New Earth cannot simply be dismissed as an aspiration of the alienated male ego. The new life of peace and joy that is pictured in the above quotation is compatible with the Bible's body-affirming and non-dualistic view of resurrection, I suggest, but not with reabsorption.[197]

It is interesting to ponder the connections between Ruether's idea of reabsorption back into God/ess and the Eastern Orthodox tradition's belief in *theosis* or the divinization of creation. A major difference in Ruether's case seems to be that this is not the final goal of the history of redemption so much as part of an ongoing cyclical process of reabsorption and individuation. Also in Ruether's theology, matter is not reabsorbed back into God.

Ruether's interest in the Eastern Orthodox tradition is clear in her Ph.D dissertation on Gregory of Nazianzus.[198] In a more recent reflection on her doctoral studies, she comments, "In spite of the stasis of its historical development, I still suspect that the [Eastern] Orthodox tradition has the most authentic vision of the union of nature and grace, self and cosmos, one that has tended to get lost in the quasi-Marcionism of Western theology."[199]

It seems likely that there is some connection between Orthodox notions of the energies of God and Ruether's emphasis on energy as the part of spirit closest to matter. Consider the "Ruetherian" sound of the following words of contemporary Orthodox theologian Paulos Mar Gregorios:

> The creative energy of God is the true being of all that is; matter is that spirit or energy in physical form. Therefore, we should regard our human environment as the energy of God in a form that is accessible to our senses. [200]

The extent to which Ruether's feminist alternatives to patriarchal theology are similar to Eastern Orthodoxy's alternatives of the theology of the West would be an interesting topic to pursue.[201]

As a concluding comment, I would like to reflect on Ruether's observation about the modern practice of getting buried in steel coffins, which she rightly links to a fear of finitude and an alienation from the earth as our true home. The Scriptures suggest a different attitude towards burial, highlighting the true relationship between humanity and the earth in a way that may help us today. When Abraham buried Sarah in Canaan (Gen. 23:19), and when the Israelites buried Joseph at Shechem (Josh. 24:32), these were acts of faith in which they laid claim to possess the land promised to them by Yahweh. Today, I suggest, we can see the burial of those who know Yahweh as their claim to inherit the New (i. e., redeemed) Earth which is promised to us.[202]

In facing death, we are confronted with one of the limit-questions of our existence. The knowledge of faith, which is revealed to us in the act of trusting what we depend on as Ultimate, and which cannot be fully reduced to what we can conceptually grasp and articulate, plays a crucial role in the way we answer such a question. In the proposed funeral liturgy from which I have quoted above, Ruether expresses her faith in some form of life beyond death by saying, "This is a great mystery which we do not pretend to understand. But [as] we trust with that faith of little children who put their hand into the hand of a loving parent, knowing they will be led aright . . . [s]o we trust in that great Creator-Spirit. . . ." It is appropriate that the God in whom we place our trust is the next and final topic in this chapter.

VIII. God
In chapter 1, I noted that Ruether not only objects to the common use of the male pronoun for God, but is also eager to draw our attention to the fact that even the word "God" has non-inclusive connotations given the existence of the word "Goddess." In her more recent writings, Ruether attempts to solve this problem by using the neologism "God/ess"—which has been present in some of the quotations I have selected for this chapter. Ruether gives the following explanation of her use of this term in *Sexism and God-Talk*:

> [W]hen discussing fuller divinity to which this theology points, I use the term God/ess, a written symbol intended to combine both the masculine and the feminine forms of the word for the divine while preserving the Judeo-Christian affirmation that divinity is one. This term is unpronounceable and inadequate. It is not intended as language for worship, where one might prefer a more evocative term, such as Holy One or Holy Wisdom. Rather it serves here as an analytic sign to point toward that yet unnameable understanding of the divine that would transcend patriarchal limitations and signal redemptive experience for women as well as men.[203]

I also noted in chapter 1 that Ruether was particularly concerned with the way in which we conceive of the Holy Being's power in relation to humanity. In fact, it is probably fair to say that it is this concern that is most central to her own positive proposals on the topic of God-language. Even as early as her book *Mary—The Feminine Face of the Church* (1977), Ruether suggested that as an alternative to seeing God's transcendence as "a 'power over' that reduces creation to a servant status," we should see it "as the ground and power for created being to exist and to be continually renewed." "God," she continues, "is thus both the ground of being and its continual power for aspiration to new being."[204]

The metaphor of the Ground of Being in modern theology, she argues, continues what was, to the best of our present archaeological knowledge, the most ancient way that humans saw the divine, which was not as the abstracted ego of male monotheism, but as an encompassing source of life which was imaged as Goddess. In this view, Ruether comments,

> We can speak of the root human image of the divine as the Primal Matrix, the great womb within which all things, Gods and humans, sky and earth, human and nonhuman beings, are generated. Here the divine is not abstracted into some other world beyond this earth but is the encompassing source of new life that surrounds the present world and assures its continuance. This is expressed in the ancient myth of the World Egg out of which all things arise.[205]

Ruether is clearly sympathetic to this ancient tradition and herself refers to God/ess as "Matrix," as we have already seen.[206] I shall explore exactly what this means in further detail below. But it would be a mistake to take this language as implying that she wishes to draw her ideas of the divine primarily from pagan sources, for she appeals to at least four aspects of the biblical portrayal of God to support her own constructive proposals.

Firstly, in contrast to the Gods and Goddesses of the ancient Near East, who are modelled on the ruling classes to the extent that they only show mercy to the oppressed "in the manner of noblesse oblige," Yahweh is "the prophetic God" who is the leader and liberator of a tribal confederation of former slaves. "The identification of Yahweh with liberation from bondage," writes Ruether with approval, "allowed this diverse group to unite in a new egalitarian society and to revolt against the stratified feudal society of the city-states that oppressed the peasant peoples of the hills with taxes and forced labor."[207]

Although Ruether is quick to point out that this tradition, which is rooted in the exodus and is so central to the prophets, does not dissent against gender discrimination, there is a development in this direction within the canon. Thus in the gospels and in texts such as Gal. 3:28, God is seen as a liberator of those oppressed not just by class but also by gender and ethnicity.

The second "antipatriarchal use of God-language" that Ruether sees in the Bible is the tradition of "the Liberating Sovereign." Here God is seen as Father and King. As we have already seen in Ruether's discussion of Jesus' use of *Abba*, such terms need not function to sacralize patriarchy but can be used to dissent against the establishment. People may assert, "Because God is our king, we need obey no human kings. Because God is our parent, we are liberated from dependence on patriarchal authority."[208]

Ruether finds many examples of this use of God-talk in church history. But she is also aware of how ambivalent such language can be. Thus she notes,

> God as father and king can be assimilated back into the traditional patriarchal relationships and used to sacralize the authority of human lordship and patriarchy. The radical meaning of *Abba* for God is lost in translation and interpretation. Instead, a host of new ecclesiastical and imperial "holy fathers" arises, claiming the fatherhood and kingship of God as the basis of their power over others.[209]

Therefore she concludes that we need language that cannot be so easily co-opted.

Thirdly, Ruether believes that the biblical proscription of idolatry is particularly important to a feminist theology. The implications of the command to Israel not to make any picture or graven image of Yahweh are clear:

Christian sculpture and painting [which] represents God as a powerful old man with a white beard, even crowned and robed in the insignia of human kings or the triple tiara of the Pope . . . should be judged for what it is—as idolatry, as the setting up of certain human figures as the privileged images and representations of God.[210]

Ruether points out that if we extend this attitude to "verbal pictures," then we are in a position to condemn literalistic uses of male imagery for God (such as "Father") which suggest that "He" is male and not female. She supports her position by appealing both to the tradition of apophatic theology, which stresses the gulf that exists between God and our God-talk, and to the Jewish tradition that even writes YHWH without vowel signs as it is so circumspect about this verbal image. This enigmatic name which means "I am what I shall be," says Ruether, can be interpreted to mean "God is person without being imaged by existing social roles."[211]

Rather than trying to achieve inclusive language for God/ess by using highly abstract images, which in practice tend to hide androcentric assumptions (such as when people say "God is not male. *He* is Spirit"), Ruether proposes that we use concrete images of God/ess as female alongside images of God/ess as male. Such "equivalent images," she points out, are not to be confused with those biblical metaphors which present us with nothing more than " 'feminine' aspects of a male God."[212]

The presence of genuinely equivalent images in the parables of the mustard seed and the leaven (where God is first imaged as a farmer and then as a woman making bread), and in the parables of the lost sheep and the lost coin (where God appears as a shepherd and then as a woman sweeping her house) is the fourth area of biblical tradition to which Ruether draws our attention. She notes that these parables are remarkable not only because of their gender imagery but also because they draw on the everyday activities of Galilean peasants.[213]

On the basis of these four traditions, Ruether draws five conclusions. Firstly, if all God-language is analogical, even the non-idolatrous use of male imagery for the divine must lose its privileged place. Secondly, if God/ess is not the creator and validator of social hierarchies, God-talk drawn from kingship and hierarchical power must also be relativized. Thirdly, images of God/ess must include female roles and experience. And fourthly, such images should be drawn from the activities of those at the bottom of society.

Ruether's fifth conclusion, which she emphasises more than the others, is that "images of God/ess must be transformative, pointing us back to our authentic potential and forward to new redeemed possibilities." This means that we should not reinforce stereotypic gender roles at the level of God-language by "[a]dding an image of God/ess as loving, nurturing mother, mediating the power of the strong, sovereign father."[214] Furthermore, we should de-emphasize the use of parental images in general as these can imply a permanent parent-child relationship between us and God/ess.

By contrast, Ruether suggests "We need to start with language for the Divine as redeemer, as liberator, as one who fosters full personhood and, in that context, speak of God/ess as creator, as source of being."[215] This is a further strength of the parables to which we have just referred because "The old woman seeking the lost coin and the woman leavening the flour image God not as mother or father (Creator), but as seeker of the lost and transformer of history (Redeemer)."[216]

Ruether distinguishes her proposal to start with language about God/ess as Redeemer rather than Creator from that of theologians committed to "patriarchal theologies of 'hope' or liberation." While Ruether is happy with the affirmation of the God of the Exodus in such theologies, she is critical of the fact that such a view of God goes hand in hand with a negation of "God/ess as Matrix, as source and ground of being." Ruether believes that in such thinking, the ground of creation has become falsely identified with the foundation of existing social systems, many of which are unjust. Therefore liberation becomes defined as "liberation out of or against nature into spirit." Consequently, "God/ess as Matrix is thought of as 'static' immanence. A static, devouring, death-dealing matter is imaged, with horror, as extinguishing the free flight of transcendent consciousness."[217]

As I noted in chapter 1, Ruether is convinced that this "dualism of nature and transcendence, matter and spirit as female against male is basic to male theology" in both its conservative and radical forms. Thus to avoid this [harsh] dualism, feminist theology must find an alternative to seeing God/ess as either "static immanence" or "rootless transcendence." To this end Ruether proposes that,

> Feminist theology needs to affirm the God of Exodus, of liberation and new being, but as rooted in the foundations of being rather than as its antithesis. The God/ess who is the foundation (at one and the same time) of our being and our new being embraces both the roots of the material substratum of our existence (matter) and also the endlessly new creative potential (spirit).[218]

My discussion of Ruether's view of God/ess in the context of her approach to personal eschatology is fully compatible with the view of God/ess embracing spirit, but it is not at all compatible with the idea that S/he also fully embraces matter.[219] On closer investigation, however, it becomes clear that this passage is not advocating a version of pantheism but a form of what might be called *partial panentheism*. She does not say that God/ess embraces matter *per se*, but merely *"the roots of* the material substratum of our existence." She is not talking about the material substratum as the equivalent of the roots of our existence. Her point is that matter has roots. God/ess, as the "Ground of Being," embraces the *foundation* or roots of being (matter) and new being (spirit). The roots of the material substratum are probably to be identified with what she calls "material energy" which is on the "inside" of matter. As I have already noted, she understands this form of energy, when "organized in patterns and relationships," to be "the basis of what we experience as visible things."[220] Our "new being," "spirit" and "endlessly new creative potential," I suggest, should be identified with what she calls "spiritual energy."[221]

The following diagram, may be helpful in clarifying this point and illustrating some key aspects of the discussion below.

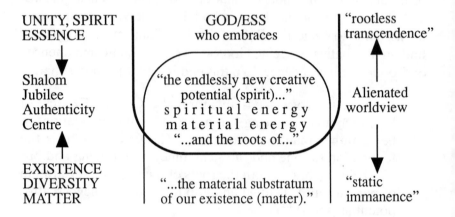

| UNITY, SPIRIT ESSENCE | GOD/ESS who embraces | "rootless transcendence" |

In terms of this diagram, the genuine point of connection between God/ess as the Ground of Being and humans would be at the *centre* where the two sides of reality meet. Ruether believes that these two sides must be held together in a healthy worldview. This fits well with the passage that I cited above from *The Radical Kingdom*.[222] There, the thrust of her argument was that we should not try to resolve "the inner contradiction of man's historical nature" by stressing either side at the expense of the other. To reduce human existence to what she there called our "thirst for the eternal which the world cannot quench," and what she here calls our "endlessly new creative potential" is to end up with the "rootless transcendence" to which patriarchal consciousness aspires. To reduce humanity to the outside of its existence, which in the passage from *The Radical Kingdom* Ruether describes as the attempt to see the human "as a totally historical being that will perish with the perishable dimension of nature" and which, in the terminology that she uses here, amounts to reducing ourselves to our "material substratum," leads to an absolutization that is equivalent to the "static immanence" that patriarchal consciousness dreads.

As an alternative to these one-sided distortions, she proposes that authentic reconnection with God/ess is found in the unity of the two sides. It is interesting, given the above diagram, that when discussing this very point Ruether actually uses the spatial metaphor of the centre, (which she also used in her comments on the Jubilee as a model for historical eschatology).[223] In her words,

> The God/ess who is the foundation of our being-new being does not lead us back to a stifled, dependent self or uproot us in a spirit-trip outside the earth. Rather it leads us to the converted center, the harmonization of self and body, self and other, self and world. It is the *Shalom* of our being.[224]

Ruether sees the goal of liberation as the harmonization and "shalomization" of all relationships, which necessarily entails a rediscovery of the true relationship between God/ess and world. Our outside (being) and inside (new being) are rooted in material and spiritual energy respectively. This energy is embraced and indwelt by God/ess. It is probably synonymous with the "primordial matrix" in which we are "reground[ed]" when we properly understand God/ess' call to liberation. Yet this matrix, which she calls "the original harmony"[225] eludes patriarchal society. In its alienation, it does not root itself in—and is thus not sanctioned by—the true Ground of Being: God/ess. Failing to see the true relationship between the two sides of reality, it erects a false system of dualisms modelled on oppressive social relationships. In attempting to pursue liberation in terms of these dualisms, it therefore furthers its own alienation from God/ess and true shalom.

An important assumption in Ruether's ontology seems to be that the relationship between God/ess and world is seen as a relationship between essence and existence. In this framework, essence is characterized by unity while existence is characterized by diversity. To reground ourselves in the primal Matrix or original harmony is to reconnect as much as creatures of diversity can to a primordial Unity which transcends us but to which we aspire and which we are called to manifest. In this sense we are like diverse iron filings which when attracted by a magnet will come together to image and reveal the shape of the magnetic field. This is what I believe Ruether means when she says, "God is the End, the Beginning, and the Center of the new being of creation that is ever seeking to become the true image of its divine foundation."[226]

If I understand Ruether correctly, to experience this unity is to encounter one's *authentic* self, as authenticity and truth are qualities of the higher or deeper side or realm. It is also to encounter God/ess, although there can be no direct or unmediated communion with the Deity as S/he is pure essence (unity) and we can never fully transcend our existence (diversity).[227] Unity and God/ess are experienced by humans in and through the overcoming of the fragmentation of everyday life, at which time some degree of unity and harmony are experienced in the "realm" of existence. This is why she writes,

> The liberating encounter with God/ess is always an encounter with our authentic selves resurrected from underneath the alienated self. It is not experienced against, but in and through relationships, healing our broken relationships with our bodies, with other people, with nature.[228]

To understand connection with God/ess as an ascetic disconnecting of oneself from one's body or from the rest of nature, in other words, is to completely misunderstand authentic spirituality and the true relationship between God/ess and creation.

I share Ruether's hostility towards all attempts to play God and the world off against each other. Creator and creation can only be affirmed in relationship to each other. This means that in the final analysis, the world-flight mentality of so much contemporary "spirituality" and the "worldly" aspirations of modern secularism are destined to lose both God and the world.

I also share many of Ruether's concerns about language for God, such as our need for concrete rather than abstract metaphors and our need to be aware of the ever present danger of their co-option for ideological and idolatrous purposes. I am also glad that she points out that calling God "Father" or "King" may function in a counter-patriarchal way—a point often missed in less nuanced discussions of this topic. Christians who are uncomfortable with female metaphors for God may at least learn from Ruether how to use time-honoured patriarchal images in new counter-patriarchal ways.[229]

Her argument for using the word God/ess is also sound. While I do use the pronoun "S/he" in this context, I continue to use the term "God" as I personally do not know anyone who finds it offensive because of its possible gender connotations. If there does come a time when this becomes problematic for more and more Christians, I suggest we use the word "Yahweh" as it can be verbalized.

I also take Ruether's point about the potential danger of too much emphasis on parental images for God, although I think their predominance is entirely appropriate for certain stages of faith development.[230] Furthermore, in a fallen world, there are no images for God that cannot be made to foster an unhealthy spirituality, so pointing out the potential for misuse is not a sufficient reason to abandon a particular metaphor for the Divine, as this can be extended to all of our God-talk. Parental images may function in a very wide variety of ways, at least some of which may be healthy at any one time. Contrary to Ruether's claim, these are not necessarily limited to ways of talking about God as Creator. Relating to God as "Mother" or "Father" may point to God as Redeemer if we think of the parable of the prodigal son (Lk. 15:11-32) or of Paul's use of the metaphor of adoption (Rom. 8:23, Eph. 1:5).

A crucial issue that greatly influences our view of language for God is the way we conceive of the Creator/creation distinction/relationship. My own position is that we need to affirm that without the presence of evil, which by its very nature makes God absent from our world in varying degrees, God and creation would be *unambiguously* distinct but *thoroughly* related. A genuine distinction should not be seen as standing in opposition to a close relationship between Creator and creation. In fact, the former is a necessary prerequisite for the latter, and *vice-versa*. This is somewhat analogous to the fact that human lovers need healthy self-identity if they are to be capable of genuine intimacy as opposed to unhealthy enmeshment. The identity and robust sense of self that I am speaking of here should not be confused with the aspirations of the would-be autonomous individualist. Healthy self-identity includes openness to others, and only develops in us as a result of intimacy with parents, family, friends, and other creatures.[231] Thus, in opposition to heteronomous theologies, creation needs to have its own identity to relate intimately with God. But it also needs to be intimately related to God in order to have its own identity, for the way of autonomy is ultimately the way of death. There can be no life that is totally outside the covenant.

Unless the total enmeshment of a thorough-going pantheism is adopted, any blurring of the Creator-creation distinction inevitably results in some of the characteristics of created reality being seen as closer to God than others. A hierarchy is thus set up within creation, even though this may not be intended. In the cosmology of the Great Chain of Being, the neo-platonic blurring of the Creator/creation distinction results in some creatures being seen as closer to God than others. In Ruether's cosmology there is no hierarchy of creatures. Instead there is a hierarchy *within* all creatures such that the inside of each is seen as closer to the divine than the outside. Taken together, the last two diagrams illustrate how matter and the human organism are not as close to God as energy and the human ego in the cosmology that she proposes, though this is quite probably in spite of her best intentions.

I believe that it is important to assert that no being, part or dimension of creation is closer to God than any other. All kinds of creatures, ways of functioning, and types of relationships are equally capable of incarnating God's presence, as I have already argued.[232] Similarly, all human language used to name such creaturely realities can be used as legitimate metaphors for God (as long as those realities are not too marred by evil in our experience).

I find support for my position in the fact that biblical language for God draws on a very wide range of "creatiomorphic" images.[233] Such language refers to God in relation to (or revealed via) creation. Biblical authors have no notion of God's "aseity" and have no interest in ideas such as "God in him/herself." Both analogical and apophatic approaches to God-talk are mistaken in their attempts to talk in this way about something for which creaturely language is totally impotent.[234] To attempt to speak of God's "essence" as Shepherd, Judge or even Love in this manner is completely and utterly nonsensical. We cannot speak of God apart from how S/he is known in the covenant with creation. In that context, however, we can use terms such as Shepherd or Judge with confidence to refer to how God relates to us.[235]

The issue of male and female anthropomorphic metaphors for God is worth investigating within the wider context of the Bible's "creatiomorphic" language, which Ruether does not explore. The following argument, which adopts this strategy, is intended to show that the case Ruether makes for the legitimacy of female language for God can be strengthened by appeal to biblical God-talk.

In her book *Womanguides*, Ruether includes a translation of Ps. 19:1-11.[236] In what is a less than careful analysis, she claims that this psalm "displays the sense of deity as Sky-father" as opposed to Earth-mother. Such a God, she claims is portrayed as "the Great Patriarch who rules from above."[237] The identification of God with the sky and thus transcendence, Ruether seems to be arguing, results from a patriarchal ideology that is alienated from the divine in nature.

Presumably, she does not think that the last three verses of the psalm are significant as she does not bother to reproduce them. The last verse, however, refers to God as "my *Rock* and my Redeemer." It is hard to imagine a more down to earth or "materialistic" image for God than a rock! This language does not have its historical origin in abstract debates among ancient Hebrew intellectuals about Yahweh's "communicable attributes"! It has its origin in "pre-theoretical" life experience as that experience is interpreted in faith. In all probability, the practice of calling God "our Rock" began when ancient Israelites went to the rocks and mountains in order to shelter from the sun and wind and to take refuge from their enemies, and in that context became aware of the dependable and protective presence of Yahweh.

By using this down-to-earth language for God, Psalm 19 does not encourage us to see God as an earth deity or Earth-mother any more than its celebration of the heavens indicates belief in God as a Sky-father. What it ultimately assumes, I believe, is that as creatures in God's world, rocks beneath our feet can mediate and reveal

Yahweh's presence just as much as the skies above our heads and the sun on our backs.

"Rock" is quite a common biblical metaphor for God (see Gen. 49:24; Deut. 32:4,15, 18, 30-31; 2 Sam. 22:2; Ps. 18:2; 92:15; Isa. 26:4). Other metaphors taken from the natural world include God as Sun (Ps. 84:11), as Spring of Water (Jer. 2:13), as Consuming Fire (Deut. 4:24), and as Dew (Hos. 14:5). Metaphors taken from the animal world include God as Lion, Leopard, and Mother Bear (Hos. 13:7-8), as a Flock of Birds (Isa. 31:5), as an Eagle (Ex. 19:4; Deut. 32:11) and as a Mother Bird (Ruth 2:12; Ps. 17:8; 36:7; 91:4). To belittle the significance of such metaphors by saying that they are less truthful than talk of God as Father (or Mother) is to fall into a humanocentric view of God.

In the language taken from human life, God is portrayed in a number of social roles. Some images, such as God as King, Father, and Husband reflect male roles. Others such as Shepherd, Judge, Friend, Warrior and Helper refer to roles that could be played by either men or women. (Goddesses were often portrayed as warriors, while Eve's role as Adam's helper may have led to God as Helper having connotations of God as Wife.[238]) There are also metaphors for God taken from exclusively female social roles. Thus God is seen as Midwife (Ps. 22:9), and as Mother (Num. 11:12; Job 38:29; Ps. 131:2; Isa. 42:14; 46:3; 49:15; 66:13; Jn. 3:5). To say that these are merely " 'feminine' aspects of a male God," as Ruether does,[239] is no more accurate or necessary than saying that metaphors taken from the animal kingdom merely present us with "animalistic" aspects of a human God!

Ruether's comment to which I have just referred would seem to assume that the biblical writers conceived of their male language for God as "literally" true and their female language as merely "metaphorical." If this is the case, then she holds a similar view of biblical God-talk to conservative theologian Donald Bloesch.[240] In response to the Bible's use of female imagery for God, he writes,

[A]lthough God is said to be like a mother, God is never called mother in the canonical Scriptures . . . , nor does mother ever occur in the vocative. The dominant names for God in the Bible

and in the history of the church are *Deus, Domine,* and *Pater.*
The God of the Bible is much closer to the Sky Father of prophetic
religion than to the Earth Mother of the fertility religions [my
emphasis].[241]

Ruether and Bloesch differ profoundly on whether this
presents a normative position. But as a description of biblical God-
talk, these words could easily have come from Ruether herself. In
this respect, both Bloesch and Ruether are wrong, in my opinion. It
is not at all helpful to project our dubious distinction between literal
and metaphorical language for God back onto the Bible. If we want
to use such terminology, then we should say that *all* biblical God-talk
should be taken as metaphorical. We can, however, speak of some
of the biblical writers' language for God as utilizing what were at
that time *privileged* metaphors. It is primarily these metaphors that
are used in the vocative case to which Bloesch refers.

The most common privileged metaphor for God in the Old
Testament is "King." In the New Testament, it is "Father," which is
also Jesus' privileged metaphor for God. Both images are drawn
from male social roles. Privileged metaphors cannot and should not
be avoided. We cannot simply use every conceivable creatiomorphic
metaphor whenever we pray! But the question arises as to whether
the Bible's privileged metaphors should be our privileged metaphors. What counts as legitimate privileging? What counts as
idolatry?

No matter how problematic the language of God as king is for
many today, it is worth noting that it has born good fruit in the past.
It has enabled the Christian community to see God as the true
Sovereign who relativizes all human rulers. It also enabled the
Israelites to see Yahweh as the faithful Suzerain who would protect
them from their enemies. In the Calvinist tradition, it has supported
belief in God as the Lord of all of life in such a way that it has helped
many to resist a pietistical reduction of their faith. Given its
numerous connotations, the kingship metaphor has enabled previous generations to explore something of the richness of their
relationship with God.

But when the privileging of any metaphor functions to under-mine this richness, that is a different story. When the metaphor of God as Friend can only be understood as a way of talking about God's Rule, then we are in trouble. If seeing God as King blinds us to the presence of God in queens, children, and slaves, we are engaging in idolatry. The fact that a given metaphor is used in the Bible doesn't make it immune from our evil.

This means that the fact that Jesus usually called God "Father" does not automatically mean that we should. What is at stake for many Christians who resist change here is the question of what it means to be faithful to the biblical tradition. This is certainly a legitimate concern, but why is this so often identified with conser-vatism? In our contemporary attempt to continue the redemptive historical drama that the Bible tells, can we be content to simply repeat what were the faithful responses of those generations that are portrayed in its pages? Or is that to bury the one talent with which we have been entrusted, because we are afraid we will lose it if we take the risk of investing it, because we are afraid that innovation will make us lose touch with our biblical heritage, be-cause we believe that change is incompatible with continuity?

Faithfulness to a tradition, for me, means fidelity to the spirit which it embodies. The relationship between God and the biblical tradition, the Spirit and the letter, is like that of the relationship between God and creation as a whole. To the extent that evil does not pollute a tradition, we need to speak simultaneously of an unambiguous distinction and a thorough relationship between it and God. In this light, Jesus' language for God, like that of the Bible as a whole, should be acknowledged as normative, by which I mean that it is a faithful response to and revelation of a norm. But it is not itself the norm for such language in the strict sense of the word. Creation may reveal God, but no creaturely revelation should be treated as though it is itself God.

To use a simple analogy, the Lord's prayer is a normative prayer but is not in and of itself the norm for prayer. I know of no Christian who believes that for any prayer to be acceptable to God it must copy or be closely modelled on the Lord's prayer. It would be distressing if Christians never used this prayer in their liturgies. It clearly reveals much to us about what it means to pray in an authentic way. But it is a human prayer to God, not a supra-creational "archetype." That is why it is not the best prayer for us to use in many contexts. Similarly, it would probably be a cause for concern if Christians completely stopped calling God "Father." But this does not mean that it is always the most appropriate privileged metaphor for God.

This means that calling God "Mother" may be just as legitimate as calling God "Father." Which are the most appropriate metaphors for God for a given individual or community must be determined by using pastoral criteria. In other words, we should call God "Mother" and/or "Father" if this builds up our confession and bears good fruit in our actions. By contrast, when the legitimate privileging of metaphors becomes illegitimate is when our God-talk begins to support idolatry, which will manifest itself in our way of life. A savagely patriarchal lifestyle, for example, may thus be evidence for calling into question a community's or an individual's male God-talk. If seeing God as Father begins to blind us to God's presence in and with women, it has to be challenged. Ruether has not been slow to recognize this.

At the beginning of this section, I claimed that the need to reconceptualize the way we see God's power in relation to humanity was very central to Ruether's approach to God-talk. We need to move away from the idea of God's power "over" us and speak instead of God's power for or empowerment of creation, she suggests. She is also aware that such a shift might reorient our notions of the right way for humans to exercise power towards one another.

It is worth emphasizing that this does not only have implications for the exercise of "ecclesiastical" power. Clericalism is only one form of distorted leadership in the wider Christian community. Christian theologians are also called to empower and serve the Church rather than pontificate to and alienate fellow believers. Female language for God is experienced by many Christians as so new and revolutionary that they react to it as they might to the idea of their spouse going for a sex change operation. It is as though God is being subjected to gender reassignment. Therefore, those of us who advocate change need to exercise pastoral sensitivity. We would do well, it seems to me, to emphasize the *continuities* that exist between the God we are learning to relate to as Mother, for example, and the same God that Christians have known and loved for almost two thousand years. When constancy and continuity are not sufficiently stressed, then too much sudden change is hard for anyone to incorporate into their spiritual journey.

Material from previous sections of this chapter suggests to me that Ruether's overall conception of God, and not just her view of God-language, so often represents a break with past tradition without a concomitant emphasis on fundamental continuities that the cumulative impact, though no doubt unintended, may be overwhelming for many Christians. In the section on evil, for example, I noted that she dispenses with the traditional idea of God's omnipotence by claiming that such talk is simply the result of modelling the Divine after emperors and despots. I suggested that it would be more fruitful to reform our thinking in this area by exploring how God is understood as All-Powerful in the Bible's language of *faith* in distinction from the *metaphysical* language of scholastic speculation—a topic to which I shall return in the conclusion. With this approach, I suspect, we may not have to pursue change at the expense of continuity.

In the section on Mariology, I noted that Ruether rejects a view of the God-creation relationship as one in which we are seen in a role of heteronomous submission. While she still speak of human reliance on God, she goes on to highlight "the radical dependence of God on humanity" such that without human faith, God cannot act. She is right that we often ignore this side to the covenant relationship. Nevertheless, left without qualification, her comments conjure up the image of a well-intentioned but rather impotent God who has to be content with waiting for humans to get their act together. This will no doubt come across as too bizarre and troubling for many Christians.

It should be admitted that our sin and unbelief do limit God. But the Bible acknowledges this while also underlining the fact that God's purposes cannot ultimately be thwarted. Ruether's point could be made by pointing to the biblical notion that the disobedience of Noah's generation and of Israel under the monarchy, for example, prevented the coming of the Kingdom of God. What the Scriptures add is that God took steps to restore the covenant we had broken and decided to try a different way of relating to us. This resulted in the promise embodied in the rainbow and in the Word becoming flesh and dwelling among us.

In the section on ecclesiology, I pointed out that Ruether's stress on the role of the faith community goes hand in hand with a diminishing of God's role, almost to the point of invisibility at times. (This makes me wonder if she has really overcome the problem of a competitive view of the God-creation relationship.) Furthermore there is no reflection on praising and worshipping God/ess. In the section on Christology, Ruether does affirm the fundamental Christian claim that God is made known to us in Jesus. But her insistence that we too are called to incarnate God (which I fully support) is made without attention to the traditional Christian concern with what distinguishes Jesus from us. I have suggested that we need to add that in Jesus we see the Word made flesh without ambiguity, while the Law is prevented from being clearly written on our hearts because of our evil.

Taken together, these various reflections on the nature of God suggest that Ruether's emphasis on change at the expense of continuity will make her attempted *reformation* sound to many as though it is a *revolution*. Seen within this wider context, her proposals for revising our language for the Divine will come across as a call to worship a different God. I do not share this reaction, but I understand why it occurs.

In their recent book surveying the God-world relationship in twentieth-century theology, evangelical authors Stanley Grenz and Roger Olson provide a good example of how many Christians might respond to Ruether's proposals when they exclaim, "Her account of God/ess is only a hairsbreath from the nature-personification Mother Goddess of the radical feminists who worship the earth and themselves."[242] On my reading this is an exaggeration. It is true that there is a blurring between God, on the one hand, and energy, the cosmic matrix, and what I have labelled *Nature-2*, on the other, but this is far from a simple pantheism.

Her view of the God-creation relationship is ambiguous, however. If Ruether understands the spiritual energy that seems to exist "between" God and creation in her cosmology as synonymous with what Teilhard de Chardin means by "the radial energy [that] effect[s] the complexification of matter,"[243] then she might communicate more clearly to some if she connected this with the Word of God. Matthew Fox's use of the Hebrew term *Dabhar*, which he translates as "the Creative Energy (Word) of God,"[244] might also be worth adopting here, especially as it may be related to the Eastern Orthodox notion of the divine *energeiai*. It would also help if Ruether clearly distinguished God/ess' sustaining-empowering-energizing of the creation from *created* energy.

More than changes in terminology are needed to remove all the problems in Ruether's view of the God-creation relationship, however. The "soft dualism" of the inside and the outside, to which I first referred in the section on anthropology and which I further explored in the sections on nature and eschatology, appears to be reflected in and supported by what I have called her partial panentheism. The privileged side of the various correlations that she proposes—the inside rather than the outside, the ego rather than the organism, spiritual and material energy rather than matter, unity rather than diversity, universality rather than individuality—are "embraced" by God/ess in a way that implies that they have some kind of transcendent, divine status, or at least have a special, extra-ordinary capacity to reveal the presence of the Holy Being. The inside and outside of creation seem to be viewed as, respectively, inside and outside the realm of the divine.

There is an important shift in Ruether's view of the God-creation relationship that occurs in her latest book, *Gaia and God*. Here, she adopts a far more thorough-going panentheism in which God and the world (Gaia) are no longer seen as two overlapping realms but have become "one" in a metaphysical sense in what she describes as her "theocosmology."[245] Ruether still finds it necessary to speak of "divine being" as "a source of life that is 'yet more' than what presently exists," and as a "deeper source of life 'beyond' the biological" that is expressed in human ethical reason. She also says that God is "the life power from which the universe itself arises."[246]

This is no simple pantheism, although some will no doubt make this accusation.

As before, the God-Gaia relationship is a macrocosm which is reduplicated at a microcosmic level in the human self-organism relationship.[247] What has changed is that these relationships are no longer understood primarily in terms of the distinction-connection between inside and outside, spirit and matter. Instead, the one reality—the theocosmos—can be viewed in two fundamental ways or directions: as the One Whole (God), or as the many parts (Gaia). Appealing to Nicholas of Cusa's notion of the "coincidence of opposites," she suggests that we may focus on the diverse parts of reality in such a way that we may encounter the Unifying Whole or hidden harmony at the heart of reality. She writes,

> As we move below the "absolute minimum" of the tiniest particles into the dancing void of energy patterns that build up the "appearance" of solid objects on the macroscopic level, we also recognize that this is also the "absolute maximum," the matrix of all interconnections of the whole universe. This matrix of dancing energy operates with a "rationality," [and in] predictable patterns that result in a fixed number of possibilities. Thus what we have traditionally called "God," the "mind," or rational pattern holding all things together, and what we have called "matter," the "ground" of physical objects, come together. The disintegration of the many into infinitely small "bits," and the One, or unifying whole that connects all things together, coincide.[248]

This shift leaves many of the cental features of my earlier analysis virtually unaffected. Unity, Universality, Essence, and the Self are still privileged over against diversity, individuality, existence, and the body. In fact, the divinization of the former realities is even more clear, as I read her, because God is now literally the Unity of "creation" (while "creation" is the diversity of God).

However, because it is the part-whole relationship that is seen as the key to the relationship between Gaia and God in this book, the inside-outside relationship, which used to play this exalted role, is now conceived differently. As I interpret her, Ruether now stops flirting with the "soft dualism" that I have identified in her previous works, and firmly rejects Teilhard's claim that spiritual energy can finally toss aside its material underpinning. While she still retains his idea that spirit is the "inside" of matter,[249] the inside-outside distinction is now monistically conceived with energy being seen as the point of their bifurcation. This "matrix of dancing energy" also functions as the privileged medium of connection with the primordial Whole that unifies the diversity of the parts.

To illustrate the shift in her view of reality, we have to imagine that the two previous diagrams have been laid on their sides. The "overlap" between God and "creation" (as well, paradoxically, as their mutual opposition) is now far more complete. Some of the dynamics of her view of the nature of history are also incorporated in a new way in this model, although the alternating movement from cosmos to chaos and back again would now seem to occur simultaneously. As we look at reality from the parts to the Whole—from right to left—we encounter the divine side of the correlation. But as we focus on the parts alone—from left to right—the world of ordinary experience comes into view. The coincidence of opposites, which corresponds to the "loop" *in this diagram*, occurs at the point

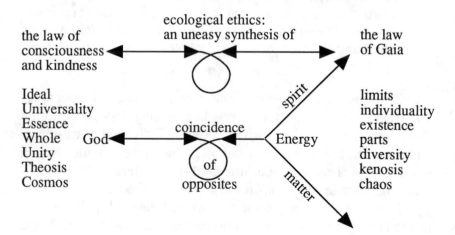

of spirit-matter bifurcation but has been separated from it for the purpose of visual clarity.

This shift leads to a new emphasis on the difference between humans and other creatures that tended to be flattened out in her previous cosmology in favour of her stress on our common possession of spiritual energy. Here she points to the fact that humans alone are capable of reflective consciousness which enables us to be "the 'mean' or mediator between the worlds"[250]—which I interpret as our capacity to be aware of both directions of the part-whole or Gaia-God correlation. Our responsibility as imagers of God includes harmonizing these apparently opposed directions of reality. We need to bring together *ideals* which reflect our awareness of the divine beyond present existence, and an attention to the *limits* which are part of the fabric of finitude. Thus she writes, "Ecological ethics is an uneasy synthesis of . . . the law of consciousness and kindness, which causes us to strain beyond what 'is,' and the laws of Gaia, which regulate what kinds of changes in 'nature' are sustainable in the life system of which we are an inextricable part."[251]

Her move away from a "soft dualism" to this complex "contradictory/harmony monism" has also affected her view of personal eschatology. The forthright challenge of her earlier works that we should simply accept our mortality has returned. What she calls the "contradiction" that is inherent in "the capacity of consciousness to roam through space and time," on the one hand, "and its utter transience in its dependence on our mortal organisms," on the other, must not be denied but can be embraced once we realize that there is a hidden harmony or resolution that can be revealed to those who can see beyond mere appearance. To do this, we must reject the egoism that keeps us caught in the multiplicity of life and blinds us to the One of which we are all parts. We need to let go of the ego in death as in life. Yet once we do this, we can value our "small selves" as expressions of "the Great Self."

As before, the Divine is pictured as "the wellspring of life and creativity from which all things have sprung and into which they return, only to well up again in new forms." She also continues to speak of God as "the great Thou, the personal center of the universal process." But at death, instead of picturing a reabsorption back into a Supra-individual Spirit, her hope for the ongoing significance of our lives after they have come to an end is that God is "a heart that knows us even as we are known" and is "a consciousness that remembers and envisions and reconciles all things."[252]

What I believe Ruether is trying to say may be clarified by an analogy. It could be said that although there is more to who I am than what I do, I am only known or revealed in my actions. Yet these actions leave behind only traces and do not live on as I do. Nevertheless, they may live on in my memory where I may continue to celebrate my achievements, learn from my mistakes, and work on resolving the pain and suffering of my past. For Ruether, I suggest, there is a parallel between the microcosm and the macrocosm. It is as though God is the self and our mortal lives are God's enactments which live on in God's memory after they have run their course.

If this is a correct reading, then as a response to evil this is no more satisfying than Ruether's earlier eschatological position. It is one thing to say that God continues and extends the work of cultural formation, liberation and redemption that we have begun in our lives, for the benefit of future generations. But to speak of the reconciliation of all things in the memory of God is quite another. The bringing about of justice and healing for those who perished in the Holocaust, for example, has to affect the concrete flesh and blood individuals who suffered—and thus requires a resurrection to life on the New Earth. This cannot be confused with, or reduced to, erecting a monument in their memory—even if this memorial is somehow located in the mind of God.

Gaia and God actually marks the *second* major shift in Ruether's view of the God-creation relationship. Her first book, *The Church Against Itself* (1967), is characterized by a neo-orthodox outlook in which she even speaks of "the 'wholly other' of God's nature."[253] By the time of her fourth book, *Liberation Theology* (1972), Ruether has begun to move towards the partial panentheism that I believe characterizes most of the material analyzed in this study. With *Gaia and God* (1992), she has moved to a more thorough-going panentheism.[254]

Some will see this as a move in the right direction, while others will see it as a gradual slide into paganism. My own reactions are mixed. What I like about Ruether's development is that it reveals her desire to see an intimacy between God and the world. This alone is enough to provoke suspicions of pantheism from some, who typically express this as a fear that God's transcendence, and thus "His" holiness, will be eclipsed. The fact that transcendence is frequently symbolized by masculinity and immanence by femininity means that Ruether's support for female God-language will tend to exacerbate such anxieties.

It is not uncommon to pay lip service to the idea of a "balance" between God's immanence and transcendence in this context. Donald Bloesch, for example, says, "The God of the Bible is utterly transcendent but also radically immanent." Two sentences later, however, he claims, "He is primarily and originally transcendent and secondarily and derivatively immanent."[255] It is no coincidence that he privileges male language for God.

Transcendence and immanence are confusing terms. Sometimes transcendence is used where I would rather speak of God's identity, and immanence is used to refer to what I like to call God's intimacy with, relationship to, or revelation through, creation. In this context, they are correlative terms and should not be opposed to one another. I confess to having no idea what it could possibly mean to make one more original or derivative than the other.[256]

In other contexts, however, transcendence refers to God's distance or hiddenness from us, while immanence refers to God's closeness and accessibility. In this context, the two terms are not correlates but should be seen as opposites. God's transcendence as distance is due entirely to the presence of evil.[257] Evil cannot incarnate, or reveal God. Thus creation is presently split apart into heaven, where God's will is done, and earth, where it is not done as it ought to be. In the biblical drama, God's transcendence in this sense—God's partial and temporary exile from the earth—will be overcome when God becomes "all in all." This has nothing to do with pantheism. God and creation will be so close that there will be no "gap" between them. In that *covenantal* sense they will indeed be "one," (in the same way that we might speak of husband and wife being one, or one flesh). God's transcendence in the sense of God's identity is in no danger of being lost. In fact, the nature and identity of God will no longer be hidden but will be clearly revealed in the eschaton. Similarly, once purged of evil and thus in full intimacy with its Creator, the true and authentic nature and identity of the world will be restored.

In this light, we need a view of the God-world relationship which acknowledges how this relationship can and will *change*. Ruether's view suggests that God and creation, as understood in her partial panentheism and now in her more consistent panentheism, are already related as they should be. The problem, however, is that we deny reality and, as a result of our alienated patriarchal consciousness, distort and misconstrue the relationship between God/ess and world, turning it into one of polarization, heteronomy, competition, and hierarchy. I don't doubt the warped nature of the dominant worldview. But it might be more accurate to say that the stress in traditional (patriarchal) theology on God's transcendence (distance) to some extent correctly describes a facet of the present relationship between God and creation, but errs in seeing that distance in terms of a spirit-matter dualism and as something that is permanent, desirable and normative. Looked at in this way, Ruether fails both in her criticisms and in her own proposals to distinguish between an authentic vision *of* the God-world relationship (as it is at present) and an authentic vision *for* that relationship (as it ought to be, and as it will be).

Whether "patriarchy" is the root cause of our present alienated and alienating worldview and way of life, as Ruether often suggests, is one of the topics that will be explored further in the next chapter. There I shall look at how some of the aspects of Ruether's systematic theology that have been explored in this chapter function in her theology of culture. I will also tackle the question of the place of feminist concerns within a global theology of liberation.

Notes

1. As with the summaries of her work in previous chapters, I will continue to draw from all of Ruether's feminist writings. I will, however, pay special attention to *SGT* as this contains her most systematic treatment of the various areas of theology.

2. Hence the subtitle in *SGT*, 109: "Toward A Feminist Anthropology Beyond Liberalism And Romanticism." The following discussion is based on pp. 102-13.

3. Ibid., 104.

4. ibid., 107.

5. Ibid., 107-108.

6. Ibid., 108.

7. Ibid.

8. Ibid., 109.

9. *FMM*, 115.

10. *SGT*, 109.

11. Ibid., 109-10.

12. Ibid.

13. Ibid.

14. *NWNE*, 193.

15. Presumably she would no longer claim, as she does in *NWNE*, 205, that "The human capacity for technological rationality is . . . the *highest* gift of nature" (my emphasis).

16. *SGT*, 113.

17. Ibid., 111 (her emphasis).

18. Ibid.

19. Ibid.

20. See ibid., 89.

21. Ibid., 112.

22. Ibid., 274, n.10.

23. Ibid.

24. Prudence Allen, *The Concept of Woman: The Aristotelian Revolution 750 BC-AD 1250* (Montreal: Eden Press, 1985), 4-5.

25. *SGT*, 110.

26. *FMM*, 83.

27. See *SGT*, 113.

28. *NWNE*, 210.

29. Patricia Wilson-Kastner, *Faith, Feminism, and the Christ* (Philadelphia: Fortress Press, 1983), 55.

30. Ruether's distinction between the inside and the outside, which will be examined below, is influenced by the thought of Pierre Teilhard de Chardin. It is significant that in his *The Phenomenon of Man*, trans. Bernard Wall (New York: Harper and Row, 1959), 143, he says, "*The essence of the real . . .* could well be represented by the 'interiority' contained by the universe at a given moment" (my emphasis).

31. Allen, *The Concept of Woman*, 5.

32. See Eph. 4:31-32; 5:21; Col. 3:12; Gal. 5:22-23 and 1 Pet. 3:8.

272 Giving Birth to the Future

33. Mary Stewart Van Leeuwen, *Gender and Grace: Love, Work and Parenting in a Changing World* (Downers Grove: InterVarsity Press, 1990), 100. This illustration is still a little dualistic as it suggests that the lower is merely the necessary occasion for the activity of the higher functions. See chaps. 4 and 5 of this book for a lucid analysis of the nature/nurture debate.
34. *SGT*, 112.
35. See *NWNE*, 151-52.
36. *WC*, 131.
37. *SGT*, 161. Cf. *GG*, 115-16.
38. See *SGT*, 159.
39. Ibid.
40. See ibid., 161.
41. *CAI*, 162.
42. *SGT*, 161. Cf. *GG*, 256.
43. *SGT*, 161.
44. *TCW*, 25.
45. *SGT*, 181-82.
46. *TCW*, 27-28.
47. Ibid., 28.
48. Ibid., 29.
49. Ibid.
50. See Nik Ansell, "The Sins of the Fathers. . . . Reflections on Tradition, Evil and the Atonement," (Toronto: unpublished paper, 1991) and the chapter on women and evil in *The Troubled Marriage Of Adam And Eve*.
51. On this important topic, see Walter Wink, *Naming the Powers: The Language of Power in the New Testament* (Philadelphia: Fortress Press, 1984) and idem, *Unmasking the Powers: The Invisible Forces That Determine Human Existence* (Philadelphia: Fortress Press, 1986). The third volume in this trilogy has now been published. In *GG*, 303 n.10, there is a reference to the first volume, but Ruether's own discussion (on p. 233) does not reflect Wink's position. On the related biblical notion of idolatry and its relevance for contemporary Christian cultural analysis, see Goudzwaard, *Idols of Our Time*.
52. This was quite clear from the way she answered a question on this topic at the ICS in 1983 in the context of giving the "Christianity and Learning Lectures" of that year. It is not easy to document from her writings however. For a recent example of liberal-conservative polarization along these lines, see David L. Edwards (with John Stott) *Essentials: A Liberal-Evangelical Dialogue* (London: Hodder and Stoughton, 1988), 107-68.
53. See Gustaf Aulen, *Christus Victor: An Historical Study of the Three Main Types of the Idea of the Atonement*, trans. A. G. Hebert (London: SPCK, 1970). This was originally published in Swedish in 1930.

54. See Reta Halteman Finger, "How Can Jesus Save. Women? Three Theories on Christ's Atonement," *Daughters of Sarah* 14 (November-December 1988), 14-18. Halteman Finger is currently a student at Garrett-Evangelical Theological Seminary where Ruether is a professor. See also Thomas N. Finger, *Christian Theology: An Eschatological Approach* vol. 1 (Scottdale: Herald Press, 1985), 303-48. I have drawn on this material in my paper "The Sins of the Fathers . . . Reflections on Tradition, Evil and the Atonement."

55. *SGT*, 152.

56. See *MFFC*, 87.

57. See *SGT*, 152-58.

58. Ibid., 153.

59. Ibid., 154.

60. Ibid.

61. Ibid., 156-57.

62. Ibid., 157.

63. Ibid.

64. I would add that Ruether's view often sounds as though it is referring to co-dependency and mutual limitation rather than co-agency. Cf. my comments in the final section of this chapter.

65. Another book which looks at Mary's role in Jesus' birth but challenges traditional interpretations in a way that is very respectful of the biblical givens, is Jane Shaberg's *The Illegitimacy of Jesus: A Feminist Theological Interpretation of the Infancy Narratives* (San Francisco: Harper and Row, 1987). This is, in my opinion, clearly the best book yet to be written by a feminist in the area of biblical studies, and I find myself in substantial agreement with her arguments. The dust jacket of the hard-cover edition and the back cover of the paperback edition quote Ruether as saying: "This is a fascinating book. Although speculative, it is very solid; the interpretation of the *Magnificat* is particularly compelling."

66. Ricoeur, *The Symbolism of Evil*, 250.

67. Hart, *Setting our Sights by the Morning Star*, 203-204.

68. For Ruether's own argument against modern ideas of autonomy, see *CAI*, 162-63.

69. Pedro Trigo, *Creation and History*, trans. Robert R. Barr (Maryknoll: Orbis Books, 1991), 52.

70. Wolfhart Pannenberg, *Anthropology in Theological Perspective*, trans. Matthew J. O'Connell (Philadelphia: The Westminster Press, 1985), 113-14.

71. *SGT*, 207.

72. *NWNE*, 80.

73. *SGT*, 207-208.

74. Ibid., 208-209.

75. Ibid., 209.

76. See ibid., 203-204.

77. Ibid., 201.
78. Ibid., 205.
79. Ibid.
80. See *FMM*, 115.
81. *SGT*, 206.
82. *WC*, 67.
83. See ibid., 57-74.
84. See ibid., 122-282.
85. Ibid., 60 (my emphasis).
86. Ibid., 62.
87. Ibid., 61.
88. Ibid., 73-74.
89. See *SGT*, 208-209 as cited on 199-200 above.
90. I am speaking here of the way she expresses herself in *SGT*, 208-209. She does not speak this way in her main work on ecclesiology, *WC*.
91. I can find no reflection of the need for or nature of worship in her writings. A small number of songs of praise are included in *WC* on pp. 174-76, 180-81, 267, 271-72.
92. On this second point, see Walter Brueggemann, *Israel's Praise: Doxology Against Idolatry and Ideology* (Philadelphia: Fortress Press, 1988).
93. See, e. g., *WC*, 32-35 and *WG*, 248.
94. See *SGT*, 193-213.
95. This seems close to what Ruether herself suggests in *NWNE*, 81.
96. See Hendrik Hart, "Cultus and Covenant," in James H. Olthuis et al., *Will All the King's Men*. . . (Toronto: Wedge, 1972), 29-60.
97. *TCW*, 56. Cf. *SGT*, 137.
98. *SGT*, 137.
99. *WG*, 112.
100. *SGT*, 138. Cf. *FF*, 238-39, 243, 246-51.
101. *SGT*, 114.
102. The following summary is based on *SGT*, 131-38.
103. Ibid., 131. I have reversed the order of the phrases in this first quotation.
104. Ibid., 138.
105. This would fit with Ruether's own observations in ibid., 36-37.
106. Although some might cite 2 Pet. 1:4 against me on this second point, see Wolters, " 'Partners of the Deity': A Covenantal Reading of 2 Peter 1:4."
107. Cf. the discussion of the meaning of "head" on 141 above and in chap. 3 n.159.
108. For additional exegetical support for a corporate Christology in Paul, see John A. T. Robinson, *The Body: A Study in Pauline Theology* (London: SCM, 1952), chap. 3, and N. T. Wright, *The Climax of the Covenant: Christ and the Law in Pauline Theology* (Minneapolis: Fortress Press, 1991), chaps. 2 and 3.

109. See Yoder, *The Politics of Jesus*, 123-34.
110. See Hart, *Morning Star*, 189-97.
111. Ibid., 196-97,
112. See *LT*, 115-26 and *NWNE*, 186-211.
113. See *SGT*, 85-92. The shift that occurs in her view of nature and in her cosmology as a whole in *GG*, is discussed briefly in the final section of this chapter.
114. Ibid., 85.
115. *TCW*, 11.
116. My use of the terms "monism" and "dualism" follows the interpretation of D. Th. Vollenhoven's ideas by James H. Olthuis and Arnold H. De Graaff in their " Models of Man in Theology and Psychology" (Toronto: ICS, 1978), 15-17. These terms do not refer to whether or not someone distinguishes between God and creation. A monist is someone who explains the diversity of creation in terms of its unity, reductionistically conceived. By contrast, dualists, if they explain the unity of life at all, do so in terms of the relationship between what they perceive as the two fundamental halves, principles, origins, substances, sides, or realms that make up reality. By "soft" dualism as opposed to "harsh" dualism, I am referring to the kind of dualism found in "monarchian" and "semi-mystic" cosmologies (see ibid., 35) as opposed, e. g., to an "ascetic spiritualist" position (see ibid., 33). Soft dualists attempt to keep their higher and lower realms together, unlike harsh dualists who favour the higher and thus tend to have a more clearly hierarchical cosmology. Following Vollenhoven, Olthuis and De Graaff, I believe that neither unity nor diversity must be over-privileged. As an alternative to monistic or dualistic cosmologies and anthropologies, we must speak of life in terms of its multi-dimensional unity.
117. Thus the fact that she employs the inside-outside (or inward-outward) distinction to advocate a *"holistic* vision of the world," in *TCW*, 11 can be interpreted in terms of Olthuis' and De Graaff's observation (in "Models of Man," 16) that "Dualisms are preoccupied with the quest for unity, cooperation and harmony." Wholism and monism do not necessarily go together. One can hold to a dualistic view of the whole.
118. *SGT*, 86. The discussion of the next two paragraphs is also based on this page.
119. It is interesting that on p. 16 of his introduction to *The Phenomenon of Man*, Julian Huxley notes the same ambiguity in the cosmology of Teilhard de Chardin—a thinker to whom Ruether is clearly indebted. Cf. Teilhard's attempt on p. 64 to avoid a "fundamental dualism" in his discussion of the two distinct components of energy.
120. I have placed "realm" within quotation marks here because Ruether does not normally use such overtly dualistic terminology. It is interesting that in the more existentially charged language of *SGT*, 257, cited on 229 below, she does

ask whether there is "some larger *realm*" in which the meaning of our lives is preserved.

121. These terms should probably be seen as Ruether's version of what Teilhard de Chardin calls "psychic" energy. He equates this with what he himself calls "radial" energy in *The Phenomenon of Man*, 143.

122. See *NWNE*, 187-88, and Rosemary Radford Ruether, "The Biblical Vision of the Ecological Crisis," *The Christian Century* 95 (November 22, 1978): 1129-32. Cf. *GG*, 207-10.

123. This freedom/necessity distinction within nature is related to a cosmos/chaos distinction. Cf. *SGT*, 75-76 and 218-19 below.

124 Cf. Teilhard's discussion in *The Phenomenon of Man*, 57 and 149.

125. *SGT*, 86 from which all the quotations in this paragraph have been taken. For an earlier example of her use of Teilhard, see *RK*, 202-12. For a more recent interaction, see *GG*, 242-45.

126. *SGT*, 87.

127. Ibid. Cf. *GG*, 227-28.

128. Ibid.

129. Ibid., 89.

130. Ibid., 90-91.

131. Ibid., 75-76.

132. *LT*, 124.

133. I wonder if on *SGT*, 78, she slips back into an anthropocentric position when she claims that in the Old Testament, "God's covenant relation with *humanity* links the human and natural communities in one creation (my emphasis)." My thanks to Brian Walsh for alerting me to this sentence.

134. Understanding the miraculous as the restoration of normative order should not be confused with the more common notion that miracles break the order of nature.

135. For an attempt to explore the agency of non-human creation, see Brian J. Walsh, Marianne Karsh and Nik Ansell, "Acid Rain, Deforestation, and the Responsiveness of Creation," paper presented at the Canadian Theological Society on May 23, 1990 at the University of Victoria and forthcoming in Steve Bishop, ed., *Stewarding Creation*, (Bristol, U.K.: Regius Press).

136. *SGT*, 87 also cited above.

137. "Transcendental" is a term used of this direction in Dooyeweerd's ontology. I prefer to speak of guiding, leading or nurturing.

138. See 90-91 above.

139. See 211 above. To say that only humans will incarnate God is to be guilty of "humanocentrism" to use one of Ruether's terms. The fact that we are created *imago dei* does not mean that we are the only creatures that reveal God. It simply refers to the unique way we reveal God by guiding the rest of creation to its destiny in history and thus continuing God's work of forming and filling the earth.

140. What I am arguing here is that Ruether's cosmology can be classified as a form of semi-mysticism, to use the terminology of Olthuis and De Graaff, ("Models of Man", 35). What is peculiar to her position is that while most semi-mystics elevate the rational mode to a special role of revelation of and connection with the Ultimate, Ruether would seem to elevate the physical or energy mode in this way. (Actually her cosmology is not quite this straightforward as the more precise explanation of what she means by energy offered on 330 below, will show.)

141. *SGT*, 87.

142. Rosemary Radford Ruether, "The Resurrection of the Body and the Life Everlasting," in Robert A. Evans and Thomas D. Parker, eds., *Christian Theology: A Case Study Approach* (New York: Harper and Row, 1976), 256.

143. Ibid., 257.

144. See 40 above.

145. See Rosemary Radford Ruether, "A Historical and Textual Analysis of the Relationship Between Futurism and Eschatology in the Apocalyptic Texts of the Inter-Testamental Period" (Unpublished B.A. thesis, Scripps College, 1958), 88 and passim, (hereafter referred to as *RFE*), *and CAI*, 29-30 (where the eschatological is identified with a transcendent norm, not as a point in time). Cf. Ibid., 56-7, 60-61, 90, 210, and *RK*, 276, 287-88.

146. *RK*, 287.

147. *TCW*, 69.

148. Ibid., 68-69. Cf. *SGT*, 254-56.

149. *TCW*, 69 and *SGT*, 255.

150. *TCW*, 69-70.

151. *LT*, 125.

152. See *GG*, 257.

153. See ibid., 139, 141 and 200.

154. *LT*, 125. This essay originally appeared in *Christianity and Crisis* 31 (December 13, 1971): 267-73.

155. *NWNE*, 211.

156. *WG*, 224.

157. *SGT*, 257.

158. Ibid., 257-58.

159. Ibid., 257.

160. Ibid.

161. Ibid., 257-58.

162. Ibid., 258. My later argument depends in part on reading Ruether's first sentence here as "If the interiority of our organism is a personal center, how much more so is [*the interiority of*] the great organism of the universe itself?"

The words that I have supplied are necessary if a *non sequitur* on Ruether's part is to be avoided. This reading is also justified, I believe, because in her essay "Eschatology and Feminism," in Susan Brooks Thislethwaite and Mary Potter Engel, eds., *Lift Every Voice: Constructing Christian Theologies from the Underside* (San Francisco: Harper and Row, 1990), the last two pages of which reproduce the section of *SGT* under investigation with only minor stylistic changes, she rephrases this sentence to read: "If the interiority of our organism is our personal center, might we not suppose that this is also true of the great organism of the universe itself?" (123).

163. *SGT*, 258. Cf. Teilhard's comments about how the end of the world defies imagination in *The Phenomenon of Man*, 273.

164. Presumably, given her cosmology, she would say the same about all creatures.

165. My emphasis. Cf. Teilhard's discussion of the Omega Point in *The Phenomenon of Man*, 260-72.

166. See *SGT*, 256-58.

167. See ibid., 1-3. I am not claiming that every time Ruether uses the word *kenosis* she is referring to this individuation process. This may be the case, however, when she uses it in the context of the relationship between God and humanity. See the section on *kenosis* in Kathryn Allen Rabuzzi, "The Socialist Feminist Vision of Rosemary Radford Ruether: A Challenge to Liberal Feminism," *Religious Studies Review* 15 (January 1989): 7.

168. *SGT*, 251. For an earlier less mystical appeal to Native Indian beliefs, see "The Resurrection of the Dead and the Life Everlasting," 260.

169. *SGT*, 257-58. Cf. Teilhard's critique of egocentrism and his claim that true personality requires the transcending of individuality in *The Phenomenon of Man*, 244 and 263.

170. *SGT*, 258. Cf. Teilhard's claim in *The Phenomenon of Man*, 271, that the Omega "by its very nature . . . escape[s] from time and space which it gathers together."

171. *WC*, 211.

172. See, e. g., Snyder, *The Christology of Rosemary Radford Ruether*, Vaughan, *Sociality, Ethics, and Social Change*, and the other works cited in section B of my bibliography.

173. *SGT*, 258.

174. "Geneticism" is a term used by Olthuis and De Graaff in "Models of Man," 18-23, to describe cosmologies or anthropologies that absolutize change and development in contrast to "structuralism" which refers to positions which overemphasize the structural contours of creation. They note that most monists are also geneticists, while dualists tend to be structuralists. The above reading of Ruether has been an attempt, for the sake of argument, to read her as a geneticistic monist.

In addition to structuralism and geneticism, Seerveld, following Vollenhoven, suggests that there is a third tradition of thinkers who have a "mythologizing" view of cosmology/cosmogony. He claims that such thinkers "hold the structurally ordered durational matrix of reality underdevelopedly undistinguished, with the result that the order is given genetic finality and genesis is given everlasting, repetitive order." (Calvin G. Seerveld, "Biblical Wisdom Underneath Vollenhoven's Categories for Philosophical Historiography," in K. A. Bril, H. Hart, and J. Klapwijk, eds., *The Idea of a Christian Philosophy: Essays in Honour of D. H. Th. Vollenhoven* [Toronto: Wedge Publishing Foundation, 1973], 137.) Ruether's view of the nature of history examined in the above section on historical eschatology has such a "mythologizing" character in my opinion. Following a discussion about Nietzsche's view of death with Mark Roques, it has struck me that Ruether's words "And so it shall ever be" at the end of the funeral sermon cited in *DQ*, 23, might indicate an "eternal recurrence of the same" motif.

175. *SGT*, 258.

176. See ibid., second full paragraph. The first two sentences read, "But what of the meaning of our lives; what of the good to be remembered and the evil redressed? Is this merely the disintegration of centers of personality into an 'impersonal' matrix of the all? If the interiority of our organism. . . ."

177. In the section on personal eschatology in ibid., 256-58 it seems to be equivalent to what I described above as Nature-1, although it may sometimes mean Nature-2. In *NWNE*, 194-95, it seems to mean Nature-3. When used as term for God, it seems to mean "source," but with connotations of Nature-2 possibly present. See *SGT*, 48 and 70. In *WG*, 216 the etymological connections between matrix, mother and matter are made explicit, but most contexts preclude a simply identification of matrix and "matter" in its modern sense.

178. See 218 above.

179. *SGT*, 71.

180. Ibid., 257.

181. Ibid., 86.

182. Ibid., 85. My emphasis.

183. Ibid., 258.

184. Ibid.

185. *WC*, 212-13.

186. "Eshatology and Feminism," 123. For another clarification in this essay that helps my reading of the discussion in *SGT*, see n. 162 above.

187. She refers to Teilhard de Chardin in *SGT*, 86-87 and to his *The Phenomenon of Man* in *SGT*, 272 nn. 12, 13.

188. See *The Phenomenon Of Man*, 260 and 271.

189. Ibid., 272.

190. *RK*, 211. Cf. *The Phenomenon Of Man* (n.30), 287.

191. *SGT,* 258.
192. *RK,* 212. This inner contradiction is worked out differently in *GG,* as I will argue briefly in the final section of this chapter.
193. On our call to be both sojourners and homesteaders, see James W. Skillen, "Politics and Eschatology: Political Action and the Coming of God's Kingdom" (Toronto: ICS, 1978).
194. *SGT,* 256-57.
195. *RFE,* 90. Cf. Ruether, "The Resurrection of the Body and the Life Everlasting," 259.
196. *WC,* 232.
197. The resurrection of the body is not a dualistic notion unless it is coupled with the idea of an intermediate state for the disembodied soul. I reject the idea of an intermediate state. The problem of the continuity of identity between a person before death and that same person at the general resurrection might be greatly relativized if we paid attention to the mystery of the continuity of identity from day to day and year to year in this life. The continuity of identity in either context cannot be adequately understood without reference to God's covenant with creation. A full exploration of this topic here would go beyond the bounds of this study.
198. This was later published as *GN.*
199. *DQ,* 37.
200. Paulos Mar Gregorios, "New Testament Foundations for Understanding the Creation," in Wesley Granberg-Michaelson, ed., *Tending the Garden: Essays on the Gospel and the Earth* (Grand Rapids: Eerdmans, 1987), 90.
201. Orthodox influence may also explain why the title of the postscript in *SGT,* 259 is "Woman/Body/Nature: The *Icon* of the Divine", rather than "Woman/Body/Nature: The *Incarnation* of the Divine" (which I would prefer). This term fits well with what I interpret as her ontological subordination of matter to spirit/energy. It is interesting that the use of icons was first defended by Christians who appealed to the cosmology of Neoplatonism. Virgil Cândea notes that "According to Neoplatonists the relationship between image and prototype is not one of sameness: images serve only as vehicles by which to approach the divine prototype, which is hidden from humans because of the limitations of their corporeality." He goes on to quote the eighth-century theologian Theodore of Studios, who said that, "veneration was not due to the essence of the image but rather to the form of the Prototype represented by the image . . . since matter cannot be subjected to veneration." See Virgil Cândea, "Icons," in Mircea Eliade, ed. in chief., *The Encyclopedia of Religion* vol. 7 (New York: Macmillan Publishing Co., 1987), 67-70. The quotations are taken from pp. 68 and 69 respectively. While some may believe that icons reflect a high view of the goodness of creation, others, including myself, see them as reflecting a denaturation of our world.

202. I owe this idea to Professor John Stek of Calvin Theological Seminary. Some may claim that 2 Pet. 3:10 negates belief in the restoration of creation, but see Al Wolters, "Worldview and Textual Criticism in 2 Peter 3:10," *Westminster Theological Journal* 49 (1987): 405-13.

203. *SGT*, 46. It is interesting that she uses "God" throughout *GG*. Is this to enhance communication to a wide audience on the ecological crisis, or does it reflect an even stronger identification of the divine with metaphysical Unity which is undermined by connotations of bi-unity in "God/ess"?

204. *MFFC*, 77-78.

205. *SGT*, 48.

206. See *DQ*, 24 and *SGT*, 85.

207. *SGT*, 62.

208. Ibid., 65. See Ruether's discussion of *Abba* on 68 above.

209. Ibid., 66.

210. Ibid.

211. Ibid., 66-67.

212. Ibid., 67.

213. See ibid., 67-68. The biblical references for these parables are Mt. 13:31-32; Mk. 4:30-32 (mustard seed), Mt. 13:33-35; Mk. 4:33-34 (leaven), Mt. 18:10-14; Lk. 15:4-7 (lost sheep), Lk. 15:8-10 (lost coin).

214. Ibid., 69.

215. Ibid., 70.

216. Ibid., 68.

217. Ibid., 70.

218. Ibid., 70-71.

219. While *NWNE*, 14 refers to the Divine embracing spirit and matter, Ruether is describing the view of early religions to which she is sympathetic but not in entire agreement. We cannot assume she is outlining her own position here.

220. *SGT*, 86. See 214-15 above. Cf. Teilhard de Chardin's claim, in *The Phenomenon of Man*, 151, that a being's visible characteristics form "merely the outward garment round something deeper which *supports* it [my emphasis]."

221. It is possible that in the passage cited above that she intends to suggest that God/ess embraces the *roots* of our new being (and thus the roots of spiritual energy). The grammar of the last sentence does not convey this, however.

222. See *RK*, 212, cited on 242 above.

223. See *TCW*, 69, as cited on 225 above.

224. *SGT*, 71.

225. Ibid.

226. *MFFC*, 78.

227. I wonder whether this understanding of God as a *metaphysical* Unity may be why she is keen to "preserv[e] the Judeo-Christian affirmation that divinity is one" in *SGT*, 46, rather than opt for a polytheism that is available to her in some of her "usable traditions." The Bible's language about the one God is confessional not metaphysical. It means that the idols that human beings worship are no-gods, while the true God tolerates no divided loyalties but requires single-minded commitment.

228. *SGT*, 71.

229. A helpful book in this context is Diane Tennis, *Is God the Only Reliable Father?* (Philadelphia: The Westminster Press, 1985).

230. Faith development is sadly not something that Ruether takes into account in any of her writings. The classic work on this subject is James W. Fowler, *Stages of Faith: The Psychology of Human Development and the Quest for Meaning* (San Francisco: Harper and Row, 1981).

231. On the intimacy/identity correlation in humans, see James H. Olthuis, *Keeping Our Troth: Staying in Love Through The Five Stages of Marriage* (San Francisco: Harper and Row, 1986), 20-48.

232. See 222 above.

233. I owe this neologism to Hendrik Hart.

234. The apophatic tradition may well be very pessimistic about such talk, but it is still playing the same game.

235. See Roy Clouser, "Religious Language: A New Look at an Old Problem" (Toronto: ICS, 1980). Cf. the revised version of this essay in Hendrik Hart, Johan Van der Hoeven and Nicholas Wolterstorff, eds., *Rationality in the Calvinian Tradition* (Lanham: University Press of America, 1983), 385-407 and his discussion in *The Myth of Religious Neutrality* (n.), 180-90.

236. See *WG*, 9.

237. Ibid., 3.

238. See Ruether's comments on the Goddess of Babylonia in ibid., 4-5. On the meaning of "helper," see 114 above.

239. *SGT*, 67.

240. See Donald G. Bloesch, *The Battle for the Trinity: The Debate over Inclusive God-Language* (Ann Arbor: Vine Books, 1985), 35 where the literal/metaphorical distinction is parallelled in his catalogy/analogy distinction.

241. Ibid., 34. Bloesch continues, "But the living God transcends and overcomes this polarity." It is hard to see how his position does justice to this claim, however.

242. Stanley J. Grenz and Roger E. Olson, *Twentieth-Century Theology: God and the World in a Transitional Age*, (Downers Grove, IL: InterVarsity Press, 1992), 233.

243. *RK*, 211.

244. Matthew Fox, *Original Blessing: A Primer in Creation Spirituality* (Santa Fe: Bear and Co., 1983), 35-41.

245. See *GG*, 247.

246. Ibid., 5.

247. See ibid., 48.

248. Ibid., 248-49.
249. See *GG*, 245.
250. *GG*, 249.
251. Ibid., 31.
252. Ibid., 251-53. The sentiments in this last quotation are anticipated in "Eschatology and Feminism," 125, where she speaks of being "preserved in [The Holy Being's] eternal memory"—an idea not present in *SGT*, 258, which is otherwise virtually identical to this part of the later essay.
253. *CAI*, 174.
254. In the terminology of Olthuis and De Graaff, "Models of Man in Theology and Psychology," this first shift is from a "monarchian" to a "semi-mystic" anthropology (p. 35). Her current position corresponds to "contradictory monism" (pp. 28-30). On this last type, see Calvin G. Seerveld, "The Pedagogical Strength of a Christian Methodology in Philosophical Historiography," in *Social Theory and Practice: Philosophical Essays in Honour of Prof. J. A. L. Taljaard*, *Koers* 40/4-6 (1975): 269-302.
255. Bloesch, *The Battle For The Trinity*, 29.
256. The impulse to insist that God's identity as God pre-existed the creation of the world comes from the influence of post-biblical Greek metaphysics. In the Bible, "God" always means *God of creation*.
257. *Contra* Bloesch, *The Battle For The Trinity*, 30, who says, "It is primarily because of our sin that we find God unapproachable and inaccessible." "Primarily" should be replaced by "only" in my opinion.

Chapter Five: The Sins Of The Fathers?

In the previous chapter, I concentrated on Ruether's proposals for various areas of theology. Here the focus will be on aspects of the cultural analysis that flows from her feminist theology and from her worldview. After raising the question of the helpfulness and accuracy of her use of "patriarchy" as a global concept, I will look at the origin, nature and development of male dominance and entertain the possibility of a "multi-faceted liberation theology" as a model that can incorporate and integrate the best features of Ruether's theology of culture while avoiding some of the limitations of her approach.

I. Patriarchy as a Global Concept

"Patriarchy" is undoubtedly one of the most central concepts in feminist cultural analysis. As can be seen in various places in her thought (and as was made clear in the section on ecclesiology in the previous chapter), Ruether often uses this word when she wants to refer to the nature of Western culture as a whole and/or when she intends to reveal the common root of our many social problems.

It is true that Ruether does not always simply equate evil with sexism. In the previous chapter I looked at the way in which she has attempted to analyze evil in terms of broken relationships—an approach with which my own sympathies lie. Even when specifically addressing the evil of sexism, she may relativize its primacy. In one place she refers to "the distortion of humanity as male and female into a dualism of superiority and inferiority" as being "*[a]mong* the primary distortions of the self-other relationship [my emphasis].[1] There is also at least one place in Ruether's writings in which she appears to speak of an alienation from God as being more fundamental than sexism, even though this only amounts to a partial relativization of the latter. She writes,

> We must begin by understanding the nature of sexism as sin. If the fall consists in an alienation between man and God that takes social form in the alienated oppressive social relationships between persons, then sexism must be seen as the original and primary model for analyzing the state of the fall.[2]

Elsewhere, this distinction between original sin and sexism is conflated.[3] In an argument in which she claims that feminists need not reject the biblical ideas of the Fall, sin, and inherited evil just because they have been used to scapegoat woman, she proposes that this "biblical religious pattern" can be legitimately interpreted to mean that "self-alienation and the transformation of the primal relation of men and women into an oppressive dualism is *the root sin upon which the crimes of history have been constructed* [my emphasis]."[4] In *New Woman/New Earth*, she goes as far as to claim that "Sexism reflects both the heart and the ultimate circumference of the many revolutions in which we are presently involved."[5] This helps make sense of why a litany that includes disaffiliation from such diverse evils as violence, racism, wealth and exploitation in *Women-Church* is referred to as "a litany of disaffiliation from *patriarchy*."[6]

Such a global use of the term "patriarchy" cannot just be assumed. We may grant that there is structural evil in all known societies. We may also grant that all known societies are "father-ruled." We may even believe that the fact that they are "father-ruled" is an evil. Yet a number of questions still remain. Why should *this* particular feature of human societies be privileged? Isn't the attempt to encapsulate the alienated and oppressive nature of a culture by calling it a "patriarchy" a serious confusion of causation with correlation? Are racism and classism less fundamental forms of oppression than sexism? These are some of the important issues which need to be dealt with.

One way of capturing the common concern in each of these questions from an explicitly Christian perspective is to propose that when she should refer to a culture as simply "fallen," Ruether tends to describe it as "patriarchal," thus giving the impression that sexism is to be understood as nothing less than the heart of original sin. Thus, in her review of *From Machismo To Mutuality*, Christiane Carlson-Thies writes,

> As helpful as Ruether's historical reconstructions are, her analysis suffers from a serious weakness. Ruether locates the origin of human brokenness in the Fall, but then goes on to characterize the essence of that event as the resulting domination of man over woman. This expression of fallen humanity is raised up, in her thinking, as the primal perversion and the cause of all other forms of social alienation (e. g., racism, militarism, disregard for our environment, etc.). Thus, in her terms, the most accurate label for our broken world is that it is "masculinist." The entire book abounds with such phrases as "male culture," "patriarchal hegemony," "male-dominated systems," and as these phrases are used, they are intended to convey the true core of all our social problems—not merely aspects of them.[7]

Ruether's tendency to conflate original sin with sexism, and fallenness with patriarchy is not consistent with her practice elsewhere of analyzing evil simply in terms of broken relationships. Both ways of talking, however, appear throughout her corpus. While I will later suggest the reason why she moves back and forth between these two positions, the focus in this chapter will be on this former strand in her thought.

Although I disagree with Ruether on this issue, I can see that there are at least two ways in which she could justify the central place sexism and patriarchy occupy in her cultural analysis. The first involves an appeal to her cosmology. The shift in Ruether's view of the world articulated in *Gaia and God* does not seem to have altered her conviction that all our social problems stem from (and reinforce) an alienated view of the world in which we falsely polarize the dialectics of essence and existence, spirit and matter.[8] We might even say that for Ruether the first commandment is: What God/ess has joined together, let no man put asunder! In this light, it becomes clear that one fundamental reason why she uses the term patriarchy so globally could be because she believes that the "divorce" within human consciousness between spirit and matter, which has had such wide-ranging and devastating consequences, has its historical origin in the rise of patriarchal cultures. Thus, while others may blame the ecology crisis on capitalism or the modern idols of Technicism and Progress, Ruether writes,

> It is not too extreme to see this denouement as inherent in the fundamental patriarchal revolution of consciousness that sought to deny that the spiritual component of humanity was a dimension of the maternal matrix of being. Patriarchy sought to elevate consciousness to supernatural apriority. Mother and nature religions traditionally have seen heaven and earth, gods and humans, as dialectical components within the primal matrix of being. Its spirituality was built on the cyclic ecology of nature, of death and rebirth. Patriarchal religion split apart the dialectical unities of mother religion into absolute dualism, elevating a male-identified consciousness to transcendent apriority.[9]

Another reason why she believes it is legitimate to use "patriarchy" in such an all-encompassing way is that she accepts the thesis, which she finds in Engels' 1885 study *The Origin and History of the Family, Private Property and the State*, that woman's subjugation is not only the first oppressor-oppressed relation, but is used as the prototype for destructive class and property relations. Thus, building on Engels' position, Ruether writes,

> Sexual symbolism is foundational to the perception of order and relationship that has been built up in cultures. The psychic

organization of consciousness, the dualistic view of the self and the world, the hierarchical concept of society, the relation of humanity and nature, and of God and creation—all these relationships have been modelled on sexual dualism. . . .[10]

In a similar vein, building on the work of Simone de Beauvoir's classic study, *The Second Sex,* Ruether observes that male-dominated societies always view woman as the "other," by which she means an antithesis over against which "authentic" or "normative" (i. e., male) selfhood is defined. The cultural impact of sexism does not stop here, however, because the female viewed as alien or deviant also functions in the eyes of ruling-class males as a model for the inferiorization of lower classes and conquered races. Because it is the same dominant group doing the naming, all subjugated groups are perceived through similar stereotypes: as sensual, irrational, passive and dependent. They are thus seen in terms of the characteristics of repressed bodiliness which are projected onto them by a dominant race, class, and sexual caste that models its own self-image after ego or consciousness.[11]

Therefore in Ruether's view, it would seem that describing a culture as sexist or patriarchal is not analogous to labelling it as racist or capitalist. It is to speak of something more fundamental. She would strongly resist the accusation that she was indulging in a simplistic or arbitrary privileging of what is merely one form of oppression among many others. To identify a culture as patriarchal, she believes, is to penetrate to the very core of its many forms of oppression. This is why she can say that "[s]exism reflects both the heart and the ultimate circumference of the many revolutions in which we are presently involved."[12]

II. The Rise and Development of Patriarchy

For anyone who shares Ruether's fundamental assumptions about the nature of sexism, tracing the rise and development of patriarchy is not just a matter of historical curiosity, for such historical knowledge promises to shed light on the origins of our current problems and may also suggest possible solutions.[13] Two very important questions in this context are, Why did patriarchy arise at all?

and Was it inevitable? While I find Ruether's answer to the first question to be inadequate, I do want to insist with her that the rise of patriarchy was not a historical necessity.

I have already mentioned in chapters 3 and 4 that the biblical Story speaks in faith of an unambiguously good creation which preceded a space-time fall.[14] Evil is not something God has built into the structure of creation or history. To believe that it is, I contend, is to legitimate evil in general and patriarchy in particular. Evil then comes to be viewed as both necessary and inevitable. Just as we can't make an omelette without breaking a few eggs, so humans, by analogy, cannot engage in cultural formation without causing oppression. In such a view, it is hard to see how creation can be liberated or redeemed. Salvation becomes an escape from those people, those parts of the creational structure, or those stages of the historical process that are seen as the root of evil (such as the Jews, the body or the rise of institutions). The eschaton is seen as making permanent the dualistic split between the Aryan and the Jew, the soul and the body, and nature and culture which the faithful attempt to anticipate now via various separatist strategies. This approach has manifested itself historically in both Christian and secular, masculinist and feminist forms. Needless to say, such a position depreciates aspects of creation in a way that is thoroughly incompatible with the kind of theology that Ruether advocates.

A second non-separatist alternative, that has become popular in recent history, takes a more evolutionary approach. What we now call "oppression," it is readily admitted, was historically unavoidable. Yet, with the advent of modern knowledge and technological expertise, it need only be a temporary phenomenon. It is as though we have now found a way of making omelettes without using eggs at all. Now that test-tube babies are possible, for example, women can be liberated from the constraints of pregnancy and childbirth and can achieve full equality with men. Patriarchy is viewed as a necessary earlier stage in the historical development of civilization in which we must not get stuck but which we must move beyond.

But this approach also depreciates the goodness of creation when it goes beyond trying to heal the brokenness and distortions that our evil has brought about and seeks to "improve" on fundamental features of our world that would seem to have their origin in the way God has made things. When used by feminists, it has a number of draw-backs. In addition to accepting the womb-less male as the normative human, a position such as that of Shulamith Firestone is unable to say that those patriarchal societies that lacked modern technology were evil.[15] This would be as anachronistic as saying that medieval society was inherently oppressive and evil because its people were deprived of telephones or washing-machines.

A vibrant Christian feminist theology, by contrast, needs to be able to affirm an originally good (i. e., non-patriarchal) creation and an historical, non-necessary fall into alienation and sin. Evil can then be seen as an alien(ating) intrusion into a creation which is "by nature" non-oppressive. It is very interesting in this context that feminist theologian Sheila Collins feels compelled in her desire to delegitimate patriarchy to go against the dominant stream of modern theology. She writes,

> Unlike Tillich and most other theologians who locate alienation in the ontological structure of things, a feminist reading of history and the feminist experience suggest that this alienation may actually have been a function of certain historical proces-ses. The Fall may have occurred *in* history, not outside it![16]

By contrast, Ruether does not believe as I do that there was ever a pre-fallen stage in human history. For her, as for Tillich, the biblical account of the fall mythologizes as an event what is really the ontological "gap" or distinction between essence and exist-ence.[17] This does not mean that she cannot believe in a pre-patriar-chal era of some kind, although it does make such a belief harder to hold.

At one point, she introduces her own view on this issue by distinguishing it from two other approaches to the origin of woman's subjugation which correspond (in reverse order) to the two positions that I have criticised above. In response to the evolutionistic posi-tion, which she interprets as claiming that "[t]hings can be changed now, but men cannot be held responsible for the past," she remarks,

"Obviously males prefer this viewpoint, but so do some women who are afraid of confrontation with the males in their lives." Of the other position which "sees the suppression of women as a great historical crime [which] [m]en have deliberately and continually conspired to perpetuate," she notes that feminists who hold this view "come close to suggesting that males, by nature, are intrinsically oppressive."[18] This, she says, leads quite logically to a feminist separatism.

Ruether describes her own view, as lying "somewhere between these two extremes." In agreement with the second position, she states, "First of all, I believe we must take with full seriousness sexism as a massive historical crime against the personhood of women." In opposition to that position, however, she asserts that "[t]his crime was neither biologically inevitable nor the expression of unconscious forces." She grants that the social division of labour along lines of biological roles in reproduction that took place as early as the tribal period "corresponded to certain necessities of survival." But what is not excusable is the fact that women did not enter into leadership roles once this emergency measure was no longer necessary. She writes,

> The social incorporation of biological roles is a cultural artifact, not a necessity of nature. Particularly once social power is freed from direct prowess in hunting and war and becomes incorporated into legal and cultural superstructures, all biological reasons for eliminating women from leadership roles disappear. The fact that patriarchal societies arise that legislate such marginalization of women is the expression of the will-to-power of a male ruling class, not a biological necessity. This marginalization, moreover, is not maintained by mere unconscious forces, but by the constant reiteration of laws and pronouncements from the guardians of the prerogatives of this male ruling class against women who seek to emerge from its limits. This is a culpable history, in the same way as slavery or racism.[19]

In agreement with Ruether, and in opposition to the first position she rejects, I too want to insist that this is a "culpable history." I also agree with her, against this second position, that the origin of patriarchy must not be identified with biological maleness. Yet her own comments raise the question as to the true origin of the male "will-to-power" that resulted in the marginalization and oppression of women.

Ruether's writings often imply that this will-to-power began to manifest itself at a particular stage of human history. At one point she claims that "[i]n prepatriarchal myth, one discerns the rudimentary elements of what might have been an alternative history, based on the dialectical interplay of the polarities of existence, rather than hierarchical dualism, which defines the 'feminine' as the unconscious side of the self."[20] If we take this together with her earlier comments about mother and nature religions, in which she contrasts them so sharply with the rise of patriarchal consciousness, it would seem reasonable to assume that Ruether thinks that there was a non- or pre-patriarchal era which coincided with the historical ascendancy of these religions, and that this can be located historically before the end of the tribal period. Whether this is in fact a correct reading of her position is a matter to which I will return in section III, below.

The most detailed and extended discussion of the rise of patriarchy in Ruether's entire corpus is still chapter 1 of *New Woman/New Earth*, which is entitled "The Descent of Woman: Symbol and Social Condition."[21] Here she suggests that we can recognize three stages to this history: the Conquest, Negation, and Sublimation of the Mother. These correspond to the three layers of sexist ideology, which were summarized in chapter 1 in the sections on anthropology, evil, and Mariology.[22]

She begins her account of "The Conquest of the Mother" by analyzing life in the tribal period when "village culture was more equalitarian, in terms of sex and class relations, than the city society that began with the urban revolution." In the early hunting and agricultural stages, she suggests, the biological differences between the sexes created a complementarity of work roles. While the men became hunters and warriors, and thus took control of the political arena and those religious rites that sanctified political power, the women's power centred in economic life. "As long as the economy was centered in the family," writes Ruether, "woman had social bargaining power, despite the development of patriarchal political systems that defined her as dependent and rightless."[23]

A critical turning point comes with urbanization. This allows for an elite group of males to rise to positions of influence and leadership on the basis of an inherited monopoly of political power and knowledge rather than on their physical prowess as hunters or warriors. Women were excluded from these positions of power while the cultural spokes*men* for the ruling-class males began to enforce their social superiority via the construction of self-justifying ideologies and other more overtly repressive measures.

While the urban revolution originally affected only a small segment of society, mass industrialization in recent history diffused urbanization over a much larger area, with the result that economic production has become separated from home and family and thus separated from women.[24] Even those women who left the home to work in the first factories "were still tied . . . to providing the procreative and domestic support systems of male work."[25] Thus, having to work a double-shift, they were handicapped as competitors with males in the public sphere.

Although both urbanization and industrialization resulted in the further marginalization of woman, Ruether clearly doesn't believe that the development of civilization *per se* made this unavoidable. "The physical advantage that males had over [women] in the primitive struggle for survival," she says, "could have become obsolete with the development of civilization."[26] Yet the males maintained their positions of political power. The exclusion of women from education was particularly effective in consolidating this power imbalance, for when more and more skills became professionalised, women were not only unable to train but became "unqualified" for tasks such as healing which they had effectively carried out for centuries on the basis of practical experience.

Technology, like urbanization, could also have helped close the gap between the sexes and helped humanity move beyond the necessities of tribal culture. Patriarchy, however, makes sure that these opportunities do not materialize. For while men benefit from technological development because it frees them from certain "biological limitations," women, by contrast, "are prevented from gaining access to technology, especially in the reproductive sphere, that could free them from biological victimization." Furthermore,

> Ruling-class males preserve and extend a hunter and warrior mystique of maleness into the civilized era, when it should have become obsolete, biasing all the development of culture in the direction of competitive aggressiveness rather than social cooperation. It is perhaps not too much to say that the Achilles' heel of human civilization, which today has reached global genocidal and ecocidal proportions, resides in this false development of maleness through repression of the female.[27]

So far, I have mentioned many of the features that Ruether sees as making up a full-blown patriarchal culture: a view of power as domination, androcentrism, hierarchy, male control of the public sphere, and the marginalization of women. Although she does not clearly separate her account of life after the urban revolution from her portrayal of life after the industrial revolution, it is evident that she believes that all of these features are present at this earlier stage. But I have yet to mention the rise of dualistic consciousness. This coincides with the classical period and is discussed as a feature of the phase Ruether calls "The Negation of the Mother."

This new stage of consciousness, she says, arises "sometime in the early first millennium B.C." in both Hebrew and Greek cultures, (but apparently nowhere else in the ancient Near East). Ruether is convinced that it is hard to underestimate the adverse influence this development has had on Western culture. What is unique about the classical stage of civilization, she argues, is that men begin to entertain the possibility of freeing themselves from dependency on nature altogether. Rather than basing themselves on it, they seek to master it by "linking their essential selves with a transcendent principle beyond nature which is pictured as intellectual and male."[28] This transcendent sphere, where males locate their true natures and ultimate origin, is a projection of the male ego which functions to give them power over the natural world, which is now seen as a lower "female" sphere. As can be expected, religion plays an important role in this process. Ruether argues,

In genesis stories created out of this view, the world is no longer seen as evolving out of a primal matrix which contains within it both heaven and earth, the organic and the spiritual. Creation is seen as initiated by a fiat from above, from an immaterial principle beyond visible reality. Nature, which once encompassed all reality, is now subjugated and made the lower side of a new dualism. Anthropology and cosmology are split into a dualism between a transcendent spiritual principle and a lower material reality. A struggle ensues against the old nature and mother religions by prophets or philosophers who portray it as immoral or irrational. Consciousness is abstracted into a sphere beyond visible reality, including the visible heavens. This higher realm is the realm of divinity. The primal matrix of life no longer encompasses spiritual power, gods and souls, but is debased as mere "matter" (a word which means "mother"). Matter is created by an ego-fiat from a transcendent spiritual power. Visible nature is posterior and created by transcendent "Mind." Sky and earth, once complementary, become hierarchical. Maleness is identified with intellectuality and spirituality; femaleness is identified with the lower material nature. This also defines the female as ontologically dependent and morally inferior to maleness.[29]

Having described the general features of this new stage of consciousness, Ruether goes on to give illustrations from both Greek and biblical literature. In this context, she cites the (so-called) patriarchal reversal myth of Gen. 2, and the Old Testament menstrual taboos which have been examined in chapters 2 and 3. She then discusses some of the misogynistic features of Christian theology, which were summarized in chapter 1. Her comments on the romanticization of woman, which constitutes the third stage of the development of patriarchy, and which she discusses here under the title of "The Sublimation of the Mother," have also been summarized in that chapter in the section on Mariology.

I can accept the basic contours of Ruether's account. I especially like her awareness that Western culture becomes increasingly masculinist as human societies become more developed and differentiated. There is, however, one part of her account that I see as erroneous. In her account of the classical stage of history, she seriously confuses the nature of Hebrew and Greek culture in a way that does grave injustice to the biblical worldview. Both Hebrew and Greek societies were patriarchal. But I can find no trace of Greek dualistic thinking in the Old Testament (as opposed to some of the intertestamental literature). Neither can I find there the Greek view of nature or matter. The prophets attack nature religion because it is idolatrous, not because "matter" must be subordinated to "spirit." Indeed as Ruether herself notes in a later chapter of *New Woman/New Earth*, "Unlike the Greek and Christian traditions, the Old Testament is patriarchal without linking this to an alienated view of creation."[30]

Neither can I find the Greek view of God as transcendent Mind in the Old Testament. That God is "transcendent" in the biblical worldview, I do not deny—if what we mean by this is that God is not creation and creation is not God, but each have their own identity in the covenant relationship. But to say this is also to say that God is neither Mind nor Body, neither Culture nor Nature—all of which are created realities.[31] From the point of view of the Hebrew Bible and Christian Old Testament, to see God as a glorified version of the human mind would constitute idolatry. And on the basis of the biblical worldview, as I understand it, I contend that it was indeed a particular form of idolatry, which I will call Rationalism, that caused the Greeks (and then certain Christian theologians) to see the Divine in this light.

It was the specifically Greek absolutization of human conceptual powers, I suggest, that led to what Ruether has identified as the dualistic separation and polarization of what she calls the "dialectical unities" of life. This same idolization of Reason also caused the leaders of that culture to do something the Hebrews of the Old Testament never did: to borrow Ruether's words, they attempted "to master nature . . . by subordinating it and linking their essential selves with a transcendent principle beyond nature which is pictured as intellectual and male." It was this, I suggest, that gave rise to the hierarchical dualism that has dominated Western thought ever since.

Theoretical reason tries to get in touch with the conditions or laws that hold for existence. By means of concepts, it focuses on universality rather than individuality, the general rather than the particular, the law-side of creation rather than its subject-side.[32] All of this is quite legitimate. In Rational*ism*, however, the law-subject correlation which comes into focus when we relate to the world by means of our rational-conceptual abilities, is taken as the most fundamental distinction of reality.[33] Furthermore, what is grasped conceptually, namely order, is given privileged status over what only non-rational forms of knowing and experience can put us in touch with.[34] Logocentrism is the result. Universality becomes more "real" than individuality.[35] Essence becomes split apart from and placed hierarchically above existence. Logical "form" takes on divine status over against demonic "matter." God becomes a bodiless Mind, and the human self becomes identified with the logical ego. It is hard to overemphasize the impact that this kind of thinking has had in Western culture and I applaud Ruether's desire to highlight the damage it has caused. To blame the Hebrews of the Old Testament period in addition to the Greeks, however, rests on an assumption that is not likely to be supported by detailed historical investigation.

One weakness of Ruether's cultural analysis, to my mind, is that she does not further explore the dynamics of Rationalism. Not only is this crucial to an understanding of the rise of Western dualism, but an analysis of its role in Western thought—perhaps along the lines of Genevieve Lloyd's excellent book *The Man of Reason: "Male" and "Female" in Western Philosophy*—sheds light on the correlation between the domination of woman and the domination of nature, because Rationalism typically results in the subordination of both.

III. The Origin and Nature of Patriarchy
Before beginning the above summary of Ruether's account of the rise of patriarchy, I suggested that she would appear to locate patriarchy's origin somewhere in the transition between tribal and post-tribal society. Yet while the transition to an urban society is a critical one in the story she tells, it would be wrong to say that village tribal life represented a pre-patriarchal stage in the history of

civilization. In *Liberation Theology*, Ruether claims that even at this stage, women were considered as aberrant, unclean and dangerous.[36] In the section we have been considering in *New Woman/New Earth*, she says, "Feminism should not idealize the tribal period as a 'golden age' for women's autonomy and power." The sex-linked complementarity of work roles that was established at that time may have been more equalitarian than any subsequent historical period. Woman's cultural image may well have been more exalted. But the problematic connection of woman's role with the domestic sphere becomes manifest when cultural differentiation relativizes the importance of the home and thus the female role that continues to be tied to it. Males, by contrast, gain control of all tasks that are no longer connected to this "female" sphere. What was "once the center of productive economic life" becomes increasingly reduced in political power and status, finally reaching "its present proportions of a purely consumer and child-raising unit." The home, in other words, becomes "a shrinking cage" in woman has been "progressively entrapped."[37]

It might seem that what Ruether is claiming here is that the distinction in male and female roles that harsh conditions made necessary in tribal society is responsible for the rise of patriarchy. This would amount to saying that the sexist nature of later periods was historically inevitable, however, and as we have already seen, this is a conclusion she wishes to avoid.

There are two ways that she can be understood that suggest plausible ways in which she might avoid this conclusion. One entails the hypothesis that she sees cultural differentiation as a "fall" (or at least a temptation) which people of the tribal and subsequent periods had or have the power to resist. Although this is not a stance that she explicitly adopts, it is possible that an identification of societal healing with cultural de-differentiation may play a role in her attraction to communalist socialism, a political option which she notes may not provide "a comprehensive solution for *complex* societies, or for any but small intentional communities."[38] This interpretation would fit with her view of history which was explored in the section on eschatology in the previous chapter. The movement from cosmos to chaos in the ongoing spiral of time, which I there related to the notion of a "fall into finitude," could be seen as cultural differentiation, while the movement from chaos to cosmos, which she calls the "return to center," could then be equated with cultural integration, (mis)understood as de-differentiation.

The second way of reading her also involves going beyond what she explicitly says. Instead of suggesting that sexism is due solely to the socialization patterns that were set up in the tribal period, she could in fact be implying that males were *already* inclined to oppress females at this time, but were so preoccupied with the struggle to survive, for which they clearly needed female help, that they had less opportunity to do so. This is a position with which I am sympathetic. It also fits well with Ruether's claim that even the mother-centred symbolic systems of tribal cultures not only failed to promote female social equality, but in speaking of the Great Mother upon whom all political power is based, reflect "the first stage of a male cooption of the female into a system of power exercised by males."[39] I think that it is probable that Ruether's position incorporates both of these ways of reading her.

Whether or not tribal culture is seen as patriarchal depends on how we define that term. I would like to suggest that a *fully* patriarchal culture has two fundamental characteristics. Firstly, it is a culture in which males dominate the "public" or "political" sphere, though this is an area or side of life that need not be as clearly differentiated as it is today. Secondly, a fully patriarchal culture is one in which the sinfulness or alienation of those (ruling-class) males increasingly shapes the nature and direction of that society as a whole by means of that political power. Israel under the monarchy, I suggest, displays both of these features, though less so than classical Greece, which, in turn, is less patriarchal in character than modern Western society. Tribal societies, however, only meet the first criterion. This does not mean they are *non-* or *pre-*patriarchal, in my view, but *proto*-patriarchal. Perhaps we may call them *proto*-patriarchal when comparing them with later societies, but proto-*patriarchal* when judging them in terms of what should have been normative from the beginning of human history.

If the fundamental origin of patriarchy, for Ruether (and here I agree), cannot be located in the transition from tribal to classical culture, or in the move from a village to an urban life-style, then the important questions of when and why patriarchy arose have yet to be answered.

Although she does give some hints in various places scattered throughout her corpus as to how she might answer this question, most of these describe a possible mechanism by which males gained power over women, or they merely push the question of origin of this male will-to-power further back. Factors she considers include the physical lightness of a woman's body and her vulnerability during pregnancy,[40] the male's abhorrence of his own body and his bodily ties to generative processes which he projects onto the female,[41] and his struggle to free himself from bondage to nature, in which he makes her a symbol of the sphere to be transcended and dominated rather than seeing her as a partner in the struggle.[42]

In one of the fullest discussions of this topic, which occurs in *Sexism and God-Talk*,[43] she argues that evil in general, and sexism in particular, come about when the self-other distinction, which is legitimate in itself, becomes confused with the distinction between good and evil. This confusion, she writes, "seems to have occurred very early in the history of human consciousness." Against Marxism, she argues that this "perception of the other as evil is not the ideological superstructure of exploitative relations" but exists prior to, and functions to rationalize, both exploitation and conquest. In her more recent book *Women-Church*, she writes in a similar vein,

> Creation is itself the original grace or blessing. Evil and aliena-
> tion arise from the distortion and twisting of our true natures.
> One might say that the "first lie" is the naming of differences
> among humans of race, gender, and ethnicity as "good and
> bad," "being and nonbeing." Upon this lie, power systems are
> erected that further injustice and oppression and block our
> access to authentic humanity and authentic relationships with
> our bodies, the earth, and God/ess.[44]

I don't doubt that Ruether's view of false naming takes us very close to the heart of sin and alienation. But even here, we may still ask, How did this false naming arise? In a section with the promising title

"Roots of Domination" in *Sexism and God-Talk*, Ruether chooses to dodge this question by saying,

> This is a book of reflections on such symbolic structures, not a book on anthropological history. So there will be no attempt to ask how this structure "happened," even if it were possible to answer that question with any completeness.[45]

This is an unsatisfactory response to a very important question.

The topic of "anthropological history," is one that she addresses nine years later in *Gaia and God*. One new factor that she adds to her analysis is the way in which the variability of the food supply in the Neolithic period could favour the male hunter role in some contexts and the female gatherer role in others. While this undoubtedly affects male and female power, Ruether does not believe that this alone can explain the origin of patriarchy. She claims that even when the female role was strong enough for the matricentric village to emerge, this was a kind of social organization that exhibited an "internal psychosocial vulnerability . . . that le[d] to its subversion by male dominance." As to the origin of this male will-to-power, Ruether suggests,

> The root problem lies in the extension of the female childbearing and suckling functions into making the mother the dominant parent, together with primary food-gathering and food-sharing roles. Males are then somewhat auxiliary to the life-sustaining processes, both in food production and in reproduction, and can experience this as uncertainty about the male role.[46]

She then relates man's resentment of woman and his insatiable quest for power and control to his need "to fill the bottomless void of male insecurity."[47]

If patriarchal tendencies can be traced to the male reaction to female dominance of food production and parenting, we need to ask once again whether this was inevitable, or the result of some prior human action? Is the evil of patriarchy ultimately rooted in the innocent but tragically short-sighted decision of our Neolithic foremothers and forefathers to arrange their lives in one way rather than another, or was human alienation and evil involved?

Ruether does offer one other reason why males tend to dominate and scapegoat women that is historically prior to the factors examined above. She points to the impact on male children of being brought up in a society in which the female is the primary parent. This has significant consequences for the stress and insecurity experienced by the male, because unlike females, the "mother-parented male . . . makes his way to adult male status through mother-negation."[48] (This would seem to be an appeal to an "object relations" understanding of human psychological development to which I will refer in more detail below.)

If I repeat my previous question about whether this psychologically and developmentally ingrained tendency was inevitable or the result of a prior evil, it seems that Ruether ends up having to opt for the former of these two alternatives. She does not explicitly state this, but she does say that "the social construction of [translating] the primacy of maternal gestation [which is a biological given] into the primacy of early childhood nurture and domestic labor by women" is "a pattern that goes back to the beginnings of hominid development *and even earlier* [my emphasis]."[49] This sounds as though patriarchy, at least in its historical origins, was an inevitable outworking of the evolutionary process because the powerful forces that led to its appearance in human life were already at work before we even emerged on the planet. While we may be able to resist this pattern now, how can we claim, given this view of history, that patriarchy has always been an expression of human sin if it was initially unavoidable for us? How can Ruether continue to claim that even its earliest human manifestation was a culpable evil when her own view of history suggests that it was merely a tragedy that could not have been avoided?[50]

Ruether's understanding of evil in this book suggests only one possible answer that I can foresee. Human sin, for her, is related to the breakdown of the crucial cosmic harmony of the parts and the Whole. Our egoism is built into the life drive itself, just as it is for creatures as structurally simple as bacteria. This, in itself, is not evil. The danger occurs when we do not balance our life drive with the drives of our fellow human beings (and fellow creatures in general) and thus fail to ensure that "the whole remains in life-sustaining harmony."[51] The "egocentric" nature that we share with non-human creatures becomes evil when its desires are maximized at the expense of "the impulse to [reflective] consciousness and kind-ness"[52] that is unique to our species, and that constitutes what we might call our "exocentric" nature.[53] Ruether could claim on this basis that while they were unavoidably tempted to continue the woman-negation process that was part and parcel of their upbring-ing on other women, the first patriarchal human males could have resisted this impulse to maximize their egos at the expense of the opposite sex by exercising their exocentric capacities. If, given Ruether's model, it is indeed possible to say that the human impulse to kindness was sufficiently evolved at this time to make this ex-ocentricity feasible, it still leaves the question of why this temptation was not resisted. Serious problems thus remain in her position.

It seems to me that a different approach is required. While the question of the origin of evil in general and patriarchy in particular must be faced, there is a sense in which it cannot be "answered." What is required is an explanation of why this is so. What needs to be said, I believe, is that if evil is not intrinsic to the way God made humanity from the beginning, then the reason why it arose must remain a mystery, for it cannot be explained as the natural outwork-ing of prior conditions or realities.[54]

The fact that humans had the capacity to sin from the beginning seems clear from Gen. 3. But "free will" is, at best, the occasion of the Fall, not its cause. The same goes for any aspect of our creatureli-ness that we are tempted to turn into the culprit. The Genesis account of the Fall narrates but does not attempt to explain its occurrence.[55] Because evil has no legitimate place in creation, even God, I suggest, is bewildered by its presence and has to ask the man where he is and how he knows he is naked (3:9, 11). This dumbfounded reaction to evil is similar to what we find in Jer. 32:35, where Yahweh responds to the Israelites by saying, "They built high places for Baal in the Valley of Ben Hinnom to sacrifice their sons and daughters to Molech, though I never commanded, *nor did it enter my mind*, that they should do such a detestable thing and so make Judah sin [my emphasis]."

If we understand evil, sin, and alienation in terms of "disconnection," then we may be tempted to ask whether one of the fundamental forms of disconnection (i. e., with self, with God, with other humans, with "nature") occurred prior to all the others. As we have seen, Ruether often seems to make alienation between male and female the root of all the others. Many Christians, especially in the Evangelical tradition, would claim that it was alienation from God that plays this role. Both approaches are mistaken, however, for they fail to note that a rupturing of any one of these relationships—with self, other, God, or non-human "nature"—immediately and simultaneously results in the breaking of all the others.

The Fall, therefore, should be seen as that first, single, unrepeatable, historical moment in which all of these relationships became ruptured for early humanity. Sexism, as a form of self-other alienation, does indeed have its beginning in this moment. Thus the ultimate roots of patriarchy are as ancient as any form of evil that expresses the breakdown of the self-other relationship. And while the roots of sexism are, in this sense, no more or less ancient that racism, we can assume that its explicit historical manifestation was earlier as our human ancestors would have encountered sexual diversity long before racial diversity. It is also easy to imagine that tension and oppression between the sexes occurred repeatedly long before the development of a clear class system. That the historical outworking and societal impact of sexism probably preceded that of racism and classism, even though its ultimate roots are no more ancient, is something to which I will return.

It is also important to note that because of the interconnectedness of life, alienation between men and women inevitably led to self-alienation, alienation from God, and alienation from "nature" for both sexes. But we can also say that alienation from self, which also had its beginning in the Fall and is therefore just as ancient and fundamental, has led to alienation between humans (including males and females), alienation from "nature," and alienation from God. The same thing can also be said about human alienation from nature.[56] My point, therefore, is that while we should recognize the ancient, perduring and all-pervasive character of patriarchy, we should not make the mistake of identifying sexism as *the* core meaning of the Fall.

This kind of analysis, however, does clarify the element of truth in such a mistaken position. It seems probable that when Ruether speaks of evil in terms of broken relationships, this is the result of reflecting on the nature of evil in general without paying explicit attention to sexism. However, it would seem that when Ruether reflects on the nature of patriarchy, her correct awareness of the fact that alienation between the sexes inevitably leads to alienation from self, God, and nature (as I argued have above), has led her to confuse the evil of sexism with the sexism of evil.

Historical research into the rise and impact of male-female alienation, while it should honour the interconnectedness of life in all its complexity, will naturally make issues of gender the centre of attention, and thus more or less bracket other dimensions of evil. This focus is both legitimate and helpful. But just as an account of the birth of a child remains incomplete until we speak of new life as a gift of God, so a Christian account of history looked at from the vantage point of male-female alienation will be deficient in terms of its own special gender focus if it does not speak of alienation from God, for this reveals the depth-meaning or ultimate significance of sexism (as well as all other forms of oppression).

Although our relationship with God cannot be reduced to any of our other relationships, neither can it be understood as a relationship that exists "alongside" all the others. We experience and relate to God in and through our other relationships.[57] Thus, when man oppressed woman for the first time, the ultimate significance of what he did cannot be grasped without speaking of that action as an act of autonomy from, disobedience to, and oppression of God. Thus while Genesis speaks of the Fall in terms of the rupturing of all the relationships in which Adam and Eve stand—with each other (3:16), with the earth (3:17; 4:11, 12), with God (6:6), and with the animals (9:2)—its special focus concentrates on the alienation that now exists between humans and their Creator as a way of capturing the depth-meaning of all evil and alienation.

This certitudinal, confessional, or fiduciary perspective highlights some important considerations which we need to bear in mind if we are to understand the true nature of sexism and patriarchy. The role of fear in the narrative is particularly important. When Yahweh calls out to the man, "Where are you?" (3:9), he replies, "I heard you in the garden, and I was *afraid* because I was naked; so I hid."[58] Once cut off from God's affirming love and presence, the story is telling us, humanity experiences a fundamental insecurity, and it is this, I suggest, that drives it towards idols in a desperate attempt to regain a sense of safety and a source of empowerment in a world from which and in which it has become estranged. Autonomy from God leads to alienation and fear, and it is this fear and emptiness—and not pride as traditionally believed—that is the root of all of our oppressive behaviour since the Fall. Thus, drawing on the insights of self psychology, James Olthuis suggests, "The proud self does not love self too much, but too little. It is deficiency of self-esteem that leads to greed and selfishness. A posture of arrogance covers over our aching emptiness and utter depravity cut off from God's affirming love."[59]

Another reason for thinking of fear as a fundamental key to understanding the human attraction to evil since the Fall is that the traditional emphasis on pride betrays an androcentric bias. As Valerie Saiving wrote over thirty years ago,

[T]he temptations of woman *as woman* are not the same as the temptations of man *as man*, and the specifically feminine forms of sin—"feminine" not because they are confined to women or because women are incapable of sinning in other ways but because they are outgrowths of the basic feminine character structure—having a quality which can never be encompassed by such terms as "pride" and "will-to-power." They are better suggested by such items as triviality, distractibility, and diffuseness; lack of an organizing center or focus; dependence on others for one's own self-definition; tolerance at the expense of standards of excellence; inability to respect the boundaries of privacy; sentimentality, gossipy sociability, and mistrust of reason—in short, underdevelopment or negation of the self.[60]

If we take the fear and insecurity that results from autonomy from God as the root of our evil actions, however, it becomes possible to recognize that both the typically "male" will-to-power and the typically "female" negation of the self have a common source.[61] As Olthuis continues,

> In the dynamics of sin we can develop a narcissistic need to retain control or be controlled by others as self-deceiving ways of holding down our fear of being out of control, powerless, lost and alone. Thus on the one hand we inflate self and play God. On the other hand we deflate self and slavishly submit ourselves to others. In the posture of pride we do violence to others in an effort to prove our autonomy. In the posture of submission we allow ourselves to be violated in an effort to obtain identity and substance from the people to whom we submit. Both postures, feeding on each other, are at heart defensive efforts to cover over our defective and fragile selves. The postures of sin are extremely appealing because, albeit in perverted and distorted ways, they are attempts to restore us to the greatness for which we were designed and to which we are called.[62]

The pattern of sin displayed by ruling class males, I suggest, is easily and correctly identified with the inflated self that attempts to play God. Indeed, the evils of predominantly male cultural leaders have so shaped our Western society as a whole that we can, with Ruether, refer to it as a patriarchy. Such terminology, however, does not reveal the deepest root of our problems and it is here that the use of patriarchy as a global concept can be especially unhelpful.

This leads me to disagree with Ruether's conception of the nature of patriarchy. In *Sexism and God-Talk*, Ruether attributes five features to "macho-masculine culture": (1) violence, (2) hierarchical and anticommunitarian bias, (3) abstractionism (when "one turns reality into theoretical fantasies that do not need to be checked and corrected by relation to real persons"), (4) consequentialism (which I will explore below), and (5) misogyny.[63] I grant that all these features are all present in our society. I will also grant that our society is patriarchal. What I resist is that our culture is this way merely or primarily because it is patriarchal.

To illustrate what I mean, I will take a closer look at Ruether's definition of consequentialism. In her words,

> It means putting theoretical goals above the actual effects created by the means used to reach the goals. Profits pursued at the expense of the impoverishment of an increasing sector of the human race, even in industrialized countries, is one such expression. Stockpiling nuclear weapons for ultimate security, weapons that can annihilate the whole human race and reduce the planet to lifeless rubble many times over, is the ultimate virulent expression of the cult of "end" pursued without recognition of the effect of the means and the processes chosen.[64]

What Ruether is describing here—especially when she speaks of the elevation of the end above the means—is hard to distinguish from what Bob Goudzwaard refers to as a central characteristic of *any* ideology that is rooted in *idolatry*.[65] (In fact he analyzes the ideology of guaranteed security at some length.) Patriarchal cultures do indeed engage in idolatry, but not merely because they are patriarchal. Here Ruether does confuse correlation with causation. Although cultural leaders are particularly responsible for the idols that grip their culture, and although the vast majority of such leaders have been males, idolatry *per se* is not a typically "male" sin. There is simply no good reason why we should assume that female leaders in a non-patriarchal society would have avoided the sin of "consequentialism."

Yet this does not mean that the maleness of the cultural leaders of the West is incidental to whatever oppression they have encouraged and engaged in. An area Christian feminism could fruitfully explore is whether the socialization of males in general has led these male leaders to become susceptible to *certain forms of idolatry rather than others.*[66]

In this context, the work of feminists indebted to object-relations theory such as Nancy Chodorow, Dorothy Dinnerstein, Lillian Rubin and Jessica Benjamin, is particularly helpful, and it is unfortunate that, with the partial exception of *Gaia and God*, Ruether shows only a minimal acquaintance with this important stream of contemporary feminist thinking.[67] As I have mentioned above,

Ruether does make reference in her most recent book to the *insecurity* that results from males being primarily nurtured by a female parent. This is a key element in an object relations analysis. There is far more to be said than this, however.

Without rehearsing all their arguments here, scholars in this school of thought pay special attention to the fact that, as a result of mothers being the primary parents, young boys unlike girls have the task of developing their sense of identity first and foremost in relation to a parent of the other sex. It is then suggested that, given the relative absence of the father, a boy's sense of masculinity develops in terms of being in *opposition* to mother. As a result, the boy (and consequently the adult male) develops over-rigid ego-boundaries which tend to separate him from his own inner emotional life and cause him to see relationships as extrinsic to his selfhood. The Cartesian view of the self set over against the body and the world can be seen as an outworking of this warped male develop-mental process. One feminist work that shows how this material can be related to the character of the dominant theological tradition is Catherine Keller's book, *From A Broken Web: Separatism, Sexism, and Self.*[68]

If all humans suffer from a sense of cosmic insecurity that results from our alienation from God, this psychological theory, which describes the impact of a virtually universal parenting pattern that itself has came about because of the Fall, can help us under-stand why males in their antipathy to intimate connection with others typically tend to hide their fear behind a posture of pride rather than one of submission. Not only does this shed light on a major reason why men dominate women, but it may also help us uncover a common psychological-developmental root behind a wide range of alienated and alienating forms of patriarchal behaviour.

Elsewhere, I have argued that the over-separate sense of self that males typically develop in opposition to a female primary caregiver has contributed to the rise, development and staying power of the idol of Rationalism in the West.[69] The stockpiling of nuclear weapons may also have roots in such typically "male" patterns of brokenness. While the attempt to find security by putting our faith in a god other than Yahweh is not a peculiarly patriarchal phenomenon, the *specific* idols that our culture decides to trust (such as Reason or the Guaranteed Security of Nuclear Weapons) may well reveal its patriarchal nature.

All this leads me to a position that is similar to Ruether's on a number of points. I am quite happy to accept her thesis that sexism is an extremely ancient form of human oppression. I am also happy to accept her suggestion that males took advantage of their wives' lesser strength and increased vulnerability during pregnancy in order to marginalize them. I see no reason to doubt that these alienated males saw themselves as normative humanity and proceeded to define woman as an "other" who then became symbolically identified with other "others" such as nature and matter. Furthermore, I believe that there is historical evidence to support the idea that the oppression of women has functioned as a model for the subsequent oppression of other groups.[70]

I also believe that the alienation of the ruling class males has made its presence felt throughout our modern world. Yet it is at this point that we must be careful. What is evil about patriarchal cultures cannot be fully explained by the sex of their rulers. We need to pay attention to the fact that the males who rule are *sinful* males. Their sin and evil does not just result in the male monopoly of power, generation after generation, but it also affects the way that power and leadership is exercised, thus influencing the nature and direction of the culture as a whole. But this is not to say that the problem with patriarchies is simply that they are led by sinners. These sinful leaders sin *as males*, in ways that manifest patterns of brokenness typical to the male sex. To put this another way, there is nothing inherently patriarchal about sin, but there are patriarchal sins and a good Christian feminist theology will be careful to make this distinction. While it will reject Ruether's suggestion that consequentialism *per se* is a patriarchal problem, for example, it might well explore the patriarchal roots of Rationalism and what Ruether calls abstractionism, which seems to be a result of Rationalism.

Yet in the position I am advocating, even forms of evil that are legitimately labelled "patriarchal" are seen as the manifestation of a fearful, alienated, defensive posture which cannot be fully understood unless we recognize that it has roots in a form of alienation/sin that is "gender-blind": autonomy from God. It is regrettable that such a prominent Christian feminist thinker as Ruether has little or nothing to say about this, for the Women's Movement will never fully understand the nature of patriarchy unless it can move beyond purely secular categories.

There is one further observation that needs to be made about Ruether's global use of the term "patriarchy." Ironically, there is a danger that it will promote an *androcentric* view of our culture by focusing, in the name of feminism, almost exclusively on male behaviour—even if this male behaviour is judged to be reprehensible.

Violence, as we saw above, is singled out by Ruether as one of the five leading characteristics of patriarchy. Yet her discussion of it is misleading because it serves to mask the reality of female violence. Let us take the case of Nazi war atrocities, the vast majority of which were committed by males. As the feminist historian Claudia Koonz writes, "The chain of command from chancellery to crematorium remained entirely within men's domain; women took no part in planning the 'final solution'; and, except for a few thousand prison matrons and camp guards, women did not participate in murder."[71] Yet even here, the evil committed was not exclusively patriarchal. As Koonz remarks elsewhere,

> Looking back at Nazi Germany, it seems that decency vanished; but when we listen to feminine voices from the period, we realize instead that it was cordoned off. Loyal Nazis fashioned an image for themselves, a fake domestic realm where they felt virtuous. Nazi women facilitated that mirage by doing what women have done in other societies—they made the world a more pleasant place in which to live for the members of their community. And they simultaneously made life first unbearable and later impossible for "racially unworthy" citizens. As fanatical Nazis or lukewarm tag-alongs, they resolutely turned their heads away from assaults against socialists, Jews, religious dissenters, the handicapped, and "degenerates." They gazed instead at their own cradles, children, and "Aryan" families. Mothers and wives . . . made a vital contribution to Nazi power

by preserving the illusion of love in an environment of hatred.
[72] . . .

It is hard to avoid the conclusion that the part that the women played was also violent in its own way.[73]

IV. Towards a Multi-faceted Liberation Theology

So far in this chapter, I have argued that while many of the specific forms of evil that our culture practises are related to the fact that we live in a male-dominated society, patriarchy, while extremely ancient and pervasive, should not be singled out as the fundamental root of all societal problems. Once original sin becomes equated with sexism, a feminist reductionism takes place which inevitably leads to a myopic view of life in which only the patriarchal aspects of oppression remain visible.

For a Christian feminist theology to remain truly in the service of liberation, it has to remember that life is infinitely richer than even our most complex and nuanced theories. It does not take a great deal of political sensitivity to realize that there are many oppressed and vulnerable groups in our society besides women. These groups include racial minorities, children, the elderly, gay people, the disabled (or physically challenged), religious minorities, and the poor. Each group contains both males and females and both men and women contribute to their oppression.

Men and women are both agents and victims of sin. Middle class white women can oppress poor males and black employees. Rich women may smoke while they are pregnant and ignore their elderly neighbours. Businessmen may beat their wives and refuse to hire the disabled. The poor may mistreat their children and look down on gay and lesbian relatives. Children may bully one another and pull the wings off butterflies. And all humans may contribute to the exploitation of the earth. Most humans, in other words, stand in a whole network of relationships and can function simultaneously as oppressors in some and as the oppressed in others. The picture becomes even more complex when we note that the brokenness we experience through oppression often, if not always, contributes to the way we mistreat others.[74]

There is of course nothing wrong with focusing in our theory construction or political action on the oppression of women. The danger is with an ideology that has so absolutized the liberation of women that the strategy of emancipation that it advocates results in the oppression of others. To borrow Ruether's term, we might call this a feminist "consequentialism."

To prevent such ideological blindspots, I suggest that work in feminist theology is best done against the backdrop of what I will here call a "multi-faceted liberation theology" which attempts to develop a model of liberation that takes the plight of all oppressed groups into account. Given her present wide-ranging interests in anti-Semitism, feminism, gay and lesbian liberation, the plight of the Palestinians, the ecology crisis, and Black liberation, Ruether herself is in an excellent position to develop such a model.

Ruether has already done some outstanding work on the complex interaction between different forms of oppression. The chapter entitled "Between the Sons of White and the Sons of Blackness: Racism and Sexism in America" in *New Woman/New Earth* is highly nuanced and penetrating in its analysis, and ranks in my mind as one of the very best feminist pieces I have read. Although her arguments for a multi-faceted feminist theology never quite amount to what I mean by a multi-faceted liberation theology, they are comparable. At one point in the essay, she writes,

> In a real sense, any women's movement which is *only* concerned about sexism and no other form of oppression, must remain a women's movement of the white upper class, for it is *only* this group of women whose *only* problem is the problem of being women, since, in every other way they belong to the ruling class [her emphasis]. But a woman who belongs to other minority groups must inevitably refuse this monolithic analysis. She must integrate her struggle as a woman into the struggle to liberate her racial and socioeconomic group. Thus it seems to me essential that the women's movement reach out and include in its struggle *the interstructuring of sexism with all other kinds of oppression*, and recognize a pluralism of women's movements in the context of different groupings [my emphasis]. Otherwise

it will tend to remain a women's movement of the ruling class that can be misused to consolidate the power of that ruling class against the poor and nonwhite of both sexes.[75]

Yet in spite of this awareness, there remains within Ruether's own thought one glaring example of feminist "consequentialism" in which women's liberation is absolutized at the expense of another vulnerable group: the unborn.[76] My disagreement with Ruether's adoption of a pro-choice position does not mean that I am an uncritical supporter of the pro-life movement. Far too many pro-life *and* pro-choice advocates appear to be blind to the complexities of the abortion issue. They make the fundamental mistake of assuming that it can be solved in principle merely by appealing to an "absolute," whether that is the "life" of the fetus or the "choice" of the pregnant woman. Although there is not the space here for me to outline a more acceptable "third way," I do want to signal that I reject both of the above positions as frequently ideological and simplistic.

The problems of "absolutism" on either side are relatively easy to see. That the life of the fetus cannot consistently be regarded as the only important consideration can be seen in the difficulty many pro-lifers have with the idea that victims of incestuous and non-incestuous rape should be legally required to carry the fetus to full term. That the woman's "right to choose" cannot be regarded as the only important criterion to which appeal should be made in any bona fide feminist position is clear from the fact that through their access to new technology which can determine the sex of a fetus in the early stages of pregnancy, some East Indian women, who have internalized the patriarchal ideology of their culture, exercise their "right to choose" by aborting their female fetuses but keeping their male ones.[77]

A "third way" position, as I see it, would work from the assumption that genuine affirmation of *life* in all its fullness must not be reduced to the absolutization of mere biotic existence. It must also include concern for issues of justice not usually cherished by the religious or political Right. It would also recognize that a genuine affirmation of *choice* should not fall into the humanistic trap of defining freedom as autonomy from all normative constraints, whatever they are taken to be.[78] In other words, the notions of "life" and "choice" need to be redefined and incorporated into a new framework.[79] A "third way" position would also refuse to accept the assumption, common to many on both sides of the debate, that what should be legal or illegal is identical with what is believed to be moral or immoral, and *vice-versa*. Both laws and morality are to be normed, but neither should be judged primarily by the standards relevant to the other.[80]

Having clarified the basic thrust of my position, I will now turn to Ruether's comments on this subject. Although I agree with many of her misgivings about the pro-life movement, I also find her pro-choice arguments unacceptable. Abortion, she writes,

> . . . is a desperate remedy for a previous evil; namely, the loss of reproductive self-determination. Any women who want an abortion (other than a small percentage who seek it because of a deformed fetus), are women who have already lost their reproductive self-determination. An unwanted pregnancy has been forced upon them against their will by a combination of ignorance, sexual coercion and inadequate medical means.[81]

I don't deny the reality of difficult cases, and I regret that this brief treatment may make it appear as though I am merely paying lip-service to them. But feminist cultural analysis must struggle to avoid minimizing both woman's victimization and woman's agency with regard to evil. Ruether's analysis is weak on the latter in this context. What I miss here, minimally speaking, is a critique of what we might call "the abortion of mere convenience." I am not primarily talking about whether this specific kind of abortion should be *illegal* (although I don't believe that this should simply be ruled out of consideration *a priori*). What I would like to see is an acknowledgment that the use of abortion as yet another method of birth-control is, or at very least can be, *immoral*.[82]

"Reproductive self-determination" is important, but like "life" it should not be absolutized. Christian feminists, I contend, while avoiding a pro-life absolutism, should reject a feminist consequentialism that reduces the fetus to an "other" who/which can be legitimately defined, by those with the power to name, as sub-human. Ruether's insistence that *every* creature is to be viewed and related to as a "Thou" who cannot be reduced to an "it" should not be conveniently forgotten at this point. If we agree with her call for the affirmation and liberation of those women who are "the oppressed of the oppressed," how can we ignore those female and male fetuses that are destined to become "the oppressed of the oppressed of the oppressed"?

I support Ruether's choice to include a rite of healing from abortion in her book *Women-Church*.[83] I would support such rituals for all forms of abortion, even those of "mere convenience." Acknowledgment rather than denial of our pain and brokenness before the face of God is crucial to any covenantal view of the Christian faith. Nevertheless, I also want to be very clear about my misgivings. Because Ruether's proposed liturgy in this context contains no hint that the choice to have an abortion may be highly immoral in some circumstances, it lends itself to a self-justifying, ideological use. That Ruether seems either unaware or unconcerned about this possibility reveals a moral blind-spot that I find worrying. I would therefore like to draw the discussion of this topic to a close by quoting from the final paragraph of the aforementioned essay, "Between the Sons of White and of Blackness," in the hope that the relevance of her wise words on this subject to the attitude we need to foster if we are to engage the abortion debate with sensitive discernment, is self-evident. Here Ruether writes,

> [W]e must recognize a certain psychological root to the tendency of both the black movement and the women's movement to ignore the structures of oppression within their own groups and to attempt to reduce "oppression" to a single-factored analysis. The Western apocalyptic model of liberation theology polarizes the world into "light" and "darkness," elect and damned, good and evil. Liberation movements draw on the same tendency to absolutize polarity, but in a reverse form. To recognize structures of oppression within our own group would break up this model of ultimate righteousness and projection of guilt upon the "others." It would force us to deal with

ourselves, not as simply oppressed or oppressors, but as people who are sometimes one and sometimes the other in different contexts. A more mature and chastened analysis of the capacities of human beings for good and evil would flow from this perception. The flood gates of righteous anger must then be tempered by critical self-knowledge. This is a blow to the ego of adolescent revolutionary personalities. But, in the long run, only this more complex self-knowledge gives us hope that liberation movements will not run merely to the reversal of hatreds and oppressions, but rather, to a recovery of a greater humanity for us all.[84]

The move from a single-factored, monolithic, black and white, two dimensional analysis to the kind of discernment that would be encouraged by a multi-faceted liberation theology may be clarified by the following analogy. Several years ago, a puzzle that was very popular with both children and adults was the Rubik Cube. The cube had six faces which were each made up of their own colour. Because the cube was made up of a number of smaller cubes, all of which could be twisted up to 360 degrees vertically and horizontally, this pattern could easily be disrupted. Realigning the six faces correctly—the process of redemption, so to speak—involved considerable lateral thinking. For while it was very easy to restore a given face to one colour, if this was done by ignoring all the other faces, they would inevitably remain disrupted.[85]

This is the danger of a feminist theology that does not see its important but limited task within the wider context of the liberation of the entire cosmos. Feminist concerns need to be relativized—that is to say related—to a truly global vision. If this does not happen, evil and fallenness will become reduced to patriarchy, while the redemption of creation will be reduced to women's liberation.

On the one hand, there are times when Ruether is guilty of such feminist reductionism and absolutism, such as in her litany of disaffiliation from patriarchy, her comments about original sin and abortion, and her analysis of "macho-masculine" culture. On the other hand, I believe that the promise of a highly nuanced feminist theology worked out against the backdrop of a multi-face(te)d liberation theology can also be seen in her writings—most clearly in what is arguably her best and most important work, *Gaia and God*. It is at those points where Ruether's liberation theology reflects her desire to promote "a recovery of a greater humanity for us all" that I believe she has made her greatest contribution to contemporary Christian cultural analysis.

Notes

1. *SGT*, 165. In *GG*, 165, she writes of early city life, "One should not assume that subordination of women is always the first subordination, only then followed by slavery and class hierarchy."
2. *FMM*, 103.
3. In her review of *SGT* in the *Union Seminary Quarterly Review* 40 (1985): 66, Angela Askew even goes as far as to say "her apparent inability to address racism in a blueprint for feminist theology, while puzzling, is perhaps symptomatic of a serious difficult[y] with this kind of liberation theological analysis. By taking sexism itself as the locus of sin and evil, Ruether has given us a theological construction which *cannot* have wider application because the limit-case itself lacks universality."
4. *DQ*, 139.
5. *NWNE*, 83.
6. *WC*, 129, my emphasis.
7. Christiane Thies, "Review of *From Machismo To Mutuality* by Eugene Bianchi and Rosemary Radford Ruether," *Vanguard* (September 1976), 26.
8. See the section on God in the previous chapter, and *SGT*, 71.
9. *NWNE*, 194-195.
10. Ibid., 3.
11. See ibid., 3-4. The influence of Simone de Beauvoir on Ruether seems to be the reason why Josephine Donovan, in her book *Feminist Theory: The Intellectual Traditions of American Feminism* (New York: Ungar Publishing Co., 1987), analyzes Ruether's work in her chapter entitled "Feminism and Existentialism." It is misleading to classify Ruether as an existentialist, however. The idea of authentic freedom as the transcending of nature, for example, is very alien to her thought.
12. *NWNE*, 83.
13. This is why she can say in *SGT*, 41 "To see patriarchy coming into existence ... is also to see it passing away."
14. See 90 and 192 above.
15. See Shulamith Firestone, *The Dialectic of Sex: The Case for Feminist Revolution* (New York: Bantam Books, 1970), 192-202.

16. Sheila Collins, *A Different Heaven and Earth* (Valley Forge: Judson Press, 1974), 164. For Paul Tillich's position, see his *Systematic Theology*, vol. 2 (Chicago: University of Chicago Press, 1957), 29-44.

17. See *SGT*, 159.

18. *DQ*, 126-127.

19. Ibid., 127-128.

20. *NWNE*, 157.

21. But see also the discussion in *GG*, 155-72, to which I will refer briefly below.

22. This is also closely related to the distinction she makes between the tribal, classical and modern eras in *LT*, 5-7.

23. *NWNE*, 6-7.

24. The split between the "private" and "public" areas of life, which she calls "male sociological dualism" (*SGT*, 113), is an important area of concern in her cultural analysis. Unfortunately lack of space prevents an exploration of this important topic in this study. But see *SGT*, 226-34, and her fine essay "Toward New Solutions: Working Women and the Male Workday," *Christianity and Crisis* 37 (February 7 1977): 3-8.

25. *NWNE*, 8.

26. Ibid., 10.

27. Ibid., 11.

28. Ibid., 13.

29. Ibid., 13-14.

30. Ibid., 188. Cf. Rosemary Radford Ruether, "The Biblical Vision of the Ecology Crisis."

31. *Identifying* God with creation is not to be confused with the belief that God is equally close to/ present with/ revealed by all creatures, types of relationships and dimensions of creaturely existence. Such an identification undermines this kind of Creator/creation intimacy as I have argued above on 255-56.

32. See Hendrik Hart, "Dooyeweerd's *Gegenstand* Theory of Theory" in C. T. McIntire ed., *The Legacy of Herman Dooyeweerd: Reflections on Critical Philosophy in the Christian Tradition* (Lanham: University Press of America, 1985), 143-66.

33. This is still a tendency in Hart, *Understanding Our World*, though this does not characterize his more recent thought, on which I am dependent at this point. See my paper, "The Trouble with Normative ... Creation Order, Hermeneutics and Homosexuality."

34. By Rationalism here, I am not merely referring to the foundationalism of Descartes, although he is in this tradition. I am using the term very broadly to cover thinkers as diverse as Plato, Aristotle, Augustine, Aquinas, Locke, Ayer, Popper and Habermas who exaggerate rational forms of knowing, and believe that theoretical thought is or should be autonomous in some or all areas of life. My comments in this context, however, are focused on the origins of Rationalism and thus on the Greek philosophical tradition.

35. "The Lion" studied by zoologists—i. e., the conditions that lions must meet in order to be lions, or to put it another way the logical object-functionality of the lions in relation to analytic subjects—become more "real" than the lions cared for by the zoo-keeper. The most extreme form of this is when universality is thought of in terms of entities called universals in Platonic realism.

36. See *LT*, 96-97. Here she is describing pastoral and hunting societies and not agricultural societies.

37. *NWNE*, 9. On not seeing the tribal period as a golden age, see also *GG*, 8. Whether this means that she believes that there was no pre-patriarchal period is not clear. What she calls "the tribal period" covers a very long period of time, and may include a pre-patriarchal phase within it. To my knowledge, however, she never makes this suggestion. Cf. n. 39 below.

38. Rosemary Radford Ruether, "Why Socialism Needs Feminism, and Vice-Versa," *Christianity and Crisis*, 40 (April 28, 1980), 103-108. This quotation, to which I have added my own emphasis, is taken from p. 108. In chap. 4 n. 174 above, I described Ruether's view of history as "mythologizing." It is interesting, in this context, that Calvin Seerveld has come to the conclusion that mythologizing thinkers typically replace the need for cultural integration with cultural de-differentiation, and understand the latter as redemptive. On the idea that cultural differentiation and integration can and should occur simultaneously, see Herman Dooyeweerd, "The Criteria of Progressive and Reactionary Tendencies in History," in *Verslag van de plechtige viering van het honderdvijftigjarig bestaan der Koninklijke Nederlandse Academie van Wetenschappen, 6-9 mei 1958,* (Amsterdam: North-Holland, 1958), 213-28.

39. *NWNE*, 13. Presumably, this is the case with the "pre-patriarchal myths" about which she is elsewhere very positive (see ibid. 157 and 293 above). In "Goddesses and Witches: Liberation and Countercultural Feminism," 843, reflecting on goddess worship in the ancient Near East, she writes, "One might argue that these historical texts of goddess religion represent the transformation of a still earlier truly female-centered pattern to a patriarchal system. But no one has yet discovered the sources for determining whether that is so."

40. See *LT*, 96.

41. See *NWNE*, 27.

42. See ibid., 25 and *FMM*, 8.

43. See *SGT*, 159-183. The following two quotations are from pp. 161 and 162.

44. *WC*, 86.

45. *SGT*, 72.

46. *GG*, 167.

47. Ibid., 170.

48. Ibid., 169.

49. Ibid., 171.

50. I wonder whether questions such as these may eventually prompt some feminists (especially those who are theists) to seriously explore the possibility that evolutionary theory in its various (conflicting) forms is itself the outworking of an extremely widely held, but nevertheless false, modern creation myth. Ironically, the fact that it is so widely believed is itself evidence, in a culture in which virtually every other belief is openly challenged, of its religious, mythic nature. But this is a topic that falls outside the scope of this study.

51. *GG*, 257.

52. Ibid., 31.

53. The egocentric-exocentric terminology is that of Wolfhart Pannenberg, who holds to a similar cosmology to the one Ruether adopts in *Gaia and God*. See Brian J. Walsh, "A Critical Review of Pannenberg's *Anthropology in Theological Perspective*," *Christian Scholar's Review* 15/3 (1986): 247-59.

54. I am in basic agreement on this issue with the approach taken by Gary Shahinian in his M.Phil. thesis "The Problem of Evil in David Griffin's Process Theology" (Toronto: Institute for Christian Studies, 1984). Cf. Hart, *Understanding Our World*, 313, "Evil does not, as such, *belong* in the world; there is no explanation for evil. We can explain whatever has a legitimate place in the scheme of things, but evil has no such place."

55. Thus, there is no speculation about the motives of the serpent. That it is one of the wild animals (3:1, 14), may be mentioned because the author is commenting on the origin and nature of idolatry, which is thus portrayed as the attempt to find religious direction for one's life by turning to a created reality rather than to God. 3:1, 14 certainly prevent us from linking the snake to a primordial chaos, as may be implied in *SGT*, 77.

56. Indeed Ruether herself alludes to the impact of these other forms of estrangement and brokenness on the rise of sexism, as can be seen in the material summarized above.

57. Cf. Ruether's comment in *CAI*, 220, where she writes, "In scripture, creation is very good; we encounter God through his creation, and not by turning our eyes away from his work to some other world which is beyond and set against his creation. There is no way of running away from the world to find God. It is God's creation which is God's manifest, and apart from his work there is no accessibility to God." It should be added that in a fallen world, creation cannot reveal God's presence to the extent that it is warped by evil. God is encountered through what is creationally good but in spite of and in opposition to what is evil. In the latter context, God may legitimately be seen as "intervening" into our world (from that part of creation called "heaven").

58. My emphasis. Jesus has the unfaithful servant who is lent one coin allude to these words in the parable of the talents (Mt. 25:24-25).

59. James H. Olthuis, "The Covenanting Metaphor of the Christian Faith and the Self Psychology of Heinz Kohut," *Studies in Religion* 18 (1989): 322.

60. Valerie Saiving, "The Human Situation: A Feminine View," in Christ and Plaskow, *Womanspirit Rising*, 37. This article originally appeared in *Journal of Religion* 40 (April 1960): 100-12. Judith Plaskow appropriately uses this quotation to introduce her book *Sex, Sin and Grace: Women's Experience and the Theologies of Reinhold Niebuhr and Paul Tillich* (Lanham: University Press of America, 1980), 1.

61. Here I am departing from Saiving (see ibid., 33) who tends to see fear or anxiety as more typically male than female. I would rather speak of typically male and female forms of fear. Her own analysis would seem to suggest that men may fear intimacy and women fear identity.

62. Olthuis, "The Covenanting Metaphor of the Christian Faith and the Self Psychology of Heinz Kohut," 322. It could be said that Olthuis' claim that our need to retain control or be controlled by others is itself a way of "holding down our fear of being *out of control* . . ." needs to be supplemented by speaking of the fear of responsibility if it is to avoid the charge of a one-sided emphasis in the direction of typically male experience.

63. See *SGT*, 179.

64. Ibid.

65. See Goudzwaard, *Idols of Our Time*, 23-25. The idol of guaranteed security is discussed on 61-77.

66. While the phenomenon of idolatry should be examined by looking at the way in which human faith guides and integrates the other dimensions of our experience, we should not only pay attention to the transcendental, guiding, or nurturing direction of influence. This is a weakness in Bob Goudzwaard's otherwise fine book, *Idols of our Time*. Because faith is founded on all the other modes of our being, the kind of idols to which we are attracted will always to be connected to economic, psychic, historical, and other non-fiduciary factors. Here we need to examine life in terms of the foundational direction. The nature of these two direction was discussed briefly on 221 above.

67. See Jessica Benjamin, *The Bonds of Love: Psychoanalysis, Feminism, and the Problem of Domination* (New York: Pantheon Books, 1988), Nancy Chodorow, *The Reproduction of Mothering: Psychoanalysis and the Sociology of Gender* (Berkeley: University of California Press, 1978), Dorothy Dinnerstein, *The Mermaid and The Minotaur: Sexual Arrangements and Human Malaise* (New York: Harper and Row, 1976) and Lillian B. Rubin, *Intimate Strangers: Men and Women Together* (New York: Harper and Row, 1983). Before *GG*, to the best of my knowledge, Ruether only refers to the book by Dinnerstein (see *SGT*, 279 n. 16). In *GG*, Dinnerstein and Chodorow are both mentioned in 292-293 n. 48. The influence of this stream of thought is clear in Van Leeuwen, *Gender and Grace*, chaps. 7 and 8. Some of these ideas are anticipated in Saiving, "The Human Situation," 30-31 and Margaret Mead, *Male and Female: A Study of the Sexes in a Changing World* (New York: The New American Library, 1955), chap. 7 (a book first published in 1949).

68. Boston: Beacon Press, 1986.

69. See the chapter entitled "Swimming Against the Tide of Male-Stream Thought: Feminism, Tradition and the Academy," in my *The Troubled Marriage of Adam and Eve.*

70. On this last point, see Lerner, *The Creation of Patriarchy,* chap. 4 esp. p. 77.

71. Claudia Koonz, *Mothers in the Fatherland: Women, the Family and Nazi Politics* (New York: St. Martin's Press, 1987), 387.

72. Ibid., 17.

73. Ruether herself notes in *SGT,* 165 that women have "collaborated with sexism in lateral violence toward themselves and other women." She does not make it clear, however, that while patriarchy is violent, violence is not intrinsically patriarchal in her discussion of "macho-masculine culture" under consideration here.

74. Who, for example, can determine with any confidence the extent to which Hedda Nussbaum was responsible for the death of Lisa Steinberg? On this subject, see Anne Summers, "The Hedda Conundrum," *Ms.* 17 (April 1989): 54, Marilyn French, "A Gothic Romance," ibid., 60 and esp. Susan Brownmiller, "Madly in Love," ibid., 56, 58-59, 61, 63-64.

75. *NWNE,* 125.

76. It is also worth noting the contradiction that results here from the fact that half the members of this group are female.

77. See, Kathleen Kenna, "Couples wanting only boys flock to MD for gender test" *The Toronto Star,* 10 December, 1990, sec. B, pp. 1, 3.

78. As I will argue in the conclusion, a biblical view of freedom, means partnership with God, not independence from Her/Him. Cf. Ruether's own comments cited there.

79. Ruether herself rightly notes, "Clearly, if one was really interested in reducing the evils of abortion, the best way to do so would be to enhance all the aspects of culture that could help women to resist unwanted sexuality and to prevent unchosen pregnancy." (*CRC,* 42-43). A "third way" strategy would encourage this, but it would also go beyond it to include, at the present time, a call to Christians and non-Christians on both sides of the debate to work together in a "choice" for "life" movement that would campaign to maximize the social conditions that help an already pregnant woman to freely choose life for her child/fetus.

Work that needs to be done in order to empower the pregnant mother, Denyse O'Leary rightly argues, includes: "a) laying the legal framework for winning more paternity cases, b) lobbying for more effective collection of child support, c) providing more rent-geared-to-income housing, d) setting up affordable day care, e) studying and reporting on experimental adoption programs where mother and child do not completely lose touch." ["The Pro-Life Movement: Coming to Terms with our Costly Mistakes," in Denyse O'Leary ed., *The Issue is Life: A Christian Response to Abortion in Canada* (Burlington: Welch Publishing Co. Inc., 1988), 57.] I can see no possible pro-life or pro-choice argument against these proposals. Perhaps those concerned about the rights and wrongs of abortion could put more of their energy into such projects instead of voicing the rhetoric of their respective positions!

80. See Paul A. Marshall, *Thine Is The Kingdom: A Biblical Perspective on the Nature of Government Today* (Basingstoke: Marshall, Morgan, and Scott, 1984), 18ff and 83ff.

81. *CRC*, 41.

82. On this point, see Kathleen McDonnell, *Not An Easy Choice: A Feminist Re-examines Abortion* (Toronto: The Women's Press, 1984). Another ethical critique of pro-choice absolutism from a feminist perspective is Jean Bethke Elshtain, "Reflections on Abortion, Values, and the Family" in Sidney Callahan and Daniel Callahan, eds., *Abortion: Understanding Differences* (New York: Plenum Press, 1984), 47-72.

83. See *WC*, 161-62.

84. *NWNE*, 132.

85. This analogy could be correlated to some extent with my ideas about orientation and reorientation in chap. 3 (see 103-13 above). There is often no simple move from disorientation to the state of orientation or eschatological reorientation. To reorient the faces of the cube sometimes involves breaking down partial realignments as part of a process towards true realignment. Thus the way the Spirit guides creation towards wholeness necessarily include temporarily leading us in directions that are sub-normative.

Conclusion

A recent survey of twentieth-century theology has described Rosemary Ruether as "[p]erhaps the most influential feminist theologian" of our day. The writers go on to say that she is "[a]n articulate and persuasive speaker as well as a prolific writer [who] has done more to promote the cause of feminist theology and Women-Churches than any other single person."[1] Whether one is an enthusiastic supporter or troubled critic of feminist theology, Ruether's importance as a contemporary theologian cannot be doubted.

In the sympathetic critique of Ruether's thought that I have offered, I have presented her as a theologian whose praxis-oriented scholarship always challenges us and usually empowers us to wrestle with key issues of our time. I have also suggested that her theology provides us with an important test-case for the possibility of developing an integral Christian feminist position (introduction). In this light, I have claimed that she has drawn on a wealth of historical knowledge to expose the androcentric and misogynous nature of traditional Christian theology, thus building an extremely strong case for our need to break with much of the past (chap. 1). I have welcomed her insistence that we *not only* need to honour contemporary experience *but must also* root ourselves in history if we are to attempt to construct a Christian feminist theology for our times (chap. 2). Even though I have developed a different approach to the biblical tradition in this context, I have still found a number of significant points of contact with her thinking (chap. 3). I have also suggested that in spite of having some major disagreements with her on certain topics such as eschatology, Ruether has made a number of insightful and suggestive proposals for a feminist reconstruction of the various areas of theology (chap. 4). While I believe that there are a number of blindspots in her field of vision, I remain convinced that she has raised some important issues with respect to how we should understand the patriarchal nature of Western culture (chap. 5). All in all, the preceding discussion should convey my conviction that no Christian cultural analyst or theologian who is concerned to interpret the world as part of the larger struggle to see that God's will is done on earth as it is in heaven, can afford to ignore Ruether's contribution.

In previous chapters, my agreements and disagreements with her thought have been closely interwoven. My aim in these final pages is to draw this wide-ranging discussion of Ruether's theology to a close by clarifying the basic ontological, epistemological and confessional differences between us. I will focus on the challenge to construct a holistic woman-affirming anthropology and cosmology and on the relevance of the biblical drama for the issues that address us. I will also reflect on how successful Ruether is in constructing a theology that is simultaneously Christian and feminist.

I. Anthropology/ Cosmology
In the preceding pages, I have often referred to what I believe is a subtle though persistent dualistic streak in Ruether's cosmology and anthropology. This manifests itself in the way she distinguishes and relates the inside and the outside, unity and diversity, universality and individuality, the infinite and the finite, spirit and matter, essence and existence. While I will not attempt to outline a detailed alternative to this view of the world (or to the more monistic conception that she begins to articulate in *Gaia and God*), I will make a few general points, focusing primarily on the last two pairs in this list.

Ruether's attempt to develop a holistic, non-reductionistic, non-dualistic cosmology and anthropology by arguing for a correlation of spirit and matter, or energy and matter, is an improvement on the positions she rejects but is still less than satisfactory. What we need, I believe, is a fresh approach to the question of the unity and diversity of created reality.

I have alluded a number of times in the preceding pages to Herman Dooyeweerd's theory of the modal diversity of creation. In this view, in the place of the rather limited categories of spirit and matter, and in opposition to the notion of "substance," human existence is made up of a number of interrelated but irreducible modes, dimensions, aspects, or ways-of-being-in-the-world.[2] Dooyeweerd claimed that there is a certain order to these modes of being, some being more foundational than others. The modal order suggested by the Dooyeweerdian philosopher Hendrik Hart, when looked at in this foundational direction, is: numeric, spatial, kinematic, energetic, biotic, psychic, technical (or formative), symbolic, analytic, social, economic, juridical, ethical, and pistic (or certitudinal).[3]

This modal diversity should not be seen as analogous to the layers of a wedding cake. That would be to emphasize the identity and irreducibility of the modes at the expense their mutual intimacy and interrelatedness. Dooyeweerd attempted, in part, to explain modal unity in terms of a complex system of "analogies" in which each mode in its own unique way reflects the reality of each of the other irreducible sides of reality.[4] The details of Dooyeweerd's thought are not important in this context. Nevertheless, because most thinkers have an awareness of some kind of modal order to reality, what interests me here is the relationship of Ruether's use of the terms "spirit," "energy" and "matter" to this ontological schema.

It seems probable that the correlation of spirit and matter, or the inside and the outside, in both the dualistic and monistic articulations of her cosmology, is a reductionistic way of distinguishing what I would call the relatively foundational aspects of reality from those situated later in the modal order. "Matter" is probably a conflation of the pre-biotic modalities, while the less foundational modes are, in effect, lumped together as "spirit."

Giving Birth to the Future

I have argued that Ruether sees energy as that part of spirit closest to matter in her soft dualist cosmology, and as the point of their bifurcation in *Gaia and God*.[5] It may seem that given the linguistic similarity, there is a close relationship between this energy and the energetic mode listed above. I believe that this is probably the case with respect to what she calls "material energy." But Ruether's discussion of Teilhard de Chardin, upon whom she is dependent, strongly suggests that what she calls "spiritual energy" is equivalent to what he calls "psychic energy," and which she, in a summary of his position, describes as "biopsychic energy."[6] "Spiritual energy" in Ruether's terminology, then, refers to what I would call biotic or psychic functioning as those modes "analogically" reflect the more foundational reality of the "energetic" aspect of reality.[7]

In my terminology, dualistic anthropologies claim that we are made up of two fundamental or irreducible sides which are either closely correlated, as in *soft* dualism, or sharply polarized, as in *harsh* dualism. Up until *Gaia and God*, Ruether's categories of spirit and matter or inside and outside function in a way that exemplifies the former kind of dualism which she then recommends as an alternative to the latter kind. In her terminology, she is positing an alternative to dualism *per se*.

Her emphasis on there being *two* sides to our humanity is better than those truncated anthropologies that would further reduce us to just one fundamental side. Nevertheless, I would prefer to speak of the *many* sides of our humanity, or better, the multi-dimensional unity of the human person. The stress on unity here is rooted in the philosophical conviction that there is no break in the modal order that separates our relatively higher and lower functions. Each mode influences all our other ways-of-being-in-the-world. Earlier modes are foundational to later modes which, in turn, guide or "open up" earlier modes. By contrast, no matter how favourably Ruether may speak of notions of "the dialectical interplay of the polarities of existence,"[8] I have yet to see real evidence in her anthropology of a genuine interaction between what she calls the inside and the outside, or spirit and matter.

Ruether identifies the inside of entities with freedom and the outside with necessity.[9] While her language of the two sides to reality appears very reductionistic when compared with a multi-sided or multi-modal ontology, it does closely echo what philosophers in the Dooyeweerdian tradition call the law-side and subject-side of creation.[10] For this tradition, when we examine phenomena in terms of the law-subject correlation, the categories of freedom and necessity (or determinism) become important. When we look at this correlation in the direction of law to subject, we become aware of the extent to which creatures are determined by creational limits and called to an existence of a certain kind. When we look at the correlation in the other direction—from subject to law—our attention is drawn to a subject's freedom, understood as the responsibility that it has within the space it has been given to work out its covenantal relationship with God and with its fellow creatures.

Because we are talking about a correlation here in which each side can only exist and make sense in relation to the other, it follows that no creature is ever fully determined or entirely free. While Ruether's position would appear to go a long way towards recognizing that this is so, her cosmology gives the impression that we are part determined and part free in the sense that what I have referred to as the relatively higher modes are seen as modes of freedom, while the more foundational modes are viewed as modes of necessity. Teilhard de Chardin, after articulating the same position, asks, "How can life respect determinism on the *without* and yet act in freedom *within*? Perhaps we shall understand that better some day."[11]

I believe our understanding will not increase if we approach the world in this fashion. When we look at human life in terms of the law-subject correlation and isolate each of the modes in turn, what we find, I suggest, is a correlation of freedom and determinism *at each level* even though the freedom of response increases and the limits of and for life become more "plastic" the further we move beyond the more foundational modes.[12]

As I have already argued, Ruether's soft dualism leads her to minimize the impact of male and female sexual difference on our post-biotic ways-of-being-in-the-world.[13] There are some slight

hints in *Gaia and God* that her shift to a more monistic cosmology
may signal a weakening of her determination to restrict our maleness
and femaleness to the "outside" of our humanity.[14] But it is still fair
to say that this lack of integrality in her anthropology has significantly shaped the character of her feminist theology as a whole.

Her critical principle of feminist theology rightly calls for "the
promotion of the full humanity of women."[15] But while her
anthropology could be said to affirm the full humanity of women as
people, it falls short, in my opinion, of doing justice to the full
humanity of women *as women*. This is a significant weakness.[16] What
her approach is in danger of missing is the way in which sex and
gender differences affect the quest for authentic spirituality. While
I cannot address the question of how this is so for women, I am
convinced as a male that the attention that James Nelson has given
to the specific nature of male gender identity and bodily structure
(in his book *The Intimate Connection: Male Sexuality, Masculine
Spirituality*) highlights important realities for men that remain invisible in approaches that focus on the generically human.[17]

Hester Eisenstein, in her introduction to *The Future of Difference*, argues that there have been three distinct phases in the
history of Women's Studies. In the late sixties and early seventies,
the differences between men and women were rejected as oppressive and basically artificial. This gave way to "woman-centred
analysis" which, far from minimizing male-female difference,
celebrated the distinctive character of women's experience. This, in
turn, gave way to an intense recognition of cultural and historical
differences between women themselves.[18] One gets a sense of these
three phases by noting the striking differences between the writings
of Simone de Beauvoir, Adrienne Rich, and recent post-modernist
feminists.

We might characterize the first phase as focusing on women as
human, the second as concerned with women as women, and the
third as drawing attention to women as black/white, lesbian/straight,
rich/poor, and so on. Each approach highlights important realities
that need to be honoured, I believe. Looked at in this light,
Ruether's theoretical anthropology seems primarily oriented to, or
perhaps stuck in, the first of these phases. While there is evidence

that she is sympathetic to the political concerns of those who prefer the third phase, her antipathy towards and lack of dialogue with the work of the second phase hinders her chances of developing as rich a framework as possible.

No anthropology is adequate, in my view, unless it also addresses the reality of the self.[19] While the self cannot be reduced to human functionality, neither does it exist apart from our ways-of-being-in-the-world. We need to speak of a self/functions correlation. In the way it is expressed and experienced, the self is multi-modal. Thus we can speak of the physical self, the emotional self, the rational self, and so on. But the self cannot be exclusively identified with any of its ways-of-being.

The shift in Ruether's view of the world in *Gaia and God* promises to modify her view of the self, although it is too early to say exactly what form this will take.[20] I will therefore limit my comments to the way our selfhood appears to be understood in her previous works. There it is related to her category of spirit, and identified with the "ego." For her, the ego is the "inside" of the human organism, which is in turn the "outside" of the ego. If we replace the category of "matter" with that of "body," we can explore the correlation of self and functions by using this terminology of spirit, inside, and outside within a different framework. As James Olthuis has suggested,

> [W]hen we desire to refer to human persons from the viewpoint of their differentiated, multi-functional, positioned existence, we can talk of "body." I am totally body. When we want to refer to human persons from the viewpoint of their unified, intentional, centred, directional, open existence, we can talk of "spirit." I am totally spirit. Each description covers the whole person, but they do so from differing perspectives. Looking at the human person as body is to look so to speak from the outside-in: looking at the human person as spirit is to look so to speak from the inside-out.[21]

Viewed in the light of this self/functions correlation, Ruether's ego/organism distinction appears reductionistic in a double sense.

Firstly, it sounds as though she reduces the self's many "bodily" ways-of-being to organic expression. Secondly, if she is using the term "ego" as it is typically used in psychological literature, then it is equivalent to the self viewed as separate from its relationships and whittled down to it rational dimension. At best, this is an abstraction. Far more insightful and anti-reductionistic is her discussion of the I-Thou relationship in which she rightly draws attention to the reality of selfhood in humans and in other creatures.[22] Nevertheless, the self appears fused with the higher or less foundational functions and is seen as closer to God than the more-or-less extrinsic organism to which it is related.[23]

In the anthropology that I am proposing, there is an order to the modalities. Yet there is no hierarchy in the sense that only some modes are considered to be modes of the self. Neither is any mode closer to God or more "divine" than any other. All of our ways-of-being-in-the-world are thoroughly creaturely. In my view, to be a creature is to be called to reveal God in terms of our creatureliness. When we love God, self, neighbour and the rest of creation, therefore, all of the modes of our humanity become ways of making God present on earth. I hear Ruether moving in the same direction when she entitles the postscript to *Sexism and God-Talk*: "Woman/ Body/ Nature: The Icon of the Divine."[24]

Looked at in this light, we might say that the calling to make God present in the way we live our lives is a calling to "give birth to God." To borrow the imagery of Rev. 12, we might say that the messianic community that is engaged in fighting the powers and principalities of our age is the pregnant woman who is about to give birth facing the dragon that is waiting to devour her child immediately it comes into the world.

Ruether's distinction between *essence* and *existence*, like her spirit-matter distinction, gets at a reality that I wish to honour in terminology that I would not choose. In her book *The Radical Kingdom*, she offers the following sympathetic description of how this distinction has functioned in Western thought. She writes,

> Classical thought identified reality with essence, and so judged existence by the standard of essence. Truth by its very nature

could not be value free, but was a value judgment upon present existence. Truth or essence was a demand laid upon existence that defined what the thing "really was" and so what it "should be." In Christian mythological language the same idea is present in the images of "Creation" and "the Kingdom." Creation is not the historical origin of present existence but stands for the true nature of things which is recovered or fulfilled only at the End. Both poles are necessary because without the creational pole the demand upon existence loses its foundation. Only with the doctrine of creation as the foundation is it clear that what the world "should be" is to become "what it really is," its true nature. Existence, by contrast, is in tension with what creation truly is.

Ruether argues that both classical and Christian "man" lived in a two-dimensional universe of tension between the "is" of existence and the "ought" of essence, a tension which has been inherited by modern critical philosophy and reinterpreted so that the historical nature of the dialectic is made clear. For such thinkers, writes Ruether sympathetically,

"Being" or "true reality" is understood as a demand laid upon existence both in negation of its present failure and an exhortation to struggle toward self-transcendence. Truth or essence is subversive of the existing order. The search for truth is sociohistorical. It is the search for the new *polis*. Historical being is a dynamic continuum of tension and negation and elan toward the "true world".[25]

Ruether utilizes this distinction in her own theology in order to highlight that what "is" should not be identified with what "ought" to be.[26] Our "true" nature to which we should aspire is a norm that judges who we are at present. Thus, while she describes "the critical principle of feminist theology" as "the promotion of the full humanity of women," she is quick to point out that this "full humanity of women . . . has not existed in history."[27]

The problem here is that this "essential" or "true" nature can sound abstract and even supra-temporal. Rebecca Chopp notes that Ruether's methodology is built on three basic presuppositions:

> 1) that there is a structure expressive of human nature that stands behind history . . . , 2) that this structure is thought to be universal, and 3) that our words about human nature refer to this extrahistorical structure. These assumptions predispose one to the commitment that when we speak of "full humanity" we can grasp something that is independent of our concrete situation. Consequently the term "full humanity," which is to liberate us for ourselves, precipitates a wandering away from our real, concrete, historical experience.[28]

Related to the problem of abstract universality is the difficulty we have in explaining what it is we are talking about. If our full or authentic humanity doesn't exist historically, then where is it?

In the Dooyeweerdian tradition in which I situate my own thinking, what Ruether is trying to get at in terms of an essence-existence framework bears striking similarities to the "law-subject" relationship to which I have already referred.[29] This is sometimes spoken of as the relationship between creatures and the Word of God to which they are subject. When a theoretical attention to the universal conditions that hold for existence is combined with questions about the normative direction in which life should go if humanity is to find Shalom, what comes into view are God's perduring, universal calls to humanity to be energetic, emotionally sensitive, imaginative, clear thinking, just, and faithful, to name some obvious examples. To disobey these calls, all of which can be summarized in terms of the one call to love God, neighbour, self and creation, will result in our dehumanization and will give birth to a world in which God's presence will become increasingly hard to find. Life in all its fullness will evade us and even our basic existence may be threatened.

What this amounts to is the conviction that to be authentically human, to bring one's true self into existence, is to follow God's will for human life. To attempt to be autonomous is to become alienated from who we are called to be. Here the Dooyeweerdian or "reformational" tradition is very close to Ruether when she writes in her first book,

> To know oneself as a creature is . . . not an ignominy and a shackle to be thrown off by man "come of age." All this is the view of creaturehood of Adamic man. No, to be a creature is sheer miracle, sheer divine grace. To throw off our being-from-God is not to soar above it, but to sink below it. Our being-in-Christ, our being in the New Covenant life of the church is, then, not a supra-creational state of being, but a renewed creational state of being. We must find our true being in Christ, not so that we can be religious men, but so that we can be men, human beings, children of God, persons and brothers.[30]

In *Sexism and God-Talk*, written sixteen years later, she writes in a similar vein, "The liberating encounter with God/ess is always an encounter with our authentic selves resurrected from underneath the alienated self."[31] Where she speaks of "the regrounding of ourselves in the primordial matrix" just before this quotation, the reformational tradition would speak of regrounding ourselves in God's Word for creation, and reconnecting with the Spirit who guides creation in history from its origin to its destiny.

With this parallel approach of law and subject, we can make some progress in determining the ontological status of the "authentic self." Given the law-subject correlation, we may understand it as the law, conditions, or Word of God that holds for the everyday self and which that self must obey and incarnate in order to be whole. Thus understood, when I experience reconnection with God, when I internalize His/Her will, I naturally experience wholeness, restoration and authenticity. I get a glimpse of my "authentic self" and I know that this is who I am called to be, and in that sense, who I really am.

Problems, however, remain. Because theoretical analysis always leads to a bracketing of individuality and change in the attempt to conceptually isolate what is universal and constant, and because the law-subject correlation, like that of essence and existence, only comes into view via such analysis, the attempt to gain access to questions of normativity via the investigation of the law-subject relationship can only put us in touch with something abstract. The calls of God, in this framework, may call for(th) varied and dynamic responses, but they are themselves universal and perduring. We are still left with Chopp's problem of a notion of normativity that "precipitates a wandering away from our . . . concrete, historical experience."[32] A possible solution to this dilemma may be found in a consideration of the nature of the biblical drama.

II. The Biblical Drama

We can speak more concretely about the authentic self if we view it in terms of the biblical drama. From this point of view, my authentic self is an *eschatological* or *future* reality; a concrete existent which the Gospel promises will only be fully realized when all creation is healed and incarnates the will of God. The law-subject (or essence-existence) relationship may give us insight into certain aspects of the relationship between what is and what ought to be, but the is/ought relationship is not static and must be viewed in the light of the historical drama of creation-fall-redemption-eschaton.

Many of the criticisms of Ruether's cosmology that I have offered in this study concern problems that are implicit in the structure of her thought rather than proposals that are explicitly stated and defended. More often than not, such problems exist in conflict with what I take to be her best intentions. Here, however, we meet a far more fundamental difference in our approaches. Unlike myself, Ruether understands the biblical themes of creation and eschaton as supratemporal realities. For her, they are merely ways of talking about the true nature of, or normative call to, historical existence. Thus, in her first book, she writes,

> In patristic and Protestant theology, . . . nature and grace, creation and redemption, are related dynamically rather than hierarchically. In the opinion of this author, this is the only authentic way the biblical dualism of the New Creation *versus* "this world," which is clearly not intended to be a neutral state of nature, but is the sphere which is dominated by the powers and principalities: i. e, the "work" of the demons. In such a view,

creation is not viewed historically but eschatologically. The primal creation is an eschatological reality, not a description of any past historical situation. Creation is always pre-historical as the New Creation is post-historical, whereas history begins with the fall. Historical existence is always "under the fall," under the law of death. Redemption, therefore, is not transcendent to creation, but dynamically continuous with it. Redemption is not rising to the "supernatural," but realising that creaturely existence which was laid on us in the beginning both as a gift and as a promise. The eschatological paradise recapitulates the primal paradise. Creation, therefore, is not a neutral state of nature between grace and fall, but grace and fall are two poles of the dynamic tension between which creation exists. Historically, creation is always fallen; essentially, its nature is grace.[33]

While Ruether is quite right to reject a view of redemption that would take us out of creation, what I have interpreted as the biblical belief in a future historical time when the world that God has made will be fully healed has no real place in this schema.[34]

The danger with Ruether's position is that, while she may speak of "gift" and "promise," all we have is the imperative of God's will laid upon us, with no hope that it will ever be fulfilled. We can expect glimpses of a world of shalom, mercy and justice in those rare moments when we overcome our brokenness. But I see no reason, given her framework, to believe that they will be anything more than fleeting moments in a world in which the forces of evil and oppression will continue to have the last word. Ironically, while the subtitles of two of Ruether's own books contain the word "hope,"[35] this is something that her own theology seems unable to provide. In fact in her recent writings, she has begun to advise us that "[w]e need ... to learn to become wise in the absorption of the tragic dimension of life, which we cannot change or control."[36] It would appear that this tragic dimension is something that even God can do nothing about—a topic to which I will return below.

The conflation of creation and fall in this understanding of human life as necessarily tragic, and present in the claim in her first book that "[h]istorically, creation is always fallen," is also evident in her latest publication. Here she writes,

> Nature, in the sense of the sum of cosmic life, was not originally paradisaical (benign for us) and is not capable of completely fulfilling human hopes for the good, in the sense of benign regard for individual and communal life, which is the human ideal.[37]

Later in this book, she makes it clear that our suffering and lack of fulfilment is not always due to our evil, but is often the inevitable consequence of the way we have been made. Thus she writes,

> There is tragedy in the finitude of the human perspective, which pursues limited good for its community and is little able to visualize the interrelated train of destruction that may be set in motion thereby. . . .[38]

This perspective is seriously at odds with the biblical worldview, as I understand it. If we view our present life within the context of the biblical drama of creation-fall-redemption-eschaton, which begins with an unambiguously good creation and ends with the promise of the New Earth, our attitude towards hope, finitude, and fulfilment will be very different, I suggest.

In contrast to Ruether, I want to insist that our finitude in not inherently problematic, as she suggests, but was created good. It gets caught up in tragedy because of our alienation from God. It is true that even well-intentioned human cultural formation has led to suffering, but this was not inevitable. We have never been "omniscient." That kind of knowledge belongs to God's side of the covenant relationship. Our finite ability to foresee the long-term consequences of our actions, which was supposed to reveal to us our need to depend on Yahweh as we set about our task of guiding creation to its eschatological destiny, has become a painful reminder of our inability to play God.

In the beginning, creation was "benign" in the sense of being a home for us in which we were safe, and "paradisaical" in the sense that we had all that we needed to fulfil our calling and thus our humanity. But it is important that the phrase "very good" that is used to describe creation in Gen. 1 is not read as "perfect" or "complete" in a static Greek sense. The call to humans to make history (as distinct from merely being historical) included plenty of room for surprise, innovation, growth in wisdom, and alternative possibilities. Thus God is portrayed, in Gen. 2, as genuinely curious to see what names Adam will give to the animals.

It is also important to note that the security of our environment was never "absolute" in the (etymological) sense of being immune from the relationships in which it stood. Nothing in creation can be regarded as self-contained or viewed as though the covenant with Yahweh is incidental to its nature. Our security was dependent on our ongoing trust in God, which was the antithesis of eating of the tree of knowledge and attempting to define good and evil autonomously.[39] Once we exchanged wisdom for folly, and thus cut ourselves off from God's revelation of how to find the way of life and avoid the way of death, all our relationships were affected. Our world immediately ceased to be a safe place for us, and became increasingly threatening and even hostile. Work turned into labour, challenge was replaced with struggle, limits became constraints, distinctions gave way to alienating chasms, and healthy self-love degenerated into self-hatred and self-worship.

Mortality can be especially threatening in a fallen world. This does not mean that it is simply the result of the Fall, any more than any other facet of our finitude. The promise of a long life not prematurely cut short that is found in the Old Testament prophets (e. g., Isa. 65:12, Zec. 8:4) points towards a different understanding of mortal limits. Furthermore the warning of Gen. 2—"When you eat of the tree of good and evil you shall surely die"—should be read within the story of the Pentateuch as a whole, and thus in the light of "life" and "death" in the covenantal sense as found in Deut. 30:15-20.

In my opinion, human life was always meant to be unto death (Heidegger) as well as beyond death (Augustine). The "beyond" here must not be seen as a translation to a different, higher realm, or as a move from time to eternity. It is "beyond" in the same sense that birth signals life beyond the womb (not beyond creation or history). Paul's image of life beyond death as being like the seed that "dies" in the ground before growing into a plant (1 Cor. 15: 35ff) suggests neither a dualistic uprooting from the earth, nor a healing of the seed from what it should never have been, but its fulfilment in a new stage of development.

Without an eschatological future, even life in an unfallen world would (as Ruether puts it) not have been "capable of completely fulfilling human hopes for the good," although I mean this in a different sense from her. While we can distinguish present and future, they are interrelated in such a way that the nature of the present includes the anticipation of what is to come. Just as adolescence is a time when we begin to have desires and ambitions that can only come into their own in adulthood, so present existence would not have satisfied all our hopes even if we had not broken the covenant.

It is becoming increasingly popular to speak of the structure of the adult personality as being built on childhood experiences which are incorporated into the adult self as one's "inner child." The same dynamics are at work in all of the transitions of life, I suggest. By analogy, the life of the resurrection does not simply discard or leave the life of the present age behind, even though it moves us beyond our present existence in ways we cannot imagine any more than an unborn baby can picture life outside the womb.

In this light, the call (or benediction) to fill and subdue the earth of Gen. 1 is good, but it is only for a time (hence Jesus' reply to the Sadducees in Mt. 22:23-33). That this present age is not the "be all and end all," and was never intended to be historically self-contained, is hinted at in the Sabbath rest mentioned before the Fall in Gen. 2:2, which is appealed to as the creational basis for the weekly rest for humans and their animals in the Decalogue (Ex. 20:8-11). Just as God's rest signified that the task of setting the stage for human life was complete (a rest which is interrupted by the Fall), so part of the significance of the weekly Sabbath for God's image bearers is as an anticipation of the fulfilment of our calling. In other words, it has a creational-historical significance that is now interwoven with, but not simply reducible to, respite from the unrest caused by our evil. This becomes visible when the theme of rest is viewed within the canon as a whole. Thus it appears not only in the redemptive-historical context of entering the promised land (e. g., Deut. 3:20), but as an important element in the eschatological reflections of Heb. 4.

Evil constantly threatens to prevent us from reaching this goal (Num. 14:30, Ps. 95:11, Heb. 7:3-19). As a result of God's redemptive work, however, creation can now move towards its eschatological fulfilment once again. If the transition to life on the new Earth is somewhat analogous to the birth of a baby, then the entrance of evil into history can be compared to a disease that attacks the health and development of the fetus and threatens to terminate the pregnancy. Redemption can then be seen as the process that restores health to the fetus and culminates in the safe delivery of the child.

Eschatological "rest" marks the end (termination) of our present unrest, and the end (goal and fulfilment) of our present work. Such an eschatological horizon can help us resist the idols that prey on our present insecurities. Once we know that the idea of the meek inheriting the earth is a promise and not an impossible ideal, we can afford to be as wise as serpents but as gentle as doves.

Ruether's rejection (or lack of serious consideration) of this kind of eschatology may be a reaction to the way belief in a future resurrection often functions to buttress an other-worldly approach to life, but this is not the kind of "hope" that I am advocating. In 1 Cor. 15:12-58, Paul works out some of the implications of his corporate Christology-ecclesiology by basing his argument for the future resurrection of believers on the resurrection of Jesus. This does not have to be read as a recipe for "pie in the sky by and by" but as a view of the future that increases the significance of the present.

In the Christus Victor model of the atonement, to which I referred in chapter 4,[40] Jesus' death on the cross is understood as a confrontation with the powers and principalities. The resurrection is seen as God's vindication of Jesus, and as the revelation that death could not hold him. This view encourages us neither to minimize nor to become paralysed by present evil. As Reta Halteman Finger explains,

Human salvation [according to the Christus Victor model] is
. . . effected by putting one's trust in and identifying with this
victorious Christ. In our world, the powers are still at work, and
we do not underestimate their pervasiveness and ability to
poison, cripple, and kill—as violently as a nuclear bomb or as
insidiously as polluted water and air. But the resurrection of
Jesus is our one hope that evil does not have the last word, and
that, in the New Creation, we will be raised like Jesus to witness
the final defeat of all powers of evil.[41]

Hope is possible here and now because the powers and principalities have been unmasked (Col. 2:15). Ruether is right to say
that we must continue Jesus' struggle against them, but is wrong to
claim that the cross represents their victory.[42] It is precisely the cross
and resurrection that reveal to the world that these powers are not
omnipotent. As Heb. 2:14 puts it,

Since the children have flesh and blood, [Jesus] too shared in
their humanity so that by his death he might destroy him who
holds the power of death—that is, the devil—and free those
who all their lives were held in slavery by their fear of death.

To the eyes of faith, therefore, death has lost its sting, ultimately
speaking (cf. 1 Cor. 15:55). Because death could not hold Jesus, we
know that in the end it cannot hold us. In that hope, we are liberated
from the temptation to escapism and empowered to combat patriarchy and the other powers and principalities of our day, even though
this may cost us our lives.

Our view of God's power is important in this context. In chapter
4, I referred to Ruether's claim that Christian notions of God's
"omnipotence" were the result of modelling the way God exercises
power after human rulers and despots who force their enemies to
surrender and submit to their will. Such false ideas, she argues, give
us the problem of theodicy. In the light of such views of God's power,
the evils of the present age make us question God's goodness. But
once we involve ourselves in the struggle for justice, she believes,
such questions will no longer be relevant for we will know that the

God who is with us and for us is not a distant sovereign but a God who, in Jesus, has made Him/Herself vulnerable to the forces of evil and destruction by siding with the poor and oppressed in the struggle of life against death.[43]

There is much here with which I am sympathetic. On the specific notion of omnipotence, however, I believe that Ruether's approach is less than satisfying, especially for those who struggle with God to promote justice and peace. What I consider to be Ruether's best proposals for theological reconstruction, such as her reflections on Mariology and Christology, are always the result of subjecting the Christian tradition to a much-needed "hermeneutic of suspicion" and then applying a "hermeneutic of retrieval" which draws on the resources of the tradition that can help us in the task of reconstruction. When she is weakest, such as in her proposals in the area of eschatology, the hermeneutic of suspicion is utilized without an adequate hermeneutic of retrieval. This, in a nutshell, is also what disappoints me about her reflections on omnipotence.

As usual, her criticisms of traditional thinking are to the point. But how might a hermeneutic of retrieval help us here? The biblical ideas of God as Sovereign and as Almighty are very different from later scholastic speculations. To confess God as Sovereign is not so much a description as a normative declaration made in faith, for in an important sense the existence of evil means that God is not fully ruling at present. But S/he is the one true Ruler. To speak of God's sovereignty in this way is to declare that the reign of the powers and principalities may be very real but is nevertheless illegitimate and temporary. Such a confession articulates and strengthens our conviction and knowledge that evil will not have the last word. To believe in God as the Almighty One is to trust that no matter how difficult the task of purging all evil from the earth, and no matter how much God's strategy of love involves risk, vulnerability and struggle, God nevertheless has all the power that is necessary to emerge victorious.

The Scriptures reveal that in His/Her covenant with creation, Yahweh has taken full responsibility for overcoming the evil which we have introduced into the world. The Kingdom of God will be established on earth. God will be all in all. If God is omnipotent or all-powerful in this sense, then the powers and principalities are not. We too can afford to acknowledge the limits of our own power and avoid the twin temptations of fatalistic resignation and heroic triumphalism.

At the end of "Mother Earth and the Megamachine," Ruether declares defiantly, "We seek to overcome the deadly Leviathan of the Pentagon of Power, transforming its power into manna to feed the hungry of the earth."[44] In a sermon reproduced in *Women-Church*, she says,

> Together, let us break up that great idol and grind it into powder; dismantle the great Leviathan of violence and misery who threatens to destroy the earth, plow it into the soil, and transform it back into the means of peace and plenty, so that all the children of earth can sit down together at the banquet of life.[45]

It is significant that in the biblical tradition, Yahweh alone is described as actually crushing Leviathan (and giving him as food to the creatures of the desert, cf. Ps. 74). In the story that the Bible tells, there are some things that only Yahweh has the power to take care of. We are called to accept such mighty acts of God as the context within which we are to live our lives in faithfulness to our side of the covenant.

The fact that God effortlessly established the earth in the beginning means that there is no need for humans to ritually re-enact a primordial victory of cosmos over chaos. (This is another part of the significance of the Sabbath for God and for humans.) That God alone establishes and knows the difference between good and evil is something we have to accept if we are not to become cut off from the tree of life. That God alone can see to it that evil in its patriarchal and non-patriarchal forms is finally overcome liberates us from the tyranny of impossible expectations to be faithful to what God calls us to do in our generation—including opposing the Leviathan of violence. We are thus set free, even in our fallen world, to embrace our finitude as a gift and as a call to keep our part of the covenant with Yahweh, as created co-creators and redeemed co-redeemers.

These reflections, like the responses that I have made to Ruether's constructive proposals in previous chapters are, for all the limits of my own argumentation, rooted in the conviction that a vibrant feminist theology is made possible not when we turn to pagan and humanistic sources of revelation, but when we ground our vision of and for life more deeply in the biblical tradition. This also means developing a profound suspicion towards what the Enlightenment tradition tells us about what modern people should and should not trust, believe in, and hope for. Such a "second naiveté"[46] might do much to close the gap that presently exists between the theologically educated elite and the "simple believer," a gap which frequently prevents what feminist theologians have to say from being taken to heart by the wider Christian community.

Communication problems here are often further compounded by differing approaches to Scripture. As I noted in chapter 3, which ended Part One of this study, those highly negative elements in Ruether's approach to the biblical tradition will function as a stumbling block to thousands of Christians in this context. As a member of the evangelical community this concerns me, for I know many Christians who will reject everything else that she says for this reason.

Some may even use her arguments on this topic to support their conviction that feminism and Christianity are incompatible. Conservative theologian Clark Pinnock, for example, appeals to *Sexism and God-Talk* for precisely this purpose, noting that "this radical feminist scholar does not believe that biblical feminism will work." He also comments,

> The writer insists that the Bible as presently constituted is the enemy of women's liberation. The only way to get feminism out of the Bible is to edit it according to a feminist criterion. This is not likely to attract many evangelicals to feminism.[47]

I hope that my hermeneutical and exegetical reflections from chapter 3 onwards may help some see that the Bible is far more supportive of the legitimacy of a feminist theology than Ruether (or Pinnock) might believe possible. Large numbers of Christians will, in all sincerity, resist the call to challenge the sexism of current Christian thought if they hear this as a call to reject fundamental tenets of the biblical faith. The case for a Christianity that is sensitive to feminist concerns needs to be made in terms of a call to a biblically inspired and biblically rooted radical reformation if we are to have a significant impact on large numbers of our fellow believers and not end up simply preaching to the converted.

Although this is a point that can be made on purely pragmatic grounds, it also relates to the question of whether an integral Christian feminism is a genuine possibility, or whether we have to be content with an uneasy synthesis.

III. Towards an Integral Christian Feminist Theology

Forming a working definition of feminism that all find acceptable is not easy. Nevertheless, it is far more accurate to define a feminist as someone who is concerned about gender justice than it is to define a Marxist as someone who is concerned about socio-economic justice. The latter is true as far as it goes. But any adequate definition of what it means to be a Marxist should also mention that it involves being committed to a certain worldview, and thus to answering all the ultimate questions that shape one's way of life in a charac- teristically Marxist way. Such questions include: What does it mean to be authentically human?, What is the nature and origin of evil and brokenness?, and How do we find healing and liberation? The lack of unanimity among feminists about how best to answer ques- tions of this kind is closer to what we would find in a group of people who share a common concern for socio-economic justice but are otherwise chosen at random, than it is to the relative agreement that we would find in any group of Marxists.

This pluralism is largely due to the fact that, unlike Marxists, feminists have to draw on the resources of traditions they have not founded or collectively reshaped in order to answer such questions and they disagree about which traditions to turn to. Thus the different kinds of feminism that Ruether has identified—liberal, Marxist, and romanticist—have come into being. Consequently, there are far fewer universally shared beliefs or practices that function as a test for "orthodoxy" or "orthopraxis." If we look at the

Women's Movement as a whole, past and present, we do not find wide-spread opposition to the idea that Christianity can be the tradition to which a feminist may turn to find answers to the ultimate questions of life. Thus, unlike Christian Marxism, Christian feminism does not necessarily involve a clash or synthesis at the level of ultimate, i. e., religious, convictions.

Just as faith guides and integrates all of the other dimensions of our experience (even as our other ways-of-being-in-the-world support and contextualize our faith), so an authentic *Christian* feminism, in my opinion, is one in which Christian commitments guide and shape our feminism and are not merely the icing on a secular feminist cake. In the introduction, I spoke more vaguely of the need for Christian feminists to nurture a positive relationship to significant aspects of the Christian tradition as they set about the task of promoting the full humanity of women. Here I am saying that this positive relationship should include relying on the Christian faith to answer the ultimate questions of life. At this level, no other source of revelation should be accepted.

Pamela Dickey Young has argued persuasively that Ruether tends to relate to the Christian tradition in general and the Bible in particular as a *resource* rather than as a *norm*.[48] In Ruether's terminology, there exist at best only *"usable* traditions," and these are not exclusively Christian.[49] Young even argues that Ruether has relativized her appeal to the biblical prophetic tradition in her more recent writings.[50] What does seem to be normative in an unambiguous way for Ruether is what she describes as "the critical principle of feminist theology." It would seem that this principle is what she uses to distinguish between the wheat and the chaff in the various resources at her disposal, including the Christian Scriptures.

Young's distinction between resource and norm is helpful. Like Ruether, I also believe that we need more than contemporary experience to guide us. I too want to utilize certain traditions as resources that I do not take to be normative but which I believe contain helpful insights from which we can benefit. The intertestamental book of Sirach (Ecclesiasticus), for example, contains material that I would be happy to preach from, but it also contains material that I believe should be preached against. Similarly, I might point to Abraham Kuyper's Stone Lectures at Princeton Theological Seminary in 1898 as a fine example of Christian cultural analysis, while denouncing his 1914 essay, "The Woman's Position of Honor," as conservative romanticism at its most infuriating.[51] Suspicion and critical distance are appropriate.

By contrast, once the Scriptures are read as the articulation of a faith that has Jesus as its focal point, and is embodied without sin only in his life, death and resurrection, the need to be critically selective that is so important when we approach other traditions, is no longer necessary in the same sense. The biblical tradition is not simply a resource within which I feel the need to distinguish between the Truth of God and the Lie of the Devil. For me it is a normative tradition.

I believe that an integral Christian feminist methodology must go beyond developing a feminist critical principle which is then applied to the Christian tradition in order to see what it has to offer. Neither is it sufficient to let one's feminism inform one's hermeneutic of suspicion and one's knowledge of the Christian or biblical traditions to inform one's hermeneutic of retrieval. At best these approaches offer what I would call a "Christian/feminist" theology.

That I have referred to Ruether's own thought in this way in the subtitle to this study indicates my belief that her feminist theology is not as integrally Christian as it could be. While Ruether's writings often give evidence of being shaped by Christian commitments, she still speaks as though the fact that her thought has developed within the Christian tradition is ultimately no more significant than the fact that she writes in English rather than Japanese or Sanskrit. Thus she says,

> Theological reflections drawn from Judeo-Christian or even Near-Eastern-Mediterranean-European traditions do not have a privileged relation to God, to truth, to authentic humanity over those that arise from Judaism, Islam, and Buddhism. Nor are they presumed to be the same. Exactly how a feminist theology drawn from other cultural syntheses would differ is not yet known. But we affirm at the outset the pos-

sibility of equivalence, or equal value, of different feminist theologies drawn from different cultural syntheses.[52]

More recently she has gone as far as to say,

> I am not sure that Christian theology will be able to develop an adequate relation to nature or to deal with feminism. It may be that the Christian system will have to be transcended, in a new synthesis with insights from other religions, to create an adequate theology for justice to women and peaceful and sustaining relationships with the biosphere. I plan to follow these concerns wherever they lead me.[53]

Such a relativization of Christianity (which she does not apply to her feminist commitments) is not a stance that I share. Because one's ultimate hopes, beliefs, and commitments are precisely those which one is unable to relativize in this fashion, this suggests that the fundamental religious convictions that shape Ruether's worldview in general and feminism in particular may be more generally theistic than specifically Christian in the final analysis.

For a feminist theology to have a distinctively Christian character, I suggest, its critical principles must be rooted, evaluated, interpreted, and applied in the light of the religious vision of the biblical Story. If we look once more at the critical principle that Ruether espouses, we can see how interpreting and transforming it in the light of the Scriptures can lead to a different way of working with it than she does. Ruether writes,

> The critical principle of feminist theology is the promotion of the full humanity of women. Whatever denies, diminishes, or distorts the full humanity of women is, therefore, appraised as not redemptive. Theologically speaking, whatever diminishes or denies the full humanity of women must be presumed not to reflect the divine or an authentic relation to the divine, or to reflect the authentic nature of things, or to be the message or work of an authentic redeemer or a community of redemption.

This negative principle also implies the positive principle: what does promote the full humanity of women is of the Holy, it does reflect true relation to the divine, it is the true nature of things, the authentic message of redemption and the mission of redemptive community.[54]

How a critical principle such as this will function in our theologizing will depend on how we interpret certain key words and phrases. If "full humanity" is understood in terms of classical notions of humans as rational animals, we will develop a very different feminist theology from one that defines authentic humanity in terms of Hinduism, modern existentialism or the New Age movement.

Ruether herself connects this full humanity to Christian notions of the *imago dei*. An exploration of how the Scriptures understand what it means to be made in the image of God, which she does not provide, would go a long way towards turning this into a critical principle of a *Christian* feminist theology.[55] In the same way, we could explicitly connect "the full humanity of women" which Ruether admits "is not fully known" in the present age, with their eschatological destiny as I have already suggested in section II.

In Ruether's theologizing, what she judges to be necessary for promoting the full humanity of women, given the raised consciousness of twentieth-century feminism, is often used as a criterion in the light of which many of the biblical authors are criticized for failing to provide us with an authentic message of redemption. A different view of the process of redemption, one attuned to the unfolding redemptive-historical drama of the Scriptures, can lead to a different way of understanding and applying this critical principle, however.

I have argued in chapter 3 that a biblically sensitive approach will encourage us to distinguish between what is creationally or eschatologically normative and anti-normative, on the one hand, and what is redemptively right and wrong, on the other.[56] To promote shalom, to move life in a redemptive direction, cannot be understood simply as a call to force it to correspond to its eschatological destiny or to the Creator's intentions from the beginning, no matter how important these may be for getting our bearings. If this was the kind of redemptive process that God was interested in, the tyranny of impossible expectations would effectively sever all contact between us and our Creator and the God of the covenant would become the Wholly Other.

Whether or not a community offers an authentic message of redemption must be judged in relation to the redemptive possibilities of its situation and not by rigid ahistorical criteria. What we need to pay attention to is whether a community is moving in the direction of life or death. This is an important consideration in our evaluation of the Bible. With time, redemptive possibilities change. When God's people are faithful these possibilities open up. When they are unfaithful for long enough, they may close down. Thus what constitutes promoting the full humanity of women also changes. Limiting some of the worst abuses of patriarchal power is the Old Testament Law's way of promoting that full humanity. That its first interpreters were doubtless completely blind to further abuses that later generations could see without any difficulty reflects an increase in redemptive possibilities that should not be mistaken for an increase in holiness. We are often called to go further than our forefathers and foremothers. In the case of the Old Testament Law, for example, we need to go beyond the Bible in the Spirit of the Bible.[57] At the same time, this does not mean that we have to conclude that the generation that first wrote down the Law "got it wrong."

The fact that God is prepared to stay with people in the redemptive process in spite of their blindspots also applies to us. Future generations will no doubt see aspects of our way of life that involve more compromise with evil than they will be able to tolerate for themselves. Even the most discerning prophet of today is oblivious to dimensions of oppression and liberation that will be obvious to the most blinkered conservative of tomorrow. But our role in the covenant involves neither omnipotence nor omniscience. This is both humbling and reassuring. We can be confident that God will be with us if we are faithful and seek to accomplish what is redemptively possible in our time.

This understanding of the process of redemption means that we should not use what we now understand as vital to the task of promoting the full humanity of women as a standard in the light of which we can judge previous generations as failing to exemplify "an authentic relation to the Divine" and articulate "an authentic message of redemption." The point is not to make our forefathers and foremothers immune from criticism, but to use far more nuanced criteria. I believe that I allow for far more *redemptive-historical relativity* than Ruether, who, in my judgment, is too quick to excommunicate many of our ancestors in the faith who articulated their understanding of authentic spirituality in our Scriptures.

It is very hard for most of us to historically relativize what we (rightly) experience today as the difference between justice and injustice. In *Sexism and God-Talk*, Ruether offers a number of suggestions why, given their historical situation, the Hebrew prophets were not more acutely aware of the problems of sexism. She strongly resists the idea that these constitute "excuses." They are merely "reasons," she says. But the question she needs to face is that if more acute awareness of sexism was not a redemptive possibility at that time, what constitutes a fair judgment? After all, she goes on to write,

> [P]erhaps it was not until the early modern period that the perception of women as marginalized by gender became stronger than the perception of women as divided by class. Only then could a feminist movement arise that protested the subjugation of women as a group.[58]

My point here is that we need to be aware of the danger of judging one generation's redemptive calling by criteria appropriate for another. This is important within the history of the Women's Movement itself. It is very significant that we do not judge harshly those feminists (Ruether included) who did not use or see the need to use inclusive language before the mid-1970's. To cite another example, let us take the issue of female language for God. In a book first published in Spanish as recently as 1986, Third World feminist theologian Elsa Tamez writes,

The name we give to God is a question that still seems strange in our context. When theologians here speak about inclusive language with reference to God, they are not speaking within a Latin American framework. I am sure that they have in mind the discussion among First World feminists. Because in both Catholic and Protestant popular Christian communities it has occurred to no one to speak of Goddess, or to refer to the God of the Bible as mother. And generally speaking this is still alien to Latin American feminist Christian women, or at least we do not consider it an important issue—yet.[59]

With a little reflection, I think that most First World Christian feminists will agree that it would be completely inappropriate for us to conclude that our Third World counterparts do not constitute an authentic community of redemption. At the same time, we experience inclusive language for humans and for God as *vital* to the task of promoting the full humanity of women in our time and culture—and so we should. When life is viewed in the light of the *unfolding* redemptive historical drama that the Bible tells and that we are called to continue, and when the *progressive* nature of revelation is thus born in mind, it is to be expected that different cultures and different generations will be called to make the Kingdom of God present on earth in different ways.

Nothing that I have said above is intended to minimize the conviction that the construction of an integral Christian feminist theology is an important task for our generation. My point is that this calling should not be raised up as a new form of orthodoxy or orthopraxis that then cuts us off from the unfinished redemptive-historical drama of the Scriptures in which we should situate it. In my view, the way Ruether uses the critical principle of her feminist theology as a super-norm demonstrates the dangers of this temptation.

The distinction between norm and resource can help us appreciate both the strengths and weaknesses of Ruether's theology. Once we have adopted a different approach to questions of normativity and normative tradition, which will entail taking a certain critical distance from her theology, we may then draw upon her work as a valuable resource with which to interact. I hope that my attempt to dialogue with her theology in this study may encourage those who have not yet done so to discover the challenge and insight of her analysis, experience the passion that animates her call for liberation, and share in her vision for a future world in which we may overcome "the alienating chasms between God and humanity, humanity and the world, spirit and body, male and female."[60]

The construction of a Christian feminist theology requires that we attempt to submit to the revelation of the Christian tradition in the context of paying attention to what women themselves find oppressive and liberating, and *vice-versa*. To take the authority of women's experience seriously in this context includes being prepared to modify or reject any Christian feminist proposals—including my own—that women involved in the struggle judge to be an inadequate response to their pain.

If we focus on the issues as Christians solely in terms of the ultimate beliefs, creeds and norms we hold dear, while cutting those beliefs off from the questions, hopes, and fears of those committed to the feminist cause inside and outside the church, our theological reflections will, at best, be superficial. To embrace the pain of those who suffer because of the sexism of the church, by contrast, can motivate us to plumb the very depths of our worldviews and sacred writings so that we are far more likely to avoid answers that are cheap and facile. Jeremiah, the prophet who embraced pain perhaps more than any other, and the false prophets of his day, who were numbed by the royal consciousness, had access to the same sacred traditions but read the signs of the times very differently.[61]

One thing that comes through very clearly in Ruether's writings is that she senses the pain of women who cannot feel at home in our churches. Even on those occasions when she does not complete the hermeneutical circle as I would wish by plumbing the depths of the biblical worldview as a way to reform theologies and practices that no longer bring life (if they ever did), I am still struck by the fact that her responses to the pain are never facile. This feature of her work gives her theological reflection a power and an integrity that any Christian feminist position should strive to reflect.

Ruether's writings convincingly demonstrate that if we are to find our full humanity as women and men then, contrary to the protests of reactionary anti-feminists, we cannot go back to Egypt but must press on to the promised land.[62] She also shows us that the journey we are on is not just an exodus but is also a return from exile, because the life and teaching of Jesus—the heart of the Christian tradition—represent a breakthrough in the affirmation of woman that has been forgotten in the subsequent history of the church. To cite Ruether's words from a slightly different context, this is a "precious legacy that needs to be separated from the toxic waste of sacralized dominion."[63]

Past and future, memory and hope, thus belong together (as do amnesia and despair). In our struggle to find the presence of God in the past, we may find the grace and strength to give birth to God in the future. It is appropriate, therefore, to conclude with the following prophesy of Jeremiah in which we hear the words of the God of the covenant to our foremothers and forefathers who were also in exile. Here, in the context of speaking of a return to once-familiar territory, Yahweh also promises to bring about a change in the relationship between man and woman that is so unimaginable in the present order that it is nothing less than a new creation.

> *Set up waymarks for yourself,*
> *   make yourself guideposts;*
> *consider well the highway,*
> *   the road by which you went.*
> *Return, O virgin Israel,*
> *   return to these your cities.*
> *How long will you waver,*
> *   O wandering daughter?*
> *For the Lord will create a new thing on the earth:*
> *   a woman will surround a man,*
> *   the woman will overcome the warrior.*

(Jer. 31:21-22)[64]

Notes

1. Grenz and Olson, *Twentieth-Century Theology*, 227.
2. For a good introduction to these matters, see Kalsbeek, *Contours of a Christian Philosophy*. See also chap. 4 of Hart, *Understanding Our World*.
3. See Hart, *Understanding Our World*, 190-98.
4. See ibid., 153-63. These "analogies," which probably provide the ontological basis for the metaphorical character of human language, are subdivided into "anticipations" and "retrocipations." Hart offers the following definition of an anticipation on p. 438, "In the actual interrelation of aspects, there will be evidence of how aspects of one kind or mode relate to aspects of another kind or mode. Some aspects support or found others, while some aspects open up, develop, and qualify others. When a function of some kind typically reflects the fact that a function of another and higher modality qualifies or opens it up, that function is called an anticipation. It anticipates the higher function." Similarly, when a function reflects the fact that a function of a lower or more foundational modality supports it, it is called a retrocipation.
5. See the sections on nature, eschatology, and God in chap. 4.
6. See *RK*, 206. "Psychic energy" is an important reality for Ruether in her early essay "Male Chauvinist Theology and the Anger of Women," 182, 184.
7. In more precise Dooyeweerdian terminology, this is the "retrocipation" of the biotic and psychic modes to the energetic. Perhaps the energetic "anticipation" of the biotic and psychic modes is also involved here.

In the more monistic cosmology of *GG*, psychic energy functions as the point of bifurcation of inner spirit and outer matter and as the medium through which the divine Whole may be experienced in the parts, as I have argued in chap. 4. It is also crucial to the revelatory power of the lower bifurcation, which is connected to our feelings of compassion. This form of revelation cannot be translated into "intellectual knowledge," because analytic functioning is placed in the higher bifurcation, which is that part of "the lenses of human existence" through which we may hear divine commands. See *GG*, 254-55.
8. *NWNE*, 157.
9. See 215 above.
10. See Hart, *Understanding Our World*, chaps. 1 and 2.
11. Teilhard de Chardin, *The Phenomenon of Man* (New York: Harper and Row, 1959), 149.
12. See Hart, *Understanding Our World*, 297-305.
13. See the section on anthropology in chap. 4.
14. I find it highly significant that while Ruether has only been comfortable in her previous works with using the terms "male" and "female" for biological reproductive role specializations, in *GG*, 254-55, she refers to the "two voices of divinity from nature" (which, in my interpretation, correspond to the revelation of the Divine by the upper and lower bifurcations of existence) as the

masculine and the feminine voice, without even using quotation marks (which are sometimes called "scare quotes"). Only her future work can reveal whether this is as significant as I suspect.

15. *SGT*, 18.

16. Some of the liturgies in *WC*, chap. 9 do affirm women as women. In this context, however, I am talking about Ruether's theoretical anthropology.

17. See James B. Nelson, *The Intimate Connection: Male Sexuality, Masculine Spirituality* (Philadelphia: The Westminster Press, 1988). Perhaps an equivalent book for women is Penelope Washbourn, *Becoming Woman: The Quest for Wholeness in Female Experience* (San Francisco: Harper and Row, 1977).

18. See Hester Eisenstein and Alice Jardine, eds., *The Future of Difference* (New Brunswick: Rutgers University Press, 1985), xv-xx.

19. On the importance of the notion of the self therapeutically, see Heinz Kohut, *The Restoration of the Self* (Madison: International Universities Press Inc., 1977). On the loss of the self in recent thought, see William Barrett, *Death of the Soul: From Descartes to the Computer* (Garden City: Anchor Press/Doubleday, 1986), and Robert C. Solomon, *Continental Philosophy Since 1750: The Rise and Fall of the Self*. A History of Western Philosophy vol. 7 (Oxford: Oxford University Press, 1988).

20. The exocentric-egocentric tension in her new cosmology constantly threatens to undermine the human self in its individuality. In *GG*, 251, Ruether continues to oppose egoism, but makes the important observation that "women . . . scarcely have been allowed individuated personhood at all." She also seems to want to distinguish the "ego" from the "person" here, probably along the lines of the egocentric-exocentric distinction. It will be interesting to see how Ruether wrestles with this problem in the future. On the problematics of the agape-eros distinction, see James H. Olthuis, "Self or Society: Is There a Choice," in Craig W. Ellison, ed., *Your Better Self: Christianity, Psychology, and Self-Esteem* (New York: Harper and Row, 1983), 202-14.

21. James H. Olthuis, "Be(com)ing: Humankind as Gift and Call," unpublished paper presented at the Canadian Theological Society, June 1986, 11. Cf. The analysis of Paul's anthropology along similar lines by Herman N. Ridderbos in his *Paul: An Outline of his Theology*, trans. John Richard de Witt (Grand Rapids: Eerdmans; London: SPCK, 1975), 115-21. This forms quite a contrast with Ruether's wrong-headed reading of Paul as "dualistic" and "quasi-Gnostic" in *GG*, 127 and 129 (which would appear to conflict with *CAI*, 163 n. 1). For Paul's notion of the "spiritual body" that Ruether makes much of in her reading in *GG*, 234, see Ridderbos, *Paul*, 539-45. On this and other aspects of Pauline anthropology, see also J. A. T. Robinson's fine monograph, *The Body: A Study in Pauline Theology*.

22. For an argument for understanding the agency of trees in terms of a self/functions correlation, see Walsh, Karsh, and Ansell, "Acid Rain, Deforestation and the Responsiveness of Creation" (Bristol, UK: Regius Press, forth-coming), section 3.

23. See the diagram on 233 above.

24. *SGT*, 259. But on the use of "icon" here, see chap. 4 n. 201.

25. *RK*, 276. This passage occurs in the context of a discussion of the work of Marcuse. That it reflects her own position, however, can be inferred from the concluding chapter (pp. 283-88). Also her talk here of the "struggle toward self-transcendence" is parallelled in her dedication of the book to "those who risk world-transcending action." (p. v).

26. In *LT*, 34 she speaks of the role of an authentic prophetic counter-culture as "the critical spokesman for envisioning and experiencing that 'still more' which is not yet achieved, and for glimpsing more perfect communion with the True, Good and Beautiful." Cf. the "is" "ought" dialectic in ecological ethics in *GG*, 31.

27. *SGT*, 18-19.

28. Rebecca S. Chopp, "Seeing and Naming the World Anew: The Works of Rosemary Radford Ruether," *Religious Studies Review* 15 (January, 1989): 10. She contrasts Ruether's method with the vision of her more recent works and argues that we must avoid this earlier appeal to the "abstract principle of 'full humanity' in order to discover together the variety of ways human beings are and become" (ibid., 11). Ruether's down-playing of variety fits with her orien-tation to the first phase of Women's Studies noted above.

29. Hart, in *Understanding Our World*, 444 defines "essence" and "nature" as: "That configuration that determines what properties an existent must necessari-ly have in order to be the thing that it is." Similarly, he defines existence as: "a basic term which indicates the reality of whatever is subject to conditions." (Cf. his definition of condition and law on pp. 441-42.) This definition is not dissimilar to the one offered by Van A. Harvey in *A Handbook of Theological Terms* (New York: Macmillan Publishing Co., 1964), 83, where he writes, "If existence refers to the concrete actuality of something, i. e., that there is a man named Peter, and accidents refer to the individual peculiarities of that being, i. e., that Peter has blue eyes and is short-tempered, essence refers to the characteristics Peter must exemplify in order properly to be called a man." Peter A. Angeles, in his *Dictionary of Philosophy* (New York: Barnes and Noble Books, 1981), 80, offers, as one of his definitions of essence, the following: "The abstract idea (or law) of a thing by which we can recognize further particular instances of it."

30. *CAI*, 162-63.

31. *SGT*, 71. In my view, Grenz and Olson in their *Twentieth-Century Theology*, 233 seriously misinterpret this sentence.

32. A problem here is that the reformational tradition has assumed that the law-subject relationship can be simply identified with the relationship between "ought" and "is." This is based on a less than satisfactory way of relating structure, direction and process which I have criticized in my unpublished paper

"The Trouble With Normative . . . Creation Order, Hermeneutics, and Homosexuality."

33. *CAI*, 188-89. I admit that Ruether's thought has changed and developed since these early writings, but her understanding of creation and eschaton in terms of an essence/existence distinction continues into her recent work, in my view.

34. I have not attempted to defend my belief in the future eschatological restoration of creation, except to argue that it is part of the biblical worldview (see 90-91 above) which is vital if we are to resist the notion that evil will have the last word (see 243 above). It should be pointed out that this is a fundamental belief of the kind that one argues *from* rather than argues *to*. Its coherence with other fundamental beliefs is easy to recognize, however. If one accepts that God created the world good, that evil is a parasitic intrusion into a good creation, and that God is committed to liberating creation from evil and oppression and has the power to do so, then it follows that the scope of redemption should be understood as creation-wide. Belief in a future New Earth—i. e., a creation purged of all evil—clearly follows from these other beliefs. I would claim that it necessarily follows from them, though its truth cannot be established in isolation from them.

35. *RK*'s subtitle is "The Western Experience of Messianic Hope." *LT*'s subtitle is "Human Hope Confronts Christian History and American Power."

36. Ruether, "Eschatology and Feminism," 123. Cf. p. 122 and *GG*, 31, 139, 141, and 200.

37. *GG*, 31.

38. Ibid., 200. She offers the salinization of soils through irrigation as an example.

39. For a helpful discussion of the knowledge of good and evil in Gen. 2-3, see Claus Westermann, *Genesis 1-11: A Commentary*, trans. John J. Scullion (Minneapolis: Augsburg Publishing House, 1984), 242-248.

40. See 193 above.

41. Finger, "How Can Jesus Save Women?" 17.

42. see *TCW*, 29 and 191 above.

43. See ibid.

44. *LT*, 125-26.

45. *WC*, 74.

46. Cf. Ricoeur, *The Symbolism of Evil*, 351.

47. Clark Pinnock, "Biblical Authority and the Issues in Question," in Alvera Mickelsen, ed., *Women, Authority and the Bible*, 53 and 55.

48. See Pamela Dickey Young, *Feminist Theology/ Christian Theology*, 31-39 and passim.

49. See *SGT*, 21-22.

50. See Young, *Feminist Theology/ Christian Theology*, 35. The appeal to Scripture in *GG* is stronger than the works Young would have in mind, however.

51. See Abraham Kuyper, *Lectures On Calvinism* (Grand Rapids: Eerdmans, 1970), and idem., "The Woman's Position of Honor", trans. Irene Konyndyk, (unpublished manuscript, Calvin College, Grand Rapids, 1990).

52. *SGT*, 21.

53. "Eschatology and Feminism," 112.

54. *SGT*, 18-19.

55. For a good discussion of *imago dei* in the Bible, see Walsh and Middleton, *The Transforming Vision*, 52-65, 83-88. There is some attention paid to the *imago dei* theme in *GG*, 222.

56. See 153 above.

57. See 117-25 above.

58. *SGT*, 63.

59. Elsa Tamez *et al*, *Against Machismo*, trans. John Eagleson (Oak Park, IL: Meyer Stone Books, 1987), 147.

60. These are the words Bernard Zylstra used to describe the aims of Ruether's theological reflection at ICS in 1983. They are cited more fully on 3 above.

61. On Jeremiah's pathos and cultural discernment, see Brian J. Walsh, *Subversive Christianity: Imaging God in a Dangerous Time* (Bristol: Regius Press, 1992), chaps. 3 and 4.

62. Cf. *WC*, 73-74.

63. *GG*, 3.

64. This is a combination of the NIV and RSV with two possible translations offered for the final verse.

Bibliography

A. By Rosemary Radford Ruether (with abbreviations in parentheses)

"A Historical and Textual Analysis of the Relationship Between Futurism and Eschatology in the Apocalyptic Texts of the Inter-Testamental Period." B. A. thesis, Scripps College, 1958. [*RFE*]

The Church Against Itself: An Inquiry into the Conditions of Historical Existence for the Eschatological Community. New York: Herder and Herder, 1967. [*CAI*]

"The Becoming of Women in Church and Society." *Cross Currents* 17 (Fall 1967): 419-26.

Gregory of Nazianzus: Rhetor and Philosopher. Oxford: Oxford University Press, 1969. [*GN*]

The Radical Kingdom: The Western Experience of Messianic Hope. New York: Paulist Press, 1970. [*RK*]

"An Unexpected Tribute to the Theologian." *Theology Today* 27 (October 1970): 332-39.

"Male Chauvinist Theology and the Anger of Women." *Cross Currents* 21 (Spring 1971): 173-85.

Liberation Theology: Human Hope Confronts Christian History and American Power. New York: Paulist Press, 1972. [*LT*]

"An Invitation to Jewish-Christian Dialogue: In What Sense Can We Say That Jesus Was 'The Christ'?" *The Ecumenist* 10 (January-February 1972): 17-24.

"Judaism and Christianity: Two Fourth-Century Religions." *Studies in Religion* 2 (Summer 1972): 1-10.

"Male Clericalism and the Dread of Women." *The Ecumenist* 11 (July-August 1973): 65-69.

"Sexism and the Theology of Liberation: Nature, Fall and Salvation as Seen from the Experience of Women." *The Christian Century* 90 (December 12 1973).

Faith and Fratricide: The Theological Roots of Anti-Semitism. New York: The Seabury Press, 1974. [*FF*]

"Preface." In *Religion and Sexism: Images of Woman in the Jewish and Christian Traditions*, ed. Rosemary Radford Ruether, 9-13. New York: Simon and Schuster, 1974.

"Misogynism and Virginal Feminism in the Fathers of the Church." In *Religion and Sexism: Images of Woman in the Jewish and Christian Traditions*, ed. Rosemary Radford Ruether, 150-83. New York: Simon and Schuster, 1974.

"Anti-Semitism in Christian Theology." *Theology Today* 30 (January 1974): 365-81.

New Woman/New Earth: Sexist Ideologies and Human Liberation. New York: The Seabury Press, 1975. [*NWNE*]

"Women, Ecology and the Domination of Nature." *The Ecumenist* 14 (November-December 1975): 1-5

"The Resurrection of the Body and the Life Everlasting." In *Christian Theology: A Case Study Approach*, ed. Robert A. Evans and Thomas D. Parker, 255-61. New York: Harper and Row, 1976.

Mary—The Feminine Face of the Church. Philadelphia: The Westminster Press, 1977. [*MFFC*]

"Toward New Solutions: Working Women and the Male Workday." *Christianity and Crisis* 37 (February 7 1977): 3-8.

"Time Makes Ancient Good Uncouth: The Catholic Report on Sexuality." *The Christian Century* 94 (August 3-10 1977): 682-85.

"The Books That Shape Lives." *The Christian Century* 94 (October 19 1977): 962.

"The Biblical Vision of the Ecological Crisis." *The Christian Century* 95 (November 22 1978): 1129-32.

"Mothers of the Church: Ascetic Women in the Late Patristic Age." In *Women of Spirit: Female Leadership in the Jewish and Christian Traditions*, ed. Rosemary Radford Ruether and Eleanor Mclaughlin, 71-98. New York: Simon and Schuster, 1979.

"Entering the Sanctuary II: The Roman Catholic Story." In *Women of Spirit: Female Leadership in the Jewish and Christian Traditions*, ed. Rosemary Radford Ruether and Eleanor Mclaughlin, 373-83. New York: Simon and Schuster, 1979.

"Consciousness-Raising at Puebla: Women Speak to the Latin Church." *Christianity and Crisis* 39 (April 2 1979): 77-80.

"Ruether on Ruether." *Christianity and Crisis* 39 (May 14 1979): 126.

"A Religion for Women: Sources and Strategies." *Christianity and Crisis* 39 (December 10 1979): 307-11.

"Asking the Existential Questions." *The Christian Century* 97 (April 2 1980): 374-78.

"Why Socialism Needs Feminism, and Vice Versa." *Christianity and Crisis* 40 (April 28 1980): 103-108.

"Goddesses and Witches: Liberation and Countercultural Feminism." *The Christian Century* 97 (September 10-17 1980): 842-47.

To Change the World: Christology and Cultural Criticism. New York: Crossroad, 1981. [*TCW*]

"The Feminist Critique in Religious Studies." In *A Feminist Perspective in the Academy: The Difference it Makes*, ed. Elizabeth Langland and Walter Gove, 52-66. Chicago: University of Chicago Press, 1981.

"Women in Utopian Movements." In *Women and Religion in America*. Vol. 1 *The Nineteenth Century: A Documentary History*, ed. Rosemary Radford Ruether and Rosemary Skinner Keller, 46-53. San Francisco: Harper and Row, 1981.

Disputed Questions: On Being a Christian. Nashville: Abingdon, 1982; Maryknoll: Orbis Books, 1989. [*DQ*]

"Feminism and Patriarchal Religion: Principles of Ideological Critique of the Bible." *Journal for the Study of the Old Testament* 22 (February 1982): 54-66.

Review of *Christ in a Changing World: Toward an Ethical Christology*, by Tom F. Driver. In *The Christian Century* 99 (April 7 1982): 416-18.

Sexism and God-Talk: Toward a Feminist Theology. Boston: Beacon Press, 1983; London: SCM Press, 1983. [*SGT*]

"The New Year—A Time for Renewal." In *Social Themes of the Christian Year: A Commentary on the Lectionary*, ed. Dieter T. Hessel, 56-62. Philadelphia: The Geneva Press, 1983.

Review of *Christ: The Experience of Jesus as Lord*, by Edward Schillebeeckx. In *Religious Studies Review* 9 (January 1983): 42-44.

"Women In Ministry: Where Are They Heading?" *Christianity and Crisis* 43 (April 4 1983): 111-16.

"Feminist Theology and Spirituality." In *Christian Feminism: Visions of a New Humanity*, ed. Judith L. Weidman, 9-32. San Francisco: Harper and Row, 1984.

Review Symposium: *In Memory of Her: A Feminist Theological Reconstruction of Christian Origins*, by Elizabeth Schüssler Fiorenza. In *Horizons* 11 (Spring 1984): 146-50.

Womanguides: Readings Toward a Feminist Theology. Boston: Beacon Press, 1985. [*WG*]

"Feminism and Peace." In *Women's Consciousness, Women's Conscience: A Reader in Feminist Ethics*, ed. Barbara Hilkert Andolsen, Christine E.

Gudorf and Mary D. Pellauer, 63-74. San Francisco: Harper and Row, 1985.

"Feminist Interpretation: A Method of Correlation." In *Feminist Interpretation of the Bible*, ed. Letty M. Russell, 111-24. Oxford: Basil Blackwell, 1985.

"Feminist Theology in the Academy." *Christianity and Crisis* 45 (March 4 1985): 57-62.

"Catholics and Abortion: Authority Vs. Dissent." *The Christian Century* 102 (October 2 1985): 859-62.

"The Future of Feminist Theology in the Academy." *Journal of the American Academy of Religion* 53 (December 1985): 703-13.

Women-Church: Theology and Practice of Feminist Liturgical Communities. San Francisco: Harper and Row, 1986. [*WC*]

Review of *Bread Not Stone: The Challenge of Feminist Biblical Interpretation, by Elizabeth Schüssler Fiorenza*. In *Journal of the American Academy of Religion* 54 (Spring 1986): 141-43.

Contemporary Roman Catholicism: Crises and Challenges. Kansas: Sheed and Ward, 1987. [*CRC*]

"Christianity." In *Women in World Religions*, ed. Arvind Sharma, 207-33. Albany: State University of New York Press, 1987.

"Feminism and Jewish-Christian Dialogue: Particularism and Universalism in the Search for Religious Truth." In *The Myth of Christian Uniqueness: Toward a Pluralistic Theology of Religions*, ed. John Hick and Paul F. Knitter, 137-48. Maryknoll: Orbis Books, 1987.

"The Development of My Theology." *Religious Studies Review* 15 (January 1989): 1-4.

"Feminism and Eschatology." In *Lift Every Voice: Constructing Christian Theologies from the Underside*, ed. Susan Brooks Thislethwaite and Mary Potter Engel, 111-24, San Francisco: Harper and Row, 1990.

"The Message and the Movement." *Creation* 6 (November-December 1990): 20-23, 37. (= "Matthew Fox and Creation Spirituality: Strengths and Weaknesses." *The Catholic World* [July-August 1990].)

Gaia and God: An Ecofeminist Theology of Earth Healing. San Francisco: HarperCollins, 1992. [*GG*]

Ed. *Religions and Sexism: Images of Woman in the Jewish and Christian Traditions*. New York: Simon and Schuster, 1974. [*RS*]

With Eleanor McLaughlin, eds. *Woman of Spirit: Female Leadership in the Jewish and Christian Traditions*. New York: Simon and Schuster, 1979. [*WS*]

With Rosemary Skinner Keller, eds. *Women and Religion in America*. 3 Vols. San Francisco: Harper and Row, 1981, 1983, 1986.

With Marc H. Ellis, eds. *Beyond Occupation: American Jewish, Christian, and Palestinian Voices for Peace*. Boston: Beacon Press, 1990.

With Eugene C. Bianchi. *From Machismo To Mutuality: Essays on Sexism and Woman-Man Liberation*. New York: Paulist Press, 1976. [*FMM*]

With Wolfgang Roth. *The Liberating Bond: Covenants—Biblical and Contemporary*. New York: Friendship Press, 1978. [*TLB*]

With Eleanor McLaughlin. "Women's Leadership in the Jewish and Christian Traditions: Continuity and Change." In *Women of Spirit: Female Leadership in the Jewish and Christian Traditions*, ed. Rosemary Radford Ruether and Eleanor Mclaughlin, 15-28. New York: Simon and Schuster, 1979.

With Herman J. Ruether. *The Wrath of Jonah: The Crisis of Religious Nationalism in the Israeli-Palestinian Conflict*. San Francisco: Harper and Row, 1989.

B. On Rosemary Radford Ruether

Askew, Angela V. Review of *Sexism and God-Talk: Toward a Feminist Theology*, by Rosemary Radford Ruether. In *Union Seminary Quarterly Review* 40 (1985): 59-68.

Bouma-Prediger, Steve. "Ecology and Social Justice: Toward an Integral Christian Theology of Nature and Human Liberation." Unpublished paper. Chicago, 1991.

Chopp, Rebecca S. "Seeing and Naming the World Anew: The Works of Rosemary Radford Ruether." *Religious Studies Review* 15 (January 1989): 8-11.

Evans, Ruth. "Woman As Other: A Study of Alienation in Rosemary Ruether, Mary Daly and Sheila Collins." M.A. thesis, St. Michael's College, Toronto, 1980.

Harrower, Vivian Jarrett. "Feminist Critiques of a Male Savior: Christology in the Writings of Mary Daly and Rosemary Ruether." M. A. thesis, St. Michael's College, Toronto, 1985.

Heyward, Carter. "Ruether and Daly: Theologians Speaking and Sparking, Building and Burning." *Christianity and Crisis* 39 (April 2 1979): 66-72.

James, George Alfred. "The Status of the Anomaly in the Feminist God-Talk of Rosemary Radford Ruether." *Zygon* 25 (June 1990): 167-85.

Leonard, Ellen. Review of *Sexism and God-Talk: Toward a Feminist Theology*, by Rosemary Radford Ruether. In *The Ecumenist* 23 (May-June 1985): 61-63.

Micks, Marianne H. Review of *To Change the World: Christology and Cultural Criticism*, by Rosemary Radford Ruether. In *Theology Today* 39 (July 1982): 214-15.

Mullins, Mary. Review of *New Woman, New Earth: Sexist Ideologies and Human Liberation*, By Rosemary Radford Ruether. In *Horizons* 5 (Spring 1979): 129-30.

Oesterreicher, John M. *Anatomy of Contempt: A Critique of R. R. Ruether's "Faith and Fratricide."* South Orange: The Institute of Judaeo-Christian Studies, 1975.

Pellauer, Mary. Review of *Sexism and God-Talk: Toward a Feminist Theology*, by Rosemary Radford Ruether. In *Theology Today* 40 (January 1984): 472-76.

Rabuzzi, Kathryn Allen. "The Socialist Feminist Vision of Rosemary Radford Ruether: A Challenge to Liberal Feminism." *Religious Studies Review* 15 (January 1989): 4-8.

Ramsey, William M. *Four Modern Prophets: Walter Rauschenbusch, Martin Luther King, Jr., Gustavo Gutierrez and Rosemary Radford Ruether.* Atlanta: John Knox Press, 1986.

Sharp, Carolyn. "A Feminist Critique of Leonardo Boff's Vision of God Based on the Works of Rosemary Radford Ruether," M. A. thesis, St. Michael's College, Toronto, 1986.

Snyder, Mary Hembrow. *The Christology of Rosemary Radford Ruether: A Critical Introduction.* Mystic, Connecticut: Twenty-Third Publications, 1988.

Tennis, Diane. Review of *Women-Church: Theology and Practice of Feminist Liturgical Communities*, by Rosemary Radford Ruether. In *Theology Today* 44 (April 1987): 139-42.

Thies, Christiane. Review of *From Machismo To Mutuality: Essays on Sexism and Woman-Man Liberation*, by Eugene C. Bianchi and Rosemary Radford Ruether. In *Vanguard* (September 1976): 26-27.

Vaughan, Judith. *Sociality, Ethics, and Social Change: A Critical Appraisal of Reinhold Niebuhr's Ethics in the Light of Rosemary Radford Ruether's Works.* Lanham: University Press of America, 1983.

C. Other Works Consulted

Allen, Prudence. *The Concept of Woman: The Aristotelian Revolution 750 BC-AD 1250.* Montreal: Eden Press, 1985.

Alsdurf, James and Phyllis Alsdurf. *Battered Into Submission: The Tragedy of Wife Abuse in the Christian Home.* Downers Grove: InterVarsity Press, 1989.

Alter, Robert. *The Art of Biblical Narrative.* New York: Basic Books, 1981.

Angeles, Peter A. *Dictionary of Philosophy.* New York: Barnes and Noble Books, 1981.

Ansell, Nik. *The Troubled Marriage of Adam and Eve.* Unpublished manuscript. Bath, 1944.

_____. "The Sins of the Fathers . . . Reflections on Tradition, Evil, and the Atonement." Unpublished paper. Toronto, 1991.

_____. "The Trouble with Normative . . . Creation Order, Hermeneutics, and Homosexuality." Unpublished paper. Toronto, 1991.

Aulén, Gustaf. *Christus Victor: An Historical Study of the Three Main Types of the Idea of the Atonement*. Translated by A. G. Hebert. London: SPCK, 1970.

Barker, Kenneth L, ed. *The NIV Study Bible*. Grand Rapids: Zondervan, 1985.

Barrett, William. *Death of the Soul: From Descartes to the Computer*. Garden City: Anchor Press, Doubleday, 1986.

Beckwith, Roger. *The Old Testament Canon of the New Testament Church*. London: SPCK, 1985; Grand Rapids: Eerdmans, 1986.

Benjamin, Jessica. *The Bonds of Love: Psychoanalysis, Feminism, and the Problem of Domination*. New York: Pantheon Books, 1988.

Bilezikian, Gilbert. *Beyond Sex Roles: What the Bible Says About a Woman's Place in Church and Family*. Second Edition. Grand Rapids: Baker Book House, 1989.

Bird, Phyllis. "Images of Women in the Old Testament." In *Religion and Sexism: Images of Woman in the Jewish and Christian Traditions*, ed. Rosemary Radford Ruether, 41-88. New York: Simon and Schuster, 1974.

Bloesch, Donald G. *The Battle for the Trinity: The Debate Over Inclusive God-Language*. Ann Arbor: Vine Books, 1985.

Bower, Susan. "Imaging God as Woman and Man Together: A Study of Genesis Two." Toronto: Institute for Christian Studies, n.d.

Brownmiller, Susan. "Madly in Love." *Ms.* 17 (April 1989): 56, 58-59, 61, 63-64.

Brueggemann, Walter. *The Creative Word: Canon as Model for Biblical Education*. Philadelphia: Fortress Press, 1982.

_____. *Israel's Praise: Doxology Against Idolatry and Ideology*. Philadelphia: Fortress Press, 1988.

_____. *The Message of the Psalms: A Theological Commentary*. Minneapolis: Augsburg Publishing House, 1984.

_____. " 'Of the Same Flesh and Bone' (Gen. 2:23)." *Catholic Biblical Quarterly* 32/4 (1970): 532-42.

_____. *The Prophetic Imagination*. Philadelphia: Fortress Press, 1978.

Bushnell, Katherine C. *God's Word to Women*. Oakland, California: Privately printed, 1923.

Cândea, Virgil. "Icons." In *The Encyclopedia of Religion*. Vol. 7, ed. Mircea Eliade, 67-70. New York: Macmillan Publishing Co., 1987.

Carr, Anne E. *Transforming Grace: Christian Tradition and Women's Experience*. San Francisco: Harper and Row, 1988.

Childs, Brevard S. *The Book of Exodus: A Critical, Theological Commentary*. Louisville: The Westminster Press, 1974.

_____. *Introduction to the Old Testament as Scripture*. Philadelphia: Fortress Press, 1979.

Chodorow, Nancy. *The Reproduction of Mothering: Psychoanalysis and the Sociology of Gender*. Berkeley: University of California Press, 1978.

Christ, Carol P. and Judith Plaskow, eds. *Womanspirit Rising: A Feminist Reader in Religion.* San Francisco: Harper and Row, 1979.

Clark, Elizabeth A. *Women in the Early Church.* Wilmington: Michael Glazier, Inc., 1983.

Clouser, Roy A. *The Myth of Religious Neutrality: An Essay on the Hidden Role of Religious Belief in Theories.* Notre Dame: University of Notre Dame Press, 1991.

_____. "Religious language: A New Look at an Old Problem." Toronto: Institute for Christian Studies, 1980.

_____. "Religious language: A New Look at an Old Problem." In *Rationality in the Calvinian Tradition,* ed. Hendrik Hart, Johan Van der Hoeven and Nicholas Wolterstorff, 385-407. Lanham: University Press of America, 1983.

Collins, Sheila D. *A Different Heaven and Earth.* Valley Forge: Judson Press, 1974.

Conn, Harvey M. *Contemporary World Theology: A Layman's Guidebook.* Phillipsburg: Presbyterian and Reformed Publishing Co., 1973.

Countryman, L. William. *Dirt, Greed and Sex: Sexual Ethics in the New Testament and their Implications for Today.* Philadelphia: Fortress Press, 1988.

Craigie, Peter C. *The Book of Deuteronomy.* Grand Rapids: Eerdmans, 1976.

Daly, Mary. *Beyond God the Father: Towards a Philosophy of Women's Liberation.* Boston : Beacon Press; London: The Women's Press, 1973.

_____. *The Church and the Second Sex.* New York: Harper and Row, 1968.

Davis, John J. and Herbert Wolff. "Judges: Introduction." In *The NIV Study Bible,* ed. Kenneth L. Barker, 325-28. Grand Rapids: Zondervan, 1985.

Dinnerstein, Dorothy. *The Mermaid and the Minotaur: Sexual Arrangements and Human Malaise.* New York: Harper and Row, 1976.

Donovan, Josephine. *Feminist Theory: The Intellectual Traditions of American Feminism.* New York: Ungar Publishing Co., 1987.

Dooyeweerd, Herman. *Roots of Western Culture: Pagan, Secular, and Christian Options.* Translated by John Kraay. Toronto: Wedge Publishing Foundation, 1979.

_____. "The Criteria of Progressive and Reactionary Tendencies in History." In *Verslag van de plechtige viering van het honderdvijftigjarig bestaan der Koninklijke Nederlandse Academie van Wetenschappen,* 6-9 mei 1958, 213-28. Amsterdam: North-Holland, 1958.

Douglas, Mary. *Purity and Danger: An Analysis of the Concepts of Pollution and Taboo.* London: Ark Paperbacks, 1966.

Edwards, David L. (with John Stott). *Essentials: A Liberal-Evangelical Dialogue.* London: Hodder and Stoughton, 1988.

Eisenstein, Hester and Alice Jardine, eds. *The Future of Difference.* New York: Barnard College Women's Center, 1980; reprint, New Brunswick: Rutgers University Press, 1985.

Elshtain, Jean Bethke, "Reflections on Abortion, Values, and the Family." In *Abortion: Understanding Differences*, ed. Sidney Callahan and Daniel Callahan, 47-72. New York: Plenum Press, 1984.

Evans, Mary J. *Woman in the Bible*. Exeter: Paternoster Press, 1983.

Farmer, Kathleen A. *Who Knows What Is Good? A Commentary on the Books of Proverbs and Ecclesiastes*. Grand Rapids: Eerdmans, 1991.

Fausto-Sterling, Anne. *Myths of Gender: Biological Theories About Women and Men*. New York: Basic Books, Inc., 1985.

Fee, Gordon D. *The First Epistle to the Corinthians*. Grand Rapids: Eerdmans, 1987.

Finger, Reta Halteman. "How Can Jesus Save Women? Three Theories on Christ's Atonement." *Daughters of Sarah* 14 (November-December 1988): 14-18.

_____. "Your Daughters Shall Prophesy: A Christian Feminist Critiques Feminist Theology." *The Other Side* 24 (October 1988): 28-41.

Finger, Thomas N. *Christian Theology: An Eschatological Approach*. Vol. 1. Scottdale: Herald Press, 1985.

Firestone, Shulamith. *The Dialectic of Sex: The Case for Feminist Revolution*. New York: Bantam Books, 1970.

Fowler, James W. *Stages of Faith: The Psychology of Human Development and the Quest for Meaning*. San Francisco: Harper and Row, 1981.

Fox, Matthew. *Original Blessing: A Primer in Creation Spirituality*. Santa Fe: Bear and Co., 1983.

French, Marilyn. "A Gothic Romance." *Ms.* 17 (April 1989): 60.

Gillman, Florence M. *Women Who Knew Paul*. Collegeville, Minnesota: The Liturgical Press, 1992.

Goldberg, Michael. *Theology and Narrative: A Critical Introduction*. Nashville: Abingdon, 1982.

Goudzwaard, Bob. *Idols of Our Time*. Translated by Mark Vander Vennen. Downers Grove: InterVarsity Press, 1984.

Greeley, Andrew M. *A Future To Hope In: Socio-Religious Speculations*. Garden City: Doubleday and Co., Inc., 1968.

Gregorios, Paulos Mar. "New Testament Foundations for Understanding the Creation." In *Tending the Garden: Essays on the Gospel and the Earth*, ed. Wesley Granberg-Michaelsen, 83-92. Grand Rapids, Eerdmans, 1987.

Grenz, Stanley J. and Roger E. Olson. *Twentieth-Century Theology: God and the World in a Transitional Age*. Downers Grove: InterVarsity Press, 1992.

Grimshaw, Jean. *Philosophy and Feminist Thinking*. Minneapolis: University of Minnesota Press, 1986.

Gundrey, Patricia. *Heirs Together: Mutual Submission in Marriage*. Grand Rapids: Zondervan Publishing House, 1980.

Guthrie, Donald. *The Pastoral Epistles: An Introduction and Commentary.* Revised Edition. Leicester: Inter-Varsity Press; Grand Rapids: Eerdmans, 1990.

Hamerton-Kelly, Robert. *God the Father: Theology and Patriarchy in the Teaching of Jesus.* Philadelphia: Fortress Press, 1979.

Hanson, Paul D. *The Diversity of Scripture: A Theological Interpretation.* Philadelphia: Fortress Press, 1982.

Hart, Hendrik. "Cultus and Covenant." In James H. Olthuis *et al.*, *Will All The Kings Men...*, 29-60. Toronto: Wedge Publishing Foundation, 1972.

_____. "Dooyeweerd's *Gegenstand* Theory of Theory." In *The Legacy of Herman Dooyeweerd: Reflections on Critical Philosophy in the Christian Tradition*, ed. C. T. McIntire, 143-66. Lanham, MD: University Press of America, 1985.

_____. "New Testament People are Responsible People: A Verbatim Transcript of a Sermon on 1 Corinthians 7." *Vanguard* 10 (March-April 1980): 10-12.

_____. *Setting Our Sights by the Morning Star: Reflections on the Role of the Bible in Post-Modern Times.* Toronto: The Patmos Press, 1989.

_____. "Surrounded By Women." Unpublished sermon, Toronto, 1990.

_____. "Those Who Have Ears...." *Vanguard* (July-August 1975): 27-28.

_____. *Understanding Our World: An Integral Ontology.* Lanham, MD: University Press of America, 1984.

Harvey, Van A. *A Handbook of Theological Terms.* New York: Macmillan Publishing Co., 1964.

Hauerwas, Stanley. *A Community of Character: Toward a Constructive Christian Social Ethic.* Notre Dame: University of Notre Dame Press, 1981.

_____ and L. Gregory Jones, eds. *Why Narrative? Readings in Narrative Theology.* Grand Rapids: Eerdmans, 1989.

Hays, H. R. *The Dangerous Sex: The Myth of Feminine Evil.* New York: G.P. Putnam's Sons, 1964.

Hill, Andrew E and John H. Walton, *A Survey of the Old Testament.* Grand Rapids: Eerdmans, 1991.

Jewett, Paul K. *Man as Male and Female: A Study in Sexual Relationships from a Theological Point of View.* Grand Rapids: Eerdmans, 1975.

Kalsbeek, L. *Contours of a Christian Philosophy: An Introduction to Herman Dooyeweerd's Thought.* Toronto: Wedge Publishing Foundation, 1975.

Keller, Catherine. *From A Broken Web: Separation, Sexism, and Self.* Boston: Beacon Press, 1986.

Kenna, Kathleen. "Couples Wanting Only Boys Flock to MD for Gender Test." *The Toronto Star*, 10 December 1990, Sec. B, pp. 1, 3.

Kikawada, Isaac M. and Arthur Quinn. *Before Abraham Was: The Unity of Genesis 1-11.* Nashville: Abingdon, 1985.

Kittel, Gerhard. *"Doxa"* in *Theological Dictionary of the New Testament*. Vol. 1, eds. Gerhard Kittel and Gerhard Friedrich, 233-37 and 242-53. Grand Rapids: Eerdmans, 1964.

Klein, Lillian R. *The Triumph of Irony in the Book of Judges*. Sheffield: The Almond Press, 1988.

Kohut, Heinz. *The Restoration of the Self*. Madison: International Universities Press, Inc., 1977.

Koonz, Claudia. *Mothers in the Fatherland: Women, the Family and Nazi Politics*. New York: St. Martin's Press, 1987.

Kramer, Heinrich and James Sprenger. *The Malleus Maleficarum of Heinrich Kramer and James Sprenger*. Translated and edited by Rev. Montague Summers. New York: Dover Publications, Inc., 1971.

Kroeger, Catherine Clark. "The Apostle Paul and the Greco-Roman Cults of Women." *Journal of the Evangelical Theological Society* 30 (March 1987): 25-38.

_____. "The Classical Concept of 'Head' as 'Source'." In *Equal To Serve: Women and Men in the Church and Home*, by Gretchen Gaebelein Hull, 267-83. Old Tappan, NJ: Fleming H. Revell, 1987.

_____. "1 Timothy 2:12—A Classicist's View." In *Women, Authority and the Bible*, ed. Alvera Mickelsen, 225-44. Downers Grove: InterVarsity Press, 1986.

_____ and Richard Clark Kroeger. *I Suffer Not a Woman: Rethinking 1 Timothy 2:11-15 in the Light of Ancient Evidence*. Grand Rapids: Baker Book House, 1992.

_____ and Richard Clark Kroeger. "Pandemonium and Silence at Corinth." *Reformed Journal* 26 (June 1978): 6-11.

_____ and Richard Clark Kroeger. "Sexual Identity in Corinth: Paul Faces a Crisis." *Reformed Journal* 28 (December 1978): 11-15.

Kuyper, Abraham. *Lectures on Calvinism*. Grand Rapids: Eerdmans, 1970.

_____. "The Woman's Place of Honor." Translated by Irene Konyndyk. Unpublished manuscript, Calvin College, Grand Rapids, 1990.

Laffey, Alice L. *An Introduction to the Old Testament: A Feminist Perspective*. Philadelphia: Fortress Press, 1988.

Lane, William L. *The Gospel of Mark*. Grand Rapids: Eerdmans, 1974.

Lerner, Gerda. *The Creation of Patriarchy*. New York: Oxford University Press, 1986.

Lloyd, Genevieve. *The Man of Reason: "Male" and "Female" in Western Philosophy*. Minneapolis: University of Minnesota Press, 1984.

Maddox, Randy L. "Toward an Inclusive Theology: The Systematic Implications of the Feminist Critique." *Christian Scholar's Review* 16 (September 1986): 7-23.

Marshall, I. Howard. *Biblical Inspiration*. London: Hodder and Stoughton, 1982.

Marshall, Paul A. *Thine Is The Kingdom: A Biblical Perspective on the Nature of Government and Politics Today*. Basingstoke, U. K.: Marshall, Morgan, and Scott, 1984.

Martin, Faith McBurney. *Call Me Blessed: The Emerging Christian Woman*. Grand Rapids: Eerdmans, 1988.

McDonnell, Kathleen. *Not An Easy Choice: A Feminist Re-examines Abortion*. Toronto: The Women's Press, 1984.

McFague, Sallie. *Models of God: Theology for an Ecological, Nuclear Age*. Philadelphia: Fortress Press, 1987.

Mead, Margaret. *Male and Female: A Study of the Sexes in an Changing World*. New York: The New American Library, 1955.

"Methodology Used to Derive Biblical Principles for Issues Relating to the Social Order." Cambridge: Jubilee Centre Publications Ltd., 1988.

Mickelsen, Alvera, ed. *Women, Authority and the Bible*. Downers Grove: Inter-Varsity Press, 1986.

_____ and Berkeley Mickelsen. "What Does *Kephale* Mean in the New Testament?" In *Women, Authority and the Bible*, ed. Alvera Mickelsen, 97-110. Downers Grove: InterVarsity Press, 1986.

Moltmann, Jürgen. *The Trinity and the Kingdom of God*. San Francisco: Harper and Row, 1981.

Mouw, Richard. *When the Kings Come Marching In: Isaiah and the New Jerusalem*. Grand Rapids: Eerdmans, 1983.

Murphy, Roland E. "Wisdom and Creation." *Journal of Biblical Literature* 104/1 (1985): 3-11.

Nelson, James B. *The Intimate Connection: Male Sexuality, Masculine Spirituality*. Philadelphia: The Westminster Press, 1988.

Oddie, William. *What Will Happen to God? Feminism and the Reconstruction of Christian Belief*. London: SPCK, 1984.

O'Leary, Denyse. "The Pro-Life Movement: Coming to Terms with our Costly Mistakes." In *The Issue is Life: A Christian Response to Abortion in Canada*, ed. Denyse O'Leary, 50-58. Burlington: Welch Publishing Co. Inc., 1988.

Olsen, Dennis T. "Numbers." In *Harper's Bible Commentary*, ed. James L. Mays, 182-208. San Francisco: Harper and Row, 1988.

Olthuis, James H. "Be(com)ing: Humankind as Gift and Call." Unpublished paper. Toronto, 1986.

_____. "The Covenanting Metaphor of the Christian Faith and the Self Psychology of Heinz Kohut." *Studies in Religion* 18 (1989): 313-24.

_____. "Finding and Forming Stories that Give Life: The Narrative Character of Interpretation." Unpublished paper. Toronto, 1990.

_____. *Keeping Our Troth: Staying in Love Through the Five Stages of Marriage*. San Francisco: Harper and Row, 1986.

_____. *I Pledge You My Troth: A Christian View of Marriage, Family, Friendship.* New York: Harper and Row, 1975.

_____. "On Worldviews." *Christian Scholar's Review* 14/2 (1985): 153-64.

_____. "Self or Society: Is there a Choice?" In *Your Better Self: Christianity, Psychology, and Self-Esteem,* ed. Craig W. Ellison, 202-14.

_____. "Visions of Life and Ways of Life: The Nature of Religion." In *Towards a Biblical View of Man: Some Readings,* ed. Arnold H. De Graaff and James H. Olthuis, 62-190. Toronto: Institute for Christian Studies, 1978.

_____ with Donald G. Bloesch, Clark H. Pinnock and Gerald T. Sheppard. *A Hermeneutics of Ultimacy: Peril or Promise?* Lanham: University Press of America, 1987.

_____ and Arnold H. De Graaff. "Models of Man in Theology and Psychology." Toronto: Institute for Christian Studies, 1978.

Pannenberg, Wolfhart. *Anthropology in Theological Perspective.* Translated by Matthew J. O'Connell. Philadelphia: The Westminster Press, 1985.

Parvey, Constance F. "The Theology and Leadership of Women in the New Testament." In *Religion and Sexism: Images of Woman in the Jewish and Christian Traditions,* ed. Rosemary Radford Ruether, 117-49. New York: Simon and Schuster, 1974.

Payne, Philip Barton. "Response to Alvera and Berkeley Mickelsen, 'What Does *Kephale* Mean in the New Testament?' " In *Women, Authority and the Bible,* ed. Alvera Mickelsen, 118-32. Downers Grove: InterVarsity Press, 1986.

Pinnock, Clark H. "Biblical Authority and the Issues in Question." In *Women, Authority and the Bible,* ed. Alvera Mickelsen, 51-58. Downers Grove: InterVarsity Press, 1986.

Plaskow, Judith. *Sex, Sin and Grace: Women's Experience and the Theologies of Reinhold Niebuhr and Paul Tillich.* Lanham: University Press of America, 1980.

Prusak, Bernard P. "Woman: Seductive Siren and Source of Sin? Pseudepigraphal Myth and Christian Origins." In *Religion and Sexism: Images of Woman in the Jewish and Christian Traditions,* ed. Rosemary Radford Ruether, 89-116. New York: Simon and Schuster, 1974.

Rad, Gerhard von. *"Doxa"* in *Theological Dictionary of the New Testament.* Vol. 1, eds. Gerhard Kittel and Gerhard Friedrich, 238-42. Grand Rapids: Eerdmans, 1964.

_____. *Genesis: A Commentary.* Revised Edition. Philadelphia: The Westminster Press, 1972.

_____. *Wisdom in Israel.* Translated by James D. Martin. London: SCM, 1972.

Ramm, Bernard. *Offense to Reason: The Theology of Sin.* San Francisco: Harper and Row, 1985.

Ricoeur, Paul. *The Symbolism of Evil.* Translated by Emerson Buchanan. Boston: Beacon Press, 1967.

Ridderbos, Herman N. *Paul: An Outline of His Theology.* Translated by John Richard de Witt. Grand Rapids: Eerdmans, 1975.

_____. *Redemptive History and the New Testament Scriptures.* Translated by H. De Jongste and revised by Richard B. Gaffin, Jr. Phillipsburg: Presbyterian and Reformed Publishing Co., 1988.

Robinson, James M. ed. *The Nag Hammadi Library.* San Francisco: Harper and Row, 1978.

Robinson, John A. T. *The Body: A Study in Pauline Theology.* London: SCM Press, 1952.

_____. *Redating the New Testament.* London: SCM Press, 1976.

Rubin, Lillian B. *Intimate Strangers: Men and Women Together.* New York: Harper and Row, 1983.

Saiving, Valerie. "The Human Situation: A Feminine View." In *Womanspirit Rising: A Feminist Reader in Religion,* ed. Carol P. Christ and Judith Plaskow, 25-42. San Francisco: Harper and Row, 1979.

Schüssler Fiorenza, Elizabeth. "1 Corinthians." In *Harper's Bible Commentary,* ed. James L. Mays, 1168-1189. San Francisco: Harper and Row, 1988.

_____. *In Memory of Her: A Feminist Theological Reconstruction of Christian Origins.* New York: Crossroad; London: SCM, 1983.

_____. Review Symposium: *In Memory of Her: A Feminist Theological Reconstruction of Christian Origins,* by Elizabeth Schüssler Fiorenza. In *Horizons* 11 (Spring 1984): 154-57.

Schuurman, Douglas J. "Humanity in Reformed and Feminist Perspectives: Collision or Correlation?" *Calvin Theological Journal* 26 (1991): 68-90.

Seerveld, Calvin G. *Balaam's Apocalyptic Prophecies: A Study in Reading Scripture.* Toronto: Wedge Publishing Foundation, 1980.

_____. "Biblical Wisdom Underneath Vollenhoven's Categories for Philosophical Historiography." In *The Idea of a Christian Philosophy: Essays in Honor of D. H. Th. Vollenhoven,* ed. K. A. Bril, H. Hart and J. Klapwijk, 127-43. Toronto: Wedge Publishing Foundation, 1973.

_____. "Footprints in the Snow." *Philosophia Reformata* 56 (1991): 1-34.

_____. *The Greatest Song: In Critique of Solomon.* Revised Edition. Toronto: Tuppence Press, 1988.

_____. "The Pedagogical Strength of a Christian Methodology in Philosophical Historiography." In *Social Theory and Practice: Philosophical Essays in Honour of Prof. J. A. L. Taljaard. Koers* 40/4-6 (1975): 269-313.

Shaberg, Jane. *The Illegitimacy of Jesus: A Feminist Theological Interpretation of the Infancy Narratives.* San Francisco: Harper and Row, 1987.

Shahinian, Gary Richard. "The Problem of Evil in David Griffin's Process Theology." M. Phil. thesis, Toronto: Institute for Christian Studies, 1984.

Shils, Edward. *Tradition*. Chicago: University of Chicago Press, 1981.

Sinnema, Donald. "The *Toledoth* of the Sons of Noah: Genesis 10:1-11:9." Toronto: Institute for Christian Studies, 1973.

_____. "The Uniqueness of the Language of Faith—With Special Reference to the Language of Scripture." Toronto: Institute for Christian Studies, 1975.

Skillen, James W. "Politics and Eschatology: Political Action and the Coming of God's Kingdom." Toronto: Institute for Christian Studies, 1978.

Sneiders, Sandra M. *Women and the Word: The Gender of God in the New Testament and the Spirituality of Women*. New York: Paulist Press, 1986.

Solomon, Robert C. *Continental Philosophy Since 1750: The Rise and Fall of the Self*. A History of Western Philosophy. Vol. 7. Oxford: Oxford University Press, 1988.

Spykman, Gordon J. *Reformational Theology: A New Paradigm for Doing Dogmatics*. Grand Rapids, Eerdmans, 1992.

Storkey, Elaine. *What's Right with Feminism*. London: SPCK, 1985.

Summers, Anne. "The Hedda Conundrum." *Ms.* 17 (April 1989): 54.

Swartley, Willard M. *Slavery, Sabbath, War, and Women: Case Issues in Biblical Interpretation*. Scottdale: Herald Press, 1983.

Tamez, Elsa *et al. Against Machismo*. Translated by John Eagleson. Oak Park, IL: Meyer Stone Books, 1987.

Teilhard de Chardin, Pierre. *The Phenomenon of Man*. Translated by Bernard Wall. New York: Harper and Row, 1959.

Tennis, Diane. *Is God the Only Reliable Father?* Philadelphia: The Westminster Press, 1985.

Thompson, J. A. *The Book of Jeremiah*. Grand Rapids: Eerdmans, 1980.

Tillich, Paul. *Systematic Theology*. Vol. 2. Chicago: University of Chicago Press, 1957.

Tracy, David. *Blessed Rage for Order: The New Pluralism in Theology*. Minneapolis: The Seabury Press, 1975.

Trible, Phyllis. "Eve and Adam: Genesis 2-3 Reread." In *Womanspirit Rising: A Feminist Reader in Religion*, ed. Carol P. Christ and Judith Plaskow, 74-83. San Francisco: Harper and Row, 1979.

_____. *God and the Rhetoric of Sexuality*. Philadelphia: Fortress Press, 1978.

_____. Review of *God the Father: Theology and Patriarchy in the Teaching of Jesus*, by Robert Hamerton-Kelly. In *Theology Today* 37 (1980): 116-19.

_____. *Texts of Terror: Literary-Feminist Readings of Biblical Narratives*. Philadelphia: Fortress Press, 1984.

Trigo, Pedro. *Creation and History*. Translated by Robert R. Barr. Maryknoll: Orbis Books, 1991.

Tucker, Robert C., ed. *The Marx-Engels Reader.* New York: W. W. Norton and Co. Inc., 1972.

Van Leeuwen, Mary Stewart. *Gender and Grace: Love, Work and Parenting in a Changing World.* Downers Grove: InterVarsity Press, 1990.

_____ ed. *After Eden: Facing the Challenge of Gender Reconciliation.* Grand Rapids: Eerdmans, 1993.

Vaux, Roland de. *Ancient Israel.* Vol. 1. *Social Institutions.* New York: McGraw-Hill Book Co., 1961.

Walsh, Brian J. "A Critical Review of Pannenberg's *Anthropology in Theological Perspective. Christian Scholar's Review* 15/3 (1986): 247-59.

_____. *Subversive Christianity: Imaging God in a Dangerous Time.* Bristol, U.K.: Regius Press, 1992.

_____, Marianne Karsh and Nik Ansell. "Acid Rain, Deforestation, and the Responsiveness of Creation." In *Stewarding Creation,* ed. Steve Bishop. Bristol, U.K.: Regius Press, forthcoming.

_____ and J. Richard Middleton. *The Transforming Vision: Shaping a Christian Worldview.* Downers Grove: InterVarsity Press, 1984.

Ware, Timothy. *The Orthodox Church.* Harmondsworth: Penguin Books, 1963.

Washbourn, Penelope. *Becoming Woman: The Quest for Wholeness in Female Experience.* San Francisco: Harper and Row, 1977.

Wenham, Gordon. *The Book of Leviticus.* Grand Rapids: Eerdmans, 1979.

Westermann, Claus. *Genesis 1-11: A Commentary.* Translated by John J. Scullion. Minneapolis: Augsburg Publishing House, 1984.

Wilson-Kastner, Patricia. *Faith, Feminism and the Christ.* Philadelphia: Fortress Press, 1983.

Wink, Walter. *Naming the Powers: The Language of Power in the New Testament.* Philadelphia: Fortress Press, 1984.

_____. *Unmasking the Powers: The Invisible Forces That Determine Human Existence.* Philadelphia: Fortress Press, 1986.

Witherington, Ben. III. *Women in the Ministry of Jesus: A Study of Jesus' Attitudes to Women and their Roles as Reflected in His Earthly Life.* Cambridge: Cambridge University Press, 1984.

Wolters, Albert M. *Creation Regained: Biblical Basics for a Reformational Worldview.* Grand Rapids: Eerdmans, 1985.

_____. " 'Partners of the Deity': A Covenantal Reading of 2 Peter 1:4." *Calvin Theological Journal* 25 (April 1990): 28-44.

_____. "Proverbs 31: 10-31 as Heroic Hymn: A Form-Critical Analysis." *Vetus Testamentum* 38 (1988): 446-57.

_____. "Thoughts on Genesis." *Calvinist Contact* (14 December, 1990), 4.

_____. "Worldview and Textual Criticism in 2 Peter 3:10." *Westminster Theological Journal* 49 (1987): 405-13.

Wolterstorff, Nicholas. *Until Justice and Peace Embrace.* Grand Rapids: Eerdmans, 1983.

Wright, Christopher J. H. *God's People in God's Land: Family, Land, and Property in the Old Testament*. Grand Rapids: Eerdmans; Exeter: The Paternoster Press, 1990.

Wright, N. Thomas. *The Climax of the Covenant: Christ and the Law in Pauline Theology*. Edinburgh: T. & T. Clark: 1991; Minneapolis: Fortress, 1992.

_____. "How Can the Bible Be Authoritative?" *Vox Evangelica* 21 (1991): 7-32.

_____. "The Quest for the Historical Kingdom." Unpublished lecture series. Oxford, 1989.

Yoder, John Howard. *The Politics of Jesus: Vicit Agnus Noster*. Grand Rapids: Eerdmans, 1972.

Young, Pamela Dickey. *Feminist Theology/Christian Theology: In Search of Method*. Minneapolis: Fortress Press, 1990.

Index

Abortion 315-318, 324-325 n. 79
Allen, Prudence 182, 185
Androgyny 35-36, 179-80
Anthropology 18-25, 174-188, 328-
338
sex-unity 182-186, 223, 359 n. 14
sex-polarity 182
sex-complementarity 182-188
(see also: Androgyny; Self, the)
Askew, Angela 319 n. 3
Atonement 190-193, 343-344
Aulén, Gustaf 193
Augustine, St. 19-22, 50 n. 112
Bible, the
authorial intention of 121, 153
and biblicism 95-96
as book of faith 91-95
"certitudinal" history in 92-94
closure/formation of canon 98-
103, 163 n. 63
different feminist approaches to
79-80
"going beyond the Bible in the
Spirit of the Bible" 110-112,
123, 153-155
Jesus as focal point of 97, 350
male and female in 113-148
orienting, reorienting function of
103-113, 148-155
relationship to the Spirit 95-103,
110, 121
roots in experience 82-85
Ruether's critique of 53-60
Ruether's use of 63-68
unity and diversity of 89-91, 112-
113, 148-149
Bloesch, Donald 258-259, 284 n. 257

Brueggemann, Walter 83-84, 103, 112
Bushnell, Catherine 119-120
Carlson-Thies, Christiane 287
Childs, Brevard 119, 161 n. 50
Chopp, Rebecca 336, 338
Christian-feminist integration 5-7,
348-357
Christology 33-36, 206-212
androgynous 35-36, 49 n. 77
patriarchalization of 34-35
Spirit 49 n. 77, 207-208, 211
Clarke, Sister Maura 244
Clericalism 32, 198-200, 261
Collins, Sheila 291
Countryman, L. William 124, 165 n.
98, 166 n. 113
Critical principle of Ruether's fem-
inist theology 17-18, 61, 152, 351-
355
Daly, Mary 34-35, 70
Donovan, Josephine 319 n. 11
Dooyeweerd, Herman 9, 45, 321 n. 38,
329
Douglas, Mary 124
Dualism 19-20, 25-26, 37-39
Ruether's opposition to 45, 212-
213, 251, 253, 288-289, 293,
296, 328-330
Ruether's "soft" dualism 184,
213-215, 219, 227-240, 242,
267, 275 n. 116, 276 n. 117, 277
n. 140, 283 n. 254, 328-330
Ecclesiology 30-33, 198-206
church/Church distinction 205-206
(see also: Clericalism; Ordination;
and Women-Church)

Eisenstein, Hester 332
Eschatology 39-41, 224-246
    eschaton/history relationship 91,
        240-242, 338-343, 361 n. 34
Essence/existence relationship 18, 91,
    184, 192, 254, 291, 298, 334-336,
    360 n. 29
Evans, Mary 165 n. 101, 171 n. 166
Evil 25-27, 188-193, 285-287
Faith-revelation correlation 85-88
Feminism
    countercultural 79-80
    eschatological 24
    evangelical 79-81
    general definition of 5, 348-349
    liberal 24-25, 174, 177-179
    liberationist 79-80
    romanticist 174-179
    virginal 22-24
    (see also: Christian-feminist in-
        tegration)
Finger, Reta Halteman 50 n. 107, 193,
    343-344
Finger, Thomas 193
Fiorenza, Elizabeth Schüssler 64-66,
    74 n. 61, 142, 154-155
Foundational and transcendental
    directions of modal order 220-
    222, 323 n. 66
Fox, Matthew 264
Gender symbolism 28-31, 36-38, 41-
    42, 195-196
God, God/ess 41-45, 246-270, 281 n.
    203
    Creator-creation relationship 86-
        87, 159 nn. 26-27, 195, 220,
        251, 255-256, 259-270
    male monotheism 41, 53-55
    privileged metaphors for 159 n.
        25, 259-261
    power/omnipotence of 44, 191-
        193, 246-247, 344-346
    transcendence/immanence of
        269-270

    (see also: Heteronomy; Trinity,
        the)
Greeley, Andrew 157
Gregarios, Paulos Mar 245
Grenz, Stanley 263
Goudzwaard, Bob 309, 323 n. 66
History
    linear view of 40, 225
    mythologizing view of 279 n. 174,
        321 n. 38
    Ruether's view of 226-227
    (see also: Bible, the, "certitu-
        dinal" history in; Eschatology,
        eschaton/history relationship;
        Nature, relationship to his-
        tory)
Hart, Hendrik 139-140, 160 n. 37, 161
    n. 47, 162 n. 56, 163 n. 67, 164 n.
    74, 197, 211, 322 n. 54, 329, 358 n.
    4, 360 n. 29
Heteronomy 103, 194-198
Keller, Catherine 310
Kenosis 172 n. 177, 195, 206, 227, 232,
    278 n. 167
Kikawada, Isaac 127-128
Klein, Lillian 126-130, 167 nn. 125,
    128, 131
Koonz, Claudia 312-313
Kroeger, Catherine Clark 146
Kuyper, Abraham 9, 45, 350
Lerner, Gerda 125
Life beyond death 41, 224, 227-246,
    280 n. 197
Limit experience 83-85, 90
Lloyd, Genevieve 298
Matrix, different meanings of 235-
    236, 279-280 n. 177
Mariology 27-30, 193-198
Martin, Faith 123-124
McFague, Sallie 159 n. 25
Monism 184, 267, 275 n. 116, 283 n.
    254, 358 n. 7
Murphy, Roland 136-137

Nature 36-39, 212-224
  as chaos/cosmos 218-219
  Dame Nature 25-26, 37
  depreciation of in modern theology 37-38
  relationship to history 215-216
Nelson, James 332
Nicholas of Cusa 265
Object-relations theory 303, 309-310, 323 n. 67
O'Leary, Denyse 325 n. 79
Olthuis, James 81, 89, 92-93, 142, 307-308, 323 n. 62, 333
Olson, Roger 263
Ordination 31-32, 198-199
Paganism 70-71, 226
Pannenberg, Wolfhart 198
Pinnock, Clark 347
Patriarchy
  as global concept 285-289
  origin and nature of 298-313
  rise and development of 289-298
Quinn, Arthur 127-128
Ramsey, William M. 2-3
Rationalism 297-298, 310-311, 320 n. 34
Ricoeur, Paul 160 nn. 35, 41, 196-197
Saiving, Valerie 307, 323 n. 61
Seerveld, Calvin 82-83, 135-136, 159 n. 31, 168 n. 138, 321 n. 38
Self, the 333-334, 359 n. 20
Shaberg, Jane 273 n. 65
Sneiders, Sandra 133
Storkey, Elaine 9
Tamez, Elsa 354-355
Teilhard de Chardin, Pierre 216, 239-240, 242, 264, 271 n. 30, 276 nn. 119, 121, 125, 278 nn. 163, 165, 279 nn. 169-170, 282 n. 220, 331
Tradition 51-53, 60-72, 78-79, 88-89, 159 n. 31
Trible, Phyllis 117, 126, 129
Trigo, Pedro 197

Trinity, the 43, 50 n. 107, 162 n. 53
Ultimate questions 85
Unclean, woman as 30-31, 57, 118-119, 124
Van Leeuwen, Mary Stewart 9, 187, 272 n. 33, 324 n. 67
Vaughan, Judith 46
Vollenhoven, D.H.T. 9, 275 n. 116, 279 n. 174
Von Rad, Gerhard 115-116, 136-137
Wenham, Gordon 124
Wilson-Kastner, Patricia 183-184
Wolters, Albert M. 138, 161 n. 49
Women-Church 201-203
Wright, N. Thomas 163 n. 66, 168-169 n. 149
Young, Pamela Dickey 6, 75 n. 85, 349
Zylstra, Bernard 3